D1521357

M. K. Gandhi, Attorney at Law

The publisher gratefully acknowledges the generous support of the General Endowment Fund of the University of California Press Foundation.

M. K. Gandhi, Attorney at Law

THE MAN BEFORE THE MAHATMA

Charles R. DiSalvo

To Judge Carr
with warm regards —
Charles DiSalvo

UNIVERSITY OF CALIFORNIA PRESS

BERKELEY LOS ANGELES LONDON

University of California Press, one of the most distinguished university presses in the United States, enriches lives around the world by advancing scholarship in the humanities, social sciences, and natural sciences. Its activities are supported by the UC Press Foundation and by philanthropic contributions from individuals and institutions. For more information, visit www.ucpress.edu.

University of California Press
Berkeley and Los Angeles, California

University of California Press, Ltd.
London, England

Library of Congress Cataloging-in-Publication Data

DiSalvo, Charles R., 1948–.
   M.K. Gandhi, attorney at law : the man before the Mahatma / Charles R. DiSalvo.
      p.   cm.
   Includes bibliographical references and index.
   ISBN 978-0-520-28015-1 (cloth : alk. paper)
   1. Gandhi, Mahatma, 1869–1948.   2. Lawyers—India—Biography.
   3. Gandhi, Mahatma, 1869–1948—Travel—South Africa.
   4. South Africa—Politics and government—1836–1909.   I. Title.
   DS481.G3D473   2013
   340.092—dc23
   [B]   2013021967

Manufactured in the United States of America

22   21   20   19   18   17   16   15   14   13
10   9   8   7   6   5   4   3   2   1

In keeping with a commitment to support environmentally responsible and sustainable printing practices, UC Press has printed this book on Natures Natural, a fiber that contains 30% post-consumer waste and meets the minimum requirements of ANSI/NISO z39.48-1992 (R 1997) (*Permanence of Paper*).

To Kathleen

CONTENTS

Introduction xi

1 · Dispatched to London 1

2 · The Barrister Who Couldn't Speak 17

3 · An Abundant and Regular Supply of Labour 31

4 · Dada Abdulla's White Elephant 36

5 · Not a White Barrister 49

6 · Formation Lessons 67

7 · Waller's Question 84

8 · A Public Man 95

9 · To Maritzburg 104

10 · Moth and Flame 126

11 · Sacrifice 138

12 · Transition and the Transvaal 146

13 · No Bed of Roses 159

14 · Disobedience 180

15 · Courthouse to Jailhouse 197

16 · Malpractice 216

17 · Courtroom as Laboratory   227

18 · Closing Arguments   249

Mohandas K. Gandhi Chronology   269
Abbreviations   273
Notes   275
Sources   311
Acknowledgments   323
Index   327

Illustrations follow page 196

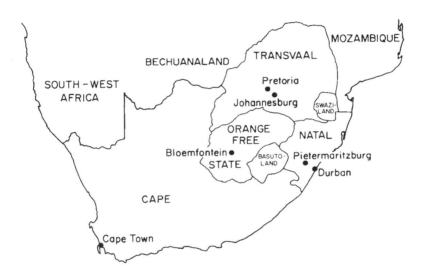

South Africa in Gandhi's time. Courtesy of Cornell University Press.

INTRODUCTION

To other countries I may go as a tourist, but to India I come
as a pilgrim.

MARTIN LUTHER KING, JR., on the occasion of
his visit to India, 1959

THE IMAGE THE WORLD HAS of Mohandas Gandhi is a stark one. Say
the name "Gandhi," and the listener invariably conjures up a vision of an
elderly, unassuming, bald-headed man. He peers at us through well-worn
wire-rimmed glasses, notable because they constitute one of the few items
owned by one who has stripped himself of virtually all material possessions. As we see him, he wears not manufactured clothing from England's
factories, but plain, white, homespun cotton from India's fields—and a
minimum of that, too. He is an ascetic man: he prays, he keeps silence, he
fasts, he refrains from wine, meat, and sexual relations. He knows the
strength he has in the political arena is derived from decidedly higher
sources: his clear and unswerving devotion to the cause of Indian freedom
and a view of life that sees the spiritual as the underpinning of the
political.

There is, however, another Gandhi. We find a photograph of him in the
Sabarmati Ashram in Ahmedabad, India. The place is Johannesburg, the
year about 1905. In this picture a tie, a starched shirt, and a three-piece suit
replace the homespun. A younger Gandhi, with a head of hair and a striking
mustache, sits with authority in an office chair placed outdoors for the occasion of this photograph. Surrounding him are four members of his staff,
including, on his immediate left, the smiling Sonja Schlesin, his longtime
secretary, and, on his immediate right, H. S. L. Polak, his trusted associate.

Dominating the picture, and found slightly above Gandhi's head, is a large opaque window in the center of a brick wall with these words carefully arranged on it: "M. K. Gandhi. Attorney."

Despite his having studied and practiced law for twenty-three years (1888–1911), this is the Gandhi about whom the world knows little.

My own image of Gandhi had always been that of the ascetic—until 1978, when I encountered a small volume entitled *The Law and Lawyers*. Gandhi was named as the author, but I quickly noted it was not a monograph by Gandhi but rather a collection of statements he made over the course of his life about the law and lawyers, ably compiled and edited by S. B. Kher. In it I learned for the first time that Gandhi himself had practiced law—for a short time in India, but chiefly in South Africa, where he worked and resided for the better part of two decades.

Curious, I headed for the library to locate a biography of his life as a lawyer. There was none. Because the library was a superb one (that of the University of Chicago Law School), I felt relatively secure in concluding that none had been written. I resorted to the standard biographies. Relying almost entirely on what little Gandhi himself had written about his time in the law, they did little more than acknowledge in passing his having studied and practiced law. No one, it seemed, had made an investigation of his long years in the law. No one had asked whether his professional experiences influenced the development of his philosophy and practice of civil disobedience. No one had explored how his legal career shaped the man. It was as if the two decades Gandhi had spent in the law had been declared irrelevant by all his many biographers. This was as stunning as it was inexplicable. Civil disobedience is the conscientious breaking of the law. Gandhi *was* a civil disobedient—and *became one while he was a practicing member of the legal profession*. Was there no relationship between Gandhi's practice of law and his embrace of civil disobedience? Was there no relationship between Gandhi's practice of law and the person he became over those years?

I set about writing this biography of Gandhi's life as a lawyer to answer those questions and to explain how Gandhi's experience as a lawyer set him on a path that would lead to his being one of the preeminent figures of the twentieth century—with a dramatic impact on the twenty-first.

Had Gandhi become the physician he wanted to become rather than the lawyer his family insisted he become, it is quite likely that the Indian independence movement would have taken an entirely different trajectory, revolutions around the globe would have more often been violent rather than nonviolent, and Mohandas K. Gandhi would not have developed into India's leading twentieth-century nationalist. But the man before the Mahatma did become a lawyer—and that made all the difference.

That and the South African legal system. Sent abroad as a novice lawyer, it was Gandhi's intention simply to earn some money for himself and his family. Before long, however, he found himself at the center of the fight for Indian civil rights in British South Africa. Because he had been trained for the bar in London, Gandhi had come to take British fair play as a settled expectation that he then projected onto the courts of Britain's South African colonies. So it was quite natural for the young lawyer to look to the legal system for help in defending against attacks on Indian rights. Gandhi's belief in the capacity of the courts to render justice was so strong that in South Africa he repeatedly knocked on the legal system's door for justice for his community. The door rarely opened. He kept knocking. The more he knocked, the less frequently it opened. This repeated, persistent, and finally predictable refusal of the legal system to render justice to South Africa's Indians slowly but inexorably frustrated Gandhi. It drove the lawyer out of the legal system—as most of us understand it—and into the arms of civil disobedience.

I say "as most of us understand it." It is true that Gandhi eventually lost faith in the traditional legal system—courts, judges, lawyers, litigation—but he never lost faith in the law. At the end of his period of experimentation with civil disobedience in South Africa, he understood civil disobedience actually to be an expression of one's highest respect for the law.

A choice presents itself to every resister who breaks the law in the course of opposing an oppressive regime: to accept responsibility and punishment or to avoid them. In Gandhi's time in South Africa, both responses to this choice were on display. The Boers (descendants of the Dutch settlers whom the British displaced) felt oppressed by the British and took up arms against them. No Boer openly opposed the British and stood by to be arrested and punished. By contrast, Gandhi and the Indians did openly oppose the British, broke South African laws, and accepted their prosecution and punishment. This put Gandhi and his followers firmly under the law's ultimate dominion—which is just where Gandhi, who had a great deal of esteem for the law, wanted to be.

Gandhi's goal was, in large part, to change the mind of the oppressor. In South Africa Gandhi was feeling his way toward an understanding of the dynamic by which civil disobedience creates social and political change. That dynamic relies on the power of willingly accepted self-suffering to awaken and convince the public of the virtue of the disobedient's cause, such that the public sympathizes with the disobedient and then puts pressure on decision-makers to redress the problem. Gandhi conceived, rightly so, of the willingness to endure suffering and accept punishment as a sign of the disobedient's continuing faith in the law—a grand system understood as transcending courts, judges, lawyers, and litigation—to do justice. And it was the willingness to be ultimately governed by the law that Gandhi saw as a critical element in changing the mind of the oppressor.

In the end, Gandhi learned how to use the legal system against itself to transform injustice into justice. From all the lessons Gandhi learned in the practice of law, this lesson that he learned in South Africa and acted on in India was the single most important key for opening the door to freedom in India.

THE LAW: A LABORATORY FOR PERSONAL CHANGE

Gandhi's experiences as a lawyer matter not only because it was in the context of his law practice that he developed his philosophy and practice of civil disobedience, but also because his time in the law readied the man for leadership in India.

A South African law practice was the perfect hothouse for raising the initially shy and retiring Gandhi into a public person. The colonial courts in which Gandhi practiced were then backwoods jurisdictions where the quality of legal talent would not easily scare a timid novice away. At the same time, being in court anywhere requires a certain amount of courage. Repeatedly advocating before judges and engaging with opponents in courtrooms and a range of other settings had their effect on Gandhi. The law provided him with confidence. The law made him a leader. The law gave him his voice.

Moreover, his South African law practice provided Gandhi with an identity. The London-trained barrister received the instant respect of his relatively uneducated countrymen in South Africa. They naturally turned to him—the only Indian lawyer in an otherwise completely European bar—for advice and leadership. Gandhi also earned the respect of some of his opponents in the bar and in politics, who recognized and valued his sincerity, his intellect, and his thoroughness.

The psychological security he derived from having a professional identity, however, did not protect him from the hard edges of law practice. It was as a lawyer that Gandhi learned how to negotiate with the most skilled bargainers. There were times when he showed real talent for it—such as when he negotiated a partnership agreement with an older, seasoned lawyer in the Durban bar. There were other times when he was sent away licking his wounds. Gandhi and the Transvaal colonial secretary, Jan Christian Smuts, spent a good deal of time together negotiating over government recognition of Indian rights—and, after a settlement had been reached, Gandhi spent a good deal of time afterward trying to figure out how he had been had. As a result, when Gandhi sat down in India with Viceroy Irwin years later to negotiate the Gandhi-Irwin Pact, he did so as one who had been schooled in negotiating with the most difficult negotiators the colonial world had to offer.

In other contexts, too, Gandhi was toughened and prepared for India. Racist magistrates before whom he constantly appeared had to be tangled with, as did racist functionaries in local and provincial governments. Liars, like the Transvaal registrar of Asiatics, Montfort Chamney, had to be confronted. Corrupt officials, like those in the Transvaal's Asiatic Office, had to be faced down. And rebels in his own camp, like the former clients who beat him to within an inch of his life, had to be endured. Battle-scarred, Gandhi emerged from all this intact—and ready for all the challenges India could throw at him.

What enabled him to survive this trying process of preparation?

Role-differentiated behavior is an occupational hazard for lawyers. The adversary system, with party pitted against party, encourages it. There is no impartial investigator of the facts in most legal settings under this system. Rather, the truth, it is said, emerges in the mind of the judge or jury when all sides to a dispute, partisan to the core, zealously investigate their cases and present them to a neutral court.

This arrangement permits lawyers to look to the system to produce justice, rather than to themselves. Importantly, it excuses lawyers from having to take responsibility for the positions they advocate. The result is a legal culture in which many lawyers believe they are not morally responsible for their professional behavior and there is no need for their professional conduct to be consistent with their personal morality. The lawyer's job is simply to play a part. Lawyers thus rationalize professional behavior that is inconsistent with their personal morality by saying that if each player in the system vigorously plays his or her role, the system will take over and sort both the truth and justice out.

There is a trace of role-differentiated behavior in Gandhi's early practice. In representing his wealthy commercial clients, he finds himself taking actions he would never take on his own as an independent moral agent. Gandhi, however, evolves. In the long arc of his practice he moves away from role-differentiated behavior. At the end, there is almost no difference between Gandhi's morality, on the one hand, and his professional behavior, on the other. Rather, they reflect each other. It is this merger in South Africa of the man and the professional that demonstrates to him the power to be gained from personal integrity and that serves as a precedent for uniting his spirituality with his politics in India.

CIVIL DISOBEDIENCE: ITS PURPOSES

The notion of civil disobedience developed by Gandhi in South Africa did not suddenly spring forth from him in its full maturity. It emerged in an evolutionary way—and did so as a result of a series of bold experiments. To understand these experiments as well as the civil disobedience campaigns Gandhi would later lead in India, an overview of the purposes to which civil disobedience can be put is necessary.

Over its long history, its practitioners have found civil disobedience useful for a variety of aims. While it is certainly true that a single civilly disobedient act often involves multiple, interrelated purposes, it is helpful for understanding Gandhi's experiments with civil disobedience to identify its most salient discrete purposes and to give examples of each. Moving from the simplest to the most complex, these are as follows.

Honoring one's conscience. While much civil disobedience has multiple motives, a disobedient might defy the law principally for reasons of conscience. Such a disobedient may have little concern for larger political, social, or cultural goals; this disobedient's primary motivation simply may be to act in a manner consistent with his or her own conscience by protesting a wrong. In this vein are those, for example, who engage in the Plowshares civil disobedience movement against nuclear weapons by trespassing on sites that have these weapons. They consistently say they are more interested in being faithful to the Christian gospel than being politically effective.[1]

Testing the law. Often the quickest—and in some circumstances the only—way to get a ruling on the validity of a law is to break the law and thus force a criminal prosecution of the disobedient. In that event, a forum is created for the disobedient to mount his or her argument to a court against the validity of the law as part of the disobedient's defense.

This was precisely the purpose for which five African Americans in 1964 entered a Louisiana public library designated by the local government for whites only. To challenge this discrimination, the men occupied the library's reading room and refused to leave when asked to do so. They were arrested for breaching the peace. In defending against this charge, the disobedients were able to attack the library's segregation as unconstitutional. Not only did the United States Supreme Court agree, but the Court also ruled that the disobedients had a constitutional right to mount their protest.[2]

Advancing the debate. When public discussion of a vital issue is stagnant or nonexistent, civil disobedience can cause discussion to occur in a higher key or to arise for the first time. A disobedient's act, if sufficiently out of the ordinary and sufficiently open, attracts the attention of the media and the public. Debate on the substantive issue often follows.

Susan B. Anthony, the great American advocate of woman's suffrage, knew this purpose well. In 1872, she attempted to vote when she knew she was prohibited from doing so on the grounds of gender. Her prosecution and trial made for front-page news all across the United States, stirring up a discussion of women's rights as no other single act had done.[3]

Creating change. Civil disobedience can be used to create a variety of forms of change—political, social, cultural, legal, and more. It often does so through what is now a fairly well established dynamic. The disobedient breaks a law; the disobedient suffers; the public takes note of the suffering and inquires as to the reason for the disobedient's action; the public sympathizes with the disobedient; the public puts pressure for change on those in power; and those in power react by enacting curative, institutional reform. While this dynamic does not fully explain every case of successful civil disobedience undertaken to create change, it does explain many such cases and it does highlight the critical role self-suffering plays in a civil disobedience campaign to create change.[4]

A leading example of civil disobedience undertaken to create change occurred in 1961 when equality activists boarded passenger buses in Washington, D.C., with the intent to travel to New Orleans and to challenge racial segregation in bus stations along the way. As the Freedom Riders moved from terminal to terminal, they drew the attention of the media, the public, and state and federal governments to the segregated terminals, particularly when they were severely beaten, their bus firebombed, and their lives threatened by racist opponents. The suffering they endured raised questions around the country about segregation, caused the public to sympathize with them, and created pressure on the federal government to intervene not only to protect the riders but also to create new law. At the insistence of Attorney General Robert F. Kennedy, the Interstate Commerce Commission issued new regulations banning racial discrimination in terminals.[5]

An important variant of this dynamic occurs when the disobedience is committed not by a small band of resisters seeking sympathy from the wider public, but by a significant swath of the population. Because government depends for its operation on the consent of the governed, when an appreciable portion of the public withdraws that cooperation through disobedience, government cannot function properly.[6] The Danish population demonstrated this principle with its widespread resistance to German occupation during World War II. In 2011, disobedient citizens in Tunisia and Egypt, as part of the Arab Spring, removed their rulers from power by withdrawing consent to their rule. Wael Ghonim, the young Google marketing director who was a key player in communicating the substance of the uprising to the Egyptian public, encapsulated the revolution's message to the Egyptian people in words Gandhi himself could not have improved upon: "This is your country; a government official is your employee who gets his salary from your tax money, and you have your rights."[7]

Gandhi's South African experiments follow this progression of purposes, though I am quite confident he did not anticipate their doing so. They begin with test-case disobedience, end with change-creating disobedience, and rest on the same foundation throughout—the need to act in concert with conscience.

GANDHI IN CONTEXT

This book focuses on the story of Gandhi's life as a lawyer, almost all of which takes place in South Africa in the years 1893 to 1911. After Gandhi leaves South Africa, he spends virtually the rest of his life (1915–1948) in India, where he devotes himself to the movement to free India from rule by the British. (British control of India began with the coming of the East India Company in the seventeenth century, accelerated with the assumption of the company's governing role by the British government in 1858, and ended with Britain's granting independence to India and Pakistan in 1947.) While it is beyond the scope of this book to address Gandhi's time in India in any great detail, a brief discussion of his work there will put this exploration of his life as a lawyer in South Africa in context.

Every schoolchild who has seen a map of Asia knows that India's landmass is vast, extending from the Indian Ocean in the south to the disputed border with Pakistan far to the north. Its history is equally vast, stretching from its millennia-old origins along the Indus River through the late-fifteenth-century arrival of the first Europeans to India's present-day parliamentary democracy.

Thrusting himself into the midst of this historical current near the start of the twentieth century was the forty-five-year-old Mohandas K. Gandhi, who, despite having spent most of his adult life in South Africa, would profoundly influence India and its history. The India that Gandhi found on his arrival home in 1915 was neither a clearly defined country nor an independent one. Its British rulers, however, had unintentionally done their best in the sixty years before his arrival to present Gandhi with a set of conditions that encouraged both Indian nationhood and Indian freedom.

Fielding a small but powerful force of not many more than a thousand men, the British Empire used its Indian Civil Service (ICS) to exercise authority throughout India, with ICS agents controlling virtually all aspects of government within their jurisdictions. David Lloyd George, Britain's prime minister from 1916 to 1922, famously credited the ICS with being "the steel frame on which the whole structure of government and of administration in India rests." That steel frame demonstrated for Indians that a competently operated administrative body could bring the subcontinent under the control of a national government.

The ICS was not the only enterprise that the empire created that paved the way for its own departure and made Gandhi's job of unifying and leading India easier. By the dawn of the twentieth century the British had put a railway system in place that was among the world's five largest. By connecting Indians to each other and to the world, Britain's investment in the railway system helped integrate India's economy. Much the same can be said of the methods of communication that the British developed in India in the second half of the nineteenth century. The postal service installed by the British served virtually the entire subcontinent, while the telegraph system reached areas where even the rail system had not penetrated. These modern systems of transportation and communication helped create a feeling of nationality as Indians from disparate parts of the subcontinent came to feel a connection to one another.

In addition to building India's infrastructure, the British educated the Indians who would come to oppose their rule. In the mid-nineteenth century, London ordained that there should be universities all across India.[8] At the same time this university system was developing, the British welcomed Indian students to Britain, where they might train for the professions—chiefly medicine and law. Gandhi, like many a nationalist leader in the making, would study law in Britain.

The supply of educated Indians soon outstripped the number of positions available. In 1884 Lord Ripon, the Crown's viceroy in India, reported the danger that education was creating: "Unless we are prepared to afford these men legitimate openings for their aspirations and ambitions, we had better at once abolish our Universities and close our Colleges, for they will only serve to turn out year by year in ever-increasing numbers men who must inevitably become the most dangerous and influential members of our rule."[9]

Ripon's fears would soon begin to be realized when in 1885 the Indian National Congress (INC)—a body of nationalists that would grow in importance and later include Gandhi—held its first meeting in Bombay (today, Mumbai). While the Congress founders who assembled then were not quite the radicals Ripon had described, they did raise their voices against the status quo, they were as influential as Ripon had predicted, and they had, courtesy of Ripon's empire, Western educations.

A small number of Western-educated elites dominated Indian intellectual life at the time of the 1885 meeting. Having been educated in British or British-influenced institutions, they gravitated toward employment in the service of the Raj or in the professions. The leadership of the INC, dominated as it was by lawyers trained in Britain, was a microcosm of this development. As a result of their education, they identified with the empire.

The demands that emerged from the first Congress meeting were predictably modest. When early Congress members sought greater Indian involvement in government, the government they had in mind was the colonial government, not that of an independent India. They considered themselves loyal sons of the empire who were simply asking for their rights as family members—a theme we will see Gandhi repeatedly articulate in South Africa as he argued for the rights of the clients and countrymen he was careful to call not Indians, but British Indians.

A favorite activity of the early nationalists was petitioning, an approach that rested on a belief in British fair play and equal justice. In his early South African days, we will see Gandhi often file petitions with South Africa's colonial governments—petitions that demonstrated a faith no less naïve than that of his nationalist counterparts in India. The similarity was not superficial. Gandhi and India's moderate nationalists shared a common understanding of the nature and role of the petition as polite, respectful, relatively restrained. Petitions fit neatly into the reigning paradigm: more Indian control of Indian affairs, yes, but within the imperial system.

This paradigm did not go unchallenged. Eventually a fissure opened in the nationalist movement, with moderates on one side and those known as "extremists" on the other. Dissatisfied with the slow approach of the moderates, the extremists engaged with the moderates in a struggle for supremacy during the early twentieth century. The strength of the movement for independence was so weakened by this internecine struggle that it opened a path for Gandhi to make his move into the leadership of the nationalist movement.

But first there was a year of relative silence while Gandhi, newly arrived in India, educated himself by traveling about the subcontinent. As he did so, he had time to reflect on his experience with nonviolence in South Africa, where his form of opposition to the government was originally called passive resistance—principally a refusal to obey the law based on conscience. Because Gandhi did not believe this term adequately captured the spirit of his movement, he held a contest to rename it. His cousin suggested *sadagraha*—"firmness in a good cause." Gandhi reacted in this wise: "I liked the word, but it did not fully represent the whole idea I wished it to connote. I therefore corrected it to 'Satyagraha.' Truth (Satya) implies love, and firmness (agraha) engenders and therefore serves as a synonym for force. I thus began to call the Indian movement 'Satyagraha,' that is to say, the Force which is born of Truth and Love or non-violence, and gave up the use of the phrase 'passive resistance.'"[10]

When Gandhi did enter into Indian politics and began to acquire a more robust national profile, it was, paradoxically, at the local level, where he conducted three attention-getting satyagraha campaigns. These early experiences—some of them involving civil disobedience—were the start of a process that caused Gandhi to become a national figure.

The journey to national prominence, however, would not be easy. Having lived abroad almost continuously since he was eighteen, Gandhi had no easy familiarity with India, its people, or its problems. In South Africa, for example, very little was made of a long-standing Indian problem: Hindu-Muslim discord. The South African Indian community, strangers together in a foreign land, was unified. In fact, Gandhi, a Hindu, conducted a very successful commercial law practice representing almost exclusively Muslim traders in South Africa. Indians, displaced from their native land, overlooked their differences and clung to each other.

On their home soil in India there was no similar motivation for unity. Conflict was the norm. Attempting to vault into the leadership of a movement deeply fractured by these differences was immensely difficult—and Gandhi clearly saw it that way. His response to this reality was to seek out issues, such as the Caliphate movement in the 1920s—that he could use to unite the two religious communities. While some judge it to have been unsuccessful in uniting the communities, in none of his campaigns—from the campaign against restrictions on Indian civil liberties in the early twenties to the pro-independence "Quit India" movement during World War II—did he succeed on as many levels as he did in the Salt Campaign of the early 1930s, a campaign in which Gandhi capitalized on the lessons he had learned in South Africa about sacrifice, suffering, and civil disobedience.

By the time of the annual Congress meeting in 1928, a split in the Congress had developed between those who favored Dominion status within the empire and those who favored complete and immediate independence. Gandhi brokered a compromise. The Congress would issue an ultimatum to Britain: either India would receive Dominion status by the end of 1929, or Congress would organize "non-violent non-co-operation" in support of complete independence.

Britain responded. In October 1929, the British viceroy in India, Lord Irwin, announced that the government had allowed him "to state clearly that . . . the natural issue of India's constitutional progress . . . is the attainment of Dominion status." Moreover, Indian representatives would be invited to a Round Table Conference to discuss "the British-Indian and All-Indian problems." The Congress saw this statement as a commitment to write the constitution for a new India at the conference; its initial reaction, accordingly, was largely positive. However, in the House of Commons British politicians rose in opposition to the idea, renewed resistance to Dominion status caused a split within the Congress, and Irwin himself was unable to guarantee the Congress that Dominion status would emerge from the conference as the Indians originally anticipated. When the Congress met at the end of 1929, it committed itself to complete independence, authorizing consideration of civil disobedience.

It was up to Gandhi to conceive of and lead the disobedience. He devised a brilliant plan calling for a tightly controlled group of ashram-based supporters to break the laws that imposed taxes on salt and restricted the free manufacture of salt by Indians.[11] Gandhi would greatly reduce the chance of violence by keeping the initial disobedience in-house. Disobedience against the salt laws slyly promoted Muslim-Hindu unity by bringing the two communities together around a nonreligious, economic issue. And, as historian Judith Brown has observed, the campaign's "condemnation of a tax on a necessity of life for all by an exploitative foreign government could serve as a mass rallying cry and would probably rouse sympathy in England and America, elevating the whole campaign to a moral plane which would embarrass the raj."[12]

Gandhi dramatized his disobedience by staging a huge buildup to it. He would undertake a long march to the sea with a band of dedicated supporters and, only after he arrived there, break the law by making salt. Before the march, Gandhi wrote to Lord Irwin sharing the details of his planned disobedience and offering a negotiated settlement.

When the British declined to settle, Gandhi and seventy-eight compatriots set off on the morning of March 12, 1930, from Gandhi's Ahmedabad ashram for the seashore at Dandi—some 220 miles away.[13] A huge crowd— one British newspaper's estimate was 100,000—lined the immediate road ahead. The plan was to stop at a different village each night and each morning. At each stop, Gandhi would speak not only against the salt tax, but for the adoption of the ideal of village life as a path toward freedom and a good in its own right. The crowds for these talks were superb, ranging from the hundreds in small villages to the tens of thousands in larger towns.

The delegation reached Dandi on April 5. The next day, Gandhi defied the empire by very deliberately stooping over and gathering up a concoction of mud and salt. His followers then boiled seawater from which they extracted salt in defiance of the law. Gandhi used the first days after this initial salt-making to speak about the injustice of the salt laws. In the meantime, illegal salt-making erupted all across the country. Many thousands were arrested.

For weeks after the Dandi conclusion to the march, Gandhi mounted a vigorous, highly public campaign against the salt law. As he did so, government officials simply did not know what to do with him. If they arrested him, they would help transform him into an even greater hero than he already was. If they let him continue his defiance, the power of the government would be progressively diminished. Gandhi had plans to make matters more difficult for the government by raising the stakes; he intended to lead a nonviolent raid on the Dharasana Salt Works. The government, with its continued credibility at stake, felt forced to act. It arrested Gandhi just past midnight on May 5. Nonetheless, the raid went on. The disobedients endured exceptionally violent treatment by the lathi-armed police. There were multiple results flowing from this violence: injuries to hundreds of peaceful disobedients—with at least two of the injured dying; journalist Webb Miller's moving reporting of Indian bravery in the face of police brutality; the inspiration for many other Indians to participate in subsequent raids; and the generation of enormous sympathy from the West for Gandhi's cause.

Even with Gandhi and his co-workers in jail—or perhaps because they were in jail—civil disobedience against the salt laws continued. Thousands of localized civil disobedience movements around the country broke out over the course of the next year, accompanied by a widespread boycott of foreign cloth. By the time the movement came to an end, some sixty thousand Indian disobedients had graced the empire's jails.

To allow them to confer over the terms of a possible settlement, the British released Gandhi and the other imprisoned members of a key Congress committee in early 1931. In February and March, Gandhi and Irwin negotiated face-to-face. They reached an agreement, commonly known as the Gandhi-Irwin Pact, in early March. By not calling for the outright repeal of the salt laws, the pact allowed the government to save face. The Indians realized many of their goals, however. In return for discontinuing disobedience and the boycott of British goods, the government would interpret the law to allow Indians to make and sell salt in their villages. Moreover, the government agreed that additional talks on constitutional reform would be held and would include representation from the Congress. In addition, imprisoned nonviolent disobedients would be released, pending prosecutions of nonviolent disobedients would be withdrawn, uncollected fines would be waived, some village officials who had resigned in protest would be reinstated, ordinances restricting civil liberties would be withdrawn, some confiscated properties would be restored to their owners, and lawful picketing could continue.

Nonviolent discipline was essential to the success of the Salt Campaign. But more important, the campaign worked because the participants engaged the dynamic that leads to social and political change. It did so in a way that revealed the two basic ways disobedience can be understood to lead to change. The salt campaigners made the sacrifice to endure jailings, beatings, and even death. When their suffering was seen by the public, including the international public, the public sympathized. This created pressure on the British government, which in turn led to curative institutional reaction. At the same time, the Salt Campaign was a massive withdrawal of consent to the salt laws as tens of thousands of people all across the subcontinent broke the laws governing the manufacture and sale of salt.

The salt disobedience is as clear an instance of success in creating change as there is in the Gandhian portfolio of disobedience. It resulted in a liberalization of the administration of the salt laws and in the withdrawal of ordinances restricting civil liberties. Even more important than a new understanding of the law, it created a new respect for the power of the Indian independence movement. As Gandhi scholar Thomas Weber has described it, the campaign "was about empowerment; it told people that they were stronger than they thought and that the rulers were weaker than they imagined."[14]

After World War II, Britain calculated that maintaining its rule was more trouble than it was worth. It finally gave India its independence in 1947, and at the same time consented to the establishment of Pakistan, a separate Muslim state, created from Indian territory. Gandhi was deeply distressed by this partition of India and his failure to ultimately bridge Hindu-Muslim differences.

Just months later, a bullet fired by a disgruntled Hindu nationalist brought his life to an end.

GANDHI'S SIGNIFICANCE TODAY

Because neither the Salt Campaign nor any of Gandhi's other civil disobedience campaigns brought about the immediate liberation of India, scholars argue about the weight to give Gandhi's contribution to the struggle for independence. Some give Gandhi the lion's share of the credit, while others severely discount his role. In some respects the criticism is quite unfair because immediate liberation was not always Gandhi's goal. His most successful campaign, the Salt Campaign, had the more limited goal of raising India's stature in the eyes of Britain and the world and of providing Indians with a sense of their own considerable power. The Salt Campaign achieved these goals and more by engaging the dynamic that connects suffering to social and political change.

In other instances the criticism is more justified. Judith Brown observes that the failure of Gandhi's civil disobedience during World War II casts "doubt on the viability of non-violence as a political mode except in very restricted, small-scale situations, where its exponents could be carefully disciplined and deployed."[15]

Professor Brown is correct to emphasize the need for nonviolent discipline. The history of civil disobedience movements is littered with the debris from campaigns that foundered on lack of discipline. Campaigns lacking nonviolent discipline play right into the hands of the oppressor, who *wants* the disobedients to use violence. The use of violence delegitimizes the resistance in the world's eyes, practically eliminates the possibility of sympathy for the disobedients, and places the contest directly on grounds where the oppressor invariably has an overwhelming advantage.

The leadership of the American civil rights movement understood this reality when it imported Gandhi's thinking in the late 1950s and the early 1960s. James Lawson, a colleague of Martin Luther King, Jr., who had spent time in India, helped introduce Gandhian thinking and tactics into the movement at large and the lunch counter sit-ins in particular. The sit-ins were extremely successful in desegregating southern lunch counters in the early 1960s in no small part because of the stress Lawson put on nonviolent discipline when he prepared sit-in participants for their disobedience. Lawson's influence also extended to the Freedom Rides, another campaign that relied on strict nonviolent discipline and one that succeeded in desegregating bus depots throughout the American South.

The leading civil rights figure of his time, King more than once acknowledged Gandhi's influence on his thinking. In a radio broadcast during his 1959 visit to India, he said: "Since being in India, I am more convinced than ever . . . that . . . nonviolent resistance is the most potent weapon available to oppressed people in their struggle for justice. . . . Mahatma Gandhi embodied in his life certain universal principles that are inherent in the moral structure of the universe, and these principles are as inescapable as the law of gravitation."[16]

At the point of the American civil rights movement in the evolving history of nonviolent civil disobedience, the argument could still be made that Gandhian civil disobedience could succeed only when it embraced nonviolent discipline and that nonviolent discipline was possible only in very controlled situations. What no one could foresee was the programmatic application of Gandhian disobedience to such a broad range of controlled situations—some involving very large numbers of participants—that it could serve as an extremely powerful and fairly reliable tool for bringing down repressive, autocratic regimes.

No one, that is, except for Gene Sharp.

For more than fifty years, it has been the mission of nonviolence scholar Gene Sharp to demonstrate that nonviolence works better than violence in toppling oppressive, nondemocratic regimes. (As used here, "nonviolence" includes civil disobedience as one of its primary manifestations.) Sharp's claim is that "all governments can rule only as long as they receive replenishment of the needed sources of their power from the cooperation, submission, and obedience of the population and the institutions of the society." He goes on to argue that nonviolence "is uniquely suited to severing those sources of power."

Sharp's inspiration came from Gandhi. His first book, published in 1960 by India's Navajivan Publishing House, was a study of Gandhi. Today Sharp and those who are carrying on his work are careful not to promote nonviolence as a morally superior path to self-reform and freedom, as Gandhi often did. Rather, their argument is straightforwardly pragmatic: nonviolence in general and civil disobedience in particular, when properly used, are tools that work better than any other in liberating oppressed populations and paving the way for functioning democracies.

And work well they have.[17] Sharp's book *From Dictatorship to Democracy: A Conceptual Framework for Liberation* is changing the world. Translated into more than thirty languages, it serves as a virtual handbook for nonviolent revolution. This is the book that was put in the hands of the young people of Serbia that helped them throw the dictator, Slobodan Milosevic, out of office in 2000. Their nonviolent resistance movement, known as Otpor (Resistance), was heavily influenced by Sharp. After Otpor defeated Milosevic, the movement praised Sharp's approach as "an astoundingly effective blueprint for confronting a brutal regime."

The Otpor lesson was not lost on young activists in Tunisia and Egypt. They studied Otpor—and they took to Sharp. Egypt's April 6 Movement created a symbol to resemble Otpor's clenched fist, and elements of the movement went to Serbia to meet with Otpor. Another Egyptian group, the Academy of Change, also relied on Sharp's work.[18] It is no exaggeration to say that Sharp was an intellectual father of the Arab Spring—and Gandhi a grandfather.

Gandhi would feel quite comfortable with King's understanding of Gandhian nonviolence as having a foundation in morality, and at least somewhat uncomfortable with Sharp's promotion of nonviolence on purely pragmatic lines. But despite this fissure among devotees of nonviolence, this much is true: Gandhi's technique of nonviolence lives on and has made a material difference in freedom movements all around the globe, from bus stations in the American South to public squares in Cairo, Egypt.

Gandhi may not have become a practitioner and theorist of nonviolence had he not been a lawyer in South Africa. Admittedly, there is a risk of oversimplification associated with seeing Gandhi's world primarily through his life in the law and the civil disobedience to which it led. In that vein, I recognize that Gandhi's motivations were always complex. To understand them, scholars over the years have isolated them. Some have written about his religious motivations, some about his philosophical motivations, some about his political motivations, some about his cultural motivations, and still others about his psychological motivations. A fair criticism of what I have done here is that my work is in that tradition. To this, I plead guilty. I will leave the legitimate and important task of broadly contextualizing Gandhi's time in the law to other scholars at other times. My object is clear—and different. One of the last great unexplored areas in the Gandhi story deals with the two decades he spent practicing law. My mission here is to demonstrate how the law played a critical role in bringing Gandhi into a position from which he was forced to invent his philosophy and practice of nonviolent civil disobedience—a signal development the consequences of which threaten oppressive regimes even to this day.

It is my hope that this book illuminates Gandhi's path to disobedience and, along the way, permits him to teach us by example what it means to have a life that brings into near-perfect unity one's public behavior with one's mostly deeply held spiritual beliefs.

ONE

Dispatched to London

> It seems strange that any man should take one of the most important steps of his life, and one on which his future happiness largely depends, without duly weighing what it means beforehand. Yet, in the case of many Barristers, this is so.
>
> BALL, *The Student's Guide to the Bar* (1879)

IT WOULD BE SURPRISING IF anyone noticed him. The person who arrived on the SS *Clyde* on September 29, 1888, at Tilbury Station, twenty miles south of London, England, was not the ascetic, politician, and saint whose campaign for Indian independence would make his loin-clothed image instantly recognizable a century later in Richard Attenborough's Academy-award winning film, *Gandhi*. Rather, the figure stepping gingerly into that inhospitably cold and foggy Saturday night was a timid, even frail, eighteen-year-old child from an obscure part of a continent thousands of miles away, dispatched from his Hindu homeland to the foreign Christian and Western culture that was nineteenth-century Britain.[1]

What transformed this shy boy into a respected leader? What drew the leader to civil disobedience? The answers, in part, are to be found in the experiences Gandhi underwent in the law. Before passing into that phase of his life during which he dedicated himself to the liberation of India from British rule, Gandhi practiced law for twenty years, at first briefly and unsuccessfully in India and then for a substantial period and quite successfully in South Africa before giving up the practice and returning to India. During the period of his legal education and then his practice, Gandhi was severely tested and, in response, found his voice and his focus. He established his identity as one who saw injustice clearly and acted decisively against it, saw truth clearly and acted decisively for it. He succeeded in conjoining his practice with his beliefs, making of the law not simply his profession but his vocation. And in the end, even as he recognized the limits of traditional legal processes, he discovered the great dynamic within the law that converts civil disobedience into social change.

The choice of career, like the choice of marriage, was not Gandhi's to make. Just as his marriage at age thirteen to Kasturba was arranged for him, so, too, was the decision to study law the product of family forces other than his own will. Gandhi's father, Karamchand Gandhi, had met with some success in ascending to positions of high bureaucratic power, serving as prime minister of the small dominions of Porbandar, Rajkot, and Vankaner. While Karamchand's political career failed to make his family wealthy, neither did the family want for the basics of life. Theirs was a day-to-day stability. Karamchand's health, however, worsened as a result of age and accident, and eventually he was forced to give up his career in government. When he passed away, he did not leave the family anything on which to live. None of Gandhi's three older siblings had the prospects required to carry the family. Accordingly, the burden settled on the shoulders of young Mohandas Karamchand Gandhi.

After completing high school, Gandhi passed the Bombay University matriculation examination and took up his studies at Samaldas College in Bhavnagar in 1887. He wasn't much of a student, being both uninterested in and unable to follow his professors' lectures. Compounding the difficulty he had with his studies were his physical problems. Gandhi complained of constant headaches and nosebleeds due, some conjectured, to the hot climate. Gandhi's summer vacation from Samaldas could not come too soon. In late April 1888, at the start of his vacation, Gandhi and his oldest brother, Lakshmidas, decided to visit a friend of the family, the Brahmin Mavji Dave. On hearing Gandhi's complaints about college, including his prediction that he would fail his first-year examination, Mavji suggested that Gandhi be sent to England to study for the bar. This, he thought, would prepare Gandhi to reclaim his father's position and income in much better fashion than would the pursuit of an ordinary college degree. The calculus being made at this time did not involve altruistic concerns. The naked purpose of providing young Gandhi a legal education was to guarantee an income for the family. It is not surprising, then, that when Gandhi was asked in 1891 why he had come to England to study the law, his forthright reply was "ambition."

There are no reports indicating just what Gandhi thought at this time of what a life in the law meant, if he gave any thought to it at all. Indeed, there are no reports indicating any resistance on Gandhi's part to the idea of training in the law, except his timid inquiry whether he could be sent to study his first love, medicine, instead of law, a proposal which was quickly discarded in the wake of his brother's declaration that it was their father's wish that Mohandas become a lawyer, not a physician. Thus it appears that Gandhi accepted the choice of profession made for him with little more objection than that he voiced to the choice of a wife his family made for him.

Regardless of the little thought Gandhi himself may have given to studying the law or being a barrister, we do know that he relished the prospect of three years in England. Perhaps this is what motivated him to overcome four serious obstacles to his studying law there: the lack of any means to finance his legal education overseas, the concerns of his wife's family, the uncertainty of his mother, and the opposition of his caste.

OVERCOMING OBSTACLES

Lakshmidas assumed the task of obtaining financing. His first attempt at securing the necessary funds was to send Gandhi off to beseech Frederick Lely, the British administrator of Porbandar state, for governmental assistance. The Gandhis hoped that their reputation with Lely, established by the late Karamchand, would lead Lely to open the state coffers. After a four-day journey to Porbandar and after elaborately rehearsing his request, Gandhi was startled when his request was dismissed out-of-hand. Lely brusquely advised him to secure his B.A. before attempting the study of law, after which Lely would consider granting some aid. Gandhi then turned to his cousin Parmanandbhai, who promised his financial support, as did Meghjibhai, another cousin. Despite their promises, there is no evidence that either of these cousins aided Gandhi; indeed Meghjibhai is on record as later angrily denying Gandhi any help. Two additional governmental representatives whom Gandhi approached were as unhelpful as Lely. Other than some small amounts of money and a silver chain that some of his friends gave him on his departure from Bombay, it appears that Gandhi received no financial help from any of his friends, extended family, or governmental officials. If Gandhi was to go to London, it would be by exhausting what capital remained with his immediate family after the death of Karamchand.

Money, however, was the least-complicated of Gandhi's problems. He was married to Kasturba, the daughter of the merchant Seth Gokaldas Makanji of Porbandar—an arrangement put together according to Indian custom by the families of the children. Now here was the eighteen-year-old Kasturba, pregnant with the couple's child,[2] about to be abandoned for three years by her husband. This did not sit well with Kasturba's parents. Gandhi spent many hours convincing them of the wisdom of his intentions and reassuring them that Lakshmidas would look after Kasturba. Speaking of the difficult project of winning over Kasturba's parents to his plan, Gandhi later said, "Patience and perseverance overcome mountains."

But an even more difficult task lay ahead—obtaining the blessing of Gandhi's mother, Putli Ba. Naturally, she had the reluctance any mother would to bid adieu to her youngest child.[3] Perhaps as an expression of this fear, but more likely as an expression of genuine spiritual concern, Putli Ba, a devout Hindu, worried that her son would surrender his Hindu practices to the English appetite for the forbidden pleasures of wine and meat. Indeed, there was an idea abroad at this time in India that wine and meat were actually necessary for survival in the English climate. Determined to go to England, Gandhi devised two ways of dealing with his mother's concerns. First, by his own admission, he exaggerated the benefits of his English sojourn. Second, to quiet her concerns about his moral purity, he secured the services of Becharji Swami, a Jain monk and a family advisor, to administer an oath to him that he would refrain from wine, meat, and for good measure, women. With these steps reassuring Putli Ba, she granted her permission.

Even with his immediate family in the fold, however, Gandhi's plan was controversial. To make his way to London, he needed to travel from Rajkot to Bombay, where he would board a steamer for England. Bombay was even more populated by members of his caste than his hometown. This was unfortunate for Gandhi; there was heated resistance on the part of his caste to the notion of any of their members going abroad. A series of incidents in which Gandhi was peppered with harassment on the streets of Bombay for his intentions was followed by an even more dramatic public confrontation. Gandhi was forced to attend a meeting of his entire caste, at which the subject of his going abroad would be addressed before the whole group. The discussion came to a head with this ultimatum issued by the leader of the caste to Gandhi: "We were your father's friends, and therefore we feel for you; as heads of the caste you know our power. We are positively informed that you will have to eat flesh and drink wine in England; moreover, you have to cross the waters; all this you must know is against our caste rules. Therefore, we command you to reconsider your decision, or else the heaviest punishment will be meted out to you."[4] Gandhi's unequivocal response was to reject the threat, saying that he was going nonetheless. The head of the caste thereupon decreed that Gandhi was no longer his father's son, ordered all members of the caste to have nothing to do with him, and declared him an outcast.

While the initial idea of taking up legal studies did not belong to Gandhi, it is clear from his determination to remain unaffected by the decision of his caste and to overcome the other obstacles to his going that once he embraced an arrangement thrust upon him by others, he advanced that arrangement with all the same energy and spirit of one who gave birth to it. Just as he had been faithful to his arranged marriage, he would be faithful to the plan to study the law, foreshadowing his faithfulness to the integrity of the legal process itself that would distinguish his career in the law.

On September 4, 1888, two weeks after being ejected from his caste, Gandhi boarded a steamship for London.

THE DISMAL STATE OF BRITISH LEGAL TRAINING

The world of legal education into which Gandhi stepped in the fall of 1888 would be almost unrecognizable to legal educators today. It is now almost universally true that there is a serious academic component in one's training for the bar, usually in a university context. It often includes or is followed by practical training in either simulated or actual practice settings or both.

Legal education at the close of the nineteenth century in London could hardly have been more different. To begin with, the student prepared for the call to the bar in something other than a traditional university setting. Since at least the middle of the fourteenth century those who wished to become barristers received their call to the bar by first enrolling in one of the four Inns of Court. The source of the term "inn" is instructive. Historian Robert Pearce tells us, "The word 'Inne' was anciently used to denote the town houses in which great men resided when they were in attendance at court."[5] From this beginning the various Inns grew into powerful voluntary associations of barristers, centered in London, the purpose of which was to control entry to the bar and to provide young men an environment within which to read the law in preparation for their bar examinations.[6] One must be quick to add, however, that there appears to have been another function of the Inns, namely to school barristers-to-be in the long-standing elitist traditions of the bar. This tradition had deep historical roots. Sir John Fortescue, the Lancastrian chief justice, speaking of the practices of the fifteenth century, said that "the greatest nobility . . . often place their children in those Inns . . . not so much to make the laws their study, much less to live by the profession . . . but to form their manners."[7]

This deep-rooted awareness of manners and social status persisted down to the time Gandhi began his studies and was no more evident than in the requirement that the student eat a minimum number of dinners with his fellow students and the senior barristers of his Inn while awaiting his call to the bar. Dinners were highly stylized affairs, emphasizing hierarchy, formality, and tradition.

At earlier points in their history, the Inns provided the students with lengthy and careful lectures, known as readings, by distinguished members of the bar. The reader prepared an elaborate discussion of an act or statute that, after being delivered, was followed by a series of arguments by barristers about the incorrectness of the reader's opinion, followed itself by the reader's rebuttal. In addition to these readings, the students were provided with the opportunity to observe mock exercises called bolts and moots.

KEEPING TERMS: DINNER AS EDUCATION

By the time of Gandhi's arrival these practices had disappeared, and the Inns, while retaining their control over admission, had, with respect to their pedagogical function, descended to institutions akin to educationally undemanding social fraternities. The practice of "keeping terms," as the dinner requirement was known, remained, but in an eviscerated form. Four terms a year were held. A student was required to keep twelve terms in all, meaning that one could complete his preparation for the bar in just under three years. During these terms, students with university educations were required to dine at least three times during each term in a dining hall run by the Inn while nonuniversity students, like Gandhi, were required to eat dinner there at least six times a term. Students and barristers would be seated at tables of four, while the "benchers" would be seated separately.[8] Although all were required to appear for dinner attired in their formal gowns, there was no requirement that any part of the dinner conversation center on the law. Indeed there was not even any conversation between the students and the benchers. There were no readings, lectures, or speeches. There were no moot exercises, the custom of conducting mock trials having been discarded long before Gandhi arrived. The only requirement was that the student, to get credit for attending, appear before grace was said and remain present throughout the dinner until a concluding after-dinner grace was said. By 1888, it appeared that keeping terms had lost any function it may once have had to impart a formal legal education to the students and was reduced to nothing more than a ceremony to inculcate in the student the manners of his profession.[9]

Apart from dinners there was no setting in which students were required to come in contact with either lecturers or practitioners.[10] The students' days were their own. A diligent student would occupy himself, perhaps in one of the Inns' comfortable libraries, with the reading entailed in meeting the only academic requirements of this process: the passage of two written examinations, one in Roman law and one in English law. *The Student's Guide to the Bar*, by William Ball of the Inner Temple, published in 1879, states that the knowledge required to pass the Roman law examination was slight, and advises that for the person with a university education, "six weeks' work of . . . six hours a day would be sufficient."[11] In the period before Gandhi arrived in England, the English law examination had developed a reputation for being not much more challenging than that in Roman law, with Ball estimating that "four months' work of . . . six hours a day ought to be amply sufficient for a University man of average abilities and education."[12] The picture changed just before Gandhi started his studies. Writing on the eve of Gandhi's arrival in London, T. B. Napier and R. M. Stephenson, authors of *A Practical Guide to the Bar* (1888), claimed that "until quite recently the difficulty of the Bar examinations was greatly underrated" and that the "percentage of men who are ploughed for the Bar examinations is tolerably large."[13] It is not surprising, then, that they advised more study than Ball, namely two to three months of steady work for the Roman law examination and more than just "a few months' reading" for the English law examination.[14]

The final condition for being called to the bar was simply that the applicant be at least twenty-one.

These were the requirements to be called to the Bar in Gandhi's day, a set of criteria so minimal that it was universally agreed that one's legal education at the Inns had to be supplemented by an apprenticeship if one was to have any chance of success as a barrister. By associating himself with a practitioner, the pupil could familiarize himself with practice not only by observing the work of his barrister but by helping in the work itself, such as by drafting conveyances and pleadings under the barrister's supervision. Opinions as to how long a pupil should read in chambers, as it was called, ranged from one to three years.[15]

THE INNER TEMPLE

Like every barrister-to-be, Gandhi had his choice of inns. Of the four—Gray's Inn, Lincoln's Inn, the Middle Temple, and the Inner Temple—the Inner Temple was the most expensive.[16] Gandhi chose the Inner Temple. Given the difficulty he had in India raising the funds to support himself in England, and given his lifelong habit of squeezing every ounce out of every rupee, a habit already well developed when he arrived in England, this is something of a surprise. Because there is no record indicating why Gandhi chose the Inner Temple, we can only speculate. Perhaps he chose it because it was the most prestigious; the Inner Temple numbers Lord Coke, for example, among its graduates. Perhaps he chose it because it had the largest membership and because he thought he could therefore expect to find there the company of a fair number of countrymen.[17] The most plausible explanation, however, is that he chose it because it focused on the common law, the study of which would aid him later in his practice in India.[18]

Whatever Gandhi's reason for choosing the Inner Temple, it was not unlike the other Inns with respect to the abysmal level of training it offered aspiring barristers. By the middle of the nineteenth century, the Inns had fallen to a very low point. Only the most minimal intellectual standards were maintained. It was not until the decade before Gandhi's arrival, in 1872, that the Inns agreed to require students to take a bar examination, and it was not until the very year Gandhi arrived in England that all the Inns required that nonmatriculates take and pass a special entrance examination. Since Gandhi had already passed the Bombay matriculation examination, he was excused from the preliminary examination to which nonmatriculates were subject. Gandhi's agenda, therefore, was clear and simple: to be called to the bar, he had only to keep terms and pass examinations in Roman and English law.

But Gandhi was still a student without a university degree, while the great majority of his fellow students were university graduates.[19] To make matters worse, Gandhi didn't even have full command of the English language. When he was unceremoniously invited to leave a swank restaurant because of what were perceived to be his bad manners, he assuaged his pain by resolving to take on Western ways and master "the task of becoming an English gentleman." As part of his plan to become more sophisticated, Gandhi began searching for a suitable program of study. The reputation of the special admission examination for nonmatriculates was that it was a pushover, requiring only minimal knowledge of Latin, English, and English history. Gandhi needed something quite different to distinguish himself. In the University of London matriculation examination he found a suitably difficult challenge.[20] In addition to the subjects tested on the bar's special examination, this examination required that the student know other subjects, including science and a modern language. Gandhi chose to be tested in French, a language with which he had some familiarity. Joining a private matriculation class and keeping meticulous fidelity to a self-imposed schedule, Gandhi undertook a five-month course of fairly arduous private study that culminated in his taking the examination in January 1890, nearly a year and a half after landing on England's shores. The results were not good. Gandhi, to use his phrase, got "ploughed in Latin."[21] Latin and French together, he later admitted, were too much for him.

Gandhi was unbowed. He renewed his studies, substituting "heat and light" for the more difficult subject of chemistry, and reattacking Latin, for which, he says, he acquired a taste. At the same time, Gandhi apparently was suffering from pangs of guilt, thinking that he was spending his family's fortune only to meet failure. Accordingly, he secured a smaller apartment and began eating more of his meals at home. The change, he says, "harmonized my inner and outer life. It was also more in keeping with the means of my family. My life was certainly more truthful and my soul knew no bounds of joy."[22] Gandhi took the examination in June 1890 and, this time, passed it. Making his accomplishment all the more noteworthy is the fact that for much of the time prior to his taking the London examination, he was also preparing for his examination in Roman law, which he took just three months earlier.

BAR EXAMINATIONS

Those in the business of advising law students at the time universally recommended that the Roman law examination be taken at the earliest possible moment, thus freeing up the maximum amount of time to study for the examination in English law that followed. Inns permitted their students to take the Roman law examination after four terms. Gandhi would have completed his first four terms with the end of the Trinity term in mid-June 1889, yet he did not take the Roman law examination until March 1890. Why the delay? The most likely explanation is that Gandhi divided his attention for a substantial period of time between his preparation for the Roman law and London examinations.[23] Whatever the reason for the delay in taking the Roman law examination, Gandhi was not hurt by it. He finished sixth out of the forty-six who sat for it. Not a bad showing for one who was not a "University man."[24]

With the Roman law and London examinations both behind him, Gandhi opened the summer of 1890 with but one more substantial hurdle: passage of the English law examination (known as the "bar finals"). This examination could not be taken before one had kept nine terms. For Gandhi, his ninth term would be completed with the conclusion of the 1890 Michaelmas term on November 25, 1890. For this examination, Gandhi was out of the gate with the crack of the starter's gun, sitting for it at the first opportunity, from December 15 to December 20, 1890. While this set of dates falls just six months after his London examination, Gandhi actually spent more time than that to prepare, pouring himself into the common law for "nine months of fairly hard labor."[25] Even accounting for a month he spent in Brighton in the summer of 1890 and accounting for the study he undertook earlier in 1890 to pass the Roman law and London examinations, the amount of study Gandhi invested in preparation for the bar finals exceeded the four months of study recommended by Ball for a university-educated person. In his autobiography, Gandhi recounts that he managed to increase his burden of preparation by forgoing the use of notes on the law that were circulating among students, choosing instead to go directly to the recommended textbooks instead. Foreshadowing the scrupulousness that would characterize his entire life at the bar, he felt that to do otherwise would be a fraud. Accordingly, he purchased and read "all the text-books . . . , investing much money in them."[26] Among the treatises Gandhi read were Snell's *The Principles of Equity, Intended for the Use of Students and the Profession*, which he found "full of interest, but a bit hard to understand" and which actually would aid him in his religious explorations later in life, and Williams' *Principles of the Law of Real Property, Intended as a First Book for the Use of Students in Conveyancing*,[27] surely the only law text in existence ever described as reading "like a novel."[28]

Gandhi's industriousness paid dividends. On January 12, 1891, he learned that he had passed his bar finals. Validating Napier and Stephenson's observation that the test had recently become more difficult than most thought,[29] 32 of the 109 test takers failed. Of the 77 who passed, Gandhi placed in the top half, finishing 34th.

Gandhi placed fairly highly, too, in the esteem of his fellow "dinner barristers," as they were then called, but not for very admirable reasons. Each table of four was allocated a set amount of wine for each meal. With the abstemious Gandhi at one's table, the wine could be split not four ways, but three. As a result, Gandhi was very much in demand as a dinner companion.

AN APPRENTICESHIP FORGONE

And dinner was his last formal obligation, for with his passing the bar finals, Gandhi had now fulfilled all the academic requirements for the call to the bar. But for the necessity of keeping the Hilary, Easter, and Trinity terms, he had no obligations between the end of his test on December 20, 1890, and the date in early June 1891 when he could anticipate being called to the bar. While an apprenticeship was not a requirement for being called, students were nonetheless strongly advised to use the half-year between the bar finals and the call, as well as a period of one to two years after the call, to learn how to practice by serving as apprentices in the offices of practicing barristers. Without the experience of pupilage, it was adjudged that the "greatest amount of theoretical or book knowledge [was] comparatively worthless."[30]

For reasons he does not explain, and apparently contrary to the general advice he later gave others, Gandhi never apprenticed.[31] Why forgo the experience? Perhaps Gandhi deemed practice in India so different from that in England that apprenticing would have been a waste of his time—an unlikely supposition in light of the court system operated by the British Empire in India. Perhaps the fastidiously economical Gandhi did not believe he could afford to apprentice; after all, it was not free. A pupil was expected to pay his barrister fifty guineas for each six months of pupilage. Perhaps Gandhi could not find a barrister who would take him on for such a relatively short period of time with no prospect of Gandhi's returning the investment with permanent employment. Perhaps Gandhi, lacking close connections to the British bar, could find no barrister at all. The most intriguing explanation, however, is that Gandhi was preoccupied with a realm of life entirely separate from the bar.

When he arrived in London, Gandhi was thrust into a world where he was a stranger looking to be accepted. The world of the Inns, with its dinners, costumes, formality, and long tradition of catering to the educated, wealthy, and noble, was an upper-class world to which this relatively uneducated boy from the colonial backwaters of India was unaccustomed, but which he was eager to explore. Gandhi's understanding of the privileged status to which barristers were entitled may have led him to see his mission in England to learn and take on the customs of the elite. After all, he had been sent to England to attain the lofty status of barrister for one reason only: to come home and provide financial leadership for the family. Thus, it is likely that Gandhi believed that becoming a barrister required of him different tastes and manners. Accordingly, he experimented in 1890 with top hats, starched collars, silk shirts, striped trousers, gold watch chains, leather gloves, walking sticks, patent leather shoes, spats, and evening suits.[32] The private lessons in dance, elocution, violin, and French that he took for a brief time can be similarly explained.[33] With time, however, Gandhi came to his senses, realizing that a dandy was not who he was, nor who he needed to be, in order to be called to the bar and to practice in India. Here his pledge to his mother to avoid wine, meat, and women might have fortified him with the beginnings of the independence he needed to escape the full grasp of British upper-class mores. Yet the attraction of belonging to a privileged group gripped him still. It was in his study of theosophy and his embrace of the cause of vegetarianism that he discovered a way to bridge the distance between faithfulness to himself and things Indian, on the one hand, and, on the other, his attraction to the higher strata of British society where, at least at the edges, theosophy and vegetarianism were thriving.

Theosophy in Gandhi's time was a religious philosophy with roots in the teachings of the Russian-born medium Helena Petrovna Blavatsky.[34] She, along with an American, Henry Olcott, founded the Theosophical Society in New York in 1875. Theosophy argued that all religious traditions "hold in common many religious, ethical, and philosophical ideas." It purported to explain the commonality of all religious thought by resort to the notion that an ancient band of "great spiritual Teachers (themselves the outcome of past cycles of evolution) acted as the instructors and guides of the child humanity of our planet, interpreting to its races and nations the fundamental truths of religion in the form most adapted to the idiosyncrasies of the recipients."[35] The truth that they passed on to Blavatsky and her followers was divine wisdom, the Greek for which (*theos* and *sophia*) gave rise to the name of this body of thought.

The openness of theosophy to all the great religious traditions included an embrace of Hindu ideas, which in turn led theosophy to a pantheistic understanding of God, an emphasis on the oneness of all people, and a belief in human perfectibility. One could see how readily each of these notions might appeal to a young Hindu stranded in an alien culture far from home.[36] Gandhi tells us he was introduced to theosophy by two friends who asked him for help in reading Sir Edwin Arnold's *The Song Celestial*, a poetic translation of the Bhagavad Gita. The friends thereafter took him to Theosophical Society meetings and eventually to a talk given by Annie Besant, a follower of Blavatsky and a leading theosophical theorist of her time, whose speeches emphasized brotherhood, tolerance, and the spiritual nature of people.[37] The talk Besant delivered the night Gandhi was in the audience defended theosophy against its critics, causing Gandhi to later write: "The words she uttered . . . as she rose to answer the charge of inconsistency have never faded from my memory. She said as she wound up her great speech that she would be quite satisfied to have the epitaph written on her tomb that she had lived for truth and she died for truth."[38] Gandhi made it a point to read Blavatsky's *The Key to Theosophy*. The effect of this reading was to stimulate in him "the desire to read books on Hinduism" and to disabuse him "of the notion fostered by the missionaries that Hinduism was rife with superstition."[39]

Despite this interest, Gandhi felt that he did not have sufficient time to continue his religious explorations while examinations were looming. Thus, it appears that the period of Gandhi's most intense involvement with theosophy came to an end sometime before December 15, 1890. And when his examinations concluded on the 20th of December 1890, it was not theosophy that reclaimed his attention, but vegetarianism.

Gandhi's initial interest in vegetarianism resulted from a blend of pragmatism and principle. To secure her blessing for the trip, he had promised his mother he would not touch meat. Keeping this pledge caused him to endure a fairly lengthy trial, stretching from the time he boarded the SS *Clyde* in early September to late October 1888, during which time he ate meals that were meatless but nutritionally inadequate for this eighteen-year-old manchild. On the *Clyde*, an English fellow passenger importuned him to eat meat, claiming that it was "so cold in England that one cannot possibly live there without meat."[40] Gandhi politely turned away the advice, saying that if what the passenger was saying were true, he would simply pack up his bags and return to India before violating his vow. Gandhi's fidelity to his pledge (as well as his fear of having to speak English) resulted for some days in his eating spartan meals in his cabin, meals consisting of nothing more than sweets and fruits brought from home, before other arrangements could be made. After finding his initial lodging in England at the Victoria Hotel, Gandhi apparently had little luck there, reporting that he paid the princely sum of £3 for his short stay and got very little to eat for it. He was forced to continue eating from his store of Indian sweets and fruits. Even after Gandhi left the hotel and secured private, less expensive rooms, he found that all the meatless dishes put in front of him were "tasteless and insipid." This, plus a serious case of homesickness, left this young man lying in bed at night, wondering whether he had erred in leaving home, pining over the loss of his mother's affections, and unable to check the rivers of tears flowing down his cheeks.

Gandhi had come to England with several letters of introduction, including one addressed to Dr. Pranjivan Mehta, a medical doctor as well as a barrister-in-training himself, who hailed from near Gandhi's hometown. Mehta quickly recognized Gandhi's need for some social context, for he convinced him to move and take on a roommate, all in preparation for eventually taking quarters with an English family. Mehta's argument was that Gandhi, after all, had come to England not so much to get an education as to gain "experience in English life and customs," something life with a family would provide. Gandhi soon thereafter moved in with Dalpatram Shukla, another law student from Gandhi's region. It became Shukla's job to train the young Gandhi in English ways—in the course of which he could not get Gandhi to eat meat. Despite his profound dislike for the landlady's nonmeat dishes, Gandhi resisted sampling her meat dishes. Seeing Gandhi's resistance, Shukla lost his temper and exploded: "Had you been my own brother, I would have sent you packing. What is the value of a vow made before an illiterate mother, and in ignorance of the conditions here?"[41] Gandhi, however, remained steadfast—and hungry. After a month of training in English ways, save meat eating, Mehta and Shukla found a family in West Kensington willing to board Gandhi. Again, he found the meals insipid and complains in his autobiography that he continued to "practically . . . starve."[42] But eventually the day came when his landlady informed him that there were vegetarian restaurants in London. Gandhi seized on this information and found, to his great happiness, the Central Restaurant off London's Farringdon Street. He related later that the very sight of the restaurant filled him with joy.

What Gandhi found for his soul, however, was to become even more important than that evening's meal. On his way in to the Central he noticed a window display featuring Henry Salt's *Plea for Vegetarianism*. He devoured not only a hearty meal but Salt's book, which, he later states, turned his life around:

> From the date of reading this book, I may claim to have become a vegetarian by choice. . . . I had all along abstained from meat in the interest of truth and of the vow I had taken, but had wished at the same time that every Indian should be a meat-eater, and had looked forward to being one myself someday, and to enlisting others in the cause. The choice was now made in favour of vegetarianism, the spread of which henceforward became my mission.[43]

His "appetite for dietetic studies" whetted by Salt, Gandhi "went in for all books available on vegetarianism."[44] Eventually Gandhi found new rooms (he was constantly moving during his London student days) in order that he might economize by cooking for himself. By mid-1890 Gandhi was able to report that he "enjoyed the best of health and had to work very hard if not the hardest as there were only five months left for the final examination."[45] During this pre-exam period Gandhi was invited by Josiah Oldfield, a leading vegetarian whose acquaintance Gandhi had made earlier, to a vegetarian conference to be held in September 1890. As a result of his participation in this conference, Gandhi was almost immediately invited to become a member of the Executive Committee of the London Vegetarian Society (LVS), an invitation he accepted. With exams looming, however, Gandhi appears not to have taken much of a role on the committee.[46]

After the completion of his final examinations, by contrast, Gandhi was a beehive of vegetarian activity. Giving a preview of the prodigious output of writing for which he would later become known, Gandhi produced a series of articles for *The Vegetarian*, the weekly journal of the LVS. First he wrote a series of six essays on the practice of vegetarianism in India. This series was followed by a series of three articles on the festivals of India. Gandhi then delivered a speech titled "The Foods of India" before the LVS and had it printed thereafter in the *Vegetarian Messenger*, the society's Manchester voice. Gandhi also gave a two-part interview to *The Vegetarian*. In addition, he found time to get embroiled in the inner politics of the LVS, to start up a local vegetarian club with his friend and eventual roommate Josiah Oldfield, and to make appearances in a number of forums on behalf of vegetarianism.

This intense round of activity closed out Gandhi's time as a student in London. In the months since his bar finals, while his fellow students were learning to draft conveyances and pleadings in chambers, Gandhi's involvement with the vegetarian movement was schooling him in ways of "organizing and conducting institutions."[47]

He also was learning something about himself with no little import for a young barrister's future, a lesson with ominous implications for the career that his family had chosen for him.

He was terrified, sometimes to the point of paralysis, of speaking in public.

TWO

The Barrister Who Couldn't Speak

No client would be fool enough to engage me.

GANDHI

FOR SOMEONE WHO CLAIMED TO be in love with London, Gandhi's behavior might easily be counted as strange. He received his call to the bar on June 10, was sworn in before the High Court on June 11, and on June 12 he was on a boat for India. Perhaps this was Gandhi the responsible son, one who knew that every extra day in London was an added burden on the family finances. Indeed, this might have been a Gandhi who knew that such expenses were doubly problematic: not only was he exhausting his family's capital, but he had no prospects of replenishing the family coffers any time soon.

UNPREPARED TO PRACTICE

Gandhi's family had sent its most promising son to England to obtain the elevated status of barrister and the lifestyle that accompanied it. Those who had sacrificed to put Gandhi through his legal training in England expected to be rewarded for their sacrifices upon Gandhi's return to India.[1] His faithful brother, Lakshmidas, in anticipation of Gandhi's arrival home as the wealthy barrister, embarked upon a course of upgrading his family's living style even before Gandhi's return,[2] a pretense Gandhi himself endorsed and furthered when he introduced European clothing and food to his family in Rajkot upon his arrival there. Surely, under these circumstances, Lakshmidas cannot be blamed for thinking that Gandhi would establish for himself and his family the comfortable life of a prestigious barrister. Gandhi, however, came back after three long and expensive years in England wholly unprepared to make a return to his family. He carried with him the title of barrister—and precious little else.

To begin with, he had no knowledge of Indian law. Despite a prolonged British effort at codification, the operation of a significant part of the legal system continued to be governed by a body of traditional Hindu and Muslim law that applied to succession, inheritance, marriage, adoption, guardianship, family relations, wills, gifts, and partition. Many practitioners would consider these basic aspects of practice, yet Gandhi had no knowledge of them.

Not only was he unacquainted with important aspects of the doctrinal side of the law, but Gandhi also had equally little knowledge of its practical side, having forgone the opportunity to apprentice. One cannot overstate the paucity of his practical knowledge. One example might suffice. The most basic written instrument in the practice of law is the complaint, the document a plaintiff files against a defendant to begin an ordinary civil suit. While Gandhi's family expected him to start up a "swinging practice" forthwith, the fact was, as he confessed to himself, "he had not even learnt how to draft a plaint."[3]

SETTING UP SHOP IN BOMBAY

Gandhi was brutally honest about his position in 1891 when he later wrote in his autobiography: "To start practice in Rajkot would have meant sure ridicule. I had hardly the knowledge of a qualified vakil[4] and yet I expected to be paid ten times his fee! No client would be fool enough to engage me. And even if such a one was to be found, should I add arrogance and fraud to my ignorance, and increase the burden of debt I owed to the world?"[5] Faced with these rather serious disabilities, and seeing nothing for an inexperienced barrister in Rajkot, Gandhi decided to shift operations to Bombay, where he hoped to accomplish three goals: to remedy his deficiency in Indian law, to obtain some knowledge of the workings of the Bombay High Court, and to pick up a few cases.

Gandhi's study of Indian law proved to be the easiest of these tasks. He set about studying Mayne's *Indian Law*, which he read with "deep interest."[6] He had no similar luck plowing through the Civil Procedure Code, a failure readily forgiven by anyone who has attempted to study civil procedure—the driest of subjects—as an abstract matter, as opposed to learning it in the context of simulated or actual cases. The Evidence Act, by contrast, held more of Gandhi's interest, perhaps because he knew that one of the giants of the Indian bar, Sir Pherozeshah Mehta, had memorized the act by heart.

Gandhi's experience observing arguments before the High Court was neither productive nor uplifting. With nothing at stake for himself or for a client in the proceedings, there was little to hold his interest. Moreover, Gandhi had insufficient knowledge of the law in general or the argued cases in particular to be able to follow, much less learn from, the line of the arguments. For any neutral party observing appellate arguments, one wit has observed, the experience is about as stimulating as being a lighthouse attendant. Thus, it is not surprising that Gandhi's main occupation while at the High Court was to sleep, a habit shared by so many other "observers" that Gandhi actually came to think it was "fashionable to doze in the High Court."[7]

Neither Gandhi's attempt to learn Indian law nor his study of the High Court's workings was a demanding enough activity to occupy his complete attention. Reminiscent of his experiments with top hats and French-language lessons, he used his free time to play the wealthy barrister. He hired one Ravishankar to cook for him at his residence. Gandhi quickly learned that Ravishankar knew little about cooking, and so, with the initiative that hallmarked so much of his life, he threw himself into running the kitchen along with his pupil, teaching Ravishankar something about vegetarianism along the way.

A FAILURE OF NERVE

With his days passing in such desultory fashion, it is no wonder that Gandhi leapt at the chance to represent an actual paying client in court when a defendant in a civil case, an individual by the name of Mamibai, asked Gandhi to represent her. Little did Gandhi realize how terribly unprepared he was by nature or experience to advocate a client's cause in open court.

To be an advocate for a client in court requires a fair amount of confidence in one's ability to engage without hesitation in the rambunctious and fractious give-and-take of the courtroom. It requires a lawyer to be a public person, one who is not afraid to stand before a judge and argue, one who is not afraid to take on opposing lawyers and parties, one who is not afraid to vigorously defend one's position or to attack an opponent's position—all in public. In sum, the lawyer as a public person is one who has no lack of nerve.

In the year 1891 twenty-two-year-old Mohandas K. Gandhi, barrister at law, lacked nerve. As a result, his representation of Mamibai ended in failure and embarrassment. Mamibai's case was being processed at the lowest level of the judicial system, the equivalent of what is called small claims court in some jurisdictions.[8] Because Mamibai was the defendant, the first task of Gandhi's courtroom career was to cross-examine the witnesses for the plaintiff. As Gandhi stood up to conduct his first cross-examination as a barrister, he was gripped with fear. He became dizzy from stage fright and his head began to reel. His heart sank. Even his eyesight failed him. He could not get control of his panic. He was unable to ask a single question. He staggered to his seat and told the client's agent that he could not go on. Then, unnerved, he stumbled out of the courtroom in disgrace.

A HISTORY OF FEAR

Gandhi's extreme discomfort in his role as a courtroom advocate was the predictable end point for a person who only rarely was able to find his voice in public. From the time Gandhi was a high school student (and probably before), public speaking had almost always reduced him to a nervous, quivering bowl of mush. Just before Gandhi set sail for London in 1888, his high school classmates in Rajkot held a farewell celebration in his honor. In his autobiography Gandhi recalls that he had difficulty reading his prepared notes, that he was dizzy from nervousness, that he stammered and that "his whole frame shook."[9] Such a reaction should have been expected from Gandhi, inasmuch as he was an extremely shy and timid youth, avoiding not only the rigors of childhood sports but even the casual company of other children.

When Gandhi boarded the steamer SS *Clyde* for London, he found it impossible to speak with other passengers. His shipmate and fellow Indian the lawyer Tryambakrai Mazmudar urged him to deal with his unfamiliarity with English by conversing in English with their fellow travelers. Interestingly, Mazmudar even pointed out to Gandhi that such practice would do him good because "lawyers should have a long tongue."[10] Mazmudar put Gandhi on notice that he was entering a profession in which speech was considered a tool of the trade. Nothing, however, moved Gandhi; he abstained from social commerce.

Little changed on his arrival in England. When Gandhi secured a room with a family in West Kensington, he found that the portions of food his landlady served him were too small. But the same mouth that craved to eat could not convince itself to speak. Gandhi found himself "as shy as ever and dared not ask for more than was put before [him]."[11]

Gandhi's involvement in the vegetarian movement brought him face-to-face with several opportunities for public speaking. He seems to have failed miserably at almost all of them. Indeed, Gandhi set a pattern: he would write out his remarks, practice them, arrive at the meeting, lose his nerve, and ask someone else to read his speech. For example, in a dispute within the leadership of the LVS, on whose Executive Committee he served, Gandhi was forced to take sides between its president, Arnold F. Hills, and Dr. Thomas R. Allinson, another member of the Executive Committee. Allinson had taken up the cause of birth control, leading to a motion by Hills to strip Allinson of membership in the society. Gandhi was opposed to birth control, but believed there should be no morals test for those who wanted to join; support of vegetarianism was enough. Gandhi decided to advocate for Allinson. He wrote out his speech but "had not the courage to speak."[12] Hills was gracious enough to find someone to read a speech attacking his own position.

On another occasion, Gandhi and Mazmudar attended a vegetarian conference in Ventnor. While there, Gandhi met the author of a famous vegetarian tract who offered Gandhi the opportunity to speak at the conference, an invitation he accepted without hesitation. Once again Gandhi wrote out his remarks, and once again he appeared to deliver them. In terms reminiscent of his description of his cross-examination effort in the Mamibai case, Gandhi states what happened next: "I stood up to read it, but could not. My vision became blurred and I trembled, though the speech hardly covered a sheet of foolscap." Once again, Gandhi was forced to find someone to read for him. While the audience received the talk well, Gandhi "was ashamed of [him]self and sad at heart for [his] incapacity."[13]

Demonstrating either his courage or his naïveté, Gandhi's two earlier failures at public speech making did not deter him from a third attempt. The occasion this time was a farewell vegetarian dinner hosted by Gandhi for a group of friends on the eve of his departure from London. The scene was the Holborn, a conventional restaurant Gandhi had convinced to host a vegetarian banquet. Again Gandhi had prepared his remarks with care. When he stood, he found that he "could not proceed beyond the first sentence."[14] Gandhi had intended to begin with a bit of humor but, as he stalled after his first sentence, found that the only thing humorous was his attempt to speak in public. He gathered up just enough composure to blurt out his thanks to his guests for coming. He then sat down, defeated, once again, by himself.

Was Gandhi's difficulty that he obsessed over his prepared remarks, to the point of paralysis? Perhaps, but he also confesses that he had no aptitude for *ex tempore* speaking either. He was inept at both. The inability to deliver prepared remarks and the inability to speak extemporaneously must be counted as significant disabilities for one who intended to earn his living by speaking. Yet, years later, when writing his autobiography, Gandhi claimed that several advantages flowed from what he called his "constitutional shyness." While he was in England, he says, he found that his shyness made it easier for him to keep his pledge to his mother to abstain from commerce with women. In the rest of his life, he found that shyness brought him the benefits of speaking little, namely that a studied silence permitted him to avoid thoughtless chatter, exaggeration, and untruths.

VAKILS ON THE RISE

It is one thing to muse about being tongue-tied in one's memoirs. It is something altogether different to be tongue-tied in fact while trying to make a living as a barrister in the highly competitive atmosphere of nineteenth-century Bombay. Gandhi's inability to speak in public must be understood as a limitation that rendered it virtually impossible for him to overcome a number of background factors that made his practice of law in India a chancy proposition at best.

When Gandhi attempted to enter practice in India in 1891, he did so at a time when the Indian legal system was in the midst of a maelstrom of changes in terms of both the organization of the judiciary and the regulation of the practice of law. The High Court at Bombay had only recently been established, along with High Courts at the other two presidency towns of Madras and Calcutta, by the Indian High Courts Act of 1861.[15] This act was part of a protracted process whereby the British government eventually took over virtually the entire judicial system in India.

At the same time the court system was evolving, the legal profession was undergoing change. The profession, which got its start when the East India Company first established itself in India, had a history of being poorly organized and regulated,[16] with a wide and confusing range of different types of practitioners, all competing for business.[17] Well before Gandhi's time, however, one clear distinction emerged—that between barristers and native practitioners. On the one hand, barristers, at first almost exclusively English, commanded enormous prestige—and enormous fees.[18] Their status and their earning power were the result of two factors: the monopoly on practice barristers held for a considerable period of time and the small number of barristers available for hire. For a good part of the nineteenth century barristers alone were allowed to appear in the highest courts, leaving native practitioners to scratch out their livings in inferior tribunals. For some time barristers capitalized on their legal monopoly by keeping their own numbers low. In Bombay, for example, there were only two barristers in 1807, with the number rising to only thirteen by 1861. As one historian has noted, "Even a new practitioner could begin earning large sums almost immediately."[19] It was with this image of the profession in mind that Gandhi's family had pooled its resources to give young Mohan a barrister's education.

In contrast, there existed a broadly defined class of practitioners trained in India, generally known as vakils, who were held in lower esteem, who commanded lesser fees, and whose practice was restricted to certain courts. These practitioners began with very limited roles in the legal system but transformed themselves over time into lawyers some of whose training was arguably better than that received by barristers in the Inn system. While the extent of his training and the precise nature of his practice are unknown, it is known that Gandhi's brother, Lakshmidas, was such a practitioner.

It was Gandhi's misfortune to enter practice at a time when the power of vakils was on the ascendancy, while that of barristers was on the decline. From the mid-1800s on, the vakils campaigned with good effect for the right to practice in all courts and for the abolition of the distinctions among and between barristers (known as "advocates"), solicitors (known as "attorneys"), and vakils. Indeed, even before Gandhi took up practice in Bombay, vakils had been permitted to appear before the High Court there, shattering the monopoly barristers once had and greatly influencing the economics of law practice. To make matters worse, it became well known by 1890 that the practice of law could be a most lucrative profession. Accordingly, the profession attracted great numbers to its ranks at just the time Gandhi arrived in Bombay—only to see so many enter the profession that the supply of lawyers exceeded the public's demand for them. With the laws of economics in play, many a young novice went without work.[20]

Gandhi's own background provided him with no assets with which to succeed at the practice of law in this changing environment. Much of the Indian economy in the 1890s was tied to the land.[21] When Gandhi entered practice, Indian capitalism was just starting to develop alongside the traditional agrarian economy. As the nineteenth century was coming to a close, these two forces, previously in balance, would interact, threatening society and the law with a tumultuous transformation that the Raj was not prepared to accept.[22] Thrust into this period of swirling change, Gandhi could have exploited it had he had ties to either the rising capitalist elements or to the traditional agrarian economy. Gandhi, however, had no ties to the landed elite that would help him obtain work representing landowning clients in litigation. With respect to business litigation, Gandhi was already at a disadvantage simply by virtue of being an Indian-born rather than a British-born barrister. Historian Samuel Schmitthener reports that from the time of the founding of the High Courts in 1862 through the end of the nineteenth century, Indian lawyers could not easily find financial success:

> The first Indian barristers . . . were disappointed to find that they could not make a success of practicing [in courts], where the lucrative commercial cases were. Work [in such courts] could only come to a barrister through a solicitor. The solicitors' firms were all British, and they did all the work for the Government departments and the . . . firms. They did not want to patronize an untried Indian barrister. Nor did the few Indian solicitors who were struggling to expand their practice wish to risk the blame that would come upon them if some inexperienced Indian barrister mishandled a case. . . . Not only British firms, but also Indians preferred to be represented by British . . . advocates—perhaps because it was believed they would have more influence with the English judges.[23]

Gandhi might have overcome the predisposition of potential clients to favor English barristers had he had some ties to the commercial, industrial, and mercantile classes. Because he had none, however, he derived no work from the business community.

To make matters worse, neither did Gandhi have any close relatives or friends in the legal profession in Bombay. This was a significant drawback because barristers in Gandhi's day obtained clients not directly through contact with them but through referrals from other members of the profession. Indeed, it was often a family matter: many barristers derived their success from having family members in positions from which they could refer cases to their favorite member of the bar. With no one looking out for young Gandhi's interests among the corps of Bombay attorneys, there was no one to send cases to this "briefless barrister."[24]

Finally, there was the matter of professional ethics. At the time Gandhi was attempting to practice in Bombay, some in the profession relied upon touts—mercenaries who would hunt down litigation and bring it to a barrister for a fee. While this practice was considered unethical, it was nonetheless employed by some of the most successful members of the Bombay bar. Gandhi, however, refused to pay touts, even if the practice was winked at and even if it meant he would earn far less than he might otherwise. Indeed, when those advising him in Bombay pointed out that one highly successful criminal lawyer paid touts, Gandhi scoffed at the idea that financial success should rank higher than professional ethics. This was a watershed moment for Gandhi as a person and as an attorney. Faced with the choice of failing with honor or succeeding with dishonor, he chose the more difficult path. This is the first indication Gandhi gives as a lawyer that the world's way was not his way. In the future he would stake out a definition of his professional life that rested upon the belief that one could find true happiness as an attorney without adhering to the profession's definition of success. It is not a belief to which he would always be faithful, as we shall see, but it provides us with the first real glimmer of the attorney he was to become. Interestingly, he was hired in Mamibai's case despite his refusal to pay the tout.

Gandhi would confound his critics from the beginning.

BACKWATERS: A RETURN TO RAJKOT

With all these factors against him, it is not surprising, then, that Gandhi's Bombay practice collapsed shortly after the Mamibai incident. The most he could manage thereafter was a case in which he drafted a memorial for free for an impecunious client. While his colleagues approved of the quality of his work in the case, Gandhi realized that he could not support himself if his practice consisted of nothing but pro bono work.

At about this time Gandhi started thinking of seeking employment overseas, but because Lakshmidas opposed such a move, Gandhi deferred consideration of it. Moreover, there was a promise of some work in Bombay in the fall of 1892. This new work, however, never materialized.[25]

New measures were required. Gandhi applied for a part-time position teaching English at a well-known Bombay high school for 75 rupees a month. At the interview, when it became apparent that the high school sought a university graduate, the school lost interest. He pleaded that his passage of the London examination should qualify him to teach, but the school would not budge.

With this door closed, there was nothing more Gandhi could do to sustain himself in Bombay. He had failed. After six months in Bombay, Gandhi closed what he called his "little establishment" and retreated to his Rajkot home.[26] There he would work with his brother, Lakshmidas, a petty pleader, in doing the low-level legal work of native attorneys that he had disdained earlier. Gandhi would be an overeducated paralegal in his older brother's shop, drafting common applications and memorials.

A BREACH OF ETHICS

Given the experiences Gandhi had had before being called to the bar, it was predictable that he would have difficulty assuming the role of public person that the job of courtroom barrister required.[27] From the time of his childhood Gandhi had been a timid person. His attempts at public speaking in high school and later in London regularly placed unmanageable amounts of stress on him—and these prior attempts at public speaking were almost always before receptive audiences of friends or colleagues. When Gandhi was forced into the courtroom, he found himself in a new setting in which all speech and all behavior are adversarial. Adversarial speech places enormous demands on the speaker to manage his emotions, his intellect, and even his body so that he can tell the most compelling story on opening statement, ask the most captivating questions on direct examination, wrestle the most hostile witnesses to the ground on cross-examination, and make the most persuasive case in closing argument, all at the same time he is parrying the thrusts of his opponent, responding to the inquiries of the judge, and following the rules of evidence and procedure. Even for those experienced in courtroom speaking, such speaking is challenging. For the young lawyer—even one trained throughout law school and apprenticeship—the prospect of such speaking is threatening. How much more challenging and threatening was it for Gandhi, wholly unprepared as he was by personality, training, and experience?

Gandhi's new work would keep him far from the courtroom. He set up an office in Rajkot where he was able to earn enough on which to live (about 300 rupees a month) by drafting applications and petitions. This work, at the lower echelons of practice, was made possible through Lakshmidas, who at the time was a member of a two-man vakil firm. Lakshmidas' partner (apparently the dominant of the two) gave Gandhi his overflow applications and petitions. The significant cases the partner kept; to Gandhi he gave the work of assisting his poorest clients. Even this work, however, proved problematic for Gandhi, for he was expected to pay commissions for these cases. He had rebelled at this practice in Bombay because it smelled of corruption.[28] Now, however, he relented so as not to give offense to his brother's partner, who apparently was gracious in agreeing to help Gandhi. Gandhi also undoubtedly wanted to help provide Lakshmidas with income inasmuch as Lakshmidas and Gandhi shared any income Gandhi generated through the partner's referrals. In this instance, then, Gandhi's feelings of loyalty to his brother and his appreciation for his brother's partner worked together to create a lapse in Gandhi's ethical standards. He was off the path.

So in 1893, Gandhi, a London-educated barrister, found himself stuck in the backwaters of Rajkot, performing low-level legal work and doing so in a fashion he considered morally repugnant. Indeed, he soon learned that petty politics, corruption, and backroom deals were the order of the day there and throughout the region. Gandhi's introduction to the political facts of life in Kathiawad was made possible by Lakshmidas, an individual who appears to have been possessed of a conscience less demanding than that of his younger brother. Lakshmidas had been the secretary to, and the advisor of, a powerful figure in neighboring Porbandar. During the course of this employment, Lakshmidas ran afoul of the authorities. Gandhi, in his memoirs, is not precise in his description of this trouble, but he is quite clear on the point that Lakshmidas expected his brother to bail him out of it. The political agent in charge of the area at that time was an officer whose acquaintance Gandhi had made in London. It was Lakshmidas' idea that Gandhi ought to go to him and, playing on the friendship, seek to put the matter to rest.[29]

Gandhi was opposed to this plan. It offended his sense of procedure and right order. But his reluctance was overcome by the importuning of his brother, who argued that decisions in Kathiawad were made only on the basis of influence and that Gandhi owed him a fraternal duty to intercede. Reluctantly, Gandhi agreed to see the agent, knowing in advance that he "was compromising [his] self-respect."[30]

His worst fears materialized. On seeing the agent, Gandhi sensed immediately that the agent knew Gandhi was there to improperly influence him
and that he was offended by this. Before Gandhi could even finish stating his
case, the agent exploded: "Your brother is an intriguer. I want to hear nothing more from you. I have no time. If your brother has anything to say, let
him apply through the proper channel."[31] With that, the agent had the protesting Gandhi physically removed from his office. Gandhi, who knew he was
wrong to be there in the first instance, immediately, and perhaps uncon-
sciously, converted his embarrassment at having done something improper
into righteous indignation at a perceived personal insult. Perhaps this was
Gandhi's way of pulling a curtain over his embarrassment. Gandhi was so
caught up in his anger at the way he was treated that he sent a note to the
agent, threatening to sue him for assault—the quintessential act of a juvenile
barrister too big for his britches. The agent's reply was wholly unapologetic,
telling Gandhi to sue if he wished. Nonplussed, Gandhi sought the advice of
Mehta, who happened to be in the area on a case. Mehta's reply was just what
one would expect from a wiser and older hand. Transmitting his advice to
Gandhi through a third party, Mehta wrote: "Such things are the common
experience of many vakils and barristers. He is still fresh from England, and
hot-blooded. He does not know British officers. If he would earn something
and have an easy time here, let him . . . pocket the insult. He will gain nothing by proceeding against the *sahib*, and on the contrary will very likely ruin
himself. Tell him he has yet to know life."[32] Gandhi took Mehta's advice,
despite its being "bitter as poison" to him.[33] "Never again shall I place myself
in such a false position, never again shall I exploit friendship in this way,"
Gandhi pledged to himself.[34] It was a pledge he was to honor for a lifetime.

A SOUTH AFRICAN OFFER

Gandhi had no hope of reconciling with the agent. As a result, he believed
this experience destroyed any chance of establishing a Rajkot practice, for it
was in the agent's court that Gandhi would have made the lion's share of his
appearances. Because Gandhi's practice depended on fees, he and his brother
recognized that Gandhi needed employment that did not rely for its success
on being in a courtroom run by a hostile judge. Salaried employment as a
government minister or as a judge, for example, would offer Gandhi an
opportunity to escape the consequences of his disastrous encounter with the

agent, but jobs such as these could not be had simply for the asking. Obtaining such positions required political intrigue, intrigue in which Gandhi now steadfastly refused to engage. His refusal exacted a price. Gandhi speaks in his memoirs of representing some clients in an effort to have their excessive land rent moderated. He failed at this and expresses dissatisfaction that the decision was based simply on the discretion of the authorities—the exercise of which he apparently was unwilling to influence in the usual Kathiawad way—and not upon a rule or regulation.

Gandhi's practice in Rajkot was earning him a modest living. But this was not the life of the successful barrister he and his family had envisioned. Indeed, everything about this work was wrong. It was routine, he had to pay commissions to get it, it did not come to him by virtue of his own reputation, and it took place in a legal and political world overflowing with rank corruption.

Lakshmidas was not blind to his brother's difficulties and to the ill effect they were having on his own fortunes. He apparently made it his task to contact his friends and business acquaintances in an effort to find a way out for Mohandas. Not knowing the momentous chain of events its offer would put in motion, a Porbandar business with ties to South Africa answered Lakshmidas' call. Gandhi recalls Dada Abdulla and Company's letter to his brother as stating:

> We have business in South Africa. Ours is a big firm, and we have a big case there in the Court, our claim being £40,000. It has been going on for a long time. We have engaged the services of the best vakils and barristers. If you sent your brother there, he would be useful to us and also to himself. He would be able to instruct our counsel better than ourselves. And he would have the advantage of seeing a new part of the world, and of making new acquaintances.[35]

Gandhi had questions about the offer. Was he expected to appear in court or simply to instruct counsel? How long was he expected to be in South Africa? What was the pay? The brothers arranged a meeting between Mohandas and Sheth Abdul Karim Jhaveri, an acquaintance of Lakshmidas and a partner in Dada Abdulla. Gandhi reports that the partner assured him that the job would not be difficult and that he envisioned Gandhi assisting the firm with its English-language correspondence. The company could offer him a fee of £105, first-class round-trip travel, the payment of all expenses while Gandhi was in the company's employ, and an assurance that the job would take less than a year.

Gandhi realized quite quickly that this was not a job to brag about. He knew that he "was hardly going there as a barrister," but "as a servant of the firm."[36] The advantages to taking this position in South Africa were numerous, however. In one stroke he could escape the political intrigue of Kathiawad, be done with the drudgery of drafting petitions and applications, avoid any further violation of the ethical proscriptions against paying commissions, send back £105 to his family,[37] take up work that appeared to call for no public speaking, and shake from his sandals the dust of the country in which he had failed as a barrister.

Without haggling over the terms of his employment, without ruing his departure except for the "pang of parting" from his wife,[38] and without evincing so much as an inkling of understanding how this decision would change his life forever, he agreed to go to South Africa.

Gandhi had had quite enough of India.

THREE

An Abundant and Regular Supply of Labour

The self-interest of the European brought the Indian to South
Africa; self-interest has sought to get rid of him from the country; self-interest, so far as this cannot be achieved, is determined
to keep him in what is regarded as his place.

J. F. HOFMEYR

THERE COULD HARDLY BE A stranger and more complex setting for the
formative years of Gandhi's public life than the colony of Natal, to which he
sailed in 1893. At the time of his arrival, Natal had all the economic, political,
and social complexity one might expect from a place populated by native
Africans, come upon by the Portuguese, and developed by the Dutch, before
being wholly taken over by the British.

Natal (from the Latin *natus*, "birth") was given its name by the explorer
Vasco da Gama, who, on his journey from Portugal to India, passed by
Natal's verdant coast at Christmastime in the year 1497. It was not da Gama's
fellow Portuguese, however, who were to leave a serious European mark on
Natal. Dutch from the Cape colony, uncomfortable with the notion of color
equality professed by the new British administration established there in
1815, entered the province in the early decades of the nineteenth century in
search of fertile agricultural lands, ample native labor, and a setting where
they could re-create a pleasant and secure way of life. This movement to Natal
peaked with significant migrations to the region in the 1830s and the establishment of the Republic of Natalia in 1839, an ill-fated, short-lived Dutch
endeavor that was never able to overcome serious financial and administrative difficulties.[1] The British, meanwhile, had established themselves along
the coast, desirous of capitalizing on the rich farmlands that lay there and the
harbor available for development at the coastal town of Durban.[2] The British
declared Natal a dependency of the Cape colony in 1843 with little opposition from the Dutch, who recognized that their experiment in government

had failed. In 1856 Natal became a separate colony from the Cape. Britain granted it responsible government in 1893,[3] the year of Gandhi's arrival.

THE NATAL ECONOMY AND ITS DEMAND FOR LABOR

The Europeans saw Natal's fertile coastlands not with the eyes of tourists but those of capitalists. There they experimented with efforts to grow maize, cotton, indigo, arrowroot, tobacco, and coffee. Eventually they learned that the area was suited for the growing of a lucrative cash crop, sugar.[4] The capital necessary to underwrite the sugar industry was available because banks had already been established in Natal. Labor, however, was another matter. The owners of the sugar plantations turned to what appeared to them a vast, untapped supply of labor in the native population, but most efforts to recruit native Africans as laborers ended in failure.[5] Frustrated, the Europeans tried a series of moves, some bizarre, to find workers. They attempted to lure English farmhands, import convicts, and attract Chinese and Malays from the Far East. All these attempts were unsuccessful in producing the large stocks of reliable workers needed to run an agricultural enterprise. The situation became desperate, with the *Natal Mercury* warning that the lack of labor would "in the near future imperil the whole country."[6]

Finally, the thoughts of the plantation owners and others who favored a supply of cheap, reliable labor turned to India. Several years after the Colonial Office at the Cape of Good Hope broached the idea with the government of India,[7] Natal in 1860 was able to negotiate a system of indentured labor that called for the importation of workers to be bound to their employers for three years, paid 10 shillings a month, and supplied with housing and food.[8] When the laborer's indenture was mature, the laborer could return to India, re-enlist for another period of indenture, or receive property equal to what it would have cost the government to ship him or her back to India.[9] After 6,445 immigrants had been imported between 1860 and 1866, the dissatisfaction of the government of India with the operation of this arrangement, together with effects of an economic depression on Natal, resulted in the suspension of immigration in 1866.[10]

After the depression of 1866 began to ease and the demand for sugar began to rise, interest in the importation of Indian laborers resurfaced. More than two hundred "Planters, Merchants and others interested in the supply of Labour" petitioned the Natal government for help: "Your memorialists are more profoundly impressed as ever with the necessity of an increased supply of labour; it is absolutely essential for carrying on the Industries of the Coast Lands, and for giving to capitalists arriving among us that security which is required in entering on enterprises involving so large an outlay which can only be successfully prosecuted by a more abundant and regular supply of labour."[11]

GROWERS VERSUS MERCHANTS

This renewal of interest in immigration troubled the government of India, concerned, as it was, over the complaints it had received about the treatment of its citizens during the previous period of immigration. The Natal government, however, gave sufficient assurances such that India permitted immigration to resume in 1874. These assurances included provisions that an indentured servant could return to India at the end of ten years (five years of service, followed by five years of freedom), that there should be no unequal treatment of Indians who remained, and that certain substantial percentages of the immigrants be women.[12] These provisions, reluctantly accepted by the government of Natal, practically guaranteed that immigration would result in a permanent Indian population in Natal, a prospect feared by important elements of the Natal economy. For years there had been tension between the coastal growers on the one hand and the merchants and traders on the other over the question of immigration. The white growers needed Indian laborers to run their farms, while the white merchants and traders were apprehensive over the increased competition from freed Indians who became hawkers, market-gardeners, and traders, and from Indian merchants who voluntarily came to Natal to profit by serving the needs of the expanding Indian community. With the agreement to renew immigration, however, the growers' needs trumped the merchants' fears, as well as the concerns of the larger white society about the social disruption the Indians' presence might cause. The conflict between the growers' interests in cheap labor for their agricultural and other enterprises and the merchant class' fear of competition would not remain submerged for long, however. As the Indian population steadily mounted, the wider white community's fear of the Indian community's political, as well as economic, power mounted with it. Indeed, as Indian indentured servants, followed by free Indian merchants, started pouring into Natal, the movement for responsible government gained more urgency. The

Europeans who demanded responsible government from the Crown knew that, freed from the Colonial Office's concerns about the Indian government's reactions over the treatment of Indians in Natal, Natal could deal with its "Indian problem" with a much freer hand.

The numbers tell the story. In 1859, just a year before the importation of indentured servants began, there were no Indians in Natal. In 1880, a mere six years after the resumption of immigration, Europeans in Natal numbered 22,654 to the Indians' 12,823, less than a two-to-one ratio. By 1891, two years before Gandhi's arrival, the ratio had become nearly one-to-one. In 1904 the Europeans' slight edge vanished: there were 103,673 Indians living in Natal to 92,597 Europeans.[13] With numbers like these, the reality was that, were they fully enfranchised, the Indians could outvote the Europeans.

GANDHI'S CLIENTS

The economic reality was not simply in the numbers but also in the spirit of the Indians who migrated to Natal. Indian entrepreneurs of all types—from lowly market-gardeners,[14] traders, and hawkers to powerful merchants—had a well-deserved reputation for business acumen.[15] It was common for Indians freed from their term of servitude to set up small shops in direct competition with Europeans, often besting them. Of far greater importance, however, were the "Arabs," mainly Gujarati-speaking Muslims from the region surrounding Gandhi's birthplace of Porbandar who called themselves Arabs to distinguish themselves from those whom they considered run-of-the-mill Indians. These entrepreneurs came to South Africa for one purpose only—to make their fortunes in business. But a small portion of the total Indian population in Natal, they constituted what historian Maureen Swan calls the "commercial elite." As such, they controlled Indian political and economic life before and after the time Gandhi arrived in South Africa. The wealth accumulated by these important figures in the Indian community was astonishing. To take one example, economic historian Zbigniew Konczacki estimates that in the period of 1903–1904 the commercial elite reaped profits and other income from trade in Natal to the tune of £502,000.[16]

By contrast, the living and working conditions of indentured Indians were deplorable. Swan describes them:

Plantation labourers were overworked (as much as a seventeen or eighteen hour day during the overlapping crushing and planting seasons), malnourished and poorly housed. These aspects of their existence gave rise to abnormally high disease and death rates. . . . In addition, the . . . indentured labour system offered little room for even such basic human comforts as family life. . . . There was . . . a serious imbalance in the male:female ratio, and the possibility of establishing or maintaining a family unit was made . . . remote by the prevalent employer practice of refusing to ration or pay any non-working Indian. In short, there is a solid weight of evidence . . . to suggest that overwork, malnourishment, and squalid living conditions formed the pattern of daily life for most agricultural workers.[17]

When the twenty-three-year-old lawyer who would later embrace voluntary poverty boarded the SS *Safari* in Bombay on April 19, 1893, he was going to South Africa not to champion the interests of oppressed Indian workers, but to represent the interests of the privileged elite.

FOUR

Dada Abdulla's White Elephant

There was not any immediate work for me.

GANDHI

WAITING FOR GANDHI AS HE disembarked was Dada Abdulla, one of the richest men of any color in Durban. Owner of an international shipping line and trading houses in both Natal and Transvaal, the Porbandar expatriate had acquired a vast fortune in South Africa. In the past year Abdulla had become entangled with another Indian businessman in a bitter struggle over a commercial transaction involving a huge sum of money. Gandhi understood that he had been invited to South Africa to give routine assistance in this piece of litigation. What he did not understand as his host greeted him in late May 1893 was that the world of relative complacency and comfort to which the wealthy Abdulla, with his flowing robes and his subservient attitude toward the European colonists, would introduce him, would slowly but inexorably give way to a world of hard choices.

Gandhi's first weeks in South Africa foreshadowed the questions that would, in increasingly loud tones, demand answers throughout his entire life in the law. As a lawyer, how was Gandhi called to work for justice? Was he called to be the insider, the London-trained barrister who would use the traditional accord given his position, the weight of precedent, and the ordinary forms of legal disputation to argue his causes? Was he called to be the insider with a conscience, one who would show no fear in openly advancing his views that the law and society had taken a wrong turn and were in need of reform? Or was he called to be the outsider, one who would advocate the abandonment and rejection of a bankrupt legal system?

Abdulla took Gandhi by the arm, and the two embarked upon a week or so of reconnoitering each other in Durban. Abdulla started with an assessment of Gandhi's fine English clothes; he quickly sized him up as one whose expensive tastes were more appropriate for Europeans than Indians who needed to work hard for their bread. Abdulla wasn't certain what was inside the man either. He feared that once he sent this twenty-three-year-old to the Transvaal, where the case was being litigated, he would fall under the influence of the Indian defendants there and become disloyal to his employer.

At the same time that Abdulla was evaluating Gandhi, Gandhi was evaluating his client. He recognized that Abdulla, while practically illiterate, was blessed with a native intellect, an education provided by the school of experience, and a worldly acumen that permitted him to make a success of his entrepreneurial work. It is not surprising, then, that the first test of Gandhi's legal mettle was set up by Abdulla.

Before addressing this incident, we must acknowledge that Gandhi's biographers have focused, not without justification, on two other incidents that occurred on a journey Gandhi was to take at the end of May 1893 from Durban to Johannesburg, incidents that woke Gandhi to the reality of race prejudice in South Africa. Prior to these better-known events, however, Gandhi experienced the sting of color prejudice at the hands of Natal's judicial system. It is to that incident we turn first, inasmuch as it was sure to have been a strong influence in shaping Gandhi's self-image as well as his understanding of the legal system in South Africa.

TROUBLE IN THE COURTROOM

On the morning of May 25, 1893, just days after Gandhi's arrival, Abdulla took his new lawyer to a Durban courtroom, introduced him around, and had him sit with his European lawyer in the "horseshoe," an area reserved for counsel.[1] While Indians were not strangers to Natal's courts, the European populace did not relish their appearance there. The colonists were annoyed by the need to interpret their language and by the perceived loquaciousness of Indian witnesses. Moreover, many believed that the greater portion of the testimony of Indians consisted of fiction, not fact. Indians, according to the *Natal Advertiser*, told the "most astounding and preposterous stories."[2] For an Indian to appear not as a witness, but as a barrister, upset every notion the Europeans had of Indians in court. An Indian barrister had never before appeared in a Durban court.

The intensity with which some Europeans disliked Indians should not be underestimated. Only a few days before Gandhi's arrival in Durban, the *Natal Advertiser* had editorialized that "coolie immigration has to be stopped. We want cultivators of our lands. But let us see to it that we only assist men of our own race to take up that calling in this country. We want more immigrants, but we want them white. . . . [D]o not let us become suffocated with the native scum of the streets of Bombay and Madras."[3]

When Gandhi entered the courtroom, he did so dressed "*a la* English,"[4] but he also wore the turban common among Hindus at the time. After Gandhi had settled himself into the lawyers' sitting area, largely vacant that morning, he quietly studied the proceedings taking place before him. Before too long, the court's chief clerk took Gandhi into the interpreter's room and advised him, on his next visit to the courtroom, not to take a seat in the horseshoe unless he first produced his credentials. Gandhi, thinking that he was safe for the day, returned to his seat. The presiding magistrate, however, began to glare at him, and eventually sent word to Gandhi that he had no business sitting in the lawyers' section. Gandhi replied that he was an English barrister. The magistrate, however, stated in open court that Gandhi had not formally presented himself to the court, he had not submitted his credentials to act as a lawyer in Natal, and by wearing his "chapeau" in court, he had failed to accord the court the proper respect. The magistrate requested that this interloper both vacate the horseshoe and, if he wished to stay, remove his turban. Gandhi declined the invitation to remove the turban, "apologized if he had done anything wrong," and left the courtroom. It is unlikely that a visiting European lawyer would have been treated with a similar lack of hospitality. Indeed, the *Natal Mercury*, in reporting the incident, accused the court of "misdirected zeal."[5]

Afraid that the newspaper notices of this incident would harm his reputation, the next day Gandhi wrote a careful letter to the editor of the *Natal Advertiser* describing his conversation with the clerk and explaining that he was assured by the clerk that he could retain his seat for the day. Gandhi apologized for what was perceived to be his rudeness.

LESSONS

After this unceremonious end to his first appearance in court and with court-watching now out of the question, there wasn't much for Gandhi to do. Abdulla's brother had done a favor for Lakshmidas, Gandhi's brother, by putting Gandhi on the firm's payroll, but there were no legal skills that the novice Gandhi had that the firm's experienced European lawyers didn't already possess in abundance. Accordingly, Dada Abdulla looked upon him as a white elephant.[6] With time on his hands and, after almost ten days in South Africa, with very little to occupy his attention, it was natural enough that the thought of establishing a practice of his own in Durban would enter Gandhi's mind. The thought must have entered the minds of the European lawyers, too; in fact, it was reported that the prospect of competing with an Indian for the business of the Indian merchant community was of sufficient concern among the established European bar to "cause quite a flutter of excitement among the legal fraternity."[7] By this time, however, Abdulla was ready to act. After observing Gandhi for more than a week, he finally consented to allow him to help in the case. The firm's Johannesburg counsel had sent word to Abdulla that the case was beginning to move and that he needed Abdulla or someone else familiar with the matter to come to the Transvaal to help work on it. Gandhi would be useful in this capacity because both the litigants hailed from Gandhi's hometown of Porbandar and thus shared Gujarati as their native tongue; Gandhi could serve as an interpreter for the firm's European lawyers, translating legal concepts with an accuracy of which only someone trained in the law was capable.

First, however, Gandhi had to acquaint himself with the case. It concerned the sale of the Transvaal branch of Dada Abdulla and Company's trading business to another Muslim merchant, a relative of Abdulla, Tayob Hajee Khan Muhammad. Muhammad and Company had defaulted on the promissory note it had given Abdulla and Company to support the sale, and Abdulla had sued to recover on the note. The case, according to Gandhi, was thus "mainly about accounts"—a subject that baffled him.[8] Gandhi did not even know what "P. Note," the shorthand term for promissory note, meant. Like a good lawyer called to work in another profession's field, however, Gandhi immersed himself in the study of bookkeeping, mastered it, and announced to Abdulla that he was ready to work. With that, Dada Abdulla dispatched Gandhi by a combination of train and coach to join the firm's counsel in Pretoria, the capital of the Transvaal.

Abdulla purchased for Gandhi a first-class train ticket for the Durban-to-Charlestown leg of the trip. Just before the train reached the Pietermaritzburg station, a European passenger brought the presence of a "colored" man in the first-class section to the attention of train officials. When they demanded that Gandhi remove himself to the van compartment, he refused and dared them to call a constable. The officials did call the constable, who promptly pushed Gandhi not only out of his first-class compartment but out of the train altogether—and threw his bags after him. Humiliated, Gandhi spent the night in the piercing cold of the Pietermaritzburg train station. His mind raced through the possibilities. Was South Africa a mistake? Should he give it up and return to India? Should he remain in South Africa, keep his head down, and do his work? Should he stay and fight? After a night of thought, Gandhi, having already survived his embarrassing eviction from the Durban courtroom, resolved to fight.

In the morning Gandhi wired Abdulla, who arranged for fellow merchants in Pietermaritzburg to tend to Gandhi during the day. That evening Gandhi reboarded the train for Charlestown on which he availed himself of a reserved berth and a bedding ticket.

After the train reached Charlestown in the morning, Gandhi presented himself at the stage coach station for passage to Johannesburg. The authorities there balked at putting Gandhi in the coach with white passengers. When they seated him outside of the coach box to separate him from the whites, Gandhi, not wanting to lose yet another day, decided to pocket the insult and take his seat alongside the coachman. This arrangement held until the coach reached Pardekoph, when the white man in charge of the coach demanded that "Sami" (a derogatory term for Indians) take a seat on the footboard so that the white man could take Gandhi's seat and enjoy a smoke. At this Gandhi refused. "It was you who seated me here, though I should have been accommodated inside. I put up with the insult. Now that you want to sit outside and smoke, you would have me sit at your feet. I will not do so, but I am prepared to sit inside." This was too much for the white man. He punched Gandhi in the head and then seized his arms in an attempt to pry him from his seat. The wiry Gandhi held on to the rails of the coach for dear life as the stronger opponent nearly broke Gandhi's wrists. The other passengers screamed for the fellow to stop. He did.

Gandhi endured the man's threats of more violence from Pardekoph to Standerton, all the while occupying the seat he refused to surrender. At Standerton he was placed in a good seat on the coach to Johannesburg. Arriving there, he was warned by an Indian merchant that in the Transvaal first- and second-class tickets were never issued to Indians traveling by train from Johannesburg to Pretoria. Gandhi, desirous of flexing his barrister's muscles, obtained the railroad's rules and studied them. It seems he could find no exclusion of Indians in the rules. So he sent word to the stationmaster that Mohandas K. Gandhi, barrister at law, would soon appear to obtain a first-class ticket to Pretoria. Gandhi arrived in "faultless English dress" complete with frock coat and necktie. The stationmaster sold him the ticket and Gandhi boarded the train. When the train reached Germiston, a train guard discovered Gandhi and ordered him to move to third class. Gandhi was saved by an English passenger who recognized Gandhi as a "gentleman" and convinced the guard to let him stay in first class.[9]

When Gandhi's long journey ended that evening in Pretoria, he had much to think about. He had gambled with resistance in Pietermaritzburg and had lost. He had gambled with resistance again in Pardekoph and had won. But in Johannesburg the English barrister had played the insider's game and had won with that approach, too—without getting beaten.

Maybe there was something in the law for Gandhi.

DADA ABDULLA & CO. V. TAYOB HAJEE KHAN MOHAMED & CO. AND MOOSA AMOD & CO.

Dada Abdulla & Co. v. Tayob Hajee Khan Mohamed & Co. and Moosa Amod & Co., the litigation that would occupy Gandhi's attention for the next year, was the high-profile case of its day because of the extraordinary sums at stake. In 1890, Dada Abdulla and Company, wishing to dispose of the Transvaal branch of its business, entered into an agreement with Tayob Hajee Khan Mohamed and Company whereby all of Abdulla's interests in the Transvaal, including its several stores, would be handed over to Mohamed in return for a promissory note. The purchase price approached £40,000, an astounding figure for the time. A dispute arose over the sale, the exact nature of which is unclear, causing Dada Abdulla and Company to bring suit in the High Court against Mohamed and Company for the balance alleged owing on the sale, £18,000. It is clear that one of the major issues concerned the question of how items in stock should be valued, with each party claiming a different date as that on which the stock should be valued. The difference in the two stock-takings ranged approximately between £4,000 and £6,000.[10]

The case was set for trial on February 9, 1893, before the High Court. Faced with a matter of some apparent complexity, the court eventually thought the better course was not to try the case immediately. With the consent of the parties, the case was referred to two accountants whose job as commissioners it was to examine all the account books, call witnesses as necessary, and issue a report of their findings to the court. Accordingly, their role might best be understood as that of special masters called in to develop a complicated factual picture. Because the account books they were to examine were not all kept in the English language, Gandhi, trained in the law and fluent in Gujarati, could be useful in interpreting the books for Abdulla's counsel during this process.

The commissioners apparently having finished their work by the South African spring of 1893, a trial date was set, and the attorneys for the parties engaged in some final pretrial skirmishing. Then the parties, in a major development, agreed to abandon the courtroom and turn the case over to an arbitrator in Pretoria for resolution. When the arbitration opened on April 11, 1894, in Pretoria, little did the lawyers for the two sides realize what a bizarre turn the case would soon take.

CARRYING BAGS

Representing Dada Abdulla was Albert Weir Baker, a successful, somewhat eccentric Pretoria attorney who had first practiced in Natal before relocating to Pretoria. Gandhi called on Baker the day after his arrival in Pretoria. The veteran lawyer lost no time in cordially but frankly giving Gandhi an idea of his role. "We have no work for you here as a barrister, for we have engaged the best counsel. The case is a prolonged and complicated one, so I shall take your assistance only to the extent of getting necessary information. And of course you will make communication with my client easy for me, as I shall now ask for all the information I want from him through you."[11]

So this was to be Gandhi's role—to carry Baker's bags. So little had Gandhi to do by way of actual work that he found the time to engage in other pursuits, one of which was to study the condition of Indian life in Pretoria and to agitate for its improvement. Gandhi began by making the acquaintance of every Indian in Pretoria, starting with his opponent in the Abdulla case, Mohamed.[12] Soon thereafter Gandhi called a meeting of the Indian community in Pretoria; most of those who attended the meeting were, like Mohamed, merchants, mainly Muslim, though with a sprinkling of Hindus among them. Gandhi wasted no time in lecturing his audience on the deficiencies in the Indian community, focusing on the need for merchants to be truthful in their business dealings and for all Indians to reform their derelict sanitary habits. Gandhi attempted to rouse his countrymen by urging them to set aside their religious and ethnic differences and to unite for their mutual benefit.

This was Gandhi's first speech in South Africa, and the contrast with his courtroom and public speaking experiences in India could not have been greater. He spoke with none of the difficulties of nervousness and even panic that had characterized his earlier efforts. His audience was sufficiently moved that regular meetings to discuss similar issues began. At least by his own account, Gandhi had made a "considerable impression" on his listeners.[13]

Gandhi devoted the vast bulk of his free time, however, to a detailed study of religion, reading some eighty books during his year in Pretoria. He was buffeted by calls for his conversion made by his Muslim and, especially, Christian friends. He admits to being "overwhelmed" by Tolstoy's *The Kingdom of God Is Within You*, but his friends' entreaties resulted only in Gandhi's tighter embrace of Hinduism, even with the faults Gandhi saw in it. He so immersed himself in his comparative study of religion, and his services were so little in demand, that he never bothered to apply for admission to the bar while he was in Pretoria.

Gandhi also had time to make the acquaintance of a number of powerful European figures in the Transvaal. Among them was Dr. Albert Krause, the state attorney and brother of the future public prosecutor. Their common membership in the Inner Temple must have served as an immediate bond for Krause and Gandhi. Krause was embarrassed by the fact that his fellow barrister, as a nonwhite resident, needed a pass to be on the streets after 9 P.M. Rather than give him a pass, something a master would provide for a servant, Krause presented Gandhi with a special letter from himself authorizing Gandhi to be out at any and all times. Gandhi, the barrister, did not refuse this privileged treatment but accepted the letter and carried it with him always.

The letter did not protect him, however, on one of his evening walks. His course took him by the home of the Transvaal president, a residence guarded by a police officer who, without warning, pushed and kicked Gandhi off the footpath. As chance would have it, a European acquaintance of Gandhi who happened to be passing by observed the incident. He urged Gandhi to sue. Gandhi resisted the invitation and, revealing a bit of the legal philosophy beginning to take shape in him, stated he would not "go to court in respect of any personal grievance. So I do not intend to proceed against him." At this point in his young career as a lawyer, Gandhi was even reluctant to bring a test case. He told his friends that he would rather first work through channels by seeking the assistance of the British agent in the Transvaal.

Gandhi's superior in the *Abdulla* case, Baker, was not so shy and traditional a lawyer. He led a busy and multifaceted life. His first career had been that of a carpenter. After becoming a member of the bar, Baker also established himself as a lay preacher and missionary. He was well known for his religious zeal and, as a member of the Wesleyan Church in Pretoria, he would employ drunkards as clerks in his law office for the purpose of helping them regain control over their lives. He tried on numerous occasions to convert Gandhi to Christianity. Although Gandhi politely declined his entreaties, he did join Baker for daily prayer. And it was Baker's challenges to Gandhi's religious thinking that spurred on Gandhi's study of spirituality. A clue to Baker's character and a sign of things to come lay in his willingness to lead open-air church services in Pretoria,[14] services that resulted on multiple occasions in his getting arrested for breaching the peace.

AN INTRODUCTION TO DEFIANCE

Baker's principled stubbornness was not confined to his defense of Christianity. On April 25, 1894, the parties to the *Abdulla* case met to engage in a hearing before the arbitrator, John Livingstone. After the parties, the reporter, the witnesses, the lawyers, and the arbitrator had taken their places, three Pretoria detectives burst into Baker's office and immediately arrested Abdulla Hajee Adam, Dada's partner, for breaking customs regulations. The detectives were not there just to arrest Abdulla; they announced that they also had a warrant for the seizure of certain materials belonging to him that were needed to substantiate the charges. The warrant, in Dutch, was translated by the multilingual Baker, who understood the document as authorizing only the seizure of books and nothing else. Baker identified for the detectives the materials belonging to the plaintiff and even identified Abdulla. But when one of the detectives attempted to seize Baker's papers in the case, the attorney resisted by attempting to stuff them into his briefcase. The two engaged in a struggle over the papers. The detectives got the best of it when a second detective came to the first's aid. The detectives then put Baker under restraints and seized everything in sight—Abdulla's books and papers, Mohamed's books and papers, documents of record in the case, Baker's private papers, and even the arbitrator's notes. The detectives then paraded the handcuffed Baker through the town to a police office, where he was charged with resisting the detectives. Baker posted bail and was released.

When the question of the lawfulness of the seizure came before the court, things did not go well for the government. Mr. Justice Jorissen was offended that the detectives had not only seized books belonging to Abdulla, but also records belonging to the court. Jorissen accused the state of a failure of good judgment, saying that the arbitration was a serious proceeding that had been unnecessarily and violently interrupted. He opined that rather than causing a raucous and costly interruption of the arbitration, the state could simply have petitioned the court for an order compelling Abdulla to turn the materials over to the state. Jorissen ordered all the materials returned; he charged Baker and Livingstone to keep custody of them.

As for the charges against Baker, the Transvaal High Court, in a unanimous decision, threw them out, citing Baker's status as an attorney and "a well-known and respectable citizen" and finding the detectives' "vulgar, cruel and mean" behavior to be without justification.[15]

None of these collateral events could distract from the attention received by the case that gave rise to them. After approximately three weeks of arbitration hearings, Livingstone announced his decision. He found the purchase price to be £37,000, prompting *The Press* of Pretoria to proclaim it "one of the most expensive arbitration cases that has been heard in South Africa for some years."[16] This was the amount owed by Mohamed and Company before subtraction of the sum, not made public, that it had already paid Abdulla and Company. On the 20th day of May 1894 the arbitrator's award was made a rule of the High Court of Justice.

REFLECTIONS

Gandhi was a prolific writer. *The Collected Works of Mahatma Gandhi* stretches out over one hundred volumes. He wrote numerous sketches of his life, later bound together as a lengthy autobiography, *My Experiments with Truth*. And yet from what must have been a rich storehouse of memories of his nearly twenty-year career at the bar, Gandhi chooses to relate his experiences in only a small handful of cases. One of those was the *Abdulla* case.

In reflecting on the case, Gandhi first draws a lesson about the relationship between truth and the practice of law. He claims that while he did earnestly pursue his interest in religion during his year in Pretoria, his primary concern was with the case—and its facts. He eventually came to know the facts, he claims, better than the parties themselves. He recalls the advice later given him by one older head that "facts are three-fourths of the law" and the observation of another "that if we take care of the facts of a case, the law will take care of itself"—propositions with which most practitioners might agree. Gandhi offers his own formulation when he states, "Facts mean truth, and once we adhere to truth, the law comes to our aid naturally."[17]

From his study of the *Abdulla* facts, Gandhi concluded that Abdulla's was a very strong case and that "the law was bound to be on his side." But Gandhi saw more than this:

> I also saw that the litigation, if it were persisted in, would ruin the plaintiff and the defendant. . . . No one knew how long the case might go on. Should it be allowed to continue to be fought out in court, it might go on indefinitely and to no advantage of either party. Both, therefore, desired an immediate termination of the case, if possible.
>
> I approached Tyeb Sheth and requested and advised him to go to arbitration. I recommended him to see his counsel. I suggested to him that if an arbitrator commanding the confidence of both parties could be appointed, the case would be quickly finished. The lawyers' fees were so rapidly mounting up that they were enough to devour all the resources of the clients, big merchants as they were. The case occupied so much of their attention that they had no time left for work. In the meantime mutual ill-will was steadily increasing. I became disgusted with the profession. As lawyers the counsel on both sides were bound to rake up points of law in support of their own clients. . . . This was more than I could bear. I felt that it was my duty to befriend both parties and bring them together. I strained every nerve to bring about a compromise. At last Tyeb Sheth agreed. An arbitrator was appointed, the case was argued before him, and Dada Abdulla won.
>
> But that did not satisfy me. If my client were to seek immediate execution on the award, it would be impossible for Tyeb Sheth to meet the whole of the awarded amount, and there was an unwritten law among the Porbandar Memans living in South Africa that death should be preferred to bankruptcy. It was impossible for Tyeb Sheth to pay down the whole sum of about £37,000 and costs.[18] He meant to pay not a pie less than the amount, and he did not want to be declared bankrupt. There was only one way. Dada Abdulla should allow him to pay in moderate instalments. He was equal to the occasion, and granted Tyeb Sheth instalments spread over a very long period. . . . [B]oth were happy with the result, and both rose in the public estimation.

Gandhi then expresses his own feelings at this result:

> My joy was boundless. I had learnt the true practice of law. I had learnt to find out the better side of human nature and to enter men's hearts. I realized that the true function of a lawyer was to unite parties riven asunder. The lesson was so indelibly burnt into me that a large part of my time during the

twenty years of my practice as a lawyer was occupied in bringing about private compromises of hundreds of cases. I lost nothing thereby—not even money, certainly not my soul.[19]

One must entertain a certain amount of skepticism about the accuracy of Gandhi's recollection of how arbitration came about. On the one hand, it stretches credulity to think that an unlicensed twenty-four-year-old bag carrier for the sophisticated and experienced lawyers in the case could single-handedly convince two major Indian businessmen to go to arbitration. On the other hand, Gandhi might have been able to gain the confidence of the parties because he was their countryman, and an educated one at that. Moreover, it makes sense that if Mohamed compromised on arbitration, Gandhi would be able to make a persuasive case to Abdulla that, with respect to the installments question, it was his turn to compromise.

MORE LESSONS

What did Gandhi draw from the Baker incident? We do not know whether he was physically present during the arrest. Surely he knew of it, however, inasmuch as it was the talk of the town. Baker displayed extraordinary courage in defiance of overreaching power when he resisted the efforts of the officers to seize his files. Baker apparently felt no shame on the occasion of this or any of his other arrests. Gandhi himself would later defy many an authority and freely court arrest. Gandhi learned something other than law from Baker.

What more did Gandhi learn from his involvement in the case of *Abdulla v. Mohamed*? He had been given a rare view into the privileged life and the benefits it brought. Even from his lower-level perch as a nonpracticing lawyer who served in a capacity more befitting a paralegal than a barrister, Gandhi could see the enormous amounts of money at play in the South African business and legal community. Abdulla's commercial empire stretched from Bombay to Durban to Pretoria and beyond. Other Indians were profiting from the trade that became available with the growth of the Indian community in South Africa. And if there were wealthy business owners, would prospering lawyers not be far behind? Wouldn't there be a special place for an Indian lawyer? And couldn't such a lawyer charge handsomely for his services? There were large amounts of money to be made, far, far more than Gandhi ever made in his failed attempts at establishing a practice in his home country.

It was no wonder, then, that the European bar in Durban eyed this prospective competitor with suspicion.

ONE MONTH MORE

Toward the end of May 1894 Gandhi packed his bags and headed for Durban, whence, it is said, he intended to sail back to India. On his arrival there, he learned that the same Dada Abdulla who had thought of him as a white elephant a year earlier now planned a farewell party for him. If we were to trust Gandhi's recollection of this event in the autobiography he wrote years later, we would be led to believe that at this occasion Gandhi, while scanning a newspaper, learned for the first time that the right of Indians to vote was coming under attack in the Natal Parliament. Gandhi recalls that his merchant hosts were unaware of this threat until he called it to their attention. The merchants, now apprised of the danger to them, asked Gandhi to stay and lead the fight against this franchise legislation on their behalf.

There is good reason to believe, as Maureen Swan has demonstrated, that this account is highly romanticized.[20] By the time of Abdulla's farewell party, the merchants had been resisting the attacks of the white power establishment on their interests for some time and were thus quite likely to be already keenly aware of any attack on the franchise. Dada Abdulla himself had served on the Durban Indian Committee, meeting with that group to discuss "important . . . political and other subjects."[21]

What does not appear in dispute is the deal Gandhi struck with the merchants. He agreed to stay, but on the condition that he not be paid for his work, arguing that no one should take a salary to work in the cause for Indian rights. If the merchants would provide him, however, with start-up funds to pay for telegrams, literature, law books, travel, and legal fees for local lawyers and also agree to make available a corps of volunteers, he would stay on for an additional month, an amount of time he naïvely judged sufficient to beat back the attack on the Indian franchise. The agreement was made and Gandhi's services were secured for a month.

Gandhi's month of service stretched on—for twenty years. Not until 1914 would he finally leave South Africa and the cause he had now embraced.

FIVE

Not a White Barrister

There is still a Natal Law Society which . . . keeps alive the bright flame of bigotry and prejudice.

Natal Witness, September 5, 1894

WITH A RISING INDIAN POPULATION in Natal continuing to alarm many of the European colonists,[1] the Natal Parliament undertook to limit Indian influence by prohibiting Indians from registering as voters.[2] When in the late South African fall of 1894 Gandhi agreed to stay in Natal and fight the legislature on this issue, the process of enacting legislation was well under way. The Franchise Law Amendment Bill had already received its second reading and was poised for its third and final reading in early July. Against insuperable odds—the bill enjoyed the unanimous support of the legislature—Gandhi began his public work by lodging with the Natal Legislative Assembly (the larger of the two parliamentary chambers) the first of many petitions he was to write while in South Africa.[3]

GANDHI AS PETITIONER

This petition, the first known formal handiwork of this novice lawyer, stands as a superb reflection of Gandhi's developing legal mind. The petition is quite well organized—much like a legal complaint—with a set of numbered paragraphs setting forth the identity of the petitioners, the gist of their grievance, and a concluding prayer for relief. The petition is authoritative, citing the writings of Sir Henry Sumner Maine, Professor Max Muller, and Sir George Birdwood, as well as the public statements of Sir Thomas Munro and Frederick Pincott. Compactly written, it is clear, straightforward, and easy to follow. Its tone is polite and deferential, yet firm. There is not so much as a hint of anger, but neither does it lack in confidence. Indeed, it is written with complete self-assurance.

The petition responds to the legislature's argument that Indians should be denied the franchise because they lacked institutions of representative government in their home country. Gandhi rests his response on the historical record, citing the long existence of local self-government in India's municipalities, the elections held for the governance of castes, the councils elected to govern trading communities, and the representative parliament established by the Indian state of Mysore. Gandhi concludes his petition by quoting remarks made by leading European figures, all in praise of the Indian character. The refined argument Gandhi makes befits an English barrister—careful, focused, and not at all strident. Conspicuously absent, however, is any appeal to conscience or universal human rights.

The petition was followed the next day by a letter from Gandhi and several others to the Natal premier and, just two days later, by a letter to all the members of the legislature. The letter was accompanied by a set of five questions. Question 4 provides the flavor of the document: "Do you think it just that a man should not become a voter simply because he is of Asiatic extraction?" Perhaps this was a rhetorical question. If, however, Gandhi expected answers to questions of this sort, he was revealing the naïveté of a novice political operative. The internal doubts Gandhi had about his capacity to represent the interests of his community rose to the surface in a letter he wrote to a senior advisor on July 5:

> I am yet inexperienced and young and, therefore, quite liable to make mistakes. The responsibility undertaken is quite out of proportion to my ability. I may mention that I am doing this without any remuneration. So you will see that I have not taken the matter up, which is beyond my ability, in order to enrich myself at the expense of the Indians. I am the only available person who can handle the question.[4]

On July 1, the same day the questions were sent, Gandhi met with the Natal governor and followed the meeting up with a letter. He then lodged two more petitions with the legislature. Despite Gandhi's prodigious output of words, the legislature passed the bill on its third and final reading on the 7th of July 1894. Gandhi then turned his attention to the governor, whose signature the bill required, presenting a petition to Sir Walter Hely-Hutchinson. The governor was not moved; he signed the bill. Gandhi then drafted a lengthy petition to the British secretary of state for the colonies, Lord Ripon, signed by about ten thousand Natal Indians.[5] Gandhi's recollection of his work on this petition demonstrates qualities that would be reflected in much of his work as a lawyer: "I took considerable pains over drawing up this petition. I read all the literature available on the subject. My argument centered round a principle and an expedience. I argued that we had a right to the franchise in Natal, as we had a kind of franchise in India. I urged that it was expedient to retain it, as the Indian population capable of using the franchise was very small."[6] In his career at the bar Gandhi would be known for his meticulous preparation and for a philosophy that held that the most principled action was usually that which was most effective. For now, however, this approach was unrefined and unperfected. Like his other attempts, the Ripon petition, too, would prove futile.[7]

THE MERCHANTS' LAWYER

In mid-July 1894, while awaiting the response of the secretary of state, it became clear to Gandhi not only that the franchise battle would be protracted but also that it represented the start of a longer and more wide-ranging campaign being waged by the colonists against Indian interests. While the colony's agriculturalists were sufficiently influential to block efforts to prohibit the continued importation of indentured servants, they were not concerned with staying the hands of those who desired to check Indian economic and political interests.

At the start of the franchise battle Gandhi had anticipated returning to India in mid-1894. With anti-Asiatic sentiment apparently on the rise and no relief in sight, what Gandhi earlier had thought to be a decisive battle he now understood to be a preliminary skirmish in a lengthy war. If he was to make a contribution to the Indian struggle in South Africa, he would have to remain. As Gandhi later recalled, "It was now impossible for me to leave Natal."[8]

If he was to remain, he also needed to look after his own interests. Accordingly, Gandhi turned to those with money, making an arrangement with the wealthy merchants who led the Indian movement in South Africa. They had wanted to hire him, at the rather handsome sum of £300 per year, as their political organizer, but Gandhi refused, saying that he could not charge the merchants for "public work." He reasoned that the work would not call on his skills as a barrister, that his main job would not be to perform work himself but to mobilize others to do the necessary work, that as a paid organizer he would have divided loyalties when raising money for the movement, that he needed to be able to speak his mind to the group without fear of economic repercussions, and that, in any event, the movement should be able to count on more than £300 a year for its operations.

Gandhi suggested a different tack. "Entrust me with your legal work," he implored the merchants, promising that, in exchange, he would do their political work without charge.[9] The merchants had some apparent reluctance to commit to this path, the reasons for which Gandhi himself recognized. "I am not a white barrister. . . . Nor can I be sure of how I shall fare as a lawyer," Gandhi confessed to them.[10] The merchants were able to set their reservations aside, however, as twenty of them agreed to give Gandhi a retainer for a year's worth of legal services. In addition, Dada Abdulla, originally a skeptic and now one of Gandhi's strongest backers, agreed to provide Gandhi with furnishings in the place of the monetary gift he had intended to present to Gandhi on his departure. He also paid for Gandhi's bar admission fees and for the law books Gandhi needed to establish his practice. Gandhi took up residence in Beach Grove Villa, a prominent European section of town. Gandhi's decision to live in an elite neighborhood was quite deliberate: "I thought that the house should be good and situated in a good locality. I also had the idea that I could not add credit to the community, unless I lived in a style usual for barristers."[11] He agreed to a retainer of £300 per year, the minimum he considered necessary to run a barrister's household.

Gandhi went about the task of setting up a practice. Despite having been called to the bar three years earlier, he had never successfully practiced law on his own. What did he know of the practice of law in Natal? His only experience in South Africa was assisting other lawyers, an experience that exposed him to but a small and rarified portion of practice and gave him very little understanding of what was required of a general practitioner. Gandhi must have reflected, too, on his failed attempt to establish a thriving solo practice in Bombay. He would not make that mistake again. So he began searching for a practice setting that would afford him access to a veteran lawyer who could counsel him on the intricacies of Durban practice. Gandhi's timing in this matter was fortuitous, for the Natal bar had recently begun to experiment with partnerships, an arrangement previously not common in the colony.

PARTNERSHIP

Gandhi's friend Louis Paul, the Roman Catholic Indian interpreter for the Durban courts, served as Gandhi's eyes and ears in this effort, bringing Percy

Evans Coakes to Gandhi's attention.[12] Although Coakes was no novice at the bar—he had been admitted to practice a bit less than seven years earlier—neither was he the seasoned veteran who could have taught Gandhi tricks learned over a lifetime of practice. Perhaps Gandhi believed that he, a barrister, and Coakes, an attorney, would make a natural fit, not only because their practices would complement each other as would those of a barrister and solicitor, but also because Coakes had sometimes worked for Indian interests.[13] Given the intensity of color consciousness in Natal, surely few white lawyers would be enthusiastic about opening their practices to an Indian barrister. A novice who brought with him the legal work of twenty Indian merchants, however, might be a different matter. In the summer of 1894, with forty-five advocates and more than one hundred nonadvocate attorneys licensed to practice in Natal,[14] a lawyer who could bring with him the legal business promised to Gandhi by his "Arab" patrons would be quite a catch, assuming one could stifle his race prejudice. Coakes, who had fought before the borough magistrate in an attempt to keep the names of registered Indians on the voters' list, seemingly had no race-based reservations and, having represented Indians, understood the benefits of representing Indian merchants. Moreover, there was stiff competition among lawyers in Natal at the time. As the *Natal Mercury* observed, "Competition in the labour market generally reduces the cost to the employer, and judging from the grumbles one occasionally over-hears, this inexorable law of political economy is making itself unpleasantly felt among Durban attorneys."[15]

Because Gandhi was aware of the leverage he had in this market, he was to be no pushover in negotiations with Coakes. The Durban lawyer first demanded that Gandhi pay a premium to join his practice. Gandhi not only turned that suggestion down flat but, playing his best poker hand, also sent word back to Coakes, through Paul, that he was preparing to leave Durban. Indeed, Gandhi instructed Paul not to "show over-anxiety to Coakes."[16] While Gandhi's courtroom skills may not have been very advanced, his abilities as a negotiator surely were.

A few days later, Gandhi, having heard nothing from Coakes, sent out word in the community that "unless everything was settled by next [week]," he would go. The prospect of losing Indian business must have been too much for Coakes. He immediately dropped his demand for a premium. In fact, he was now willing to give Gandhi a share of the practice's proceeds! So confident was Gandhi in his ability to consummate the deal with Coakes on his own terms that, on hearing of Coakes' new position, Gandhi that same day made an inquiry to the registrar of the Supreme Court about licensing. On the following day, Paul announced that Coakes had agreed to see Gandhi.

In a three-hour meeting, the Durban lawyer offered Gandhi a 25 percent share of the partnership's profits during the first six months and 30 percent during the last six months of their yearlong agreement. Gandhi refused the offer and instead proposed that he receive a flat third for the entire year. Two days later, Coakes conceded once more, agreeing to this percentage.

Coakes sent Gandhi a draft of a written agreement to which Gandhi made alterations and additions, sending it back to Coakes. Gandhi demanded that he be given some credit for the cases that he brought in to the practice but that were to be conducted by Coakes. Again, Coakes conceded this point to his younger partner-to-be, and the two affixed their signatures to their agreement on August 4.

OBJECTION

With the partnership agreement now in place, Gandhi turned his attention to getting himself admitted to the bar—and attention this process needed. The bar was divided about his admission. Attorney General Harry Escombe, who had done some legal work for Dada Abdulla,[17] had shown some solicitude for Gandhi's welfare when, earlier in the year, he had urged his young friend to take out his advocate's license,[18] advice Gandhi would soon follow.[19] Escombe's welcome, however, was not representative. Natal's lawyers did not look kindly upon allowing Gandhi entrance to the profession. The degree to which this opposition was based on Gandhi's skin color, rather than the threat he posed to the economic well-being of the white bar, is uncertain. It is not difficult to imagine, however, that there must have been a renewal of the fear Gandhi's first appearance in Durban a year earlier had caused, a fear that an Indian barrister would take Indian work away from the province's European barristers.[20] Indeed, the *Natal Witness* surmised that it "was the loss of fees that prompted the opposition, and that has been the common verdict of the public."[21] Whatever the motivation, the bar establishment settled upon a strategy for keeping Gandhi out of the law business: it would not oppose Gandhi's application on grounds of color, but would instead seek technical grounds on which to base its opposition.[22]

While the bar was nominally a divided bar—that is, one entered it as either an attorney or as an advocate—in practice "there was a joint bar."[23] The rules at the time permitted most attorneys to practice as advocates, and most advocates as attorneys. This arrangement was known as "dual practice."[24] Attorneys were akin to solicitors—office lawyers who focused principally on noncourtroom matters, such as the drafting of contracts. Advocates were akin to barristers—courtroom lawyers appearing without restriction in trial courts of their choosing to argue cases.[25]

Gandhi, admitted in England as a barrister, applied as an advocate. Prior to 1893 the requirements for admission were undemanding, but with the promulgation of a new set of rules in 1893, the requirements were strengthened. Natal would now require that the applicant pass a preliminary examination, serve two to four years of a clerkship, and then pass a final examination in Roman law, Roman-Dutch law, Natal law and statutes, and evidence. Gandhi was able to escape these relatively rigorous new admission requirements, however, by virtue of his having achieved barrister status in England. Rule 23 of the new rules governing admission stated that the Court could dispense with the usual requirements if the applicant had already been admitted as a barrister in England. Perhaps the bar's opposition to Gandhi was heightened by resentment that this "colored" lawyer was not only applying for admission but doing so by virtue of an exemption surely not drafted with anyone other than whites in mind.

A member of the Durban bar with the unforgettable name of Gustave Aristide de Roquefeuil Labistour was appointed to represent the Law Society in the matter of Gandhi's application for admission. At age thirty-eight already a leading member of the Natal Law Society, Labistour would later rise to the office of attorney general and be elevated to the rank of King's Counsel. Labistour was initially suspicious of Gandhi because of Gandhi's failure to tender, in support of his application, the original of his certificate of admission to the Inner Temple in London. Gandhi was unable to produce this document because he had given it to the Indian authorities when he enrolled to practice before the Bombay High Court prior to his ill-fated attempt to establish a practice in India in 1891–1892. It was another issue, however, which occupied Labistour's attention when he met with the young applicant in Labistour's office on August 20.. The Natal attorney peered through his spectacles at the one who would be Natal's first Indian barrister and demanded that he produce certificates showing the good character of his family, as well as a statement from Albert Baker as to Gandhi's fitness to practice law. Labistour also expressed his dissatisfaction with the two certificates of character Gandhi had obtained from Natal merchants of European descent, claiming that they knew nothing of his character. Labistour advised Gandhi that he needed to produce evidence of his good character from people who knew him, like Dada Abdulla, rather than European merchants who had only a recent knowledge of Gandhi. Gandhi noted that he had made Abdulla's acquaintance only in Natal, to which Labistour responded that since they hailed from the same region of India, the Gandhi and Abdulla families should at least have some knowledge of each other. Labistour then promised Gandhi that should Gandhi produce an affidavit from Abdulla, Labistour, who himself had done some legal work for Abdulla, would withdraw as counsel for the Law Society, his objections having been satisfied. Deeply disturbed by Labistour's demands, Gandhi noted to himself that had he produced Indian affidavits, the bar would have demanded European affidavits. He bit his tongue, however, and produced the required affidavit from Abdulla and, for good measure, additional affidavits from Moosa Hajee Adam and Haji Dada, as well. Labistour, true to his word, withdrew and was replaced by the attorney and advocate Edward Mackenzie Greene, one of the more senior members of the Natal bar. Labistour would later prove to be a genuine friend of the Indian cause.

In keeping with the tradition whereby the attorney general, as the leading lawyer in the bar, represented applicants for admission,[26] the long-bearded, severe-looking, and intellectual Harry Escombe rose before the Natal Supreme Court on Monday, September 3, 1894 to move Gandhi's admission.[27] Escombe recounted Gandhi's call to the bar in England and his subsequent admission to the Bombay High Court of Judicature. Anticipating the Law Society's argument, Escombe explained that Gandhi had tendered the original of his Inner Temple admission certificate to the High Court of Judicature when he was admitted to practice before that court as an advocate. Greene, in opposition, argued that Gandhi had not fulfilled the requirements for admission, because he had not tendered the original of the certificate, producing instead an informal "copy of the certificate . . . being merely signed by one J. H. Farrell."[28] Greene argued that this copy was insufficient. In a maneuver that spoke volumes, Greene cited previous cases in which two European applicants, Stephenson and Beatson, had been denied admission because they failed to "produce certificates that they were still on the roll." Greene added that "the practice had been for barristers and solicitors to produce their certificates, and not simply sign an affidavit that they had been so admitted." Greene thus anticipated an attack that the society's position was motivated by Gandhi's color. His argument would seem to mischaracterize

Gandhi's application inasmuch as the signed copy of his Inner Temple certificate that Gandhi produced was significantly more substantial than a self-serving affidavit. Nonetheless, Justice Walter Wragg, first puisne judge, stated that he thought Greene's objection was proper, noting that he, Wragg, had produced his own Inner Temple certificate when asked to do so. The *General Rules for Admission of Advocates or Attorneys and Candidate Attorneys to the Supreme Court of Natal*, in effect at the time and promulgated just the previous year by Wragg and the other two judges now sitting on Gandhi's case, did not actually require an original certificate.[29]

Remarkably, no one on the bench made any reference to any standard by which the case should be decided. Wragg's colleagues on the bench seemed, however, to sense that the society's certificate argument cloaked its true reasons for opposing Gandhi's admission—and with good reason. Even before Gandhi applied for admission, the local press reported that the Law Society was considering opposing Gandhi.[30] It is quite unlikely that the society would have known in advance of Gandhi's application that Gandhi would tender a copy rather than the original of his Inner Temple certificate in support of his application. Accordingly, if the decision to oppose Gandhi was arrived at before the Law Society could have known of the alleged deficiency in his supporting documents, the society's reliance on this deficiency was a pretext. Because the bar offered no ground for its opposition before the Supreme Court other than the deficiency in Gandhi's certificate, it is reasonable to conclude that its actual grounds for opposition were ones that could not be publicly defended—race, economic self-interest, or both.[31]

Perhaps Justice John Turnbull, second puisne judge, sensed the bar's actual motives when he differed with Wragg, stating that he had never heard of an original certificate being required. The chief justice, Michael Gallwey, joined this attack on the society's position by noting that when he himself had applied for status as Queen's Counsel, his representation that he was a barrister was accepted without the proof of a certificate. He undercut Greene's misplaced reliance on the argument that affidavits were unacceptable by observing that Mr. Gandhi was not being tried for perjury. Justice Wragg, either persuaded or embarrassed by his brethren's points, eventually embraced Justice Turnbull and Gallwey's skepticism as to the society's opposition, stating that he believed Gandhi's representations and "did not wish to place any obstacle in his way."[32]

The Court, now unanimous in its rejection of the society's objections, granted Escombe's motion, admitted Gandhi, and swore him in on the spot—but not without conditions. The court instructed Gandhi to remove his turban to conform to the rules of the Court. The same turban that Gandhi had refused to remove while in the magistrate's court he now removed. While his friends would voice their misgivings about this act of obedience, Gandhi decided that his admission victory and his turban defeat constituted an outcome with which he could live. He bowed low and left the courtroom.[33]

NATAL: A LEGAL WORLD APART

Few places in 1894 could have matched the unusual texture of the legal world Gandhi was then entering. The system of prevailing law was anything but simple and pure. When Jan van Riebeeck claimed the Cape of Good Hope for the Dutch in 1652, he brought with him the Roman-Dutch law tradition then prevalent in Holland. When the Voortrekkers left the Cape for Natal nearly two centuries later, they carried with them not only this same Roman-Dutch legal tradition, which their forebears had inherited, but they also brought a touch of Cape legislation. Soon afterward, as the trekkers' short-lived Republic of Natalia gave way to British control, the British chose not to install their own common law system. Rather, in keeping with the British policy of initially permitting former Dutch colonies to retain their legal regimes, England ordered in 1845 that "the system . . . called the Roman-Dutch Law . . . be . . . established as the law of . . . Natal."[34] Shortly after Natal was given home rule by the British and just two years after Gandhi's admission to the bar, the Natal legislature passed the Supreme Court Act of 1896, in which the supremacy of Roman-Dutch law was affirmed by the colonists themselves.

The Roman-Dutch system that formed the historical foundation of Natalian law was of a hybrid character, built of one part Roman law and one part derived from German influences.[35] The South African version of Roman-Dutch law had a tradition of differing from the English common law system in that, while hardly ignoring relevant previously decided cases, it gave somewhat less weight to precedent. Furthermore, South African Roman-Dutch law did not separate law from equity, nor was it codified. Ironically, after Roman-Dutch law was discarded in Holland, it maintained enough life in South Africa that its practitioners were forced to cite centuries-old treatises for the most recent authority.

This is not to say that Roman-Dutch law was immune from change. To the contrary, from the mid-nineteenth century onward, the Natalian version of Roman-Dutch law came under a clear, distinct British influence.[36] Legal historian Peter Spiller has observed that from the 1850s to the 1900s "Natal advocates tended to ignore Roman-Dutch law and acted on the assumption that English law prevailed in Natal."[37] Indeed, one contemporary writer took the position that in "Natal the anglicising process has been carried so far as to obscure Roman-Dutch principles."[38] In some areas, the trend was not simply to obscure Roman-Dutch law but to supplant it; for example, the South African inheritors of the Roman-Dutch tradition adopted the English law of evidence and civil procedure.

The organization of the legal profession in Natal was similarly lacking in clarity. Natal inherited from Roman-Dutch law the Roman division of the profession into attorneys and advocates. In Natal, however, this distinction existed in name more than in practice, as the line between these two types of legal professionals was regularly crossed by practitioners. Finding itself in the backwaters of the legal world, Natal could not be too demanding of those it admitted to the profession. As Peter Spiller has demonstrated, "Natal did not generally attract advocates of sufficient training, ability or flexibility of mind to cope with local demands." Spiller ascribes this to several factors. Natal's apparent emphasis on Roman-Dutch law scared practitioners away from England; Cape lawyers, who might consider moving to the Orange Free State or to the Transvaal, would not consider life in Natal's primitive legal world; and the public's low opinion of Natal's lawyers prevented the profession from charging fees equivalent to those elsewhere in South Africa. This state of affairs caused Chief Justice Gallwey to remark just a year before Gandhi's admission that "few advocates, as such, could earn more than a mere subsistence."[39]

These conditions resulted in low standards for admission to practice. They also resulted in the right of dual practice. Until the requirements for admission were substantially strengthened in 1893, all manner of poorly qualified men were admitted to the bar.[40] No examination was required. In 1863 the rules for admission were altered, but not significantly strengthened, to permit persons without a university education to enter the bar as advocates if they simply sat in court for two years. This system was roundly criticized until, in 1893, the requirements were stiffened considerably. From 1893 on, the quality of the bar began to improve and many more applicants were admitted on the basis of their training at the Inns of Court.[41]

That Gandhi was in this first wave of London-trained barristers provided yet another reason for the local bar to oppose his admission. Not only was this applicant "colored," not only was he going to steal away business generated by Indian merchants, but he presented himself for admission on the basis of credentials far superior to those of many in the local bar. The *Natal Witness*, reflecting on the argument over Gandhi's admission, editorialized on this point: "The application of Mr. Gandhi's admission was made by the present Attorney-General, and had the support of the ex–Attorney-General; and when those two gentlemen, with a few others who might be counted on the fingers of one hand, are subtracted from the Bar of Natal, the residuum does not exactly command admiration."[42] It is no wonder that Gandhi received a less than warm reception.

The conditions under which Gandhi and his new colleagues at the bar practiced law in 1894 were less than ideal. The courthouse in Durban was an abysmal place. Its acoustics were terrible, it was decrepit, it was poorly maintained, and it was so poorly built that the wind could be heard "whistling [through it] on a winter's day."[43] The courthouse did not even contain a law library. Indeed, there was not a single law library in the entire city.[44] But perhaps a run-down courthouse and the absence of a law library were fitting for a bar that did not hold itself to particularly high standards.

This unpolished legal setting matched the rough character of Gandhi's partner's practice. There was no limit to the ways the resourceful Coakes devised to make money. He did criminal defense work; represented Indian merchants; appeared in bankruptcy matters; pursued collection actions; loaned money and sued when it wasn't repaid; represented landlords wanting to eject nonpaying tenants, as well as tenants resisting payment; represented natives, Europeans, and Indians alike; engaged in commercial litigation; and, even before Gandhi was admitted, appeared in court to represent the rights of Indian voters. Coakes was not reluctant to demand his fees from his clients or to attack other lawyers trying to steal his clients. He gave no quarter. While his aggressiveness provided him a living, eventually it would land him in ethical trouble with the Law Society and the Supreme Court.

The quality of justice being dispensed in Durban was a paradoxical admixture of rank prejudice and British fairness. On the one hand, Indians were unsparingly mocked for their supposed mendacity as witnesses,[45] and Indians and natives were arrested far more often in relation to their proportion to the total population than Europeans. On the other hand, there are numerous reports of judges showing no favoritism to Europeans over Indian or native litigants. For example, shortly after Gandhi was admitted, a European supervisor at a sewage plant was accused of assaulting one of his charges, a native. Despite the European defendant's denial of the charge and the support the defendant received from the testimony of a second European witness, the magistrate showed no hesitation in finding the defendant guilty.

BARRISTER GANDHI

While he was principally occupied with his political work in the weeks leading up to his admission to practice, Gandhi also performed a variety of mundane legal tasks for the Indian community—rendering advice to Abdulla, performing translation work, and drafting and reviewing documents for his merchant clients. Gandhi also took up Abdulla's offer to purchase furniture and law books for him and to pay the fees associated with his admission. He read a little law, bought a suit for court, and looked at rooms and houses to rent, eventually settling on a handsome villa at Beach Grove.[46] Gandhi brought out the negotiating skills he had deployed against Coakes and reduced the monthly lease payments from an initial asking price of £8 to £6, 10s. In keeping with his elevated image of himself, Gandhi chose to pay this still rather steep price to ensconce himself in an area usually reserved for prestigious Europeans. Most notable among his neighbors was Attorney General Escombe. He saw to it that he would be able to support himself in this style by collecting his retainer fees from the Natal merchants who had pledged that they would underwrite his practice.

After his admission, he did routine office work for Coakes—interviewing a potential client here, drafting a document there—before making his first formal appearance in court. On September 14, 1894, the newly admitted barrister appeared in court to represent, not surprisingly, Dada Abdulla. If Coakes and Abdulla were worried about Gandhi's ability to handle the case, it wasn't apparent from the amount of money involved here—the then-handsome sum of £204. Indeed, Coakes may have given Gandhi a case with high stakes to test the young barrister's range at the start so that he would know what work he could entrust to the new man. Dada Abdulla had sold goods and advanced cash to Gopee Maharaj, taking a promissory note in return. When the defendant defaulted on the note, Abdulla asked Coakes to bring an action against Maharaj.[47] He did so, with Mohandas K. Gandhi, barrister-at-law, then trying the case without a jury before Assistant Resident

Magistrate James Francis Dillon of the Durban Court and bringing home a judgment, with costs, for his client in his very first trial.[48] Gandhi was so successful that the £263 judgment he secured was greater than the amount for which he sued. There must have been celebrations in the chambers of Coakes and Gandhi.

But they were soon enough tempered as neither October nor November was kind to Gandhi. In early October an Indian storekeeper on one of Durban's busiest thoroughfares, West Street, had come to the new Indian advocate and asked Gandhi to represent him. It seems that when a native pulled out his leather purse to pay for some fruit, he dropped a 10 shilling piece in amongst the storekeeper's produce. The costumer claimed that the storekeeper had not only refused to allow him to search for the coin but also threatened to "thrash" him if he did so. The native brought a charge of theft against the Indian, and the case came before the resident magistrate, Captain Gould Lucas, on October 3, in Durban Criminal Court. The native called as a witness his employer, who testified that she had paid the complainant his wages of 10 shillings the day before the incident, and also stated that during the complainant's three years with her he had exhibited a good character. At best, this evidence offered only mild support for the Crown prosecutor. In turn, Gandhi put his client on the stand. The storekeeper claimed that he had actually allowed the complainant to search for the coin. He testified further that some bystanders also helped the complainant look for the coin. The magistrate was unimpressed and likely believed that the Indian was taking advantage of the situation to gain a windfall. In his first trial appearance in South Africa on behalf of a defendant in a criminal prosecution, Gandhi saw his client promptly convicted and fined £2.

In late October a native police officer came upon three women engaged in a brawl on Pine Street in Durban. The officer claimed that when he attempted to arrest the defendant, a young Indian woman, she hurled insulting and obscene language at him, resulting in a charge of "swearing at a constable." After the officer's testimony before Magistrate Dillon, Gandhi produced several witnesses who were one in saying that the girl was unable to speak English. The conclusion of the case was not a good one for Gandhi's client. The magistrate gave the defendant her choice of a 5 shilling fine or five days in jail.

When Gandhi was studying law in England, he used a letter of introduction to gain an audience with Frederick Pincutt, the Conservative member of Parliament. Gandhi confessed to Pincutt his fear of the practice of law.

Never, he believed, would he be able to replicate the skill of the famous Indian barrister Sir Pherozeshah Mehta, who "roared like a lion in the law courts."[49] Pincutt, in an attempt to calm the young man, assured him that to earn success at the bar only "honesty and industry" were required.

Did Gandhi reflect on Pincutt's advice at this early stage of his career as he sustained these defeats? Did he believe his criminal clients to be innocent? Was his storekeeper trying to take advantage of the native, or had it been the native who engaged in a scam? Did the young Indian woman actually not swear at the constable? Or was her denial of any knowledge of English an evasion of the real issue and a convenient way of seeming to be innocent? Did Gandhi feel comfortable or awkward with the high level of moral ambiguity in these cases?

As if these losses in criminal cases were not enough, in November Gandhi lost his next civil case, small as it was. He represented an Indian creditor against an Indian borrower in an effort to collect £5 in principal and interest. Gandhi lost, and to make the defeat all the more bitter, he lost to someone even less experienced than he, Eugene Renaud, the young Mauritian who had been admitted to practice less than two months before.

BALASUNDARAM TODAY, SCHEURMANN TOMORROW

It was at or near the end of this string of losses that a client appeared in Gandhi's office with a matter so compelling as to decisively take Gandhi's mind off his own troubles. Gandhi looked up from his desk to see a poor man, a native of the Tamil-speaking area of India, who clearly had been set upon. The man, whose name was Balasundaram, appeared with an injury to his face that was so severe he was unable to speak. Instead, shaking and crying just from the memory of the incident, he wrote down the account of his story on a piece of paper and handed it to Gandhi's Tamil-speaking clerk. The clerk explained to Gandhi that the fellow was a servant indentured to a local European. The man had somehow provoked his master's anger, and a brutal beating had followed. When Balasundaram limped off to the nearby home of the colony's Protector of Immigrants, he was turned away. The Protector would only see him during his normal office hours. The Indian, however, was undeterred and took his complaint to the magistrate.

The magistrate was taken aback by what he saw. The Indian had been beaten so badly that his front teeth were protruding through his upper lip.

The man's turban, removed from his head and cradled in his hands, was drenched from the profuse flow of blood. The magistrate arranged for Balasundaram to go to the hospital, but kept custody of the turban as evidence. After several days of treatment, he was released—and went straightaway to the office of the new Indian barrister he had heard about.

Balasundaram's request of Gandhi was that he end his indenture by prosecuting his master. Perhaps thinking that it would be quite difficult to mount a successful attack on a European master on behalf of a lowly Indian servant in a European court, and unfamiliar with the magistrate's predisposition in cases of this sort, Gandhi instead suggested a more moderate course—that the indenture be transferred to another master. Perhaps on the advice of the more experienced Coakes, Gandhi wisely sent Balasundaram off to see a physician in order to further document the state of Balasundaram's injuries.

When Balasundaram agreed to Gandhi's proposal that they try for a transfer, Gandhi proposed the notion to the master, who was at first uncertain, but then agreed. His agreement was short-lived. After talking with his wife and hearing her argue that Balasundaram's services were too valuable to surrender, the master proceeded to the Protector's office to withdraw his agreement. With the transfer route foreclosed, the Protector arranged what he promoted as a compromise whereby the servant would withdraw his complaint and the master would take the servant back. Gandhi would later say that the news of the supposed compromise "sent a shock through my body," for Gandhi sensed what would be in store for this servant who had challenged his master. Gandhi rushed out the door of his office to the Protector's office, where the Protector placed before Gandhi Balasundaram's written withdrawal of his complaint, conveniently attested to by the Protector himself. Stating the obvious for the purpose of discouraging Gandhi, the Protector took the position that had Balasundaram wanted any other result than to return to his master, he should not have signed the document.

Gandhi was not about to concede defeat. He had one other card to play. Gandhi threatened to take the matter before the magistrate. The Protector called Gandhi's hand, saying that the written withdrawal of the complaint would make a trip to the magistrate fruitless.

Upon his return to this office, Gandhi moved on the litigation and negotiation fronts simultaneously. He instituted proceedings before the magistrate while also writing to the master with a renewed suggestion that the servant's indenture be transferred. When the master persisted in his refusal,

Gandhi pressed his case before the magistrate. After Gandhi submitted Balasundaram's testimony, the direction of the court's sympathies was clear. It was apparent that the magistrate, having seen the effects of the master's savage treatment of his servant, would come down heavily on the master. Gandhi took this opportunity, however, not to prosecute his case to its successful conclusion, but to renew in open court his suggestion of a transfer.

The magistrate stepped in to help Gandhi. He indicated to the master that acceptance of the offer was a better result than the "serious consequences" to the master that would result from litigating the case to its conclusion. To drive the point home, the magistrate offered his opinion that Balasundaram had been brutalized. To the master's response that Balasundaram had provoked him, he retorted, "You had no business to take the law in your own hands and beat the man as if he were a beast." This said, he adjourned the matter to give the master time to think, a maneuver that had its intended result: the master shortly thereafter agreed to the settlement. But one matter remained to be disposed of—the Protector insisted that the new master be an acceptable European. For this assignment Gandhi recruited his friend Oswald Askew, at once an attorney and a Wesleyan minister, to take on Balasundaram "out of charity." This done, the case was concluded.

Gandhi had recognized the rapids and falls, steered Balasundaram through them, and brought him to a safe landing. Neither theatrical speeches nor withering cross-examination brought him this success, but a right reading of the strength of his case and an insightful management of the system.

In his autobiography, Gandhi begins his account of the Balasundaram case by stating:

> Service of the poor has been my heart's desire, and it has always thrown me amongst the poor and enabled me to identify myself with them.... Balasundaram's case reached the ears of every indentured labourer, and I came to be regarded as their friend. I hailed this connection with delight. A regular stream of indentured labourers began to pour into my office, and I got the best opportunity of learning their joys and sorrows.[50]

Gandhi may have learned their joys and sorrows, and he may very well have quietly helped poor Indians in a manner not involving the legal process. Indeed, at a farewell party for Gandhi on the eve of his 1896 visit to India, Parsee Rustomji, an activist for the Congress cause, saluted Gandhi, saying that "words could not express the kindness shown by Mr. Gandhi to poor Indians."[51] If the public records left behind are any indication, however,

Gandhi the barrister did not provide them many legal services. Rather, his practice was principally focused on serving the legal, economic, and political interests of Natal's affluent Indian merchants.

Shortly after the Balasundaram case was successfully concluded, Gandhi experienced an easy win in civil court for the most prominent Indian merchant company. Max Scheurmann was the proprietor of the German Cafe, a combination restaurant and bakery located on premises leased to him by Gandhi's client, Dada Abdulla and Company. Scheurmann was not much of a businessman, however. He fell behind in his rental payments to the company, which then commissioned Gandhi to pursue the German in court. Gandhi sued and recovered a judgment of just over £38, plus costs, against the hapless and undefended businessman, who made no attempt to fight the suit. Gandhi also succeeded in having the court order the almost immediate ejectment of Scheurmann from his business premises.

Scheurmann had been vanquished by the same lawyer who rescued the impoverished Balasundaram. It would be the straw that broke the businessman's economic back. Ten days after his eviction and just a few days before Christmas, 1894, Scheurmann was in Durban Circuit Court, begging for bankruptcy protection for himself and his wife.

SIX

Formation Lessons

The Indians are to be considered a necessary evil at present; we cannot do without them as labourers; we cannot do without them as storekeepers.

RICHARD ALEXANDER, Superintendent of Police

IN 1894 GANDHI TRIED HIS first criminal cases in South Africa. We have no record of his having reflected on the moral questions that work raised. He also performed compassionate work for Balasundaram and uncompassionate work against Scheurmann. We have no record of his having reflected on the contrast. One might conclude, however, that Gandhi, with his strong conscience, turned these matters over in his mind.

What Gandhi likely did not appreciate—almost no young lawyer does—is that the experiences a lawyer undergoes in the first few years of practice help form, in a disproportionately influential way, the character of the lawyer's entire future practice. The lawyer's first experiences at the bar help answer two overarching questions. What types of clients will the lawyer represent against what types of opponents? And will the lawyer's professional behavior comport with the lawyer's personal morality?

As 1895, Gandhi's first full year of practice in Durban, opened, these two pivotal questions—as well as several secondary questions—faced this twenty-six-year-old lawyer. His career and his legal persona, then both very much in formation, would be shaped by his answers to these questions as he faced a remarkably challenging array of opponents and experiences for a beginning practitioner.

A BAD FIRST EXPERIENCE: GUILT BY ASSOCIATION?

The year began with what one must conclude was a shock for Gandhi. The lawyer with whom he chose to practice, Percy Evans Coakes, was revealed to be a cheat, a liar, and a disgrace to the profession. That Coakes would find himself in public ethical trouble should have been at least somewhat predictable. Coakes' work life seems to have had one and only one purpose: to make as much money as possible. In this single-minded pursuit, his practice appears to have embraced questionable areas—for example, he mixed a rather unsavory money-lending business with his practice of law.[1] Then, too, Coakes' moral and ethical lapses in 1895 might have been brought on, in part or whole, by the distraction of his father's lingering illness and painful death in late 1894.[2]

Coakes' troubles grew out of his representation of the defendant in the case of *Kate Hillary v. T. B. MacKenzie*, in the course of which representation Coakes appears to have engaged in a number of deceptions designed to protect his own financial interests.

Coakes' behavior propelled the opposing attorney to seek from the Supreme Court an investigation into Coakes' conduct. The Court turned the matter over to the Law Society, which, at a hearing before the Court on March 26, 1895, disclosed its findings. It reported that Coakes had "knowingly and deliberately defied" a court injunction, had deceived his opposing party in the case, and had acted in a manner that frustrated the operation of the judicial system. In Coakes' defense his attorney, Farman, made the feeble argument that Coakes, who had been appearing in Natal courts nearly seven full years, was "still young in years."

While the society's lawyer, Henry Bale, appeared uncomfortable prosecuting a colleague—disciplinary actions for ethics violations were something of a novelty in Natal at this time—the court flatly rejected Farman's preposterous argument. Chief Justice Gallwey remarked that Coakes' actions were ones "no honest man could approve of, and which no professional man could follow."

At the conclusion of the hearing, the Court unanimously agreed to suspend Gandhi's partner from the practice of law for six months.[3]

The same public that observed Coakes being punished for dishonesty and deception surely was now predisposed to make certain unwelcome conclusions about his law partner, as well. Gandhi's conduct would almost always be internally regulated by his highly scrupulous conscience. With Coakes' dishonorable behavior a matter of official record and public conversation, there would now be external pressure as well.

OPPOSING THE CROWN: TRIAL BY ERROR

During the time Coakes was being investigated and prosecuted by the Law Society, Gandhi was busy being boxed around in Durban's courts. On

February 13, 1895, he appeared in defense of an indentured Indian named Arookian who was being charged with housebreaking and theft. The victim was the family of Reverend and Mrs. W. M. Douglas, in whose service Arookian was employed as a cook. The prosecution's case was built on less than strong evidence. The Crown had no eyewitnesses and no evidence directly tying Arookian to the crime. The Crown's case rested entirely on the facts that the crime appeared to have been an inside job and that Arookian, being in the employ of the family and in debt to a money lender,[4] was familiar with the layout of the house and had a motive to commit the crime.

Reverend Douglas testified for the prosecution first, describing how a window, through which entrance had been gained, appeared to have been unlocked by a person who had earlier been inside the house. He also described finding both his cashbox emptied of its approximately £7 in contents and a screwdriver apparently used to pry it open.

The first rule of cross-examination is to cross-examine only when doing so will aid one's case. Gandhi actually helped his opponent with his cross-examination of Douglas. From him he elicited the information that the family had found Arookian to be dishonest and that, given the construction of the house, the crime must have been committed by someone familiar with its layout.

After Mrs. Douglas testified, Gandhi, not satisfied with the stinging he had just received from her husband, stood up to cross-examine again. After obtaining a helpful concession from the witness that other Indians had been in the house on occasion, the effect of this point was lost when Gandhi's next questions resulted in the witness telling the court that she suspected that previous thefts of eggs, milk, and fowls had been committed by this same servant Arookian. The cashbox crime was simply the first one she felt she could prove.

The Crown then called several other witnesses. Gandhi wisely chose to limit the damage he was doing to his own case by forgoing any further cross-examination. When it came time for the defendant to present his case, Gandhi declined to put his client on the stand and, in fact, presented no evidence at all. Judging by the support, albeit limited, for Gandhi's client in the final verdict, Gandhi's closing argument must have been at least somewhat effective in contending that the prosecution's case was too weak on which to convict. The damage, however, had been done. The jury returned after a fifteen-minute deliberation with a 7–2 verdict in favor of the Crown. Gandhi's client, Arookian, was sentenced to a term of imprisonment of two years.

Why didn't Gandhi put any proof on? Why didn't he call his client to the stand to testify in his own behalf? The answer is obvious: Arookian was guilty. Gandhi appears to have rested his case on the argument that the government had failed to prove his client's guilt—not that he was innocent. For a scrupulous Gandhi, such a defense allowed him to avoid speaking untruths. Having to hide the full truth about his criminal clients, however, appears to have been so uncomfortable for Gandhi that it contributed to his doing few ordinary criminal cases after 1895.

CONFRONTING MR. JUSTICE WRAGG

Shortly after losing the *Arookian* case, Gandhi suffered through a very public belittling.

An Indian, Hassan Dawje, had died without leaving a will. Fredric Tatham, the lawyer for the estate, did not know how "Mohammedan law" (as Islamic law was then termed) called for the property in the estate to be distributed under this circumstance. Chief Justice Gallwey stepped in and suggested to Tatham that he call on Gandhi and some Muslim clerics to advise him. The plan suggested by Gandhi was approved by the master in the case, but when Tatham presented the plan of distribution to the Court for its approval,[5] Justice Wragg—the justice who had initially opposed Gandhi's admission to the bar—took the occasion to publicly belittle Gandhi. Here is how the *Natal Witness* reported the dialogue between Wragg and Tatham on March 22, 1895:

> Wragg: . . . Mr. Ghandi [*sic*] knows nothing of Mohammedan law. He is as great a stranger to Mohammedan law as a Frenchman. For what he has stated he would have to go to a book as you would; of his own knowledge he knows nothing.
> Mr. Tatham said that a plan of distribution had been obtained from the priests and from Mr. Ghandi. Where else they were to go he did not know. . . .
> Wragg: The portion which Mr. Ghandi states should go to the brother of the deceased, should, according to Mahommedan Law, go to the poor. Mr. Ghandi is a Hindoo and knows his own faith, of course, but he knows nothing of Mohammedan law.[6]

Gandhi, undoubtedly recalling Wragg's hostility to him in the bar admission case,[7] did not sit still for this public humiliation. With his legal acumen attacked in the press by a prominent figure, and already in the process of having his reputation sullied by his association with the about-to-be-suspended Coakes, he struck back forcefully and publicly. In a letter to the *Natal Mercury* Gandhi defended his position. He divided his defense into two parts. First, he took up the question of role. In the colloquy between Tatham and Wragg, Wragg had perceived a difference between Gandhi's interpretation of the law and that of the Mohammedan priests whom Tatham had also consulted; Wragg had then told Tatham that the priests' interpretation should be followed over Gandhi's. In responding, Gandhi attributed to Wragg a notion implicit in the justice's position: that only a Mohammedan could render an expert opinion on Mohammedan law. Gandhi, showing a great deal of courage in publicly taking on a sitting Supreme Court justice, then held this notion up to ridicule: "Were I a Mohammedan, I should be very sorry to be judged by a Mohammedan whose sole qualification is that he is born a Mohammedan. It is a revelation that . . . Mohammedans know the law intuitively, and that a non-Mohammedan never dare give an opinion on a point of Mohammedan law."

Having disposed of this issue, Gandhi then dealt with the substantive question of Mohammedan law. He attacked Wragg and defended his own position on all fronts by setting forth a list of authoritative points of law and fact. Gandhi concluded his statement with a policy argument: "It will be a manifest hardship if the portions rightly belonging to the relations of a deceased Mahommedan [*sic*] are to be locked up until they can show that 'they represent the poor'—a condition never contemplated by the law or sanctioned by Mahommedan usage."[8]

Because Gandhi's argument was economical, forceful, well organized, authoritative, and comprehensive, it was highly persuasive, bringing even a European columnist for the *Mercury* to his defense. We can attribute Gandhi's excellent work to a talent for writing solid legal arguments—a skill that stood in sharp contrast to his lack of agility in the courtroom—and to the desire he must have had, during this time of his partner's very public troubles, to sharply distinguish himself from Coakes.

Wragg never responded.

CHALLENGING THE POLICE

Fresh from his public relations triumph over Wragg, but simultaneously with the embarrassing ethics prosecution of Coakes, Gandhi undertook a civil action for damages against a police officer that carried both racial and political implications. The plaintiff whom he represented, Ismail Hajee Adam, was a storekeeper who procured his merchandise at a Durban fruit auction. On one occasion of his attendance, Ismail earned the ire of the European auctioneers when he persisted in nodding, winking, and speaking in ways that led the auctioneers to believe he was bidding, when in fact he was not. Despite warnings from the auctioneers to cease this behavior, Ismail engaged in it three times on one day in March 1895. The auctioneers grew weary of this conduct. The assistant auctioneer, F. A. Pearce, testified that "on the third occasion"—despite Ismail's protestations that he had not bid—"the bananas were knocked down to him." Pearce then asked the plaintiff to pay the shilling that he appeared to have bid. The plaintiff refused.

At this point, the stories of the parties diverge strictly on racial lines. Gandhi elicited the testimony of the plaintiff, who swore that he had bid only 10 pence, not a shilling. When he refused to pay, said the plaintiff, the auctioneers called in the defendant, Police Constable Tuohy, who forcibly removed the plaintiff's coat, which contained money, and his hat.[9] Later, Tuohy "took hold of [Ismail's] throat and called him by an opprobrious epithet." For these acts Gandhi sued Tuohy on Ismail's behalf for £53—£3 for money that was in the coat and never returned and £50 as "compensation for assault and insult to his religious tenets."[10]

The story of how Tuohy came into possession of the plaintiff's clothing was completely different as rendered by the defendant and his witnesses. The defendant called European witnesses who testified that Ismail had peaceably surrendered his clothing and that Tuohy had used no force.

There the case rested for a week. When it resumed, Gandhi and Tuohy's lawyer, Palmer, had a surprise for the magistrate—they had settled. The defendant would return the hat and coat and pay the plaintiff a nominal amount—one shilling. Each party would bear his own costs.

There is reason to believe that Gandhi settled because he saw that he was going to lose before the magistrate. Every European witness had testified against Gandhi's Indian client. Gandhi had solely Indian witnesses, who were generally regarded as untruthful by European colonists. As it turned out, Gandhi's decision to settle was the right one. The press later reported that Dillon was prepared to give costs, and presumably judgment, to the defendant when the parties settled.[11] Palmer, unbeknownst to him, had beaten Gandhi in court, but he had miscalculated. The victory belonged to an opponent who, while perhaps less talented than Palmer in the courtroom, was the shrewder of the two.

DEFYING THE RAILWAY: NO WOOD, NO WORK

Many of the cases Gandhi handled throughout the South African fall and winter of 1895 were equally undemanding, perhaps as a deliberate matter so that Gandhi might be as free as possible to work against the Indian Immigration Law Amendment Bill, then pending in the Natal Legislative Assembly, and for the rights of British Indians in the South African Republic cities of Pretoria and Johannesburg.[12] In April and May he continued his representation of creditors against small debtors, represented a few Indians who were charged by the police with making a racket with their drums,[13] and appeared in a bankruptcy case in which he failed to properly prepare some paperwork. His trouble in the bankruptcy case should have shown Gandhi that routine cases were not without their dangers for a novice advocate, but he failed to learn this lesson the first time around. Just a few months later Gandhi was publicly embarrassed when the press reported that he had filed a divorce application that showed his ignorance of an elemental point of divorce law.[14] He had made a basic mistake typical of beginners. Gandhi, usually meticulous, would learn to be even more careful.

This series of low-level cases experienced two significant interruptions during the winter of 1895. The first concerned labor matters. As historian Maureen Swan indicates, prior to 1909–1910, collective action by Indian workers was infrequent.[15] The year 1895 constituted a small, but important exception. It had been the custom of the Natal Government Railway to furnish its Indian employees with cooking fuel. When the railway decided to cut its costs by substituting coal for firewood, the workers found that they could not easily light the coal for lack of kindling. Frustrated, on May 17, 1895, the workers liberated a quantity of wood from the railway yard and were in the process of taking it home when they were noticed and arrested by the police. A melee of some sort followed, with a few police officers allegedly suffering injuries. When the workers' leaders were hauled into court the following day, about a hundred of their co-workers assembled outside the courthouse and threatened to encamp there until their leaders were released.

The Protector of Immigrants supported the workers. He described the workers' plight to Magistrate Dillon in sympathetic terms, stating, "For

17 days past they had been without means of cooking their food." Dillon responded in equally sympathetic terms, agreeing with the Protector that the men were "labouring under an enormous grievance." While he found them "clearly guilty of taking that which they had no right to take, and afterwards behaving improperly to the police," he released them without "any punishment whatever."[16]

Apparently, the railway did not immediately concede, for the next day the workers felt it necessary to engage in a short, but successful strike when 250 of them left their jobs and marched to the office of the Protector of Immigrants to protest the railway's failure to supply them with firewood. There they lodged their complaint and stated their intention to remain away from work until their demands were met. The railway pledged that it would supply the workers with firewood at once, at which point the rejoicing workers returned to their posts.

It is unclear whether Gandhi acted as counsel to the workers in these matters. In his long letter to the *Natal Advertiser* complaining about the paper's inaccurate coverage of the first firewood episode, it is unclear whether he had represented the Indians in court, but he does report so much of the court dialogue as to indicate that he was at least present as an observer, if not as the workers' advocate.[17] What is more important is that Gandhi was on hand to observe the transforming power of disobedience. He would undergo other formative experiences that would shape his views on the power of disobedience to create social change; the courageous railway workers, however, can lay claim to having planted the seed of the idea in Gandhi.

This lesson was extended a month later when Gandhi did represent the workers, this time in a dispute over the amount of rations to which they claimed to be entitled. Two hundred fifty railway workers left their jobs on June 25, 1895, and marched once more to the office of the Protector of Immigrants to complain of their treatment. They were arrested and charged with violating Law 25 of 1891, which barred employees from leaving work in a body, for which the penalty was a fine of £2 or a maximum of two months' jail time. Gandhi, as he had done in other cases, tried to smooth things over by suggesting that with a postponement of the hearing the case could be resolved as a private matter between the workers and the railway officials.

The magistrate in this case was not the understanding Dillon but Resident Magistrate Gould Lucas. He declined the invitation to permit the parties to settle, stating that the defendants had been brought before him for a violation of the law and he "could not go behind the law." Alfie Hammond, head of labor for the railway, agreed with Lucas, saying that he "did not feel disposed to withdraw the charges."

Lucas asked Gandhi whether the men would deny the charges. Gandhi could have put the Crown to its proof, as he had done in *Arookian*. He did not. This was not an ordinary criminal case. Lucas offered the Indians leniency in the form of a sentence of a 1 shilling fine or three days in jail. In a move that would foreshadow Gandhi's own typical reaction to charges of disobedience some years later, he instructed his clients to plead guilty as charged, and the whole body of men marched off to the jail, refusing to pay the fine and insisting on jail time instead. After accomplishing their mission of demonstrating their resolve and simultaneously putting a scare into the authorities as to how they would cope with this massive influx of prisoners whom they would have to bed and feed for three days, the men paid their fines. Satisfied with the magistrate's assurance that the railway would provide more generous rations, and having accomplished the change they set out to effect, the men returned to work that day—and Gandhi had another lesson in the power of disobedience.

SUING THE COURT: THE LIMITS OF THE LAW AS A TOOL FOR SOCIAL CHANGE

An important case for Indian civil rights—and the second major case to interrupt the winter—arose not in Durban but in Estcourt, a small town in Weenen County that lay on the rail line halfway between Durban and Charlestown to the northwest. There on the previous November 26th an Indian storekeeper, Cassim Abdulla, had entered the courtroom of Resident Magistrate Thomas Bennett wearing his customary turban. According to Abdulla, he salaamed to the magistrate upon entering the prisoner's box, whereupon he was ordered by the magistrate to remove his turban, which he "refused to do, stating it was contrary to custom." The magistrate reacted by ordering a bailiff to take the defendant from the courtroom, remove his turban from his head, and return him to the courtroom. The bailiff, alleged the plaintiff, violently dragged him from the prisoner's box and took him outside where his turban was forcibly removed and thrown to the ground. When the plaintiff attempted to retrieve it, the bailiff wrestled it away from him.

The incident came to the attention of the Natal Indian Congress, an advocacy organization for Indian rights of which Gandhi was the secretary and a leading figure.[18] The Congress turned to a prominent member of the bar, Henry Bale, an advocate since 1881. Bale agreed to represent Abdulla. The Congress undoubtedly retained Bale because he had successfully represented an Indian in a somewhat similar case, *In Re Regina v. Camroodeen*, just a few months before. Ironically, Bale was the law partner of Edward Mackenzie Greene, the same attorney who argued against Gandhi's admission before the Supreme Court just the previous year. Even more ironically, Bale was assisted in the *Abdulla* case by Gandhi himself.

The two brought suit in the Supreme Court against Magistrate Bennett on behalf of Abdulla, claiming £50 of injuries to mind and body.[19] The Court found for the defendant on July 16, 1895. Gallwey and Acting Justice Beaumont found that judicial immunity applied, with Gallwey stating, "It has been said in all Courts that no action could be successfully brought for the exercise of judicial authority." With respect to this point of law, Justice Wragg disagreed: "Had it been that the man had been forcibly and violently removed from the dock, it might have been the duty of the Magistrate to interfere, but the evidence is all the other way." And with this assessment of the failure of the plaintiff to prove his facts, the other two justices agreed. None of the three justices believed that the plaintiff had proved "that he was dragged out of the dock."

Gandhi and the Congress later professed not to be surprised by the decision.[20] Despite their protestations to the contrary, however, they must have had some very substantial hope for a victory, given the Court's recent decision in *Camroodeen*. In *Camroodeen*—a case from Weenen County, the very county in which Estcourt was located—the Court had held that an "Indian need not remove his head covering or his shoes when he enters a Court of Justice in this Colony. It is enough if he make the usual salutation on entering the Court and also (if a witness) when he goes into the witness-box."[21]

But the Court in *Abdulla v. Bennett* was able to rule against the Indian cause without coming into conflict with *Camroodeen* by grounding its decision on the magistrate's immunity and by unanimously finding for the defendant on the facts. In the wake of *Abdulla*, *Camroodeen* lay undisturbed—and unused. Gandhi, knowing that *Abdulla* represented a political setback that had also cost the Congress a fair amount of money in legal fees and expenses, attempted to put the best face on it: "We know exactly what we should do should a similar case occur in the future."[22] The fact was, however, that *Camroodeen* had already provided all the guidance one could want. *Abdulla* was filed for political gain in an attempt to capitalize on the progress made in *Camroodeen*. Ill-advised from the start, *Abdulla* must be charged against Gandhi and the Congress as a disappointing defeat and a costly lesson in the limits of the usefulness of colonial courts in advancing the Indian cause.[23]

DEFENDING THE CONGRESS BY EXPOSING LUCAS

September 1895 would bring with it more trouble in the law courts for the Congress and a great deal of unwanted press attention as well. The controversy had its roots in a charge of assault brought by an Indian named Moroogasa Pillay against four of his countrymen. During the course of the case, styled *Regina v. Poonsamy Pather and Three Others*, it was contemplated that a witness, Mahomed Ibrahim Asgara, would be called to testify for the prosecution. Before appearing to testify, however, Asgara claimed to have been approached by one Rangasamy Padiachy, who threatened to beat him if he, Asgara, testified for the Crown. Asgara also alleged that Padiachy, who was his landlord, threatened to raise his rent if he failed to cooperate and offered to lower it if he would refuse to testify.

Upon these facts a criminal charge of witness intimidation was brought against Padiachy. The defendant secured the services of an attorney, Alfred Millar. Gandhi assisted Millar during the course of the proceedings and then publicly defended the Congress in the court of public opinion afterward. The Congress needed to be defended because the presiding magistrate, Lucas, permitted the introduction of a piece of completely irrelevant testimony, namely, that on the same day of Padiachy's threats Asgara was called to a meeting at which were present Mohamed Camroodeen, Dada Abdulla, and Dowd Mahomed along with "two or three strangers."[24] There the group asked Asgara whether he intended to testify and what he intended to say. He told them he would be testifying, but refused to answer any further questions and left. What made this testimony irrelevant was that the defendant in the matter before the court, Padiachy, was not present at the meeting, nor could he be tied to it. After Asgara had been examined and cross-examined without so much as mentioning the Congress, Lucas himself questioned Asgara and drew from him the first mention of the Congress.

Lucas was clearly biased against the Congress. In his decision finding Padiachy guilty, he stated that "it appears that the Indian Congress is of a nature of an association of conspiracy—pernicious and fraught with danger to the whole community in the Colony of whatever race."

The Supreme Court later overturned the conviction, stating that the "case bristle[d] with irregularities from its inception."[25] But damage to the Congress' reputation had been done, and it was up to Gandhi, in his capacities as secretary to the organization, chief political organizer for Indian merchant interests, and the community's lawyer, to fix it. He did so by striking at the magistrate. In a letter to Sir John Robinson, the colonial secretary in Pietermaritzburg, he attacked the bona fides of Lucas: "I venture to submit that . . . the Magistrate was biased. In the case of Poonsamy Pather and three others, without a particle of evidence, he has remarked in his reasons for judgment that the defendants are members of and have been backed up by the Congress. As a matter of fact, all of them are not members of Congress and the Congress had nothing whatever to do with the matter."[26]

He challenged the government, if it should have any concerns about the Congress as the result of Lucas' statements, to investigate it. If Gandhi had ended his letter with this demand, we might call him astute. But then Gandhi made a move that showed his naïveté. He went on to say that if the government was satisfied that the Congress was blameless in the intimidation case, it should issue a statement to that effect. Either Gandhi had a strange notion of what the relationship was between the executive and judicial branches, or he was simply, and sadly, unrealistic about how the government would react. The government, of course, declined to be drawn in by Gandhi's gambit, replying that it would take no position on the matter. Gandhi, not satisfied, wrote again to the colonial secretary in December and renewed his request for an investigation or a statement clearing the Congress. Not surprisingly, the government stood pat and did neither.[27]

Gandhi may have been naïve, but he was not afraid of power. Most novice lawyers would never contemplate attacking a judge, especially one before whom they expected to appear again. Just as he had taken on Wragg earlier, now he took on Lucas.

For Gandhi, courage was getting to be a habit.

LEARNING WHEN NOT TO SPEAK

On October 1, 1895, shortly after the intimidation trial came to a close, the following item appeared in the *Natal Advertiser*:

LEGAL NOTICE
Mr. P. E. COAKES
has resumed practice as
Attorney and Notary
AT 388, WEST STREET
(Old Town Hall Chambers)[28]

It appears that when Coakes resumed his practice, it was without Gandhi, who had moved on to associate himself with Oswald Askew. Recall that it was Askew, both a minister and a lawyer, who had agreed to take on the indentured servant Balasundaram. Askew was a novice, having been admitted as an attorney only a little more than a year earlier. Why hadn't the senior bar competed for the chance to associate with the barrister who could bring in substantial amounts of Indian work? Gandhi simply was not the catch he was in 1894. Since then he had established himself, through his organizing work for the Durban merchants and the Congress, as a thorn in the side of the European community. And perhaps it was Gandhi who wanted to practice with someone who had an ideological commitment to the Indian cause. Askew was the only European who had attended Congress meetings; moreover, Askew was not reluctant to represent Indians in court.

It may also have been that Gandhi could now afford, psychologically and financially, to operate in the absence of a well-established partner. After a year of practice, perhaps he was gaining his sea legs around clients and, to a lesser extent, in courtrooms. As for income, the one year of retainers he had received in 1894 from the Indian merchants who wanted him for their political work had been renewed for another year.

Gandhi's work for the merchants was not confined to the Durban courts. Verulam, on the rail line northeast of Durban, had its own magistrate court. There Gandhi obtained a judgment for one Indian merchant against another in a collection action (*Bedat v. Akoom*) for goods sold and delivered. Gandhi's inexperience and his exercise of extremely poor judgment, however, cost him the win on appeal. The merchant whom he represented kept his books in Gujarati, Gandhi's native tongue. On appeal to the Durban Circuit Court, the losing defendant complained that after the evidence had closed in the trial of the case in Verulam Magistrate Court, "the Magistrate had allowed an unauthorized interpreter to go into his chambers, and, in the absence of the parties, translate the books, which were in the Ghujerate [*sic*] language."[29] The "unauthorized interpreter" was none other than Gandhi himself, the plaintiff's own lawyer. Gandhi did not see what most any law student would: that a translation offered by an attorney for one of the parties created an intolerable conflict of interest between the lawyer's duty of zealousness to his client and his duty of impartiality to the court. Gandhi also did not see that a translation should not be carried out in the absence of the opposing party. The appellate court had no trouble finding that "it was altogether wrong in principle that an interested party should put in a document which no one else could test."[30] Accordingly, the court sent the case back to magistrate court to be retried. When Gandhi inquired as to any directions the appellate court might have for the retrial, the court first scolded the merchant for keeping his books in a language almost no one in the colony could understand. Then it instructed Gandhi that, if he wished to offer his translation, he would have to "be entirely free from the case."[31] There was no option of Gandhi staying in the case and bringing in a new translator, because, according to Gandhi, there were no certified translators of Gujarati in the colony.

When Gandhi was admitted to the bar in 1894, he had also sought a translator's license as well, but was turned down by the Supreme Court on the ground that it would be unseemly for an English barrister to be performing translation work. But now the *Bedat* court suggested that Gandhi reapply for his license despite the indignity of conducting such low-level work.[32] Gandhi followed the Court's advice, and on January 23, 1895, the Court approved his application for a license as a sworn Gujarati translator. Chief Justice Gallwey was not pleased, however, by the sight of a barrister stooping to translator's work: "It is a question of etiquette, and if Mr. Ghandhi [*sic*] likes to commit a breach of professional etiquette, he can become a translator." Then, to make the supposed indignity a bit more stinging and to highlight Gandhi's error in *Bedat v. Akoom*, Justice Mason issued this warning: "Mr. Ghandi [*sic*] is not to be connected in any way with a case in which he is a translator."[33]

This verbal beating that Gandhi took without comment must have had some effect in conditioning him for the days to come when he would be berated by other courts for his civil disobedience in pursuit of Indian rights in South Africa and, later, Indian freedom from British rule in India. Gandhi learned in Durban's courts when to speak in defense of himself and, just as important, when to allow silent suffering to speak instead.

DEFEATING THE SUPERINTENDENT
OF POLICE—TWICE

In early 1896 Gandhi became involved in a highly publicized case controversial for its effect on race relations. Gandhi's clients were not merchants, but two Indians, John Lutchman Roberts and Samuel Richards, who had adopted Western names as was the custom of Christian Indians during that era. The two were strolling home on West Street at 9:30 one evening when they were stopped by a police constable who asked them for their curfew passes. In 1896 Durban enforced a curfew law which provided that "a coloured person found wandering between the hours of 9 P.M. and 5 A.M. without a pass from his employer, or not giving a good account of himself, may be arrested."[34]

The two young men, well attired in Western dress, explained to the constable that they were walking from Durban's gardens to their home, which lay just a few minutes away. They offered the additional information that they were employed, one as a clerk in Mr. Gandhi's office and the other as a schoolteacher. Despite this explanation of their behavior, the constable arrested them.

When the case came before Magistrate John Parker Waller on February 20, 1896, the Crown was represented by none other than the police superintendent himself, Richard Alexander. Gandhi appeared to represent his clerk and his walking companion.

Alexander, not a lawyer, put on the Crown's case. When he was done, Gandhi called Richards to the stand. In the course of Gandhi's direct examination of Richards, the defendant testified that the constable laughed at him when he gave his Westernized name. Alexander saw the significance of this point in providing a motivation for an otherwise unwarranted arrest and cross-examined Richards. In an interview with the *Natal Advertiser* a few days after the trial, Alexander re-created the cross-examination:

Superintendent: How long have you had that name?—Eighteen months; since I was converted.

What were your parents?—Indentured Indians: father a dhoby.[35]

Try and imagine yourself on police duty in West Street during the night. A coloured person passes you, what would you do?—Ask his business.

And if he gave the answer your friend gave, that he was a clerk to someone, what would you do?—Go and see that some one to make certain.

If that someone lived outside the borough, or even a mile away, would you leave your beat to ascertain?—No answer.

If he gave your excuse, that he was a teacher, would you say, "Pass, teacher, and all's well?"—No answer.

The Court: Why don't you answer like a man? You know well that you could not take such answers from men you did not know.

Superintendent: Since your family name was not good enough for you, did you inform the police that you had taken an English name that would excuse you from Indian laws?—No.[36]

This was not an especially clever cross-examination; another witness might have turned it around on Alexander. Richards, however, did not help himself. The examination did serve to reveal the contemptuous attitude toward Indians Alexander held at this time. Later, in a *Mercury* interview, Alexander would call Roberts and Richards "these young upstarts." Indeed, Alexander gave the interview in which he re-argued his case against the defendants to "give the public a fair idea of what things were coming to." He quoted Waller, with approval, as saying that "we could not allow bare-footed black men prowling about our thoroughfares on dark nights under the pretence of going home." Alexander concluded the interview with these comments: "If an Indian is permitted to evade the law by changing his religion and his name, I am afraid we shall have the whole Indian population doing the same, especially those whose names are so familiar in the court and gaol records."

The fatal weakness in Alexander's case was obvious to Gandhi. The law permitted an Indian to be about without a pass as long as he could "give a good account of himself." Gandhi's argument was simple and, according to one press report, "eloquent": these Indians had, in fact, given a good account of themselves and as a result they should not have been arrested.[37] The magistrate agreed and dismissed the defendants on the spot. Gandhi was not done, however. He had tried to settle previous cases by getting the parties to compromise. Now, with his victory in hand, he made a play to prevent similar future disputes, urging the police "to become a little charitable and considerate towards the Indian community."[38] Alexander responded to this invitation by giving the vitriolic *Mercury* interview. Gandhi would not allow the discussion to rest there. He composed a lengthy, forceful, and well-written letter to the *Mercury* in which he conclusively rebutted Alexander, point by point, in clear, lawyerly style.[39]

In the end Gandhi scored two victories over Alexander in this racially charged case—one in court and the other in the press. It was one of Gandhi's best experiences in Durban and the latest in a string of confrontations with the most influential players in the world of Durban law, business, and politics. In a very short span of time, Gandhi had publicly taken on the government, two magistrates, a police constable, the Natal Government Railway, a superintendent of police, and a Supreme Court justice.

Fearlessness had quickly come to be the leading characteristic of this young lawyer's life and practice.

He was afraid of no one.

SEVEN

Waller's Question

> To see the universal and all-pervading Spirit of Truth face to
> face one must be able to love the meanest of creatures as oneself.
> And a man who aspires after that cannot afford to keep out of
> any field of life.
>
> GANDHI

IN SEPTEMBER OF 1895, at a Natal Indian Congress meeting attended by
upwards of one thousand people, Gandhi announced his intention to make
a trip to India to promote the South African Indian cause and to bring back
more Indian barristers to Natal to assist in the effort. It was also his desire,
now that he "had established a fairly good practice," to "go home, fetch [his]
wife and children, and then return and settle out."[1]

Gandhi could take his temporary leave from Natal in mid-1896 knowing
his movement for Indian rights had recently achieved some limited satisfac-
tion from the secretary of state for the colonies. Joseph Chamberlain had
notified the Natal legislature that the British government was not pleased
with the specific exclusion of Indians from the rolls that the Franchise Act
had worked and that for this reason the act was not acceptable.
Unfortunately for the Indian position, Chamberlain indicated that a more
general exclusion might be acceptable. The legislature, accordingly, enacted
a new bill that prohibited persons from voting if they hailed from "countries
that have not hitherto possessed elective representative institutions founded
on the parliamentary franchise." This language would be used against
would-be Indian voters. Gandhi opposed this provision to no avail; the
British government eventually approved it. Gandhi, in an excess of optimism, cast the issue in wider terms that allowed him to see the new bill as a
victory: "We have all along contended that it was not political power that
we wanted, but that it was degradation which the first franchise Bill
involved that we resented, and our protest has evidently been respected by
Her Majesty's Government."[2]

With this issue behind him, Gandhi had the freedom to travel to India.
Before he could go, however, this still-developing lawyer would first pass

through an experience that would not only add several critical attributes to a growing portfolio of professional and personal characteristics, but also answer the question of whether his professional behavior would be consistent with his personal morality. Just a few weeks after the conclusion of the straightforward Roberts and Richards vagrancy case, Gandhi would be tested by the most complex, difficult, and public case of his young career. Of his time in Durban Gandhi would later write, "Practice as a lawyer was and remained for me a subordinate occupation."[3] There is reason to doubt this recollection as a general proposition, and there is very good reason to doubt it was the case in April of 1896.

WHO WRONGED WHOM?

Dada Abdulla and Company, one of Gandhi's major clients, counted among its wide business interests a steamship line that carried both freight and passengers between Natal and India. The previous year the company was in the market for someone to captain one of its ships, the SS *Courland*, when it settled on James Matthew Adams. Adams accepted Dada Abdulla and Company's offer of £16 per month and took charge of the ship on August 19, 1895.

Adams captained the ship from Bombay to Durban without incident or complaint from his employer. On the return trip a series of incidents occurred that caused the company to lose faith in Adams.[4] When Adams anchored in Bombay, the company fired him. The captain believed he had been mistreated. On his return to Durban, Adams went to the law offices of Farman and Robinson, where he hired Ernest Farman to sue the company for £413, representing damages for wrongful discharge and reimbursement of sums spent in the operation of the ship. Gandhi, representing the corporate defendant, filed an answer as well as a counterclaim for £453.

The case went to trial in April and consumed parts or all of eight days stretching out over several weeks. During this time Gandhi had to deal with three very specific challenges: a difficult legal problem, ridicule heaped on him by his opponent and the public, and a hostile judge. His response to these challenges would help form both the man and the lawyer.

It was the company's central argument that Adams had attempted to cheat the company. The ship captain had submitted a bill in Bombay for the provisions he had purchased for the *Courland*, a bill calculated in Indian rupees. When the company attempted to pay the bill presented by Adams in Bombay, he inexplicably refused the company's offer of payment. He then traveled back to Durban and submitted a higher bill there. This second bill was calculated in pounds at an exchange rate unfavorable to the company. The company refused to pay this second bill.[5]

From Gandhi's perspective, the question of what the company owed Adams was the battleground issue in the case. In aid of his argument that the company was not obligated to pay the second, inflated bill, he desired to take evidence from witnesses who were outside Natal. To do this, he needed two things: time and the permission of a higher court.

At the conclusion of the plaintiff's case-in-chief, Gandhi obtained an adjournment of the proceedings from Magistrate John Parker Waller so that he might apply to the Durban Circuit Court for leave to gather evidence outside the colony.[6] Chief Justice Gallwey, sitting as the judge of the Durban Circuit Court, refused Gandhi's application on the grounds that the Supreme Court had ruled that there was no authority for granting such applications and the circuit court was not about to contravene a ruling of the Supreme Court. When Gandhi pointed out that an identical order had been granted recently in another case by Justice Wragg, sitting as a circuit judge, "his Lordship enquired if the case was reported in the Law Reports, and on being told that it was not, observed that it was not worth reporting." The press noted that this remark was followed by applause by those present in the courtroom. Adding to this humiliation, Gallwey ordered Gandhi to have his client pay the other side's costs in the application hearing.

When the trial of Adams' claim resumed before Magistrate Waller on April 15, Gandhi asked for another adjournment for the purpose of appealing Chief Justice Gallwey's ruling to the entire Supreme Court bench.[7] Waller was incensed. He told Gandhi that the company knew nothing about the shipping business and that its sole intent was to bring Adams, his wife, and his children to ruin.

An angry Waller then made Gandhi an offer: he would permit an adjournment only on the condition that the company pay Adams for the six months Waller expected Gandhi's appeal would take. Gandhi, generally a skilled negotiator, began to accept Waller's proposition, but not without his own condition: "We are willing to keep him with the proviso that if the judgment is given against him—"

Waller cut him off. "There must be no proviso."

Waller's dislike of the defendant then boiled over uncontrollably. He recalled the statements of the company's representatives that it provided no more than a shilling a day per passenger for food and excoriated Gandhi's client: "I would like to see . . . any respectable shipping agent in Durban go into that witness box and say anybody could feed first-class passengers at that small figure, when some £45 was charged for first-class passengers to England."[8]

Gandhi begged to differ, explaining that the shilling was for food only and that the company incurred separate costs for fuel, stewards, and other expenses. This was Farman's cue to join the court in mocking Gandhi's client. He "would like to live on land for that sum," said Farman, a sentiment with which Waller agreed.

Gandhi would not relent. Actually, he countered, it would be easy to keep a passenger fed for as little as 6 pence a day. Then Gandhi moved for an adjournment yet again. "Denied," said Waller, undoubtedly exasperated with Gandhi's persistence. "We will resume testimony on Saturday." And with that Waller rose and left the bench.

WALLER'S QUESTION

When Saturday arrived, there was Gandhi—*again* asking for an adjournment. This time he came to court equipped with an affidavit "to show that it was impossible for the defendants to substantiate their defence or support their claim in reconvention [their counterclaim] without the evidence of parties now out of the Colony."[9] Waller, not believing his own ears that Gandhi was applying once more for an adjournment, asked Gandhi rhetorically, "You want me to sit on my own decision?"[10]

When Gandhi explained how the evidence would provide a basis for a judgment for his client, the magistrate was, surprisingly, interested enough to make an inquiry. "By how much did the two accounts differ?"

"£204," said Gandhi, explaining that Adams' bill jumped by that much from the time he submitted it in Bombay to the time he submitted what should have been the same bill in Durban. "Why didn't you settle the account in Bombay, then?" asked Waller. "Because Adams refused to do so," replied Gandhi. Then, as Gandhi started to read the affidavit aloud to the court, Waller turned on Gandhi again, repeatedly interrupting him to make fun of the minor technical mistakes Gandhi had made in the affidavit. Gandhi was not able to finish reading it to the court, because Waller again interrupted to chastise Gandhi and his client for allowing the case to come to court in the first place. Then Waller confronted Gandhi with these words:

"Have you read your shipping law?"

The courtroom must have fallen perfectly silent as all heads turned to see how Gandhi would respond to this bold and accusatory question.

In fact, Gandhi had not read his shipping law, an uncharacteristic failure of preparation on his part. In the time between the question and Gandhi's answer, what were the thoughts racing through Gandhi's mind? "I could lie and attempt to bluff my way through the remainder of the trial or I could tell the truth and take the consequences." Gandhi cast his lot with the truth.

"No."

Waller jumped on this astounding admission. "If the defendants did not know shipping law they must pay for their experience, and not try to make the plaintiff pay for it."[11]

Faced with yet another expression of the magistrate's judgment on the merits, Gandhi finally attempted to cut his losses by offering to withdraw his counterclaim. Farman said that he was prepared to accept Gandhi's offer, but on the condition that judgment be entered on it for the plaintiff. Gandhi knew, however, that this meant that Farman would be awarded his costs on the counterclaim. Costs could be substantial. He withdrew his offer and proceeded with his case, calling several witnesses—two to testify as to the relative cost of provisions in Durban and India, a company clerk who reported on his observations of Adams' misdeeds,[12] and then the captain himself.

To call an opposing party during one's own case-in-chief is a risky maneuver, though somewhat less so for the defendant than for the plaintiff. In either event, however, great care must be taken to keep the witness under control, for otherwise the witness will divert the court's attention away from the damaging points the questioning attorney wishes to pursue and instead to affirmative evidence for the witness' own case. Recall that Gandhi had been blocked by Waller from obtaining evidence outside the colony that would help prove the discrepancy in the two victualing statements Adams had tendered. Finding himself with the need to prove his case in part through

Adams, Gandhi wisely confined his examination of Adams to the "accounts he rendered in Bombay and in [Durban] as to the victualing of the S.S. Courland."[13] Because he could stick to numbers and avoid evaluative or normative concepts, Gandhi's decision to examine the captain in the midst of his own case demonstrated what may have been Gandhi's understanding of both the dangers and limits of calling one's opponent as one's own witness.

Having survived Adams' testimony, Gandhi called a representative of his own client, Abdulla Karim, a partner of Dada Abdulla and Company and the president of the Congress in 1896. Abdulla Karim testified, putting in "a voluminous quantity of accounts with regard to victualing."[14] During his testimony, Gandhi also wanted to put into evidence a letter the defendant had written to its office in Bombay. Farman objected to this piece of hearsay. The colloquy that followed showed a struggle between the two lawyers for the last word—and for control of the courtroom.

Farman, after objecting, complained about all the time Gandhi was taking to put in his proof. The letter was yet another of Gandhi's delays. Speaking of what he expected to be the court's denial of Gandhi's motion to admit the letter, Farman insisted, "I will have nothing else."

Gandhi retorted: "I know you have all you want, and now you try to shut me up."

Farman replied: "That's what I'm here for."

Those in the courtroom were amused and laughed aloud with Farman as he made light of Gandhi, Gandhi's case, and the trial process. There is no evidence that Waller called for order in the room. The magistrate then surprised no one by ruling the letter inadmissible.

Gandhi persisted in arguing with the judge after the ruling was made, a maneuver guaranteed to irritate even the most patient of judges, in whose ranks Waller could not be counted.

"Without going into the facts your worship refuses to admit it!"

The steely response from the bench: "Yes; are you ready to go on?"

Gandhi then started shuffling through the pile of documents he had brought to the courtroom that day. After what must have seemed an interminable delay, Waller offered a gratuitous comment in Gandhi's direction: "You have got too many papers." This brought about an apparently facetious suggestion by Farman that the court stand in adjournment until Gandhi was ready to resume his questioning.

That afternoon, when Gandhi had tendered all his available evidence in response to Farman's case, he asked for yet one more adjournment. On this occasion he explained that he had telegraphed Delagoa Bay for certain documents—a butcher's receipt and a check—and that it would take two or three days to receive them. Farman once again objected, and the magistrate once again upheld the objection and denied Gandhi's application.

On this note, Gandhi rested his case.

A QUESTION OF TRUST

Farman then called two witnesses in rebuttal, after which he rested his case. This was Gandhi's signal to pop up again with *another* request for an adjournment, this time to provide himself with the opportunity to read the court's notes before giving his closing argument. Waller was flabbergasted at the audacity of this request, denied it without any prompting from Farman, and advised the lawyers to appear the next morning for closing arguments. Gandhi then asked Waller if he could at least review the documents that had been admitted in evidence. With no objection from Farman, Waller said that if Gandhi wanted to read the documents before court resumed in the morning he could do so.

When court resumed at 11 o'clock on the morning of Thursday, April 23, 1896, Farman was on his feet for the plaintiff. Farman's theme was that this was not a case about money. It was a case about dignity. "There [are] items on the record of the court of charges against the plaintiff, which, if proved, would make him strictly unfit to hold the position of master mariner. There was not the slightest foundation for the suggestions of fraud, dishonesty, and misconduct which would justify the charges against the plaintiff being placed on the record of the court. . . . The question the court would be called upon to decide would be—Were the defendants justified in dismissing the plaintiff in Bombay?"

After further attacks on the company, some of which were racist, and an hour-and-a-half after he had begun, Farman concluded by expressing the hope that the "the decision of the court would be so favorable to the plaintiff that he would have no cause to regret the fierce examination to which his character had been subjected, or the vague and wicked suggestions which had been thrown out against him."[15]

Now it was Gandhi's turn to address Waller. The conventional wisdom is that one should always begin a closing argument on a strong, affirmative note. Gandhi, however, began on a defensive one. In fact, he began by attacking not Adams, but the judicial system. How could he present his best case when the courts had prevented him from obtaining the testimony he needed? Gandhi then briefly addressed Farman's case before reviewing for the court the grounds on which the company had relied to dismiss Adams.[16]

Finally, Gandhi got to the heart of his argument. He laid out Adams' expenses in Bombay, which Adams incurred in Indian rupees. He then described the exchange rate, rupees as against the British currency then in circulation in Natal. Gandhi explained Adams' ploy. He incurred his expenses in rupees in India at one exchange rate, but then wanted to be reimbursed in Durban in pounds at a different and substantially higher rate. This the company refused to do. The difference, argued Gandhi, came to over £200.

How could the company keep on an employee, such as this, in whom it had no trust?

After Gandhi had addressed a number of other issues, the magistrate launched another attack on him and his client. He pointed out that after charging Adams £78 for the passage of his family back to Durban, the company had the audacity to also charge them an additional fee for their meals.

Farman, wishing to point out that the company expected Adams to bill in rupees while the company itself chose to bill Adams in pounds, pushed the dagger in a bit further: "And the charge is made in English currency." Gandhi explained that the company gave its passengers a choice: they could provide their own food or the company could provide it for them at an agreed-upon price. He was silent on the issue of the double-standard. The magistrate was still incredulous: "After you make £78 profit from these people, you charge them for food?"

Waller shook his head. "I am taking this case under advisement," he told the parties.

Gandhi sat down.

There was nothing to do but wait.

A PARTIAL WIN

Before the trial came to an end, Gandhi showed his lack of appreciation for the task before Waller when he asked the magistrate whether he would be deciding the case from the bench at the trial's conclusion. When the decision was rendered by Waller on May 15, 1896, his opinion ran to thirty-two pages.

Given Waller's oft-expressed sentiments that the company had mistreated Adams, it was no surprise at all that Waller found that Adams had been improperly dismissed. He awarded him the damages he sought, £96, representing six months of salary.

The issue that was open was the question of the rate at which Adams should be reimbursed for supplying the ship with its provisions. Because this item constituted the single largest item of damages in Adams' case, the parties were undoubtedly anxious about what Waller would decide. Here is what the magistrate wrote:

> The charge made by the plaintiff for victualling in his account rendered to the defendants in February differs from the charge made by him at Bombay on the 15th January. In that account the charge is at the rate of one rupee and eight annas per head per diem, whereas in the account rendered to defendants in Durban the charge made is at the rate of 8s 6d. per head per diem. . . . I have . . . come to the conclusion that the plaintiff cannot alter the charge in the manner in which he has done. I think he is bound as to the rate by the account rendered in Bombay. . . . I . . . will reduce the amount of the victualling charges by £141 5s.

To get out-of-colony testimony, Gandhi had applied for adjournment after adjournment. When his efforts failed, he used the testimony of the witnesses he was able to call to paint the best picture he could of Adams' chicanery. Even without being able to take the testimony of all the witnesses he felt he needed on this issue, Gandhi had prevailed on the key issue in the case.[17] After Adams' damages were offset by the £21 that Waller ruled Adams owed the company on the counterclaim, the final amount of damages to which Waller found Adams entitled stood at just over £237, just slightly over half of what Adams had claimed he was owed. Gandhi had prevailed in the biggest issue of the trial and even had won a bit of his counterclaim. Because of his doggedness, he had kept Adams' damages to the smallest amount reasonably possible under the circumstances of the case. Of the many traits Gandhi took from his law practice to his independence work in India, tenacity was one of the foremost.

But not the only one.

Toughness was another. He had persevered against insult and ridicule from the court. He had managed not to be discouraged by the applause from those present at trial when he was humiliated by the magistrate. And he had stood toe-to-toe with Farman.

All this time he never took his eye off the central issue in the case. And when he prevailed on that issue, he did so without surrendering one other defining characteristic that would remain important to him for the rest of his life.

TRUTH

The proceedings in *Adams* concluded in late May. Just a few days later, on the morning of June 5, 1896, Mohandas K. Gandhi arose at his house at Beach Grove to the most remarkable sound. It was the noisy buzz of a crowd of some five hundred Indians, led by several of the most influential Indian merchants, there to escort Gandhi to the water's edge on this the day of his departure for India. As Gandhi boarded his ship, loud, wild cheering erupted.[18] What were Gandhi's thoughts as he stood on deck, watching this tumultuous sight fade into the distance?

It was surely a time for taking stock. His first thought might have been of one of his most recent experiences—the Tuesday-night gathering at the new Congress Hall, where an enormous crowd had gathered to toast him. In response to the cheers he received from those present, he had stood on his feet before the assembly and delivered a speech that lasted two hours—a physical and intellectual feat of some substance. Could this have been the same Gandhi who nearly collapsed from fright in his first court appearance in India?

And surely some of his experiences at the Durban bar came to mind. In later years, Gandhi spoke, thought, and wrote more passionately about truth than any other subject. His unswerving allegiance to truth was one of the pillars of both his personal and political philosophy. In the 1920s, he would write in *My Experiments with Truth*, his autobiography: "My uniform experience has convinced me that there is no other God than Truth. . . . The little fleeting glimpses . . . that I have been able to have of Truth can hardly convey an idea of the indescribable lustre of Truth, a million times more intense than that of the sun."[19]

What had Gandhi learned about the truth from his practice of law in Durban?

Percy Coakes, the man Gandhi chose for his first partner and mentor, prevaricated and, largely for that reason, was humiliated, chastised, and suspended from practice—all in the full, glaring eye of the Natal press and public. As any human being would, Gandhi must have asked himself how Coakes' troubles reflected on his own probity—and the public's estimation of it. As an Indian barrister, one of a kind, he already drew an unusual amount of attention. From the beginning, he knew he needed to be above reproach if he were to successfully represent the Indian community in South Africa. Now, he must have thought, if he did not act to counter the injurious effect of Coakes' suspension on his own reputation, his entire effort for Indian rights could be ruined.

Gandhi's first fully public opportunity to distinguish himself from Coakes was undoubtedly fresh in his mind. It arose in the Adams trial when Magistrate Waller focused Gandhi's attention on a single, sharp question. "Have you read your shipping law?" demanded Waller in a case that was all about shipping law.

"Have I read my shipping law?" Gandhi stood alone in a public courtroom, with reporters from the Natal papers scrutinizing his every move, being forced by the judge to make a fundamental choice about who he was, as both a man and a lawyer. He could say he had not read it and show himself to be embarrassingly unprepared, or he could claim that he had and find Coakes reborn in himself. Gandhi's answer would help set his life's direction.

"No."

Gandhi chose the truth and never let it go.

EIGHT

A Public Man

In taking leave of Mr. Gandhi, the reporter laid stress on the very strong feeling against him at present in Durban, and advised him, for his own sake, to be exceedingly careful in regard to dis-embarking, since he was determined to land.

Natal Mercury, January 16, 1897

One, whom God wishes to save, cannot fall even if he will.

GANDHI

GANDHI WENT TO INDIA IN 1896 to promote the South African Indian cause, to recruit Indian barristers to assist in the Indian rights movement in Natal, and to relocate his family to South Africa. An unintended conse-quence of the Indian experience, however, was that it would shock Gandhi into an accurate understanding of how far he still had to go before he could count himself an accomplished public person.

FAILURE REDUX

While in India Gandhi made it his business to visit Bombay and several of its leading legal figures, among them Sir Pherozeshah Mehta, a distinguished lawyer whose advocacy skills had earned him the title "the Lion of Bombay" and whose nationalism had earned him yet another title, "the uncrowned King of the Presidency." When Gandhi pleaded with Mehta to bring the cause of the South African Indians to Bombay's attention, Mehta agreed to call a public meeting in the city to give Gandhi an audience. Mehta instructed Gandhi to report back to him on the day before the meeting.

When at 5 P.M. Gandhi appeared as requested, Mehta asked him for a copy of his speech. Gandhi confessed that he had none and stated that he intended to speak extemporaneously. Mehta made it very clear that this would not do, for the Bombay press was not capable of getting a speech right without having a text. Mehta dispatched Gandhi to write his speech. After a long night's effort, Gandhi turned in his manuscript to the printer and retired shortly before midnight.

When Gandhi arrived at the meeting hall the next day, he found a huge crowd, the very size of which astonished and frightened him. In the face of the challenge of speaking to this enormous group, which Gandhi would appear? The Gandhi who had been gaining so much confidence in South Africa that he could hold forth in public for two hours at his Durban send-off party? Or the Gandhi who collapsed in fright at his first court appearance in India several years earlier?

The answer was soon apparent. As he attempted to speak, Gandhi's body shook beyond control. His voice failed to project outward to the large crowd. Over and over, Mehta importuned him to speak louder. Mehta's urging was of no help; in fact, Gandhi only became more conscious of his failure.

Before long Gandhi gave up. In despair, he surrendered the text to a friend. Keenly aware of what was going on, the audience, however, called out for one of Mehta's associates, Dinshaw Edulji Wacha. Adding to Gandhi's embarrassment, Wacha, having engaged in no preparation, performed superbly in his place, with the crowd paying rapt attention and punctuating the talk with applause and cries of "Shame!" The speech was a hit with Mehta and the audience, even if the original speaker was not.[1]

Gandhi learned a hard lesson. He may have been a successful public figure in the backwaters of provincial Natal where, by his own admission, "forensic talent [was] not of a very high quality,"[2] but he was an unpolished pretender in mother India. He could write a good speech in the quiet of an office, but he could not deliver it in the face of a huge crowd. He would need more time to develop his skills and self-confidence out of sight in South Africa before he would be ready to take the Indian stage.[3]

A COALESCENCE OF FORCES

Gandhi would soon find out that South Africa was ready to give him all the preparation for public life he could handle. Because of his status as a British-educated barrister, he had been treated far better in Natal than his country-men. It was often written and said by Natal's whites that were all Indians of Gandhi's caliber, there would be no "Asiatic problem." Unbeknownst to Gandhi, however, several disparate forces were coalescing to test his physical and emotional courage. The coming together of these forces would also reveal that just below the community's superficial respect for Gandhi lay bitter hostility.

The first of these forces was a reaction to Gandhi's own writing. On his voyage to India Gandhi had written a long propaganda piece arguing the case of South Africa's Indians.[4] (Because its formal title, *The Grievances of the British Indians in South Africa: An Appeal to the Indian Public*, was so lengthy, it quickly became known as the Green Pamphlet for the color of its cover.[5]) The Green Pamphlet was the work of a lawyerly mind, methodically exposing the abuses to which Indians were subjected and referring repeatedly to court cases in which Gandhi and others had attempted to defend victims of European abuse. In the pamphlet, Gandhi specifically disavowed any intention to focus attention on the poor treatment of indentured Indians. He was interested only in the legal disabilities to which the colonists were subjecting all Indians. In this respect, the pamphlet was a powerful and effective statement of the Indian case.

Gandhi sought to give the Green Pamphlet the widest possible currency and, accordingly, had ten thousand copies printed and distributed. He also made it his business to promote it with newspaper editors in India, one of whom operated *The Pioneer*, an English-language newspaper in Allahabad. There he received a hospitable welcome. Later the paper printed a summary of the Green Pamphlet, which was itself then summarized in a bulletin by Reuters to London. There it was summarized once more by Reuters in a bulletin to South Africa. By the time this latest version arrived in South Africa, it had Gandhi writing fairly inflammatory material—which, in fact, he had not.[6] In typical Gandhi fashion, the pamphlet's actual tone was strong but respectful. Indeed, Gandhi said nothing in the pamphlet that he had not already said openly in Durban. As the Natal reaction would soon demonstrate, however, there were those in Durban who did not appreciate Gandhi's washing the colony's dirty clothes in public.

At the same time that the press was exaggerating the tone of Gandhi's writing, the Durban working class was revolting against the continued importation of Indian laborers. Tradesmen and artisans feared that the Indians would take away their jobs and depress wages. Grassroots protest organizations sprang up, and mass meetings of disaffected workers issued demands that the government protect the economic interests of the European common folk.

The final element in this drama was provided by the plague. The Durban papers regularly reported its eruption in India and helped stir fears among the colony's European population of its transmission to Natal via Indian immigrants.

WALKING WITH LAUGHTON

Gandhi and his family left India for South Africa on November 30, 1896. When Gandhi's ship, the *Courland*, arrived in the port of Durban on December 12, it met with the full force of all three of these developments. To make matters worse, by happenstance a second Dada Abdulla ship, the *Naderi*, entered the port simultaneously. Together the two ships held 617 Indian passengers. When the European workers learned of this, they quickly organized against the landing of the Indians. At numerous mass meetings, they resolved not to let the Indians ashore, not knowing that only a small minority of the 617 were newcomers bound for Natal.[7] The Europeans threatened violence against Gandhi and the passengers if they attempted to land, bluntly—and accurately—stating that they had "thousands of men . . . ready and waiting to oppose their landing."[8] In the meantime, the authorities kept the ships at sea by imposing a lengthy and quite baseless quarantine on the ships, justifying this action by referring to the plague present in India.

At this point, Attorney General Harry Escombe appeared on the stage. Escombe played a delicate middle game. He was intent on currying political favor with the European protestors while at the same time doing what he could to prevent violence against the Indians. Escombe, Gandhi's Beach Grove neighbor, openly met with a committee representing the protestors. Escombe stated that the protestors might "show the force they possessed, but it was the men who possess the force and could use it without making ill use of it, who gained their ends." He argued that he and the government were sympathetic to the concerns of the "anti-Asiatics," but that there was little the government could do immediately about the ships then in the harbor. Were it a matter of cost, the government would gladly pay the £10,000 it would take to ship the Indians back home. Were it a matter of honoring the wishes of the Durban protestors alone, that could be done, but the Durban protestors represented but one aspect of a larger constituency to which the government was accountable. Escombe's fundamental message was that the protestors were correct to call the problem of Indian immigration to the government's attention, but that they should go home and let the government respond in due course. In particular, he intimated his support for a special session of the Natal Parliament to deal with the issue, while at the same time urging the protestors to permit the passengers on the two ships to land.

At a public meeting of protestors following the committee's meeting with Escombe, plans for a demonstration against the landing of the Indians were discussed. The meeting chairman, a Durban butcher named Harry Sparks, acceded to Escombe's desire that there be no violence, but with what appears to be a reservation directed squarely at Gandhi: "The demonstration would be a peaceful demonstration as regards of the Indians on board; as regard to one man it would be left to the leaders . . . to deal with him down there." The press reported that this sentiment was greeted with "loud cheers and laughter."[9]

The Natal health authorities gave the captains of the two ships permission to land, and arrangements were made to do so on January 13. Trumpets sounded the call for the European protestors to assemble. Escombe addressed the mob and succeeded in cajoling the demonstrators to go home. Thanks in large part to Escombe's intervention, the demonstration of 3,500 to 5,000 protestors remained peaceful.[10] Although the passengers landed without incident shortly after noon, they did so without Gandhi. He stayed on board, weighing the conflicting advice he was getting from two different lawyers. One, the attorney general, aware of the protestors' pronounced hatred of Gandhi, advised him to land under cover of darkness and be escorted home by the port superintendent. A *Natal Advertiser* reporter also warned Gandhi to be careful in disembarking. Indeed, there were explicit threats of violence against him.

A second lawyer, Frederick Laughton, a highly skilled forty-two-year-old Natal advocate, a former partner of A. W. Baker, now a partner in a leading Natal law firm,[11] and a lawyer with professional ties to Dada Abdulla and Company, took a more sanguine view. Laughton forecast that Gandhi would not be hurt because the crowd of whites had dispersed and the scene had quieted down. Laughton, whom Gandhi would later describe as "powerfully built,"[12] urged Gandhi to let him accompany him ashore during the daylight, but in a party separate from the other members of Gandhi's family. Should there be some violence, Laughton's view was that Gandhi "should not sneak into Durban like a thief in the night, but that he should face the music like a man and like a political leader." It was Laughton's hope that his (Laughton's) "presence would save him from insult."[13]

In the days leading up to the disembarkation of the Indians, Laughton, acting for Dada Abdulla and Company, had been tangling with Escombe over the quarantining of the ships and the looming European demonstration.

After a personal meeting and an exchange of letters, each effectively accused the other of not telling the truth.

With Laughton identified with the Indians and Escombe with the Europeans, it is not surprising that it was Laughton's advice that Gandhi took. Without first informing the police, he came ashore with Laughton under an overcast sky shortly before 5 P.M. on January 13.[14] Laughton and Gandhi planned to make their way on foot to the store and home of Parsi Rustomji, a distance of some two miles. Because this was a summer day in South Africa, there was still a fair amount of daylight left. There was no crowd, but Gandhi and Laughton were soon spotted by several children, who immediately alerted others in the area with their shouts of "Gandhi! Gandhi!" When the children were joined by a half-dozen adult men, Laughton, hoping for a quick escape, called for a rickshaw. Gandhi hesitated; he believed it was wrong to be pulled about by a human being. Finally, he agreed, but by then the crowd was too much for the rickshaw operator Laughton had hailed. He fled, sparing Gandhi, as he would write later, of the "shame of a rickshaw ride." Now he and Laughton were left to the mercy of the growing crowd. The two lawyers were able to make their way from Stanger Street to West Street, a main thoroughfare, at which point the size of the crowd restrained their progress. Laughton attempted to keep the attackers at bay, but the effort was doomed. A man who could match Laughton's own strength attacked Laughton and separated him from Gandhi. Those in the mob administered a thorough beating to Gandhi. One enterprising citizen took a riding whip to him, while others entertained themselves by stealing away his turban. Still others made him the object of pelts of mud, stones, rotten eggs, and stale fish. A stone struck Gandhi in the temple, causing his head to bleed. The mob, which had grown in size to two hundred men, eventually reduced Gandhi to a dazed and bleeding pulp, forcing him at one point to hang on to a fence railing for dear life. As luck would have it, however, Jane Alexander, the wife of the police superintendent, happened upon the scene and, by placing herself between Gandhi and his attackers, saved his life.[15]

A band of police eventually arrived and escorted Gandhi to the Rustomji establishment, where he was treated for his injuries by an Indian physician who had been on board the *Courland*. A boisterous mob of several hundred people soon surrounded the store, calling for Gandhi's neck. Richard Alexander, the police superintendent to whom Gandhi had been conciliatory after thoroughly defeating him in the Roberts and Richards vagrancy case, was present and took command of the scene. Alexander cleverly devised and carried out the stratagem of spiriting Gandhi away under the disguise of an Indian constable. Eventually rain began to fall, the crowd disbanded, and the incident came to an end.[16]

TO STAY OR FLEE?

There is no evidence of what the convalescing Gandhi was thinking in the immediate aftermath of this episode. Surely he must have considered how his past behavior toward his adversary, Alexander, had influenced the superintendent's willingness to step in to save Gandhi's life.[17] As for the future, the choice before him was clear: either flee the colony and abandon his professional and public work, or stay and subject himself and his newly arrived family to the risk of more violence. Gandhi knew that the mood in Natal posed a clear threat to one who would be a controversial public figure there. In writing to an Indian barrister whom he had attempted to recruit to South Africa during his recent Indian tour, Gandhi admitted that "such a man's life in Natal is, at present, in danger. I am certainly glad that you did not accompany me."[18]

On the other hand, in South Africa Gandhi had begun to establish himself as both a barrister and a leading public figure, success that was quite out of reach for the foreseeable future in his homeland. Moreover, he and his family, were they to stay, would not face the wrath of the Europeans alone but would be surrounded by a large, supportive Indian community.

Gandhi stayed. Indeed his staying in the face of danger was noteworthy enough for the *Natal Mercury* to run two stories on his decision. The first, on January 16, 1897, reported that Gandhi intended "to resume work in a day or two." The second, on February 10, 1897, noted that Gandhi "appeared in court for the first time since his return from India."[19]

While the *Mercury*, generally a pro-government newspaper, did not mention in these reports the assault Gandhi had recently withstood, it was very much on the minds of the British and colonial authorities. The secretary of state for the colonies, Joseph Chamberlain, sent word to Escombe that he wanted Gandhi's assailants prosecuted. Alexander threatened to arrest anyone harassing Gandhi. At the same time, there was a fair amount of public speculation that Gandhi was preparing to sue for damages as a result of the quarantine to which the *Courland* and *Naderi* passengers had been subjected.[20] Gandhi, who felt he had "narrowly escaped being lynched,"[21] had made it quite clear in a newspaper interview that he was not interested in litigation:

> The statement has been made that I have been advising people . . . to institute . . . proceedings against the Government for unlawful detention. That . . . statement . . . has no foundation in fact. My object throughout is not to sow dissension between the two communities, but to assist at creating harmony between the two. . . . I do not return here with the intention of making money, but of acting as a humble interpreter.[22]

As for a possible criminal prosecution, Gandhi had this to say in a meeting with Escombe:

> I do not want to prosecute anyone. . . . I do not hold the assailants to blame. They were given to understand that I had made exaggerated statements in India about the whites in Natal and calumniated them. If they believed these reports, it is no wonder they were enraged. . . . I do not want to bring anyone to book. I am sure that, when the truth becomes known, they will be sorry for their conduct.[23]

Escombe, under pressure from Chamberlain, urged Gandhi to think this decision through, consulting Laughton, if necessary. But thinking of his own political interests, he also gave his own advice to Gandhi: "If you waive the right of bringing your assailants to book, you will considerably help me in restoring quiet, besides enhancing your own reputation."

Gandhi did not hesitate: "I need not consult anyone. I had made my decision in the matter before I came to you. It is my conviction that I should not prosecute the assailants, and I am prepared this moment to reduce my decision to writing."[24] Gandhi's easy certainty about this decision stemmed from his understanding of self-restraint in this circumstance as a religious discipline.

This refusal to prosecute his attackers is a foreshadowing of the nonviolent ethic he would later, and more deeply, experiment with in South Africa. His decision was the fulfillment of the sentiment he expressed while still on board the *Courland* when he stated that he hoped God would give him "the courage and sense to forgive them and to refrain from bringing them to law." And just as Gandhi had no interest in a criminal prosecution, he had no interest in a damages lawsuit on behalf of his fellow passengers, saying that his intention was not to sow dissension between Europeans and Indians, but "to bring about an honourable reconciliation between them."[25] This was the saintly side of Gandhi. At the same time, the lawyer in him understood that the unmerited suffering he had undergone and his refusal to prosecute would benefit him both politically and professionally as both the European and Indian populations would come to see his courage and his dignity. Years later, in his autobiography, Gandhi would reflect on his refusal to prosecute as a contributing factor that "enhanced the prestige of the Indian community in South Africa and made my work easier. . . . The incident also added to my professional practice."[26]

Gandhi's clarity on this issue should not have been surprising to anyone who saw him bear up under the attack. The *Mercury's* own reporting confirmed Gandhi's resolute and courageous demeanor during the attack when it observed the day afterward that "he bore himself stolidly and pluckily through the trying ordeal."[27] The *Advertiser* noted that Gandhi was calm as the police escorted him. Laughton later commented that "throughout the trying procession [Gandhi's] manliness and pluck could not have been surpassed." Laughton added: "He is a man who must be treated as a man. Intimidation is out of the question, because if he knew the Town Hall were going to be thrown at him, I believe, from what I saw, that he would not quail."[28]

The man who was frightened by the friendly crowd in the lecture hall in Bombay had more inner resources than even he knew.

NINE

To Maritzburg

A fire broke out in two [Indian] stores in West Street last night.
A huge crowd gathered and the scene was greatly enjoyed. Cheers
were raised at every fresh outburst of flames.

Natal Witness, March 8, 1897

Impose what sanitary restrictions you like on us; let our books
be kept in English, if you will; introduce, if so minded, other
tests which we may reasonably be expected to fulfill; but, after
we have complied with all the requirements, allow us to earn
our living and, if there be interference on the part of the Officers
administering the law, give us the right of appeal to the highest
judicial tribunal in the land.

GANDHI

HARRY ESCOMBE HAD MADE A deal with the devil.

He had succeeded in convincing the anti-Indian mob to go home. He had
prevented a violent attack. He had defused a certain amount of palpable
racial tension.

But it cost Escombe. In return for peace, he had pledged to the demonstrators that, if they would leave the Indians on the *Courland* and *Naderi* alone,
the government would address their concerns through legislation.[1] Gandhi
looked on as the threat of violence purchased new laws. He himself would
use the threat of nonviolence to defend Indian rights.

AN ARRAY OF ANTI-INDIAN LEGISLATION

When the Natal Legislative Assembly convened about a month earlier than
normal, on March 18, 1897, the task of paying Escombe's debt stood at the
top of the agenda. The Assembly, however, needed no encouragement.
Gandhi and the Indian community had many enemies and but a few

friends in the legislature; most of Natal's legislators must have been grateful to the Demonstration Committee for forcing them to address "the Asiatic question," as Europeans called it, in dramatic and bold terms. They promptly took up four pieces of anti-Indian legislation: the Quarantine Act, the Uncovenanted Indians Act, the Immigration Restriction Act, and the Dealers' Licenses Act. These measures were designed to block Indian immigration, make life uncomfortable for Indians already in the colony, and extinguish the capacity of Indian entrepreneurs to compete with Europeans. They constituted a broad and forceful assault on Indian interests that would dictate the course of Gandhi's life for the next several years, causing him to dedicate almost all of his professional and political energy to answering it.

Although Natal enjoyed responsible government, it was not fully independent of Great Britain. Under unusual circumstances, legislation could be disallowed by the Crown. In fact, the British had made it clear on earlier occasions that legislation that was *overtly* racial would not be approved. Legislation had to be race-neutral on its face. Natal's legislators played along. None of the four acts specifically mentioned Indians. The openly discussed premise of the legislation, however, was that the acts would be enforced exclusively against Indians.[2]

The Quarantine Act would prohibit the landing of any person on a ship coming from any place infected with the plague or other disease.[3] The legislature did not intend this act to be used to isolate passengers temporarily until the danger of disease erupting among them had passed, a practice regularly applied to European and, heretofore, Indian passengers, as well. Rather, it was intended that this act be used to permanently keep Indians out of the colony. As Gandhi would point out, it was actually an anti-immigration bill dressed up as a health measure.

Indentured servants who left their estates without permission were subject to arrest. Zealous police officers, however, would sometimes arrest free Indians, being unable to easily distinguish them from servants on the street. The Indians had asked the authorities to caution the police to use better judgment in making their arrests. What they got instead was the Uncovenanted Indians Act, under which free Indians could purchase and carry passes showing their status. The Indian community saw little benefit and much inconvenience in a pass system. What was more problematic, the act went on to immunize police officers against liability for wrongful arrests. The Indians, fearing the behavior this provision would encourage among the police, protested the act as giving "almost a license to arrest with impunity any Indian they choose."[4]

The Quarantine Act and the Uncovenanted Indians Act were quite mild measures in comparison to the Immigration Restriction Act (IRA) and the Dealers' Licenses Act (DLA).[5]

For years tension had existed in the colony between agricultural interests that wanted to see the continued importation of large numbers of indentured servants to work the colony's plantations and mercantile interests that saw free Indians as ruthless competitors steadily putting European establishments out of business. Allied with the merchants were tradesmen who feared not only the in-migration of free Indians but also Indians coming out of indenture, all of whom were a threat to work for low wages. The rough accommodation made by these interests was that importation of servants would be continued but that Indians coming out of indenture would be discouraged from staying in the colony. To this end a £3 tax was levied on free Indians who chose to remain.[6]

The IRA added to this accommodation by permitting the continued importation of Indian indentured servants, but prohibited the immigration of two classes of persons: paupers and those unable to write "the characters of any language of Europe."[7] Designed to stop the flow of all Indians but indentured servants, the act made illegal immigration punishable by six months' hard labor.

As racist as the IRA was, it was the DLA that posed a greater, indeed a mortal, danger to the interests of Gandhi's clients. This act required every wholesale and retail business to have a license. Town councils were authorized to appoint licensing officers from whom applicants might seek licenses. The act instructed licensing officers to deny permits to those who could not maintain their books in English and those who intended to operate their businesses in facilities that were either unsanitary, "unfit for the intended trade," or "not affording sufficient and suitable accommodations for salesmen, clerks, and servants, apart from the stores or rooms in which goods and wares may be kept."[8] Beyond these somewhat imprecisely drawn grounds upon which licenses had to be denied, however, the act established no standards to guide the decisions of licensing officers. Rather, the legislation simply entrusted the officer with the unchecked "discretion to issue or refuse a wholesale or retail Licence."[9] Without even the subtlety of a wink and a nod, the town councils would send out their licensing officers to accomplish the legislature's mission.

The DLA further strengthened the hands of licensing officers by prohibiting disappointed applicants from appealing to a court for review of the officer's decision. The only appeal allowed was to the town council—the very body that appointed the licensing officer.[10] There was no pretense here of an unbiased, objective process overseen by an impartial judiciary. Rather, as Henry Bale, a prominent member of the Assembly and soon to become the new attorney general, plainly put it when the act was being considered by the legislature, the discretion described in the act was to be "exercised by those who represented and voiced public opinion."[11]

A scheme more lacking in due process and more openly the instrument of racial prejudice could scarcely be imagined. The act, without explicitly stating its goal, was crudely but clearly designed to effectuate its purpose of putting Indians out of business. If it were allowed to go into force, many of Gandhi's merchant clients, as well as many lower-level Indian entrepreneurs, would be devastated.[12]

PETITIONING AS FAITH IN REASON AND BRITISH FAIR PLAY

Gandhi's reaction to this wave of legislation would mark the beginning of a distinct shift in his understanding of the relationship between law and political power. Up until now, Gandhi's efforts to resist anti-Indian discrimination had relied almost exclusively on petitioning—incessant, persistent, unrelenting petitioning. His petitions came in all forms. They were signed by thousands, they were signed by a handful. They were directed to London, they were directed to Maritzburg. They were long, involved treatises, they were short jabs. What they had in common was Gandhi's belief that each of them would work. With his faith in reason matched by a similarly resolute expectation of British fair play, Gandhi believed that once the Indians demonstrated the unfairness with which they were treated in South Africa, either the colonial or the imperial government would order the situation corrected.[13] Despite the repeated failure of this tactic, Gandhi did not give it up easily, even as he himself began to see its futility. It was a slow transformation that would result in his eventually moving the fight from legislative and executive chambers to courtrooms, from legislation to litigation, from politicians to judges.

In the first part of 1897 the petition was still Gandhi's preferred instrument of opposition and one with which the still somewhat timid lawyer felt at ease. Petitions do not call for public speeches. Petitions can be written—written well by someone with Gandhi's enormous skill at composition—in the sanctuary of one's office. Petitions can be circulated without fanfare among one's own friends and associates. Petitions played to Gandhi's strengths and avoided his shortcomings. So he set about storming the colonial and home governments with petitions.

The Colonial Office had the responsibility of approving or disapproving colonial legislation. Thus Gandhi directed his first petition to Secretary of State for the Colonies Joseph Chamberlain. The prospects of persuading him to disapprove the legislation were not good; Chamberlain, not wishing to alienate the colonists whom he foresaw federating into an independent union, was distinctly less friendly to the Indian cause than his predecessor, Lord Ripon. The likely outcome of his effort seemed not to matter to Gandhi, however. He poured himself into the work, taking at least six weeks to produce a massive document that takes up fifty-four pages in the *Collected Works*, exclusive of an appendix that contains more than two dozen documents.

The great bulk of the petition is an excruciatingly drawn-out description of the *Courland* and *Naderi* incident. Only when he is near the end of this lengthy petition does Gandhi even raise the issue of the proposed anti-Indian legislation. He makes three short points in support of the proposition that the legislation was unnecessary or inappropriate: that the number of Indian immigrants was minimal, that the Indians were not competing with European tradesmen, and that the Indians were a benefit to the colony. Gandhi then provides the texts of the bills, after which he employs the last few paragraphs of the petition to argue for his constituency. His first argument appears defeatist. He says that while the proposed acts do not mention the Indians by name, they are, indeed, aimed at Indians. If Indians were to be restricted, he writes, it would be "infinitely better that it were done so openly"[14]

He shows that while Europeans objected to free Indians taking up residence in Natal after completing their indentures, they were intent on having indentured servants. Gandhi then writes, "The most fatal objection, however, against those Bills is that they are intended to check an evil which does not exist." There is no follow-up argument to, or even explanation of, this statement.[15] Rather, he parades before the secretary the prospects of future legislation, not yet introduced into the Natal legislature, that would restrict Indians to "locations" (certain geographically separate areas to which Indians would be confined by law for purposes of residence or trade); further restrict the issuance of trade licenses; and bar property ownership by Indians.

Finally, in the last substantive paragraph, Gandhi makes a plea for some vague relief, asking the secretary to issue a statement on "the status of the Indian British subjects." In the alternative, he asks for a confirmation of an earlier statement from Ripon that the British government desired that Indians be treated equally.[16]

Gandhi's endless recounting of the factual details of the *Courland-Naderi* incident undoubtedly tried the patience of a busy Colonial Office. Moreover, this extended history obscured the arguments Gandhi made at the document's tail. Most damaging, Gandhi did not even mention his strongest argument—that the Indian community would work to cut off the importation of indentured servants if the government permitted the proposed legislation to go into effect. In short, this petition lacked the crispness, forcefulness, and organizational clarity of his earlier petitioning against the Franchise Act. While it reflected an enormous effort, it was not Gandhi's finest work as an advocate.

Gandhi apparently did not see it that way, thinking the petition worthy of wide distribution. He circulated it in London with a cover letter that was more persuasive than the copy of the petition accompanying it. The letter was short, well organized, and compelling. Gandhi also sent it to key figures in India and a confederate in London, urging the recipients to act. "*Now* is the time," Gandhi wrote in uncharacteristically apocalyptic terms, "or it will be *never*."[17]

Less than two weeks after writing the Chamberlain petition, Gandhi peppered both chambers of the Natal Parliament with petitions. The petition to the Legislative Council was a short, polite, even deferential argument against the Uncovenanted Indians Act. The petition to the Assembly contains the strongest single argument Gandhi makes in any of his petitions against the 1897 legislation. In protesting against the provision of the DLA that forbade an appeal of the licensing officer's decision to a court, Gandhi writes:

> To deny a subject the right to appeal . . . against . . . decisions . . . guided and carried away by popular feelings or prejudice would be deemed to be an arbitrary measure in any part of the civilized world; in the British Dominions, an insult to . . . the Constitution which is rightly termed the purest in the world. Nothing . . . can be more disastrous to the stability of British rule . . . than anything that takes away the right of the subject to ventilate his grievance . . . before the highest tribunals of justice in the British Dominions, which have, under the severest trials, vindicated their fame for absolute impartiality.[18]

The balance of the petition lacks the elegance and sensibility of this argument. It suggests that the Assembly defer action on the bills until it could first investigate whether the Indian was an aid or hindrance to the colony. Anyone who thought that the legislature would do such a thing had a greater faith in reason than the prejudices of the time justified. In Gandhi's defense, he may have filed these petitions with the Natalians in part to later make the point to Chamberlain that he had given the colonials the chance to mend their ways before he approached London for relief from their actions.

That might also be the explanation for Gandhi's lengthy April 13, 1898, letter to the *Natal Mercury*. It argued that Europeans should not fear the Indian. In it Gandhi displayed a technique familiar to thoughtful lawyers—he took his weaknesses and turned them into strengths. European businesspeople regularly complained that they could not compete with Indians, whose supposed low standard of living resulted in abnormally low costs and prices. Gandhi's response was to argue that it was a *benefit* to Europeans for Indians to live and sell cheaply because, in doing so, Indians were able to offer retail prices affordable to Europeans of limited means. In response to the claim that if Indian retailers did not exist, European ones would take their places, Gandhi argued that it was the Indian retailer who made the world bright for European wholesalers, wholesaling being "a stage higher" than retailing.

With respect to complaints that Indians lived and worked in unsanitary conditions, Gandhi's argument showed both the lawyer and the saint at work. If Indians were unsanitary, that problem could be solved by strictly enforcing the sanitation and licensing laws. The Europeans would be prepared to do this, Gandhi claimed, only if the "European Colonists, as Christians, look upon [Indians] as brethren or, as British subjects, look upon them as fellow-subjects." Then Gandhi advised the Europeans that "instead of cursing and swearing at the Indians as now, they [should] help them to remove any defects that there may be in them, and thus raise them and themselves also in the estimation of the world."[19]

THE END OF PETITIONING?

It was not surprising that Gandhi's petitioning and letter writing failed to convince the Natal Parliament. All four bills were passed and their texts promulgated in the *Government Gazette* on May 5 and June 1, 1897. Gandhi immediately wrote to the Natal colonial secretary, advising him that he would be sending a petition to Chamberlain and requesting that the secretary not transmit the bills to London for approval until the Indians had an opportunity to complete the preparation of their petition. But Gandhi was too late; the bills had already been sent. Gandhi, normally extremely attentive to details, had not prepared the new Chamberlain petition in time. Surely this could not have been for lack of notice, for it was clear from the start that the bills would pass. Gandhi was reduced to requesting that Chamberlain defer consideration of the bills until the Indians could state their case again.

Chamberlain waited and Gandhi wrote. What Gandhi wrote, however, was an ordinary, tired, and unimaginative piece of work. He restated almost verbatim arguments he had made before, he filled the document with long passages from the press supporting his point of view, and he made virtually nothing of his strongest argument, that the DLA, bereft as it was of standards, deprived British subjects of elemental due process. In the one strong paragraph that he wrote, couched unfortunately in his odd specificity argument, he did draw the secretary's attention to the Queen's Proclamation of 1858, guaranteeing equality for all her subjects:

> If Her Majesty's Government decide that, in spite of the Proclamation of 1858, a . . . Colony can legislate to the prejudice of British Indians . . . and, if they are satisfied that the number of Indians in Natal is increasing at an alarming rate, and that the presence of the Indians is an evil to the Colony, it would be far more satisfactory that a Bill specially applicable to the Indians would be introduced.[20]

Finally, he took the Indians' single point of leverage—the suspension of the importation of indentured servants—and mentioned it only in passing at the close of the petition.

As had been his practice with previous petitions, Gandhi sent copies of this one to pro-Indian leaders in Britain and to leading nationalist figures in India. His cover letter is remarkable for the desperation it shows:

> Unless there is a powerful public opinion against the disabilities that are being heaped upon the Indians in Natal our days are numbered. Natal beats both Republics [the Boer-controlled Transvaal and Orange Free State] in its studied persecution of the Indians, and it is Natal that can least do without Indians. She *must have* them under indenture. She *won't have* them as free men. Would not the Home and the Indian Governments stop this unfair arrangement and stop indentured emigration to Natal? We have but to request you to redouble your efforts on our behalf and we may yet hope to get justice![21]

Perhaps Gandhi's approach to the writing of the second Chamberlain petition was shaped by his understanding that there was little likelihood the secretary would disallow the acts on the basis of yet another Indian petition. Perhaps Gandhi understood petitioning itself was not the tool he once thought it was. When London turned a deaf ear to the Indians' plea and refused to exercise its disallowance power with respect to the four anti-Indian acts, perhaps Gandhi understood it was time for something different—litigation.

THE START OF SOMETHING NEW: THE CASE OF THE DUNDEE INDIANS

To this point, Gandhi's practice of law had been fairly apolitical. His work was that of a business lawyer. He helped his commercial clients transfer property, collect debts, and sue on back rent. Those few cases with political overtones—Balasundaram's case comes to mind—were exceptions, not the rule. In 1897, however, a convergence between Gandhi's professional and political work began to develop that would signal the start of a slow but radical change in the nature of his practice.

It is not clear, however, that litigation was a strategy intentionally chosen by Gandhi and the Natal Indian Congress (the merchants' political arm of which Gandhi was the moving force) or whether the strategy chose them. After his defeat by the legislature and following his last plea to Indian and European figures that they urge London to disallow the anti-Indian bills, Gandhi seemed to lose focus. There is almost no evidence of political activity by Gandhi from early July to late September 1897. In mid-September, however, he was called upon to intervene in a case that had been developing in Dundee.

Seventy-five Indians trying to enter Natal from the Transvaal had been arrested at Dundee for violating the IRA. They were promptly jailed. Two local European attorneys, Hugh Anderson and Albert Smith, pled with the Dundee immigration officer for their release, arguing that the men were Natalian citizens. While a few were released on this basis, the great majority of them were held for the local magistrate. He refused to grant the lawyers' request for bail. When after two days of hearings the lawyers renewed their request, the magistrate simply renewed his ruling. The day after the hearing ended, Anderson and Smith once more applied for bail and the magistrate once more denied the request. When Gandhi arrived in Dundee to take up the Indians' cause, he joined in the request for bail, and this time it "was immediately granted by the Magistrate with permission to approach the Immigration Officer."[22] Gandhi apparently had come from Durban armed with records indicating the innocence of at least some of the prisoners, permitting him to convince the magistrate.[23] Preparation was sometimes Gandhi's strong suit. The immigration officer, however, still would not budge, so Gandhi returned to the magistrate. According to the *Natal Mercury*, "The same objections were raised by Mr. Gandhi as were raised by the attorneys, but this time the Magistrate decided to liberate the whole of the men. The legal circle here is much annoyed at the course adopted in refusing two attorneys what they allowed to the third (Mr. Gandhi)."[24]

This was a rare circumstance for Gandhi—succeeding in court where European lawyers had failed. But it was more than that. It was preeminently a heady, though temporary, victory of the law over racism. Might the courts be used to defend against, and even attack, anti-Indian legislation?

THE DEALERS' LICENSES ACT

The IRA proved to be ineffective and highly unpopular. As some had predicted, the result of the legislation was to keep out far more Europeans and far fewer Indians than its proponents had hoped. The Uncovenanted Indians Act created a nuisance with which the Indians were resigned to live for the moment. The Quarantine Act would become an issue only when the danger of plague arose. The DLA, however, was another matter altogether. It was quickly, repeatedly, and ruthlessly implemented to put existing Indian businesses out of commission and to prevent new ones from beginning. Its vesting of virtually unchecked discretion in licensing officers and its bar on appeals to the courts made decisions that were nakedly race-based, easy to render, and easy to defend. A license denial did not have to be specifically authorized in the law. A license *could* be denied on sanitary grounds or because the applicant could not keep books in English. These bases were specifically mentioned in the law. But the law did not restrict denials to these grounds alone. A licensing officer could deny a permit for any reason he chose.

Nor did the act require the licensing officer to justify his decision with reasons. The act required neither the licensing officer nor the town council to provide reasons. A denial could be based on any reason or on no reason.

It did not take a keen eye to spot the arbitrariness the act permitted. By late 1897, town councils were getting their first taste of appeals from the decisions of licensing officers. On October 27, the Durban Town Council entertained several appeals from decisions of the officer denying businesspeople licenses to operate. In an appeal by one applicant, the mayor stated that the licensing officer need not present reasons for his denial of the application. After some discussion of the unfairness of not providing reasons, the officer stated that the applicant had earlier failed in his attempt to obtain a restaurant license and the officer considered this a back-door attempt to obtain such a license. The council disagreed and unanimously granted the license. The applicant was European.

The second applicant was Chinese. One council member, Daniel Taylor, stated that "it was time that they put a little check on these undesirables. . . . [I]t would be a disgrace to the community if they gave a . . . licence to this man, or any other man of the same nationality. In Australia . . . Chinese had proved to be parasites, and sucked the lifeblood out of the European population."[25] Another member of council, however, would benefit financially from the grant of a license; he was to be the applicant's landlord. The majority of the council approved the license.

The final applicant was Indian, applying on behalf of a partnership. The licensing officer claimed that the person who appeared before the town council was not the same partner who had applied for the license, prompting one council member to remark that it was impossible to follow "these people" through their partnership relationships. The council upheld the license denial.

None of these decisions, reported in a paper that Gandhi scrutinized daily, was made on a principled basis or had a firm basis in reason. But each found support in a DLA that handed over to town councils unchecked discretion and near-total freedom from accountability.

Gandhi would also look on as the Durban licensing officer issued more denials of Indian applications as well as denials to applicants who were Chinese and Jewish.

DEFENDING MOOSA

Soon enough Gandhi found himself with a licensing case. Moosa Hajee Adam operated a small fruit and vegetable stand in a passage that connected West

Street to Durban's Indian mosque. The stand was not a fixture, but removable. Moosa would set out his produce on his wooden stand during the day, transfer it indoors at day's end, and throw a canvass over the stall for the night. The city's licensing officer, W. H. Dyer, spotted Moosa operating this business, found he had no dealer's license, and cited him for violating the DLA.

When Moosa appeared before Resident Magistrate Saunders on December 9, 1897, Gandhi was at Moosa's side equipped with a clever argument for his client's innocence. Gandhi claimed that the DLA did not displace Ordinance 3 of 1850, from which the city's right to require licenses under the DLA flowed. Natal legislation of this era was notoriously poorly written,[26] and in this case Gandhi was determined to take advantage of the Parliament's failure to coordinate the DLA with the ordinance.[27] While it was true that the DLA was written to apply to "retail dealers," Gandhi argued, Ordinance 3 permitted the city to require licenses only of those who operated retail "shops." Moosa's stand, on which he set up and dismantled his business every day, had no permanence to it, concluded Gandhi. It failed to qualify as a "shop." Strengthening this argument, Gandhi reminded the court that "all laws passed in restraint of trade and liberty of the subject had to be strictly interpreted against the prosecution, and very liberally in favour of the defendant."[28]

Magistrate Saunders was not convinced. He found Moosa guilty and, accepting Gandhi's representation that this was a test case, levied a nominal fine of 5 shillings.

Moosa appealed to the Supreme Court. Gandhi rarely appeared before the Court on his own. Perhaps he was still too timid. Perhaps he was sensitive to the criticism that the arguments of a political figure such as himself would not be given their full weight by the court. In this instance, Gandhi brought in forty-eight-year-old Kenneth Hathorn to argue the case for the Indian side. The English-born Hathorn had been in practice since 1871 and was an experienced Supreme Court advocate. He would later go on to serve in the Parliament and on the Natal bench.

Hathorn echoed Gandhi's argument: "In this case the licence in question is described in Ordinance 3, of 1850, as a 'licence to keep a retail shop,' and the entire question at issue is 'does the appellant keep a retail shop?' . . . The only way in which he could be required to have a licence was if he kept a retail shop, under Ordinance 3, of 1850."[29]

Hathorn's opponent, R. F. Morcom, saddled with defending an indefensible position, satisfied himself with arguing that there was a distinction between the "question whether he can take out a licence" and the question of "whether he can carry on a business without a licence."[30] The Court, consisting of Chief Justice Gallwey and Justices Wragg and Finnemore, rejected the city's argument, unanimously ruled for Moosa, and set aside the magistrate's judgment.

This relatively easy win could only have encouraged Gandhi, as well as his friend and colleague Frederick Laughton, who joined Gandhi in the fight against the act. Laughton would later describe the DLA as a "dishonest and discreditable piece of legislation" and a "concession to an anti-Indian mob."[31] Laughton attempted to strike at the heart of the act in early 1898, after his Indian client had been denied a license by the licensing officer in Newcastle, a decision sustained by the Newcastle Town Council. Against the grain of conventional wisdom, which held that the act prohibited appeals to the courts, Laughton headed to Maritzburg to lodge an appeal with the Supreme Court.

TO MARITZBURG

Laughton was a particularly skilled lawyer. Amongst a bar that was at best mediocre, Laughton's ability to engage in sophisticated legal analysis easily distinguished him. Of course, he had an advantage. Unlike many of his colleagues at the bar, he read the law. In fact, he read it carefully and closely. In *Vanda v. Newcastle* his careful reading of the act led him to develop the novel argument that while the DLA clearly prohibited appeals from *licensing officers* to the courts, it just as plainly did not prohibit appeals from *town councils* to the courts. Nowhere did the act address itself to appeals from the town council. The vacuum on that point, Laughton argued, was filled by previous legislation. Section 8 of Law 39 of 1896, passed just two years earlier by the Natal Parliament, vested the Supreme Court "with jurisdiction to review the proceedings of all Inferior Courts of Justice or tribunals."[32] Laughton claimed that "all" meant all—that it included town councils that were, in his view, judicial bodies for the purposes of the act.

Justice Mason challenged Laughton: "Surely it was playing with words to say that they were not to review the decisions of the Licencing Officer, but were to review the decision of the Court sustaining it."[33]

Laughton, quick on his feet, responded: "Supposing the Town Council had said, 'You are entitled to a licence, but inasmuch as there is no appeal, we won't grant it.' Did their lordships mean to say that there was no appeal to that Court, in view of what was laid down in Section 8 of the Supreme Court Law? . . . The Town Council of Newcastle had said 'We will get rid of Indians in this town.' and had the Court jurisdiction in such cases? Every Court of law was jealous in sustaining its jurisdiction, not in throwing it away."

The argument of Mr. Watt, representing Newcastle, was simple, if incorrect: "The law was not ambiguous, but was perfectly clear."

The chief justice was convinced by Laughton's argument. Justice Mason, who had disagreed with Watt's point that the act was clear, was not: "How can it be maintained that this Court can review the decision of the Town Council on the granting or refusal of a licence, and yet at the same time neither review, reverse, or alter the granting of the licence itself?" Finnemore agreed with Mason that the act was clear enough to determine that the legislature's intent was to bar appeals of the sort contemplated by Laughton.

The act, which was susceptible of two reasonable interpretations on whether the Court had jurisdiction, had yielded a split decision. It was a defeat for the Indian side, but not a final one. Two avenues of recourse were yet open. The decision could be appealed to the Judicial Committee of the Privy Council, the body in London responsible for hearing appeals from courts in the colonies. The Indians did, in fact, take such an appeal.

Laughton and Gandhi knew that the Privy Council took a long time to issue its decisions, so in the meantime, they paid attention to a section of Mason's opinion that, surprisingly, suggested a second avenue of action: "Where either a licensing officer or a Town Council proposes to exercise powers with regard to trade licences which it does not possess, the position of this Court would in all probability be very different."[34]

Mason was as much as inviting the Indians to bring to the courts any irregularities of procedure to which they were subjected.

REDEEMING MASON'S PLEDGE

Gandhi, like Laughton, could read. When he appeared four weeks later at an appeal hearing before the Durban Town Council, Gandhi was ready. Despite having received a satisfactory sanitation report, his client, Somnath Maharaj, had been denied a license for property he intended to rent from the Congress. The involvement of the Congress, an institution controlled by Gandhi's wealthy merchant clients, signals that this case was part of a planned campaign of litigation against the DLA.

Gandhi immediately attacked the process. He had asked to be provided with the reasons the license application was denied and for a copy of the licensing officer's report. He had been refused on both counts. Gandhi pointed out that the council was acting in the nature of a court and that

> there was nothing in the law to provide that the ordinary rules of procedure were to be subverted. It was only common sense to presume that if the right to appeal was allowed the subject, the ordinary procedure that guarded the conduct of such appeals should be observed. If it was not to be so, it would simply mean that the law gave a right to a subject with the one hand and snatched it away with the other, and the right to appeal became a phantom.[35]

Gandhi went on to say that, unless he was provided with the reasons for the denial, "how on earth" was he going to argue his case?[36] Gandhi demanded that the council rule on his request for a copy of the record in the case and for the reasons for the refusal. He knew that a specific council ruling would provide him with a clear and crisp appellate issue.

To his legal strategy he added indignation: Maharaj "had been practically opposed by the whole machinery. Every obstacle was placed in his way—he had to anticipate reasons, come to the Council and spend a lot of money, and then perhaps be told that the Licencing Officer's decision was upheld.... [Was this] an appeal under the British Constitution?"[37]

The town council then adjourned the public portion of the hearing to huddle in private with Dyer, the licensing officer. There the officer provided the council with his reasons for denying the application. When the council emerged from this meeting, it attempted to skirt the issue of what information Gandhi was entitled to and go directly to a decision on the appeal itself. Councilman Brown moved that the licensing officer's denial of the license be affirmed. The motion was no sooner seconded than Gandhi interrupted to say, "I have not been heard." Gandhi then pressed his demand: "I have not yet got the Council's decision whether I am entitled to a copy of the record."[38] The mayor was forced to respond: "The decision of the Council is against that."

Gandhi now had his issue for appeal on the record.

With his appellate issue secured, Gandhi moved on to lay bare the motivations of Dyer and the council. In this case he had proved that Maharaj was solvent, that he could keep books in English, that he had run a business elsewhere for several years, and that he had been responsible enough to make a full settlement with his creditors before disposing of that business. The only faults that could be attributed to Maharaj were that he had not held a Durban license before and

> that he had a brown skin. . . . [I]f a man having a brown skin was not to have a licence, that . . . savoured of a great deal of injustice. It was certainly un-British and un-English. There was nothing in the law to show that licences had to be refused on account of nationality.

Gandhi concluded:

> In exercising the [licensing] power . . . , the Council would take away the bread from hundreds of respectable and deserving men, who had given their best services to the Colony. [Maharaj] had come to Natal at the wish of the Colony. He came under indenture and was told that he would better his prospects. He had given the best part of his life to the Colony for a miserable pittance, and then he was refused a livelihood because his skin was against him.[39]

Gandhi sat down. His petitioning had always been characterized by circumspection. One would strain to find a harsh word in any of his petitions. Starting with this case, litigation would change him.

Gandhi's frankness left Daniel Taylor, one of the most racist public figures in Natal, unmoved. The councilman proposed that the appeal be dismissed. Councilman Clark seconded. Maharaj's appeal was dismissed without a single vote in dissent.

AGAIN TO MARITZBURG

Laughton and Gandhi headed straight for Maritzburg, the colonial capital where the Supreme Court sat, seeking a writ of mandamus—a type of order compelling a governmental agency to carry out a duty.[40] Intent upon redeeming Mason's pledge, they had behind them the editorial support of the *Natal Advertiser* and an unusually friendly headline—"Mr. Gandhi Eloquently Appeals"—in the *Natal Witness*.[41]

Laughton rested the Indians' case on several narrow points, arguing, for example, that the appointment of a licensing officer who was also an employee of the city created an improper bias. Laughton did not argue that it was improper for the council to recess and discuss the case in private. Sensing that the issue would be on the minds of the justices, however, Thomas Garlicke, the Durban town solicitor,[42] raised the question and made a modestly persuasive argument that the council had the right to do so. Laughton must have been surprised when Justice Wragg, now the acting chief justice, interrupted Garlicke's argument to make a key distinction: "They have a right to retire and to take their legal advisor with them, but what they did in this case was to hear evidence in private, and refuse all information to the appellant." Wragg's comments were a strong indication of how the court would rule. Mason also interrupted to inquire whether it was "not an abuse of terms to call what took place an appeal?"[43]

In his opinion deciding the case, Wragg stated that the court would not decide whether the licensing officer's employment by the council created an impermissible bias; he did advise the council, however, that "it would be better that some person who is more or less distinct, should be the Licencing Officer." Wragg went on to base his vote to invalidate the council's action on the council's refusal to provide reasons and a copy of the record. In Wragg's view, the council also acted improperly when it retired and took evidence from the licensing officer "without giving the appellant a chance of hearing what that evidence was." In the face of the provision in the DLA prohibiting appeals, Wragg then set forth Mason's earlier pledge in *Vanda* as a point of law: "Where a very great irregularity takes place, this Court has the power to set aside the proceedings."[44] Justices Mason and Finnemore joined with Wragg to unanimously overrule the council, with Mason pointedly calling the town council proceedings "not only oppressive, but . . . a disgrace to the Town Council."[45]

The Court had been true to its word. While it would not invalidate the provision of the DLA barring court appeals, it would see to it that whatever proceedings were held before town councils offered appellants at least one characteristic of fair hearings—notice of the grounds for the denial.

DUE PROCESS

When Gandhi, armed with his Supreme Court decision, renewed his appeal of the licensing officer's decision against Somnath before the Durban Town Council, the council read aloud the record of the case. Gandhi then pushed the council, inquiring whether any other reasons existed for the denial of the license. By a 4–3 vote, the council required Dyer to state his reasons, which he articulated as follows: "That the applicant had no claim whatever upon

Durban, as the class of trade he was engaged in was sufficiently provided for in the town and borough."[46]

Gandhi knew this was a pretext.

> The only reason the licence was withheld was because [my] client belonged to a class who were not much in favour in Durban, or for that matter in the Colony. The reason now submitted by the Licensing Officer was . . . not sufficient to warrant the Council to reject the appeal. The man, being Indian, could not change his skin.[47]

Gandhi wanted the real basis for the decision on the record.

Councilman Farman, in an effort to avoid such unseemliness, first tried to adjourn the council to executive session, where he could more freely argue with his colleagues about the basis of their decision. That attempt failed. Then he obtained the mayor's permission to examine the applicant. This would be fatal for Somnath's application. Farman quickly demonstrated that Somnath was incapable of taking the oath because he could not speak English. Farman, his goal of avoiding an openly race-based decision now in sight, reminded the council that the act required "that the applicant should be able to keep his books in the English language."[48]

The rebuttal to this point was in plain view of anyone who had read the act. It did not require that the applicant *personally* keep his books in English, only that they *be kept* in English. A bookkeeper who knew English would do.

Gandhi, however, was speechless. Before he could open his mouth, Councilman Henwood's motion to deny the license was approved by unanimous vote. The Somnath case was lost.

The council took up a second appeal that Gandhi presented, this one an appeal on behalf of Mahomed Majam and Company. It was only then that Gandhi offered the obvious response to Farman's point that an applicant could keep his books "by means of an accountant."[49] Gandhi, however, was too late. The council ignored his point and promptly turned Majam and Company down too.[50]

In *Somnath*, the Supreme Court had forced town councils to offer disappointed Indian applicants some measure of due process when it required councils to state the reasons upon which denials rested. In the *Majam* appeal and in Gandhi's second appeal of the *Somnath* case, the Durban Town Council had complied with this mandate. It had stated reasons—and then dismissed the appeals. Gandhi got his due process—and nothing else.

If this new regime was not clear to Gandhi the day he lost the *Somnath* and *Majam* appeals, it would become unmistakably clear when he pursued yet another appeal some three months later on behalf of Dada Osman. Because Dada Osman was a Congress activist, this case, like the *Somnath* case before it, has the mark of being part of a deliberate campaign of litigation against the act.

The town clerk notified Gandhi of the hearing date at 4:30 P.M. the day before the hearing. Gandhi found it impossible to get his client to Durban on such short notice and appeared before the council to ask for a two-week continuation of the hearing. The mayor indicated to Gandhi that notice of the hearing was posted on the Town Hall notice board five days before the hearing. Gandhi argued that this notice was insufficient; no one could be expected to keep checking the board constantly, and, in any event, attorneys for the parties were entitled to individual notice. The town clerk replied that the notice from the previous day was Gandhi's individual notice. Daniel Taylor moved that the appeal be dismissed. Councilman Evans countered with a motion that the hearing be postponed for two weeks. This motion passed.

Gandhi then asked the council to provide him the reasons for the denial. Taylor moved that the officer not be required to state his reasons. This time it was Councilman Collins who countered with a motion that Gandhi be provided a copy of the reasons. Collins' motion carried. If Gandhi wanted his due process, a majority of the council was prepared to give it to him.

When the council resumed the hearing two weeks later, the council complied with Gandhi's request for reasons. The town clerk read aloud the licensing officer's statement:

> The Act of 1897, as I understand, was passed with a view of placing some check on the issue of trading licences to certain classes of people, generally regarded as undesirable, and, as I believe I am right in assuming that the applicant in question is one that would be included in that class, and, moreover, as he has never before had a license in Durban, I have felt it to be my duty to refuse the license.[51]

This statement was read after the council had already conceded that sanitation was not an issue.[52] Accordingly, Gandhi's strategy, in the face of this statement, was to show the absurdity of classifying Dada Osman as "undesirable." To do so, he called witnesses to speak to the applicant's capability as a businessman and his upright character.

He first produced an established Durban merchant, Alexander McWilliam, a European who vouched for the applicant, saying that over the past twelve or fourteen years he "had considerable business dealings with him," and that he "knew him as a clever businessman, and a good linguist and correspondent in the English language." Moreover, added McWilliam, the premises intended for the applicant's business were suitable, and as a tax-payer he had no objection to Dada Osman holding a license.

It was likely no coincidence that, were he to obtain a license, Dada Osman's landlord would be Abdul Cadir, a partner in the large Indian trading firm Mahomed Cassim and Company. Abdul Cadir was an important figure in the Congress, and Cassim and Company was a steady Gandhi client. Abdul stated that he owned several properties in Durban, worth between £18,000 and £20,000, one of which he desired to rent for £10 a month to Osman, whom he described as a capable, desirable, and honest tenant. Were Osman's license to be denied, Cadir would "lose the rent of that particular store."[53]

Gandhi also called upon Dada Osman himself to speak. He informed the council of his long history as a businessman in the colony, much of which had been spent in agreeable professional relationships with several European businessmen in addition to McWilliam. He indicated that he was fluent in English, could write English, and understood both single- and double-entry bookkeeping. Indeed, the licensing officer had already inspected and approved his bookkeeping.

Gandhi had put together an impeccable factual record. The premises were sanitary. The applicant himself could keep sophisticated books in English. There was no question of the applicant's business integrity and capability. He had a good record of dealings with well-established European businessmen. Moreover, were the license to be denied, the economic interests of a prominent landlord would be harmed.

The only issue was "desirability." Gandhi argued first that the DLA spoke not one word with regard to the "desirability" of persons applying for licenses and, accordingly, judgments about an applicant's desirability constituted an improper basis for the decision on whether a license should be issued.

The licensing officer had based his decision on "desirability," however, and Gandhi knew he must address that question squarely. Gandhi relied on the authority of no less a figure than the secretary of state for the colonies, Joseph

Chamberlain, who the previous year had spoken out against colonial legislation that explicitly discriminated on the basis of race and color. Gandhi quoted Chamberlain as saying, "It was not because a man was of a different colour from themselves that he was necessarily an undesirable immigrant, but it was because he was dirty, or immoral, or a pauper, or had some other objection which could be defined."

Chamberlain's statement provided Gandhi with an authoritative set of characteristics that defined "undesirable." Gandhi argued that because the proof had convincingly demonstrated that Dada Osman was neither dirty, nor immoral, nor a pauper, he was not, by definition, "undesirable." It was a sound argument. To it, Gandhi added a policy argument. The licensing officer himself had said that Dada Osman would conduct a sanitary business. If the council now "refused this license, it would go forth among the Indian population of Durban that the desire of the Council was not really that the Indians should conform to the sanitary requirements of the Council, but would as soon have them live in contravention of those orders."[54]

The only remaining possible reason for the denial, Gandhi concluded, was that Dada Osman was an Indian. In Gandhi's view this would be a clearly impermissible basis for the denial.

That was not the view of the town council. Councilman Collins was forthright: the council would refuse the license "not because the applicant or the premises were unsuitable, but because the applicant was Indian." Collins explained: "Parliament, representing the community of Natal, had come to the conclusion that it was undesirable that the Indians should increase their hold on the trade of Durban, and it was on that account that [the council was] practically called upon to refuse the licenses which were not otherwise objectionable."

Collins added a personal note. He "considered the refusal of the license a grievance to the applicant, who was a most suitable person to appear before the Council to ask for a licence, but it had been found expedient as a matter of colonial policy that these licences should not be increased."[55] With that, Collins seconded the motion of Daniel Taylor to confirm the decision of the licensing officer. Councilmen Evans, Labistour, and Hitchins had arrived at the meeting a few minutes before and were ineligible to vote. Labistour, the lawyer who had refused to oppose Gandhi's application to the bar in 1894, wanted to speak his mind. He expressed his disgust with the "dirty work" the council was called on to do. He said he had deliberately stayed away from the first part of the meeting because he did not want to participate. Labistour lectured the council: "If the burgesses wished all such licenses stopped, there was a clean way of going about the matter, namely, getting the Legislative Assembly to enact a measure against the granting of licences to the Indian community, but, sitting as a Court of Appeal, unless there were good grounds to the contrary, the licence should be granted."[56]

Labistour's advice was ignored. Taylor's motion was put to a vote and passed easily. Dada Osman would not get his license.

There is no doubt that Gandhi had put on a superb case. Even the Natal press had to confess that Gandhi was "to be complimented for the able defence . . . he made of his client's application for a license."[57] Because the case was a deliberate project, Gandhi had time to plan it carefully. And so he did. By the testimony of his witnesses and the force of his arguments, he defeated every substantive objection to the application that the council could muster. He even garnered the unexpected sympathy of Collins and the support of Labistour. None of this, however, was sufficient to win the day.

The Supreme Court had proven itself to be the one governmental institution to which the Indians could turn with the expectation of receiving a fair hearing. Laughton had convinced the chief justice, if not the full court, that appeals to the judiciary from town council decisions under the DLA should be allowed. Gandhi had obtained a ruling that held the authorities in check in terms of how a retail shop was defined. The two lawyers had also succeeded in convincing the Court to force town councils to provide an important measure of due process to applicants. But in the end Gandhi and Laughton must have realized that the Court's reach was limited. While the Supreme Court had forced town councils to extend significant procedural rights to the Indians, Gandhi and Laughton never asked the Court to rule on the ultimate question: would the law permit a town council to deny an applicant a license solely because the applicant was Indian?[58]

Perhaps they were afraid of the answer.

TEN

Moth and Flame

I was afraid that my main business might become merely
money-making.

GANDHI

IN LATE 1898 WORD CAME from London that the Privy Council had
handed down its decision in the case of *Vanda v. Newcastle.*[1] Laughton's argument that an applicant for a dealer's licence should be permitted to appeal an
adverse town council decision to the Natal Supreme Court had been rejected.
There would be no appeals of licence denials to the courts.

The fight against the DLA was now limited not only by the conservatism
of the Natal Supreme Court but by this devastating Privy Council ruling as
well.[2] The cause of Indian civil rights in South Africa was stymied. As town
councils continued to enforce the DLA, the owners of shops and trading
firms who were Gandhi's clients would suffer significant hardships. With
new men unable to secure licences, extant business owners could not sell
their businesses or hand them down through inheritance. Nor could they
establish new locations or split up a business among its partners. Indians
freed of their indentures and who wanted to start small businesses were also
greatly hurt.

Gandhi had been hired by Natal's prosperous Indian businessmen to stop
the erosion of their rights, not to preside over their destruction. He had
invested enormous amounts of his time in organizing meetings, writing petitions, and finally, litigating. Nothing worked.

FULFILLMENT

Gandhi would continue to struggle mightily against discrimination by the
European colonists, but as the end of the decade drew near, he found himself
taking refuge in activities that offered him clearer rewards than did his politi-

cal work. One such opportunity was opened to him during this time when a leper appeared at Gandhi's door. Gandhi took him in, fed him, dressed his wounds, and sheltered him before sending him off to a government hospital. The experience introduced Gandhi, who as a youth had been interested in medicine, to the fulfillment he might experience in caring for the ill. As a result, he began work as a volunteer at a hospital for Indians. On each visit Gandhi spent up to two hours interviewing patients, briefing their physicians, and dispensing medicines the doctors prescribed for them. The practical effects of this hands-on work constituted an achievement that could be easily seen and just as easily enjoyed.

Similarly, Gandhi's private practice of law offered him some tangible indicators of success, at least as the world measures success. Gandhi had never valued his practice above his political work (insofar as these were separate domains), but now, in the midst of his losing battle against the DLA, his practice filled a vacuum in his life. It offered him an opportunity to succeed.

His practice was demanding. Much of his time was consumed, as he described it later, with "office work, conveyancing and arbitration."[3] The importance of this work in Gandhi's mind might be reflected in his having spent practically no effort in his memoirs to describe it. A letter-book, mentioned by the compilers of *The Collected Works of Mahatma Gandhi* and containing some thousand exemplars of Gandhi-client correspondence, would likely have given us a detailed understanding of Gandhi's office work. That evidence, however, appears to no longer exist. What evidence does remain appears to indicate that Gandhi did, in fact, spend a good portion of his time in chambers, doing the sort of ordinary work one might expect of a lawyer with a busy civil practice. The record as we have it gives us some hints as to what this work was. Some work involved negotiating the rental, purchase, and sale of property and attending to the routine legal work that surrounded such transactions.[4] Gandhi was also frequently occupied in obtaining opinions from other practitioners in their areas of expertise on the rights of his Indian clients.[5] And he seems to have spent a fair amount of his time engaged in correspondence in which he dealt with the financial aspects of his practice, sometimes quarreling with others about what he or his clients owed them.[6]

Although his autobiography, written decades later, seems to downplay his courtroom practice, it is clear from the record that Gandhi was no stranger to the courtroom in the years immediately following his work with Laughton against the DLA. The fact is that, because he had established himself as a responsible and respected figure in the eyes of the colonial establishment, Indian clients were drawn to him as one who had credibility and, perhaps, even influence with those in power. Accordingly, he had no shortage of clients for whom he was called upon to litigate. His courtroom work covered a wide range of matters from mortgage bonds to promissory notes to personal injury and more. He even made an occasional but rare foray into criminal law.

So much was going on in Gandhi's office that there was enough work for two lawyers. Accordingly, in mid-1899 he took on the second Indian lawyer to come to Natal, Rahim Karim Khan. Like Gandhi before him, Khan had gone to London to undergo his legal training in the Inns of Court. Khan had been a member of Lincoln's Inn and was called to the bar in 1898. Like his employer, he had come to South Africa as a novice. Unlike his employer, he submitted an application for admission that was not opposed by the bar.[7]

As soon as Khan was admitted to the Natal bar in July 1899, Gandhi began to funnel some of his routine cases to the young barrister, freeing himself to make his money doing more interesting things. Within days of Khan's admission, Gandhi left the office in the hands of his new Muslim colleague and traveled to the Transvaal, where the Boer government was attempting to require licences of Indian traders and to segregate Indians to rural locations out of town. Gandhi met with the public prosecutor, pleaded the case of the Johannesburg Indians to the state secretary—and collected a fee for his advocacy.

On his return, he was quickly reminded of the level to which the struggle for Indian civil rights in Natal had sunk. An Indian had been selling vegetables from what the city nuisance inspector called a "building," which, the inspector charged, was erected without the requisite permission of the city council. Gandhi was called upon by his client Dada Abdulla and Company, the owner of the premises and the Indian's landlord, to represent the defendant in the lowest court in the judicial system. There Gandhi argued that the defendant was not operating out of a building at all, but rather that the shop, by virtue of its wheels, was actually a moveable van. Gandhi's star witness, a European architect, testified that to call the van a building "was absurd on the face of it." Answering the question "when is a building not a building?" the court ruled that the shop was not housed in a permanent structure and therefore did not fall under the building laws; it dismissed the charges.

This prosecution dealt with a ridiculously trivial issue, but Barrister Gandhi found himself ensnared in it because Dada Abdulla was a major client and because opposing the city on this matter was one of the few remaining ways left for fending off the continued harassment of the Indian community. This case does not get a mention in Gandhi's memoirs.

It must have come as no small relief for Gandhi to be shortly thereafter thrown into some private business litigation of a rather substantial magnitude. M. C. Camrooden and Company, a partnership, was, in Gandhi's estimation, "the premier Indian firm in South Africa."[8] Camrooden had trading interests in Natal and the Transvaal, as well as large amounts of real estate in Natal. In June 1899 a major battle erupted within the partnership when one of the partners, Mahomed Ebrahim, desiring to retire from the firm, exercised what he believed was his right to dissolve the partnership. Ebrahim wanted a *curator bonis* (a guardian of property) appointed to oversee the dissolution and the distribution of what he intended to be a cash payment to him of £7,000. Gandhi, pairing himself again with the more experienced Laughton on behalf of the partnership, resisted dissolution and the appointment of a guardian, arguing that dissolution would be fatal to the business. When Ebrahim's application for the appointment of a guardian came before the Supreme Court, Laughton argued that Roman-Dutch law controlled, providing that the dissolution of an at-will partnership cannot occur except "at a seasonable time."[9] With the Boer War clearly on the horizon and with the company having interests in both Natal and the Transvaal, Laughton and Gandhi had a strong argument that the timing of the dissolution was not seasonable—if the Roman-Dutch law applied. The two lawyers also asked that an arbitrator be appointed to settle matters between the parties. The Court agreed in a 2–1 decision that Roman-Dutch law did apply. It then referred the case to arbitration for the arbitrator to determine which time was, in fact, seasonable for dissolution and to address "all disputes and differences."[10] It was a good win for Laughton and Gandhi.

WAR

This litigation would not conclude quickly, not only because of its complexity but because the attention of the entire colony, including that of Gandhi, was about to be diverted in a very substantial way.[11] Tension had existed for a long time between the British, who controlled Natal and the Cape Colony, and the Boers, who controlled the Transvaal and the Orange Free State. So great was the animosity between these two opposing forces that the British government, indifferent at best to Indian rights in Natal, consistently opposed Boer anti-Indian legislation in the Transvaal as a part of its overall resistance to Boer influence throughout South Africa. When war broke out in October of 1899, the allegiance of the Natal Indian community to Britain was severely tested.[12] The inclination of Gandhi and many other Indians was to favor the Boers, whom they perceived as suffering under the same oppressive British boot. Gandhi had repeatedly argued, however, that Natal's Indians deserved treatment equal to that of other colonists because Indians were British subjects. To support the Boers now would give the lie to this position. Gandhi's own profession added yet more pressure on him to support the British as huge numbers of his colleagues at the bar abandoned their practices to join the British war effort. In the end, Gandhi concluded that it was important to the future of Indian rights that his community show its fidelity to Britain in its time of need. A demonstration of Indian loyalty during the war would earn Indians the respect of Britain and the colonists, who, Gandhi reasoned, would have to show greater respect for Indian economic and political rights after the war.[13]

With this philosophy in mind, Gandhi suspended his practice and organized a volunteer Indian Ambulance Corps in support of the British. In this effort he had the political support of both Escombe and Laughton and the active participation in the corps of Khan. Gandhi induced more than a thousand Indian men to serve. Of these about seven hundred were indentured servants whose employers had consented to their service. The remaining members were free Indians. While the corps included a sprinkling of professional men and a few artisans, virtually none of the volunteers came from the merchant class. Gandhi's clients were prepared to give money, but not their lives.

The men of the corps served with great distinction and bravery.[14] They earned the praise of the British authorities as well as the Natal press. Gandhi's postwar hopes were, however, to be shattered. While the colonial establishment was happy to accept the Indians' service during the war, it was just as quick to point out after the war that their service would not result in any heightened recognition of Indian rights.[15] Gandhi and the Indian community were particularly aggrieved by the position of the British home government that all the anti-Indian legislation enacted by the previous Boer regime in the Transvaal would remain on the books and be fully enforced by the new Transvaal government.[16]

There would be no more respect for the Indians after the war than there had been before the war. Gandhi's Boer war strategy was a spectacular failure.

INDENTURED SERVANTS

One happy result of Gandhi's decision to raise the Indian Ambulance Corps, however, was that it brought him into close contact with Indians who were of a social class quite different from that of his business clients. From his arrival in South Africa in 1893 to 1900, when the corps was disbanded, Gandhi rarely represented indentured servants or lower-class Indians who had been freed of their indentures, preferring instead to limit his clientele to wealthy merchants.[17] Indeed, he had sustained public criticism for failing to unite the Indian community. Within months of the disbanding of the corps, however, he was in court on at least four different occasions, defending indentured servants against charges made by their masters. The defenses mounted by Gandhi were not routine, lackluster defenses raised by a lawyer who was in the case out of a sense of obligation. Rather, these were robust, full-throated defenses.[18]

Gandhi's association with the indentured servant class in 1900 foreshadows the turn to nonmerchant Indians that he would make just a few years later in the Transvaal. For present purposes, however, his turn to the poor and the powerless must be seen in context. From the late 1890s until he departed for India in 1901, Gandhi's work with mistreated indentured servants, like his caring for the sick in the hospital and in the corps, was balm on the wound left by his failure to defeat the DLA.

THE ART OF APPEAL

So, too, was his entire private practice. In the months after his return from the war, he began to achieve more success than ever before. The key to his success could be found, in good measure, in his having been a good student of Laughton. Gandhi's senior by fifteen years, the more experienced Laughton was among Natal's best lawyers. He knew the law of procedure better than any of his contemporaries—and he was committed to using that knowledge as a powerful weapon against his opponents. It was his habit to rigorously square the actions of those whose decisions he challenged—whether a town council or a trial judge—against the procedures that they were bound to follow, rather than to challenge decisions on their merits. Laughton was particularly skilled at using this approach in appeals. He understood the dilemma all appellate judges face: they are concerned with fairness, but are substantially limited by their roles to reviewing lower-court decisions for errors generally having nothing to do with the equities. Laughton was especially good at developing compelling procedural arguments for parties who had been treated unjustly on the merits. He thus made it possible for a judge, sympathetic to Laughton's client on the merits but unable to reverse a lower court on those grounds, to rule for his client in the context of correcting a procedural error on the part of the original decision-maker.

This is an approach he handed down to Gandhi—and the student became quite adept at the master's art. Gandhi lost only one appeal in 1900. In addition to winning several indentured servant appeals, he won a reversal of a magistrate decision against one of his merchant clients, won the reversal of another magistrate decision in a property dispute, and won yet another reversal of a magistrate decision in a security case—with all of these victories coming on procedural grounds. This string of successes makes the middle of 1900 Gandhi's greatest sustained period of success at the bar to date. Gandhi knew, of course, that appellate courts were not free to relitigate the facts of a case but had to accept those from the trial court. He understood, however, what Laughton was teaching him: that when confronted with an appellant who had been the victim of some injustice, the appellate court would seize on procedural error as a convenient ground on which to reverse and do the fair thing. So, like his mentor, it was procedural error Gandhi used over and over to obtain equitable results. He was beginning to understand how the appellate game was played.

At the same time, there was good evidence that, when it was appropriate, Gandhi was unafraid to compromise with his clients' opponents in the service of fair settlements. Laughton applauds him for his openness to compromise, and the press hails him as a mediator. In his autobiography he happily tells of his affection for settling cases out of court.

With the disruption brought on by the war greatly lessened, and at the same time that Gandhi was beginning to win in court, the Camrooden partnership case began to stir back to life. Gandhi was a significant player in this dispute, appearing before the District Circuit Court by himself and before the Supreme Court with his mentor, Laughton. In addition to his courtroom work on behalf of the business, it is quite likely that Gandhi was also involved in the out-of-court arbitration work that was involved in the proposed dissolution of the partnership that would eventually take place. This case, involving one of South Africa's leading Indian businesses, meant not only lots of work but lots of fees for Gandhi.

Indeed, every indicator points to Gandhi's income having been quite substantial at this point in his career—he had major businesses for clients, he was able to take on an associate, he had significant cash flow, and he was able to offer others financial assistance.[19] And all this came in the context of record-high legal activity in the Durban courts[20]—activity that was practically monopolized by Gandhi and other Natal practitioners who had the advantage of superior English training in a bar whose "forensic talent," by Gandhi's own estimation, was not "of a very high order."[21]

A DIGNITARY

These were heady times for Gandhi: he was chalking up appellate victory after victory, he was making great amounts of money, and his services were sought after by the largest entities in the Indian business community.[22] With this success came demands for the presence of the prominent Indian barrister at public events. Beginning shortly after the disbanding of the Indian Ambulance Corps, Gandhi began regularly appearing at ceremonies taking place in the Indian community. He appeared in a variety of settings—at a celebration of early British victories, at a sports banquet, at several Indian school events, and at tributes to an Indian war hero, to the commander of British forces, and to the late queen. In addition to standing on the dais, Gandhi was frequently asked to speak. He spoke effectively; his speech on the Indian famine was praised as "touching" and as making a "deep impression."[23] He spoke to masses of people without being paralyzed by fear; the crowd to which Gandhi spoke on February 4, 1901, about the passing of Queen Victoria was estimated to be as large as five thousand.

Gandhi had arrived. He was a "dignitary," something the man who earlier had tried to learn to speak French and play the violin must have found, in some respects, satisfying. Would Gandhi's identification as a person of standing in the community, however, affect his interest and effectiveness in advocating for Indian rights? The unrelenting racism of the European colonists provided Gandhi with an opportunity to answer this question.

With the automobile not having fully arrived in 1900, Durban teemed with rickshaws. More than seventeen hundred of these hand-pulled carts were licensed to ply Durban's streets for fares at the turn of the century. The carts were usually operated by natives, but owned by others. When the town council enacted a by-law prohibiting Indians from owning rickshaws, Gandhi organized a petition to the governor, signed by a number of leading Indians.[24] Remarkably, the town council withdrew the by-law in the wake of Gandhi's protest. The council's work, however, was not done. Constructing a policy reminiscent of the discrimination against which Martin Luther King, Jr., and others would later campaign in the American South, the council then enacted a by-law establishing carts for use by "Europeans only." Gandhi did not encourage opposition to the by-law when it was first proposed. His view was that "it would be inconsistent with the self-respect of the Indian community to wish to insist on having the right to use the same ricksha used by the Europeans if the latter objected to share it with Indians, so long as the same kind of vehicle was available to the Indians also."[25]

In others words, Gandhi was prepared to accept separate-but-equal treatment of Indians. And, indeed, for a short time after the by-law went into effect, there were sufficient rickshaws without racial restrictions to serve the needs of Indians. Moreover, Indians found that those among them who were neatly dressed could get rickshaws. It was not long, however, before the town council gave the police instructions to strictly enforce the by-law, and soon enough Indians were without service. Gandhi recognized that he had made a mistake in not opposing the by-law at the start.

Europeans objected to riding in carts that had carried "dirty" Indians.[26] Gandhi approached the town council, asking not that it repeal the by-law, but that it relax its enforcement by permitting rickshaw operators to restrict their passengers not to Europeans but to those who were clean and well attired. Despite Gandhi's new bond with the Indian underclass, he was still prepared to sacrifice their interests for those of the upper class. His request, nonetheless, was denied. Accordingly, he once again petitioned the Natal governor, who earlier had approved the by-law, asking that the by-law be canceled or amended.[27] Gandhi forwarded a copy of the petition to the town council, which discussed Gandhi's request but took no action. Nor did the governor accede to the Indians' request that the by-law be canceled or amended. It remained on the books and the police continued to enforce it.

In both his letter to the town council and his petition to the governor, Gandhi stated that he believed the by-law to be invalid. For his authority he cited Section 75 of Law Number 19 of 1892. That section stated that municipal by-laws are invalid if they fail to meet certain procedural requirements or are repugnant to "the general spirit and intent of the Laws in force within the Colony."

Gandhi did not argue, as Laughton might have, that the by-law violated any of the procedural requirements of Section 75. Perhaps Gandhi did not have the facts in his corner to support a procedural argument. Rather, he argued that the by-law was invalid because it was "opposed to the general spirit of the British Constitution and the Laws of the Colony."[28]

Gandhi did not act on this argument. He and his clients did not take the issue of the legality of the by-law to the courts. There was no litigation. If there could be no hope of persuading the courts to invalidate the DLA on the grounds that race discrimination was at odds with the fundamental law of the British Empire, how could there be any hope of invalidating the rickshaw by-law on the same grounds? Yet invalidation was the relief that Gandhi implicitly threatened to seek in the courts. Theodore Roosevelt once counseled that one should "speak softly and carry a big stick." In this instance, Gandhi spoke loudly and carried no stick.

INDIA ONCE MORE

For the next year Gandhi's practice of law becomes quite ordinary. He appears before the Supreme Court twice in the same case—and loses both times. He slogs through the Camrooden partnership dissolution matter. He does some bankruptcy work. He continues to have Khan assume some of his lower-level work. Within three days in May, Gandhi loses two substantial commercial cases, both contract cases for his merchant clients. Strangely, he is the victim of his own procedural errors both times.

By September, with the bar celebrating the ascension of Henry Bale to the chief justice's seat with an elaborate dinner and with Gandhi's attendance being noted by the local press, Gandhi realizes that something has gone awry. His attack on the DLA has failed in the end.[29] As for the rickshaw controversy, he has resurrected the petition strategy in opposition to the town council's rickshaw rules only to achieve an unhappy result: Indians have to walk. They are not even allowed to ride in rickshaws they themselves own.

As for his private practice, he is aware of what it is doing to him. It is making him rich.

This is not what Gandhi had intended. Just five years earlier, in writing to a lawyer whom he was attempting to recruit to join him in South Africa, he had said:

> I cannot be too plain in saying that no one in our position should go to South Africa with a view to pile [up] money. You should go there with a spirit of self-sacrifice. You should keep riches at an arm's length. They may then woo you. If you bestow your glances on them, they are such a coquette that you are sure to be slighted. This is my experience in South Africa.[30]

Gandhi did not always follow his own advice. His wealth had caused him to embark on what he called a life of "ease and comfort."[31] He notes, in particular, that he had furnished his house "with care." Feeling uncomfortable with this style of living, he undertook efforts to simplify his life and keep his wealth in perspective. He notes in his autobiography that he began to launder and starch his own shirts and cut his own hair, but that his initial efforts were less than completely successful, earning him the ridicule of his bar colleagues.

Gandhi was, as he says, "impervious to ridicule."[32] He was not, however, impervious to the tide of money and approval washing over him, nor was he impervious to the frustrations he was suffering by his inability to gain equality for his race.

He decided to return to India. He would turn his practice over to R. K. Kahn and leave his role in the movement to Khan and Mansukhlal Nazar.[33]

By 1901 Gandhi was an important leader in South Africa's Indian community. Indians looked up to him as an educated, articulate, and influential professional who had helped many of them as individuals when they were in need and had fought for the rights of the entire community. Not surprisingly, then, there was a huge outpouring of affection for Gandhi upon his departure. The forms in which this affection was expressed, however, did nothing but discomfort him and confirm him in his decision to leave. At an elaborate farewell ceremony, the Indian community—his clients prominent among them—deluged him with gifts: a plaque of gold and ivory, a diamond ring and pin, a gold necklace, watch, chain, coins, and, according to the *Natal Advertiser*, "many more presents." He also received the praise of the establishment figures in attendance—one judge stated that he "wished they had a thousand Gandhi's appearing before the bar"—as well as congratulatory notes from, among others, the premier, the colonial secretary, and the justices of the Natal Supreme Court.[34]

The practice of law, in tandem with his political work, had brought this thirty-two-year-old barrister great wealth, universal approval—and an immense sense of loss.

It was time to retreat. It was time to go home to India.

ELEVEN

Sacrifice

> I think it is wrong to expect certainties in this world, where all
> else but God that is Truth is an uncertainty. All that appears and
> happens about and around us is uncertain, transient. But there is
> a Supreme Being hidden therein as a Certainty, and one would
> be blessed if one could catch glimpse of that Certainty and hitch
> one's wagon to it.
>
> GANDHI, reflecting on his call to South Africa

THE NATAL IN WHICH GANDHI practiced law was a backwater colony
with a backwater legal arena. Gandhi achieved material success there not
only because of his hard work and the loyalty of the Indian community to
one of its own, but also because his competition at the bar for business and
prestige was limited both in number and in intellectual sophistication.

THE INDIAN STAGE

Things were different in India. Rajkot and Bombay, the two places Gandhi
would eventually attempt to set up law practices, were thick with all manner
of practitioners, with many of the country's leading attorneys practicing in
Bombay. Aside from his British education, there was nothing to distinguish
Gandhi from his many competitors at the bar. The natural monopoly he
enjoyed in South Africa was set on its head in India.

Nor did he have the benefit of preeminence in political leadership. The
Indian National Congress was a well-established institution led by giants of
Indian nationalism who were hardly aware of the existence of lawyer Gandhi
and his Natal Indian Congress. Despite these realities, Gandhi set about to
enter nationalist politics at the highest level and to earn a living as an Indian
advocate.[1]

In both of these endeavors he was hobbled by the need to recover from his
experience in South Africa. In some way that Gandhi never fully discloses,

his health was seriously damaged in Natal to the point that his physician and friend, Dr. Pranjivan Mehta, recommended in early 1902 that Gandhi take "complete rest" for at least two or three months.[2]

Prior to this recommendation and just weeks after arriving in India, Gandhi managed to get the South African Indian question on the agenda of the upcoming Congress meeting in Calcutta. On the train from Bombay to Calcutta, he lobbied his fellow advocate Sir Pherozeshah Mehta for his help in having the Congress pass a resolution in support of the South African Indian cause. Mehta was less than encouraging, telling Gandhi "it seems nothing can be done for you. Of course, we will pass the resolution you want. But what rights have we in our own country? I believe that, so long as we have no power in our own land, you cannot fare better in the Colonies."[3]

In Gandhi's prepared remarks in support of his resolution, he identified what the Congress could do for South African Indians. Gandhi explained that the British had not yet decided whether to enforce the anti-Indian rules the Boers had in place prior to their defeat in the war. The Congress could help put pressure on Secretary of State for the Colonies Joseph Chamberlain to decide in favor of the Indians.

Gandhi had a second substantive point. Without seeing the irony of it, he urged the professional men in his audience, including barristers, to move to South Africa to help in the fight for Indian civil rights.

It is unlikely Gandhi's audience heard this plea. At nearly 11 P.M. the Congress meeting was drawing to a close, with the delegates growing restless and unanimously passing resolutions while paying virtually no attention to them. It was under these circumstances that Mehta had to be reminded by Gopal Krishna Gokhale that Gandhi's resolution still needed to be presented.

With Mehta's permission, Gandhi approached the audience and, trembling, read his resolution. Like the resolutions before his, it passed unanimously—and mindlessly. Now Gandhi had five minutes to speak to an impatient audience about the resolution. What happened next was painfully reminiscent of Gandhi's other attempts to speak in India. In his own words: "The morning found me worrying about my speech. What was I to say in five minutes? I had prepared myself fairly well but the words would not come to me. I had decided not to read my speech but to speak *ex tempore*. But the facility for speaking that I had acquired in South Africa seemed to have left me for the moment."[4]

Gandhi was still struggling with his remarks when the bell indicating that the speaker had two of his five minutes left rang. Mistakenly thinking that the bell signaled his time was up, he broke off his talk and took his seat. It had been more than nine years since his nervousness had made him unable to conduct a small trial in an Indian courtroom, and more than five years since his nervousness had made him unable to deliver a speech to a public meeting in Bombay. Now, at thirty-two years old and with almost a decade of law practice under his belt, he found that he was still not ready to act on the large Indian stage.

Gandhi's failure at high-pressure public speaking might have misled some of his listeners to think that there was nothing inside the man worth noting. Three episodes, closely linked in time with Gandhi's failed speech, would have proved them wrong:

- Sanitation at the Congress meeting site was horrible. The delegates shocked Gandhi by their failure to use and maintain latrines. To the astonishment of his fellow delegates, Gandhi cleaned his own latrine— work that the others thought belonged to scavengers.

- Stunned by the Congress' disorganization, he asked whether there was work to do. A Congress functionary, not knowing Gandhi was a barrister, gave him some trivial clerical work. Gandhi threw himself into it without complaint.

- The month after his failed Congress speech, Gandhi drew on his courage and gave another talk in Calcutta. The record does not disclose how Gandhi dealt with his nervousness. A press report, however, recounts Gandhi's remarks: "The hatred of the Colonials against them [South African Indians] was no doubt intense, but what Mr. Gandhi proposed was to conquer that hatred by love."[5]

These themes of humble service and uncompromising good will toward the opponent would appear with great frequency and be developed in depth first on Gandhi's return to South Africa and then later in India.

While Gandhi's attempt to make the treatment of South African Indians an issue for the Congress failed, he was able to establish a relationship with one important nationalist leader, Gopal Krishna Gokhale. Gokhale's influence over Gandhi was both personal and political. Gandhi was struck by the efficiency and single-mindedness with which Gokhale conducted his affairs. Gandhi would later write: "To see Gokhale at work was as much a joy as an education. He never wasted a minute. His private relations and friendships were all for the public good."[6] Gokhale provided a model that the already quite efficient and single-minded Gandhi could emulate.

Gandhi was also taken with Gokhale's admiration for a number of prominent figures in the Indian legal community. Gokhale impressed upon Gandhi the devotion these men had both to their profession and to the nationalist cause, a devotion with which Gandhi could certainly identify.

Gokhale and Gandhi became quick and close friends, and while Gokhale was easily able to introduce Gandhi to a number of leading public figures in the Indian community, he apparently could not help Gandhi with a larger and more immediate crisis.

Gandhi had no money.

DUNNING IN RAJKOT

After a month of living with Gokhale, after many weeks of touring India and Burma in early 1902, and after he had handed over the savings he had accumulated in Natal to his extended family (greatly exceeding the amount it had expended in seeing him through his London legal studies), the barrister lacked not only good health but now financial resources too. Moreover, he did not even have access to the basic tool of his trade—a decent typewriter.

After more than three months in India, Gandhi managed to open a practice. Gokhale had urged him to practice in Bombay, where he could help with the work of the Congress, but Gandhi lacked the confidence needed to practice in the Bombay environment. He was plagued, as he would later write, by the "unpleasant memories of past failure." In addition, he "still hated as poison the use of flattery for getting briefs." He resolved instead to practice in the less challenging surroundings provided by Rajkot, in his home state of Gujarat.

His first order of business was to drum up some money by dunning his South African clients. When he wrote to the Natal managing partner of Camrooden and Company, Gandhi was plain: "You have not acknowledged any of my letters. I shall thank you to let me have [a] draft for the balance of my bill which I need badly."[7] In early June, after almost another month, he wrote to Nazar and Khan, asking them to have the NIC send him money to cover his expenses on behalf of the South African Indian cause. In the course of this letter he stated that he had not expected his "pecuniary position to be so bad as it is."[8]

Fortunately for Gandhi, his health, while still far from good, had improved sufficiently for him to take on some litigation in Rajkot. Kevalram Mavji Dave, the vakil who on the death of Gandhi's father had advocated that Gandhi train in the law, referred three cases to him. Two were low-level appeals, both of which Gandhi won. The third was an original case in Jamnagar, a town to the west of Rajkot. While we know nothing about the substance of the case, we do know that it was a "rather important" one in Gandhi's estimation, causing him to question his ability to undertake it. Dave assured him by saying, "Winning or losing is no concern of yours. You will simply try your best, and I am of course there to assist you."[9]

Gandhi's preparation for the case was typical of his best work in South Africa. He prepared with his usual meticulousness, meeting extensively with Dave and drawing on his recently acquired knowledge of the Indian Evidence Act. In emulation of Pherozeshah Mehta, whose success Gandhi believed was based in large part on his mastery of evidence law, Gandhi had studied the act on his voyage from South Africa. Now that knowledge, as well as his seasoning in South Africa, stood him in good stead. He won the case and "gained some confidence."[10]

CONFIDENCE IN BOMBAY

The win made Gandhi think he might be able to survive in Bombay, after all. Not entirely certain of his prospects there, however, he continued to stay on in Rajkot. Eventually Dave came to him: "Gandhi, we will not suffer you to vegetate here. You must settle in Bombay."[11] There were now two influential people in Gandhi's life urging him to go to Bombay.

Gandhi's concern about having enough work to keep him afloat there was met with Dave's assurance that he would help provide him with sufficient work: "We shall bring you down here sometimes as a big barrister from Bombay and drafting work we shall send you there. It lies with us vakils to make or mar a barrister. You have proved your worth in Jamnagar . . . and I have therefore not the least anxiety about you. You are destined to do public work, and we will not allow you to be buried in Kathiawad."[12]

Gandhi was hesitant; Mehta had warned him that Bombay would eat up any savings from Natal he might have. Accordingly, he wanted a little more money to use to set up shop in Bombay. At the time Dave urged the move upon him, Gandhi was expecting a remittance from Natal. Two weeks later he received an amount in excess of 3,000 rupees.

He was off to Bombay. When he leased a room on the second floor of the Aga Khan building, opposite the High Court, for 20 rupees a month, it was Gandhi's intention to give Bombay "a year's trial."[13]

He seems to have had a bit more time for unproductive activities than he wished. He attended court-sponsored moots and also took in High Court arguments—but not to learn anything, as he later candidly admitted. He was in the well-ventilated courthouse, "like other fresh barristers," to enjoy "the soporific breeze coming straight from the sea." He "loung[ed] about the High Court" for a somewhat more elevated reason, as well: he wanted to make contact with solicitors who could send him clients.[14]

By November of 1902 Gandhi had been practicing in Bombay for about five months. During this time, he never had a case before the High Court. He seemed, however, to have finally jettisoned the lack of confidence that had haunted him earlier, for he felt that it was but a matter of time before he would have a case requiring him to appear before the High Court, despite the warnings of local solicitors who told him he would have to wait a long time to get cases from them.[15] Even as early as August, when the work was "uphill," he had a certain confidence. He appreciated the "regular life and the struggle that Bombay impose[d]" on him.[16]

After a few months he felt he was doing well enough financially. Just as work from the big trading firms in South Africa had carried him there, so too did it in Bombay. His former clients sent work his way. This work and the drafting work sent to him by D. B. Shukla, Gandhi's Rajkot barrister friend, provided him with enough work such that he could say in November that his income was sufficient to meet his expenses. While his expenses were higher than he had anticipated, and while he was not overflowing with confidence, Gandhi was "not . . . anxious about the future."[17] One senses that Gandhi believed his practice would grow and prosper.

SOUTH AFRICA CALLS

When Gandhi left Natal, his fellow Indians there had extracted from him a promise to return to South Africa "if, within a year, the community should need [him]."[18] Gandhi was not happy about this pledge. He understood from the beginning how disruptive keeping it would be. In fact, shortly after he arrived in India, he wrote to his colleagues in South Africa, asking "that, if our people propose to enforce the promise made by me, it should be done while my plans are yet unsettled, though . . . there is no such condition attached to the promise."[19] Then, at the end of March, he wrote to Khan and Nazar, repeating this request and stating that it "would be a gracious act to free me unless it is to be enforced in the near future."[20]

The request that Gandhi dreaded came just as he felt he was finally settling down. The South African Indians wanted him to first visit London on their behalf and then come to South Africa. His immediate response was to say "no—unless it was absolutely necessary." In support of his resistance, he cited his children's illness and his own lack of strength. Adding mystery to the exact nature of the condition he had brought with him from South Africa, Gandhi stated that "I do not yet feel strong enough for the mental strain a visit to London and South Africa would require."[21]

Gandhi negotiated by telegram with his correspondents in South Africa, who appear to have addressed, if not fully allayed, his concerns about the strain. He also seems to have eliminated the London leg of the trip. It was Gandhi's understanding that the South African Indians wanted him back principally to help them lobby Secretary of State for the Colonies Chamberlain, whose visit to South Africa was imminent.[22] This was an attractive mission to Gandhi. When the South Africans remitted the funds necessary for Gandhi's travel, there were no reasons left for Gandhi not to come.

Except deeply personal ones. He was in the process of establishing himself professionally in Bombay. He had secured a nice suburban home for his family. His children needed his attention. He had a comfortable existence, taking a first-class train every day to a job that did not seem to overly tax him. But his countrymen needed him and he felt a sense of obligation to them. He would go.

Gandhi, however, wanted help. He wanted to take as many as six barristers back to South Africa with him. He lobbied his friend Devchand Parekh and other bar colleagues to throw their lot in with him, assuring them that if they "were to come with one eye on their living and the other on public work, much of the burden may be distributed—not to speak of the relief in the pressure here."[23] Gandhi's entreaties fell on deaf ears. No one would come with him.

His immediate family, too, would stay behind, with Shukla looking after them. After all, Gandhi thought, he would only be gone for a year or so.

What Gandhi could not foresee was that there was something important in South Africa for him. His work as a barrister in Bombay had no political aspect to it. It was simply a way of earning a living. While he had failed in India to get heavily involved in nationalist work, South Africa was calling him to do so. In South Africa he could use a good deal of his professional skill and time to serve the cause.

In India, his practice was his job.

In South Africa, it would become his vocation.

TWELVE

Transition and the Transvaal

> If we are swamped by these people, trade by Europeans will be impossible, and we shall one and all become subjected to the horrible danger inseparable from close contact with a large body of uncleanly citizens, with whom syphilis and leprosy are common diseases, and hideous immorality a matter of course.
>
> *The Press*, Pretoria, South African Republic, April 5, 1895

> The Transvaal Government have gone so far in their prejudice, that the whole of the Republic, although the soil is very fruitful, remains a desert of dust.
>
> GANDHI, May 18, 1895

WHEN GANDHI OPENED HIS LAW office in Johannesburg in 1903, it was a time of new beginnings for the thirty-three-year-old lawyer. His Durban practice was behind him, as was his struggle to establish himself in India. It was also a time of new beginnings for the Transvaal. The last armed elements of a stubborn Afrikaner resistance had been extinguished and the South African Republic with it. The Transvaal was a British colony.

BOER RULE

Before, during, and after the British, there were the Afrikaners, the descendants of the Dutch who settled South Africa beginning in 1652. Having migrated to the interior from their original settlement in the Cape, the Boers, as they are sometimes also known, named their country that lay beyond the Vaal River the South African Republic. The Republic, established in 1858, took in a land of vast mineral resources. The Afrikaners did a poor job of managing their new government, however, resulting in British annexation of the area in 1877.

This phase of British control did not last long. A war for Afrikaner independence broke out in 1880, resulting in an odd 1881 settlement that permitted the Afrikaners to have internal independence while the British controlled external affairs.

In the 1880s and 1890s, the country's extraction industries began to mature. Diamond production was concentrated under the wing of the powerful company DeBeers Consolidated, and gold mining, taking off from the 1886 discovery of gold on the Witwatersrand, came under the control of a few large entities. Just as the plantations in Natal demanded a large supply of labor, so did these mining industries. Unlike Natal's natives, however, the Republic's natives did not resist employment under the European yoke. They manned the mines. When a shortage of labor did develop (natives often worked just long enough to raise the funds to buy farms), the Europeans did not replicate the Natal strategy by bringing in waves of indentured Indians. Rather, the Republic turned to China, which, unlike India, did not demand that its workers be permitted to stay in South Africa after their terms of work were complete.[1] Many of the first Indians who did come to the Transvaal in the early 1880s were merchants in search of profit,[2] or Natal Indians who had served out their terms of indenture and were now in search of employment in the Transvaal. The lack of reliance by the European establishment on indentured Indian labor, and the subsequent absence of discriminatory legislation aimed particularly at them, would, as historian Maureen Swan points out, have an enormous effect in later years on Indian politics in South Africa and on Gandhi's ability to mobilize the lower classes of the Indian community.

With control of the Cape Colony and Natal in British hands and control of the South African Republic and the Orange Free State in Afrikaner hands, the stage was set in the 1890s for a struggle over who would control the whole of South Africa. When Joseph Chamberlain took the reins of the British Colonial Office in 1895 as its secretary, he was clear in his intent to establish British paramountcy over South Africa. To achieve this ambition, he used as his proxy Cecil Rhodes, then not only the force behind DeBeers but also the prime minister of the Cape. It was Rhodes' plan to invade and conquer the South African Republic by using police from Bechuanaland, led by Leander Jameson, while simultaneously instigating an uprising among the non-Afrikaner English-speaking population (known as "uitlanders") of the mining region in the Republic.

The Jameson party was captured by Transvaal forces when Rhodes was unable to rally the uitlanders. In the wake of this embarrassment, Chamberlain took another tack. In 1897, he appointed Alfred Milner as

Britain's high commissioner for South Africa. Milner harbored a deep dislike of the Afrikaners and possessed an equally intense allegiance to the notion of British superiority. Milner's first hope, that the Republic would disintegrate from within, faded when he watched Paul Kruger easily win his fourth term as president of the Republic in 1898. He also found himself unable to flood the Transvaal with enough British settlers to dominate the political system. Milner's fallback plan was to find "fault with every action taken" by the Republic and to refuse "any compromise" and reject "every concession the Republic offered."[3] The high commissioner's goading worked. Sensing that the British were preparing for war, the Republic and the Afrikaners struck first, attacking the British on October 11, 1899. In the end, however, the Afrikaners were no match for the British. By 1900 the British had established control over Johannesburg and Pretoria, and by 1902 they had overcome the last traces of Afrikaner military resistance.

The Afrikaners lost the war, but they won the peace. They negotiated a peace treaty with the British that expressed an "expectation of ultimate political autonomy." Indeed, it was under the shelter of this expectation that the British, who had sometimes protested against the discriminatory treatment of nonwhite British subjects under the Republic's rule, permitted the Afrikaners to continue to enforce certain racial legislation after 1902.

LAW 3 OF 1885

South African Republic Law 3 of 1885 was the most prominent of the old republic's racial laws.[4] Subtitled "Coolies, Arabs and other Asiatics," the legislation unapologetically discriminated against "persons belonging to any of the native races of Asia, including the so-called Coolies, Arabs, Malays, and Mahomedan subjects of the Turkish Empire." The act denied these classes of people citizenship rights, prohibited them from owning fixed property, required registration and a £25 registration fee, and, notably, permitted the government to restrict Indians and others to certain locations determined by the government.

To understand the legal and political environment of the Transvaal into which Gandhi entered in 1903, it is necessary to understand something of the history of Law 3 and Gandhi's eventual involvement with it.[5] The agreement that ended the 1880 war for Afrikaner independence was known as the Pretoria Convention of 1881, later amended by the London Convention of

1884. Article 14 of the London Convention granted full citizenship rights in the South African Republic to "all persons, other than natives."[6] In early 1885 a question arose as to whether Article 14 prevented the Republic from discriminating against the growing Indian population. Europeans took the position that Article 14 did not give Indians citizenship rights. Acting in conciliatory fashion, the British response was to suggest an amendment of the convention that would permit the Republic to deprive Indian manual laborers (pejoratively known as "coolies") of citizenship rights just as it did natives. The British were opposed, however, to any restriction of the rights of Indian merchants—persons who belonged, according to the British, to "a superior class." Because the Republic wanted to discriminate against all Indians, the parties did not come to an agreement on this point, and the convention was not amended.

The Republic's Afrikaners then moved the issue to the Volksraad, the Republic's parliament, which was the target of complaints from European citizens that Indians were unsanitary and that Indian merchants were a threat to the livelihood of white merchants. The result was Law 3 of 1885, which, after it was amended in 1886, granted the government of the Republic "the right, for sanitation purposes, to point out for *habitation* by them ["Coolies, Arabs, Malays, and Mahomedan subjects of the Turkish Empire"] fixed streets, wards and Locations."[7]

Three years after its enactment, the law was challenged by an Indian business, Ismail Suleiman and Company. Suleiman had applied for a license to do business in the Middelburg district of the Republic, but the landdrost (a type of district magistrate) turned the company down. The landdrost offered to give Suleiman a license for a location outside of town. Not satisfied with this decision, Suleiman went to the Republic's High Court in the late summer of 1888 and asked it to order the landdrost to issue a license for his original Middelburg location.[8]

George Morice, Suleiman's attorney, argued that the government did not have the authority under Law 3 to restrict Indian businesses to specified locations. He rested his argument on the clear text of the act, which plainly and only stated that the government possessed the power to specify locations for "*habitation*."[9] Morice thus demonstrated the obvious distinction between living ("*wonen*"), which was regulated by Law 3, and trading, which was not.

The court's response to this argument was patently disingenuous: "Such a distinction cannot be drawn, for it cannot be said that a person does not *live* in a place simply because he does not sleep there; otherwise the portion of a town where traders carry on business, but where they do not sleep, might be described as an uninhabited locality."[10]

Ignoring the unambiguous text of Law 3, Chief Justice John Kotze, writing for a unanimous court, buttressed this response by relying on grounds that were more honest, but not more legitimate: "It would be inconsistent with the spirit of the law to draw such a distinction. The intention of Law 3 ... was to draw a broad distinction between Asiatics and Europeans in the Transvaal and therefore the interpretation must be against the Indians rather than in their favour."[11]

This decision, which flew in the face of Law 3's plain meaning, was a defeat for the Indian business community and a victory for European businesspeople who feared competition. If Indian merchants could be kept at a distance from the main body of the population, the markets would fall under the complete domination of European interests.

ARBITRATION AND ABSURDITY

The *Suleiman* decision was not regarded at the time as a test case and did not receive much attention.[12] As a result, the question of how Law 3 ought to be interpreted continued to fester. Seven years after the High Court issued its opinion in *Suleiman* and ten years after the enactment of Law 3, the British and the Afrikaners were still quarreling as to its meaning. To break the impasse, the two sides agreed in 1895 to submit the matter to binding arbitration.[13] Because of his reputation among some Europeans for impartiality, the parties turned to the chief justice of the Orange Free State, Melius de Villiers, as the arbitrator. The Indian merchant community's cry that de Villiers was biased against Indians was ignored by the British high commissioner.[14]

The British were represented in the arbitration by advocate Malcolm W. Searle. The Indians, choosing not to be represented by Gandhi, who was unlicensed outside Natal and inexperienced, hired prominent Johannesburg advocate Charles Leonard.[15] Leonard does not seem to have taken any formal part in the arbitration proceedings—not surprising, since the Indians were not a formal party. The South African Republic was represented by Ewald Esselen, the state attorney.

With straight faces, the Afrikaners claimed that "for habitation" meant "places of business as well as the sleeping places of the coloured persons mentioned in the law" and that the Republic was therefore entitled to prevent

Indians "from carrying on businesses in villages or other places than those pointed out" by the government. Moreover, the Afrikaners argued, the original intent of the parties in agreeing to Article 14 of the London Convention was to include "only Europeans and their descendants" within the meaning of the term "persons."[16] When Article 14 was written, the parties were only contemplating two groups, Europeans and natives. The Afrikaners believed that the British were unfairly using a change in circumstances—the influx of British Indians—to interpret Article 14 to protect a racial minority never intended by the parties to be protected.

Concerned that the new law would indeed be used to force Indian merchants in Pretoria, Johannesburg, and elsewhere in the Republic to move to out-of-the-way locations that would effectively put them out of business,[17] the British argued that Law 3 violated the London Convention. To this the British added what should have been the obvious point that there was "nothing in the law which prevents Her Majesty's Asiatic subjects from carrying on their business or trade in any portion of a town" and that "for habitation" should be construed to refer to "the dwelling places of such traders and not to places of business."[18]

De Villiers heard the arguments of the parties and received documentary evidence in hearings conducted on March 16, 18, and 19; he rendered his opinion less than two weeks later, on April 2.[19] The opinion was a masterpiece of evasion, ambiguity, and indecision. The parties, who were looking for an arbitrated decision, did not get what they paid for.

On the one hand, de Villiers held that because it might possibly have been the intention of the British to protect the interests of British Indians by agreeing to the "all persons" language of Article 14, the British were correct when they "insisted upon a literal interpretation of Article 14."[20] On the other hand, the arbitrator found that the British had given their assent to Law 3 and that by doing so, "they were bound by the indisputable principle that the legislative enactments of a country are subject to the exclusive interpretation of the tribunals of that country, and they must be held to have acquiesced in that principle.... [P]ersons who settle in a foreign country are not only subject to its laws, but also to the interpretation of those laws by the legally appointed tribunals."[21]

De Villiers concluded his opinion by holding that

on the questions that have arisen ... in the application of Law No. 3 ... , with reference to the interpretation and effect of that law, the decisions of the competent tribunals of the South African Republic must be considered as decisive. . . .

As regards the question whether the words "for habitation" . . . have reference only to dwelling places, and not to business premises, . . . it will be with the tribunals of the . . . Republic to give the necessary decision thereon.[22]

The South African Republic, which surely could have availed itself of its own presumably partisan courts, had instead agreed with Great Britain to refer to a neutral arbitrator the very question the arbitrator had now referred back to the Republic, on grounds that the Republic could decide the question by itself! The decision, Gandhi was to later correctly observe, "left the Indians entirely where they were."[23]

Within days of the decision, Gandhi was called upon by several leading merchants to take action on their behalf. He drafted a rather brief petition to the British agent in Pretoria in which he pointed out that any decision of the High Court of the Republic would be a "foregone conclusion" in light of the *Suleiman* case. The Indians were destined to lose. Gandhi then argued that "the Arbitrator did not decide the question in terms of the reference to him," suggesting that the British government should therefore reject the decision.[24] The British agent submitted the petition to the high commissioner, who, in turn, sent it to the British government.

Approximately two weeks later, Gandhi produced a far more substantial petition, this one to Lord Ripon, serving his last year as colonial secretary in London and known for his sympathies to the Indians. This petition, unlike the first, was on behalf of the entire range of Indian economic interests, from laborers in hotels to the largest trading houses. After attacking de Villiers as biased, Gandhi amplifies the argument he made in the first petition that the decision was void. Gandhi's argument is clear and tight. It concludes with the assertion that the ruling was void on two grounds: it went beyond the limits of the charge given the arbitrator (to rule on Law 3) and it delegated the decision when the arbitrator had no authority to do so.

Why does Gandhi fail to raise the most basic—and compelling—legal argument available to the Indians? Gandhi could have made a simple but powerful textual argument, namely, that the wording of Law 3 does not provide for segregated *trade* locations, only for *residential* segregation. In Gandhi's defense, it might be said that he realized that the substance of the arbitration case could not be relitigated and that the most persuasive argument was one that attacked the procedural correctness of the decision—a là Laughton.

While Gandhi might be faulted for leaving out his most telling point, credit is owed him for having a realpolitik understanding of the controversy. He spends more than half of this lengthy document rebutting the given reason for trade segregation, the insanitary habits of the Indians. Here Gandhi is at his lawyerly best, supporting his petition with affidavits from European physicians and businesspeople, all attesting to the cleanliness of the Transvaal Indians. Having dispatched the sanitation argument, Gandhi names the real reason for the Republic's discrimination against the Indian—"trade jealousy."[25] The Indian trader was able to live more cheaply than the European trader; hence, his overhead was less, his profit margin smaller, and his prices lower. The Europeans simply could not compete with the Indians. One hundred years before it became a household world, globalization had struck the Republic's European traders.

UNSEEMLINESS

The petition also reveals a shocking and unsavory side to the Indian perspective, one articulated by Gandhi on more than just this occasion. The petition quotes with approval an editorial from the *Cape Times* of April 13, 1895, which states that it is difficult to understand why some would place the Indians "in the same category as the half-heathen Native and confine him to Locations, and subject him to the harsher laws by which the Transvaal Kaffir is governed."[26] Gandhi himself attacks the inclination of some Europeans to "degrade the Indian to the position of the Kaffir."[27] Later Gandhi would write that Indians were "undoubtedly infinitely superior to the Kaffirs"[28] and would publicly protest that the actions of the Republic had resulted in merchant Indians being "generally classed among the raw Zulus."[29] In an 1896 speech in Bombay, he had this to say: "Ours is a continual struggle against a degradation sought to be inflicted on us by the Europeans, who desire to degrade us to the level of the raw Kaffir whose occupation is hunting, and whose sole ambition is to collect a certain number of cattle to buy a wife with and, then, pass his life in indolence and nakedness."[30]

Here is an argument based not on the status of Indians as British subjects, but on class and race. Gandhi is arguing that because the Indian is in a higher position than that of the native African, the Indian ought to be treated better. As Maureen Swan points out, Gandhi's Indian merchant clients in Natal had promoted their case to the British in large part by distinguishing themselves from Indian laborers. In the Transvaal, with far fewer Indian laborers than Natal, Gandhi and the merchants took pains to distinguish the merchants from natives.

Gandhi, who would later lead a campaign in India on behalf of India's "untouchables,"[31] and whose philosophy and practice of nonviolence would later inspire Martin Luther King, Jr., and the movement for African American civil rights,[32] was blind to the irony in his own argument in 1895. He seized upon European prejudice toward Africans as a convenient weapon in his own fight against European prejudice toward Indians. The pragmatist in Gandhi led him to speak in racist terms to a racist government. There was no saintly rising above the sinfulness of the time.

A CHALLENGE TO LAW 3

In the end this particular aspect, and indeed the whole, of the Indians' argument won them nothing. Chamberlain accepted the legitimacy of de Villiers' decision (known as the Bloemfontein Award) and dismissed the Indians' plea for help, rejecting what the British authorities themselves conceded was Gandhi's very able legal argument that the decision was void.

In the wake of the Bloemfontein Award, the Republic felt that it had a free hand in dealing with the Indian community, imposing restrictions on the use of sidewalks and public transportation by Indians,[33] and, of greater import, enacting a restrictive immigration law that targeted Indians. The response of Gandhi and the Indians was surely one of desperation. They sought an interpretation of Law 3 from the High Court of the South African Republic that would be favorable to the Indian community.

At first it was their hope that this test case would be financed by the British government.[34] In pleading his case with the British agent in Pretoria, Gandhi sought funding from the British on two principal grounds. He argued that it was only the foolishness of the British in deciding to go to arbitration and in ignoring the Indians' protest of de Villiers as the arbitrator in that case that created the very necessity for the test case. Gandhi also pled poverty, an odd argument from one who would later argue against the relocation of his Transvaal business clients on the grounds that relocation would jeopardize his clients' sizeable collective assets—assets totaling £375,000.[35]

What makes Gandhi's argumentative writing so often effective is his unusual fidelity to the truth, a devotion that has him admit the strength of his opponents' arguments and the weaknesses of his own. This straightforward approach suited Gandhi's nature and earned him many an open ear. It is not clear why he deviated from this course in his letter to the British agent. What is clear is that this incident, while not as weighty a matter as Gandhi's earlier use of a racial argument, marks another occasion on which Gandhi uncharacteristically permits his ends to dictate his means.

In any event, neither argument was successful. British high commissioner Alfred Milner also weighed in, arguing two points to his superiors: one, the British, already committed to having an attorney hold a "watching brief," would incur no extra costs by representing the Indian cause; and two, the Indians would receive competent representation from counsel hired by the British. Chamberlain was unpersuaded. He believed that the Indians would represent themselves well and that, if they lost, the Indians would have only themselves to blame. Chamberlain also was wary of the diplomatic repercussions that would flow from direct British involvement, a strange consideration from an administration doing everything it could to assert British paramountcy in South Africa.[36] In the end, the British refused their help and left the Indians to proceed on their own.

After a number of delays, the case was brought on February 28, 1898, in the name of Tayob Hajee Khan Mohamed, a Pretoria-based entrepreneur with a variety of business interests in the Republic. Ironically, this was the same Mohamed whom Dada Abdulla had sued earlier in the decade over a dispute involving the Mohamed firm's acquisition of the Abdulla firm's Transvaal assets. It was this lawsuit that had originally brought Gandhi to South Africa on behalf of Dada Abdulla and against Mohamed. Gandhi's earlier good work of reconciling those parties helped bind the Indian community together. Now, in 1898, relations between Gandhi and the Transvaal businessman were so good that the plaintiff Mohamed and the advocate Gandhi were able to work together. Gandhi's efforts at reconciliation had paid both spiritual and practical dividends.

IMPLAUSIBILITY

Gandhi, however, did not represent the plaintiff in the test case, not because of any conflict of interest arising from the previous litigation, but quite probably because he was not yet a member of the Republic's bar. Rather, the plaintiff was represented by advocate James Weston Leonard. In the early spring of 1898, however, Gandhi did attempt to assert himself in the preparation of the case by composing two set of notes to the European lawyers representing the Indians.

Gandhi wanted them to argue that Law 3 simply did not apply to Indian merchants. Clause 1 of the Law read as follows: "This Law is applicable to the persons belonging to one of the aboriginal races of Asia, among whom are comprehended the so-called Coolies, Arabs, Malays, and Mahomedan subjects of the Turkish Empire."[37]

In his notes Gandhi claims that "the meaning of the various expressions in the clause to be accepted by the Court will be the meaning which a standard work, as for instance, a Dictionary, would give them, and not the meaning given them by the populace, either through ignorance or prejudice . . . in the absence of a definition of these expressions in the law itself."[38]

Gandhi then turns to several scholarly sources to show that Indians are of Indo-Germanic stock and thus not aboriginal to Asia. He goes on to argue that the plaintiff could not possibly be an Arab, because he was a British subject, a native of India, and completely without connection to Arabia and Turkey. And, Gandhi contended, the plaintiff certainly was not a "coolie," that pejorative term being reserved for Indian field workers. In sum, Gandhi wanted Leonard to argue that the High Court should interpret the language of the statute not as it was popularly used by Europeans in the Republic, but as it was defined by scholars.

There was simply no justification for Gandhi's position either legally or politically. His turn to the academic authorities might have made legal sense if the statute had been ambiguous. It was not. As a matter of law Gandhi's argument is defeated by the very text of the statute. It did, in fact, define what it meant by "aboriginal races" when it said "among whom are *comprehended* the so-called Coolies, Arabs," and so forth. Moreover, the insertion of the phrase "so-called" before the listing of the discriminated-against classes made it clear beyond a shadow of a doubt that the Republic's legislature was not making an academic reference but a popular one. Gandhi's insistence that the insertion of this phrase would not alter his argument was plainly wrong.

In addition to the implausibility of Gandhi's argument from the text, it is impossible to see how Gandhi's argument could have succeeded as a matter of politics. The Republic's judicial system had just come through a bruising battle with the executive and legislative departments over the question of whether the judiciary had the power to review legislative acts, a battle that it had decisively lost and that had left it in a greatly weakened position.[39] Chief Justice Kotze, deeply influenced by the American constitutional experience in which the United States Supreme Court had established its power to rule legislation unconstitutional,[40] resisted the president and legislature and refused to renounce the testing right. Kruger dismissed him from office on February 16, 1898.

Less than two weeks later, with the wreckage of the High Court of the South African Republic before them, Gandhi's forces filed their lawsuit. Gandhi's argument that counsel for the Indians should take the position that this Court should interpret, on behalf of a racial minority, an act of the legislature in a manner completely opposite from its clearly intended meaning made little sense when he first articulated it in 1897 and made even less sense in February 1898. Watching the Republic's judiciary being brought to its knees, the Indians' hired counsel rejected Gandhi's advice.

Rather, Leonard made an argument to the Court that cleverly relied on the Volksraad for authority, but was unavailing.[41] Judgment was for the defendant, with costs to be borne by the Indians.

This was truly an Alice in Wonderland result. The High Court ruled that there was no difference between where an Indian resided and where he conducted business. There being no other court to which the Indians might appeal this travesty of justice, and in light of the many complaints that the Republic's Europeans had brought against the Indians, one would expect that the removal of Indians would have taken place forthwith. This was not to be so. Several attempts by Republican officials to remove the Indians to locations floundered because of British counterpressure, governmental bungling, and, finally, the start of the South African War between the British and the Republic's Afrikaners in October 1899.[42]

Anti-Indian animus, however, was deeply rooted and remained strong. In the course of his opinion in the test case, Justice Morice demonstrated just how deep and strong it was:

> There is not ... an equality between the whites and persons of colour, and we are bound to accept, as a principle, that every right possessed by the white man can only be exercised to a limited extent, or not at all, by the person

of colour. . . . [T]he principle of an extensive interpretation in favour of the legislature must be followed, and thus, in case of any doubt or ambiguity, against the person of colour.[43]

When Gandhi opened his law office in the Transvaal four and a half years later, he did so as a "person of colour."

He was not a welcome figure.

THIRTEEN

No Bed of Roses

He [Mr. Loveday] asked if . . . it could ever have been contemplated that the Indian trader could come into this country and have the same rights as the white man. He contended that the whole spirit of the law was against anything of the kind.

Indian Opinion, reporting the remarks of Hon. Richard K. Loveday
on the floor of the Transvaal Legislative Council

The deprivation of a man's right to trade without any compensation . . . is very much akin to robbery, which is miscalled law when it is done under cover of statute.

GANDHI

IS HISTORY THE PRODUCT OF strong-minded individuals who impose their will on the forces of society? Or is it the product of the forces of society that impose themselves on individuals? Or, as many think, are there no clear lines?[1]

GANDHI STAYS

It is easy enough to divide Mohandas Gandhi's career at the bar into two seemingly distinct phases—the Natal phase and the Transvaal phase. This division has the look of intentionality. When Gandhi returned to South Africa at the very end of 1902, however, it was not for the purpose of resuming his profession. Rather, he was there to lead the Natal Indian deputation that was to meet with Chamberlain. When, after the meeting, Chamberlain headed to the Transvaal for a meeting with Indians there, Gandhi did so too, intending to head the Transvaal Indian deputation. He would be excluded from the meeting by the government, but would go on to articulate the Indians' grievances in a written statement.

Gandhi reminded Chamberlain that when the Afrikaners were in control of the Transvaal, the British criticized them for their resistance to providing

Indians the respect the empire expected for its subjects. In fact, the British cited the Afrikaners' poor treatment of Indians as one ground justifying the South African War of 1899. This British advocacy on behalf of Indian rights led the Transvaal's Indians to believe that their situation would be vastly improved under a British postwar administration.

It was not to be. Once in power, the British performed an about-face. They shocked the Indians by not only enforcing the old regime's discriminatory laws but also enforcing them with a zeal unmatched by even the Afrikaners.[2] In fact, the government established a special Asiatic Department to oversee the administration of anti-Indian laws.

The central issue was trade, just as it was in Natal. Indian merchants consistently undercut the prices for goods offered by rival European merchants, an ability attributed to the Indians' comparatively frugal mode of living. Rather than reduce their wants so as to reduce their prices, the European merchants preferred to drive their competition out of the field. To this end they had long ago concocted the idea of locations. The Europeans believed that if they could drive Indian businesses from their towns and into the distant countryside where they would be limited to selling to their own community, to native Africans, or to no one at all, their problems would be solved.

When Gandhi arrived in the Transvaal, Law 3, empowering the government to establish locations, had been on the books for some time. As described earlier, the Indians had unsuccessfully challenged the ability of the government to segregate Indian trade under Law 3 in the South African Republic's High Court. Even with that victory in hand, however, the Republic was lackadaisical in its enforcement of the law.[3] When war broke out in late 1899, the government's attention was further diverted from the Indian question.

The tone changed after the war. The Transvaal Indians feared that the laws restricting them to locations, forcing them to pay a special £3 tax, and barring their ownership of real property would remain "unrepealed."[4] These fears were more than confirmed when, in late April 1903, the Transvaal issued Government Notice 356, popularly known as the "Bazaar Notice."[5] "Bazaar" was a euphemism for "location." Except for certain Indians who had been permitted to trade before the war, Indian merchants were ordered by the new government, now under British control, into these government-created ghettoes.

Gandhi, who felt this noose tightening well before the notice was issued, was thrown into a state of temporary confusion and indecision. On the one hand, he longed to return to India. On the other, the Transvaal, now a

Crown colony, presented him with an opportunity to preserve rights for his countrymen that had been effectively lost in Natal. Moreover, Africa, with its less competitive legal environment, offered him another chance to prosper in his profession.

Before the end of January 1903, and in evident preparation for a possible application for admission to the Transvaal bar, Gandhi had sought a certificate from the Natal Supreme Court attesting to his good standing as an advocate in that colony. In early February 1903, however, Gandhi professed his indecision with regard to whether he should return to India or take up the fight in the Transvaal. In a letter to Chhaganlal Gandhi, his cousin's son, he wrote: "There is great uncertainty about me. . . . If it is not possible to stay on here, I may leave in March. . . . I shall make every possible effort to return home. It's no bed of roses here. I cannot offer more definite news."[6] Later in February, he confided to his mentor Gokhale that because the "old laws [were] being enforced," "it probably means my having to stop here longer than March."[7]

Over the following month, Gandhi made his decision. He explained himself to his co-workers in South Africa:

> The work for which you had called me is practically finished. But I believe I ought not to leave the Transvaal. . . . Instead of carrying on my work from Natal, as before, I must now do so from here. I must no longer think of returning to India within a year, must get enrolled in the Transvaal Supreme Court. I have confidence enough to deal with this new department [the government's Asiatic Department]. If we do not do this, the community will be hounded out of the country, besides being thoroughly robbed. Every day it will have fresh insults heaped on it. The fact . . . that Mr. Chamberlain refused to see me . . . [is] nothing before the humiliation of the whole community. It will become impossible to put up with the veritable dog's life that we shall be expected to lead.[8]

He would stay, open a law office, and fight again for the rights of South African Indians, all in the knowledge that the struggle was "far more intense" than he originally expected.[9]

RACISM IN THE LAW SOCIETY

Among his first tasks in Johannesburg was deciding whether he wanted to make application to the bar as an advocate or as an attorney. When Gandhi arrived as a newly minted barrister in Natal, there was an insufficient supply of both advocates and attorneys. As a result, he, like many of his Natal colleagues, was permitted to engage in dual practice. Such a privilege did not exist in the Transvaal, where there was a heightened sensitivity to the divisions within the profession.[10] By the terms of the Administration of Justice Proclamation of 1902, practitioners were forced to enroll either as advocates or as attorneys, a distinction that mirrored the traditional British distinction between barristers and solicitors. Advocates in the Transvaal had what was called the "right of audience"—the unlimited right to appear in all courts, high and low, on behalf of clients. By contrast, attorneys in the Transvaal, while permitted to appear in some low-level courts, were not authorized to appear in all courts. Rather, like solicitors elsewhere, their principal work was that of rendering legal advice, assisting with the purchase and sale of property, and dealing with a broad range of the legal needs of businesses, among many other things. A client who had a problem requiring a court appearance would first contact an attorney, who would then bring the case to an advocate. Attorneys had a front-line relationship with clients, while barristers did not.

As an English-trained barrister and an experienced Natal advocate, Gandhi could have applied either as an advocate or as an attorney. He chose to apply for admission as an attorney, later explaining that "as an advocate I could not have come in direct contact with the Indians and the white attorneys in South Africa would not have briefed me."[11] He does not mention that the attorney's role would also allow him to more often avoid the public-speaking pressures of the courtroom.

In a petition filed in Pretoria on March 31, 1903, Gandhi applied for admission to the Supreme Court of the Transvaal as an attorney. He tendered to the court, along with his Natal certificate, a certificate of good standing from the High Court of Judicature of Bombay and the same Inner Temple certificate, attesting to his having been called to the bar in England, that had given the bar the pretext to oppose him in Natal.

Gandhi's earlier uncertainty about whether it would be possible to remain in the Transvaal was likely founded, at least in part, on his apprehension about whether the Transvaal would admit him to practice.[12] In any event, the bar did not oppose him. On April 14, 1903, the Court granted the application, directing Gandhi to appear in the chambers of Mr. Justice Wessels in Johannesburg to take his oath as an attorney.[13]

The bar's surprising lack of formal opposition should not be taken as a sign of welcome. In fact, the members of the Transvaal bar were not pleased with

Gandhi's appearance among them. Eight days after Gandhi's application for admission was approved by the Court, the Council of the Incorporated Law Society of the Transvaal met in the boardroom of the Exploration Building in Johannesburg. Gandhi was on the minds of those assembled. The society's minutes of that meeting are astonishing for what they unabashedly reveal about the bar's distinct racial attitudes:

> re: Admission—M.K. Gandhi: It was reported that this gentleman, who is an Indian, had been admitted as an Attorney of the Supreme Court of this Colony, but as his qualifications were sufficient and as there was nothing in the Administration of Justice Proclamation against the admission of such persons, the Council did not think anything could be done in the matter.[14]

The bar had apparently scrutinized Gandhi's admission application for deficiencies and studied the proclamation in search of a provision that might be used against this dark interloper. Neither exercise bore fruit. It seems beyond question that had the bar found defensible grounds on which to base an objection to Gandhi's admission, it would have seized upon them. None being found, the Transvaal bar was saddled with this Indian attorney.

Gandhi was free to practice law.

If Gandhi sensed any prejudice against him by his colleagues at the bar— as he certainly must have—he defied it. Just days after his admission, a large meeting of practitioners convened in Johannesburg. Gandhi appeared at the meeting, presenting himself to the very people who had just recently noted that they were unable to keep him out of their midst. The subject of the meeting was one that would have interested Gandhi. The meeting had been called to protest the government's licensing tax of £40 per year on attorneys. When the president of the law society pledged that the organization would "agitate, agitate, agitate, until we get reform," it was a sentiment with which Gandhi could surely identify. He and his new colleagues voted unanimously in favor of a resolution protesting the tax.[15] Later that year, the bar assembled again, this time to give encouragement to law students in the Transvaal. Gandhi apparently felt no reluctance in joining with some of the most powerful members of the bar for this purpose.

The law society was not the only association into which an unwelcome Gandhi thrust himself. The Johannesburg Parliamentary Debating Society met weekly to listen to its members give speeches about the issues of the day.[16] One of its members caused a stir by moving for Gandhi's admission. There was some controversy over the propriety of admitting an Indian member.

Gandhi's status, as it was pointed out, as a person of "culture and refinement" was sufficient in the eyes of the membership to overcome his status as an Indian. The motion, in the end, passed.[17]

Gandhi's aggressiveness in locating himself in organizations prominent in Johannesburg public life was matched by his aggressiveness in locating his law office. Assisted in his search for space by friends whom he encountered in Johannesburg's theosophist circles, he opened his office on Rissik Street at 25–26 Court Chambers, conveniently located near the courts and in the very heart of the town's legal center.

From that location, the young attorney started to make trouble.

THE ASIATIC DEPARTMENT

Even in light of his joining with Laughton in their attack on the DLA, Gandhi's practice in Durban was, relative to what his experience in the Transvaal would be, fairly apolitical. Gandhi's future in the Transvaal would be very different from his Durban experience. The rights of the Transvaal Indian merchants, Gandhi's clients, would get caught up in an uncertain postwar administrative environment and in the postwar struggle for supremacy between the Transvaal's defeated Afrikaners and the imperial British administration. The defense of his clients' economic and political interests would require Gandhi, with more frequency than ever, to act not only as a business lawyer but as a cause lawyer, a movement lawyer, a civil rights lawyer. To be sure, Gandhi's office would continue to generate a very substantial income from his conventional representation of his clients' property and business interests. At the same time, however, his law office would become a hub of Indian resistance to white discrimination.[18]

The Asiatic Department was discrimination in the flesh. The postwar government had established this agency for the specific purpose of administering the colony's anti-Indian laws. One principal focus of the office was to regulate the readmission of Indian refugees into the colony. These were Indians who had fled the Transvaal at the outbreak of war and were now trying to return to their homes and businesses. Department agents harassed returning Indians not only by subjecting them to what seemed like endless bureaucratic red tape, but also by extorting bribe money from them for the performance of their duties. According to Gandhi, "There grew up an army of intermediaries or touts, who with the officers looted the poor Indians to the tune of thousands."[19] It is not surprising, then, that the department was on the receiving end of Gandhi's most pointed criticism. He called it "a terror to the people" and described its purpose as inventing "new engines of torture."[20]

Gandhi, who had detested the department from the time it prevented him from leading the Indian party that met with Chamberlain in early 1903, plotted his attack on it from his Johannesburg law office. Teaming with members of the Chinese community that had recently grown up in Johannesburg, and working with a lawyer's eye for evidence, he set about gathering proof of bribery and corruption on the part of the department's officers. The suspects were soon on to Gandhi's activities and began shadowing his movements. Undeterred, Gandhi went about his work. When he had collected what he believed was indisputable evidence of the guilt of two of the officers, he presented it to the police commissioner, an honest public servant. The commissioner soon thereafter arrested Cecil Jackson, the supervisor of Asiatics in the Asiatic Permit Office, and Charles Walton, a clerk in the same office, on charges of taking bribes.[21] Walton had earlier fled the jurisdiction and had to be forcibly returned to the Transvaal. By November 1903, proceedings against the two had begun, with Indian witnesses testifying they had given hundreds of pounds to the pair for the issuance of permits. But the jury, which even had the benefit of knowing that Walton had tried to flee, appears to have accepted a rather unbelievable story concocted by the defense to account for the exchange of funds between the defendants and permit applicants.[22] In the face of what Gandhi considered "strong evidence" against them, the jury acquitted both defendants.

Nonetheless, some justice was done. The responsibility for processing permit applications was transferred to others, and the defendants were discharged from their employment.[23] The demonstration effect of the prosecution and firings was a healthy one; Gandhi was able to later declare that "the Asiatic Department became comparatively clean."[24] In the end, it was a considerable win for a lawyer who had only that year arrived in the Transvaal.

RELOCATION

At the same time Gandhi was fighting the corruption of the Asiatic Department, the government was busy opening another front against the Indians. The government and major elements of the Transvaal business community remained intent on driving Indian merchants out of business. Their strategy was to revive the notion of locations. As indicated earlier, the ability of the government to segregate Indians into locations had its roots in Law 3 of 1885. It prohibited Indians from owning property outside these locations and also required Indians to live and, as interpreted by the courts, trade in locations. Much of Gandhi's work in the Transvaal in the early part of his practice there dealt with resistance to this attack on Indian interests.

The Indians discovered soon after the war that the 1885 prohibition on property ownership outside locations would be enforced. Gandhi was first approached by his clients on this issue in 1903. He swung into action by instructing the advocates who would represent the Indians in this matter— and did so in a revealing way. He defined the issue solely as a question about the contract rights of the Indian purchasers.[25] At this time, he did not raise the question of whether Law 3 itself could be challenged. While Gandhi was still in India, several Indian merchants had secured the opinion of Seward Brice, a high-profile member of the Johannesburg bar, that statutes such as Law 3 were "certainly unconstitutional and without precedent in our legal history." Brice went on to offer the Indians a plan of action, recommending they petition first and, should that fail, litigate. Gandhi likely was aware of Brice's opinion but chose not to act upon it.[26] While we are not privy to Gandhi's thinking on this question, it is clear that he did not take the 1903 case to the Supreme Court, and its outcome is unknown.[27]

A case raising the same issue, however, did wind its way up the court system; the Supreme Court rendered a decision on the question in 1905. Gandhi was the instructing attorney for the plaintiffs, who were once more represented in court by J. W. Leonard, the well-respected advocate of whom Gandhi speaks highly in his autobiography. The facts of *Lucas' Trustee v. Ismail and Amod* were that Lucas, a European, held property in his name at the request of some Indian friends who understood that Law 3 prohibited Indian property ownership. The Indians paid for the property. Lucas, who made no financial or other investment in it, eventually went bankrupt. While he was in bankruptcy, the government seized his property and paid his bankrupt estate £2,000 for it. The Indians claimed this money, arguing that Lucas was their trustee and they were the beneficial owners of the property.

The Supreme Court of the Transvaal refused to accept the Indians' argument. The Court stated that under Law 3 the Indians could not own the land themselves nor could they claim to be the beneficial owners. The Court refused to grant them the £2,000 they sought, but did permit them to claim

£650 from the estate for improvements on the property. As for the £1,350 difference, Chief Justice Innes was less than clear on this question, saying that the Indians could lodge a claim for that money against the estate, but that their right to do so might "be affected by the further question whether their claim is defeated by the fact that they attempted to commit an illegality."[28] It appears that the Indians never tried to assert this claim. In the main, then, this case was a serious loss for the Indians. That is not how Gandhi painted it, however. Gandhi wrote that it seemed from the decision that "the holding by Europeans of land for Indians is not illegal." This conclusion is unjustified in light of Innes' statement. Gandhi did recognize that Indians who entered into agreements with Europeans ran the risk of losing their investments, but he nonetheless called the decision one that "takes the Indians a step further in their fight, and renders Law 3 ... still more ineffective as a weapon to be used against them."[29] While that assessment might have been somewhat accurate, the decision was no cause for rejoicing. In this instance, optimism triumphed over realism.

ASIATIC TRADING COMMISSION

The locations issue arose with full force when the infamous "Bazaar Notice," requiring compliance by the end of the year, was published in April 1903. It angered Europeans as well as Indians. Indians were upset because the notice represented a mortal threat to their very livelihoods. Europeans were upset because the policy contained exceptions. It essentially exempted "those Asiatics who were trading outside Bazaars at the commencement of the late hostilities." It also allowed higher-class Indians an exemption for out-of-location residences. Emotional, rhetoric-filled protest meetings of white colonists occurred all over the colony, with commercial interests demanding strict enforcement of the notice. The British colonial secretary resisted, expressing reservations about dispossessing Indian merchants who had traded before the war with either tacit or explicit governmental approval.

When the Legislative Council met in December, this argument came to a head. Some members wanted to allow Indians who had traded before the war without permits to continue to do so, while other members feared that allowing these Indians to resume their businesses would lead to a flood of Indian traders.[30] This difference was papered over by a decision of the Legislative Council "to appoint a Commission to investigate the cases of those Asiatics who traded in towns before the war without licenses, and to report what vested rights or interests they may reasonably claim in respect to such trade."[31] This compromise did not resolve the question of how harshly the Indians were to be treated; rather it simply passed the question on to the commission—and it did so in a way that failed to clearly articulate the commission's charge.[32]

When the Asiatic Trading Commission held its opening meeting at the Royal Courts of Justice in Pretoria on March 15, 1904, Gandhi was present with an immediate and pressing question for the commission. The notice appointing the commission spoke in terms of Indian merchants "who were trading in the Transvaal in towns outside locations without licenses *at and immediately before* the outbreak of hostilities"[33] (emphasis supplied). Substituting "or" for "and," Gandhi asked for a ruling on the meaning of the phrase "at or immediately before the outbreak of hostilities." The chair, J. W. Honey, dodged the question and replied that "a concise ruling could not be given on that point at the present moment."[34] When the commission's proceedings resumed on March 17, not only were the body's purpose and scope unclear, but so was its procedure. Present were three commissioners, a secretary to the commission, a representative of the Pretoria Chamber of Commerce, and two lawyers for Indian claimants—a Mr. Rees, who represented one claimant, and Gandhi, who appeared on behalf of twenty Indian merchants who had traded in the Transvaal before the war.

After the commission heard and rejected Rees' argument on behalf of his client, Gandhi brought on the case of Joosub Hajee Valee, an Indian merchant who had traded on his own until 1896 and who then went to work for another merchant. Chairman Honey, who earlier had refused to give Gandhi any guidance on the terms of the commission's appointment, pounced on these facts: "Three years before the war cannot be termed at or immediately before the outbreak of hostilities."[35] This comment revealed a gap of huge proportions between what the commission saw as its purpose and what Gandhi conceived it to be. The commission believed it was limited to determining which Indian merchants were deprived of their then-extant businesses *by the war* and recording the merchants' requests for compensation. Implicit in the commission's understanding was the notion that these merchants would then move on to locations.

Gandhi, by contrast, argued for a less literal meaning of the notice and claimed that the commission had a broader, underlying purpose, namely to determine which merchants had been "allowed to trade in defiance of the law and were granted protection under the late regime,"[36] a determination that should then permit them to trade outside locations under the current government. Gandhi believed that, in light of the debates in the Legislative Council that had resulted in the commission's creation, the "and" in the notice appointing the commission ("at *and* immediately before") could not be read literally, for that would result in the unreasonable conclusion that only traders who were trading on the very day the war broke out could be eligible to make a claim. Rather "and" should be read as meaning "or." Even the chair of the commission, in what was likely an unintentional concession, provided some support for this reading when he argued that 1896, in Joosub Hajee Valee's case, could not be considered "at *or* immediately before" the war.

Gandhi himself recognized that the commission had a strong case in the text of the appointment notice, admitting to his readers in *Indian Opinion* that "the Commissioners had absolutely no choice" and that the "wording of the reference leaves no loop-hole."[37]

It was not surprising, then, that the commission rebuffed Gandhi's argument. In response, Gandhi announced that he was withdrawing the claims of all twenty of his clients.[38] Then, in an apparent attempt to buy time for this dispute to be mooted by a test case,[39] he asked the commission to adjourn until after Easter. The chairman rejected Gandhi's suggestion and stated that the commission would resume hearing Johannesburg cases in four days, on March 29.

Just as the hearing was ending, J. F. Rubie, one of the commissioners and an advocate whom Gandhi respected, spoke up. The *Rand Daily Mail* reported the exchange between Advocate Rubie and Attorney Gandhi that brought the hearing to a close:

> Mr. Rubie informed Mr. Gandhi that, after consideration, some of the claims might be reinstated on application.
> Mr. Gandhi smiled in reply, and did not think, as things stood, that such was possible.[40]

Gandhi was quite likely smiling because his faith in the court system was, surprisingly, still alive.

CIVIL DISOBEDIENCE: THE FIRST SUGGESTION

When the postwar Transvaal government began to get serious about forcing Indian traders into locations, Gandhi and his clients had three choices before them. One option was to resist by refusing to apply for permits. Indeed, this was a possible course of action Gandhi described to the readers of *Indian Opinion* in January 1904. In addition to establishing the Asiatic Traders Commission, the government had required Indian merchants to apply for temporary permits from the Receiver of Revenue, to whom the merchants had to supply the same proof of prewar trading that they submitted elsewhere. Gandhi was infuriated by this duplication of effort, by the increased costs involved, and, most especially, by the government's duplicity. Here he is in his own words, raising for the first time the prospect of civil disobedience:

> What, then, is to be the attitude of the British Indians amid such a crisis? To our mind, it is quite clear what it should be. The Indians must keep themselves absolutely cool and remain patient, still relying upon justice being ultimately done. They must make respectful representations to the Government, but they should also firmly decline to give proof to the Receivers [*sic*] of Revenue, offering to do so before the Commission that is to be appointed. It may be that prosecutions will take place for carrying on trade without licences, and if summons are issued and penalties imposed for carrying on trade without a licence, the persons prosecuted should rise to the occasion, decline to pay any fines, and go to gaol. There is no disgrace in going to jail for such a cause; the disgrace is generally attached to the offence which renders one liable to imprisonment, and not to the imprisonment itself. In this instance, the so-called offence would be no offence at all, and it would be a most dignified course to adopt.[41]

With its call for patience and its expression of faith in the system to ultimately provide justice, this was a cautious excursion into the notion of principled lawbreaking. It was also a temporary one. After the government signaled that it would not prosecute Indians pending the completion of the Asiatic Traders Commission's work, talk of civil disobedience was not revived.

Two other courses of action were left for dealing with the location question. The Indians could attempt to bargain with the government for a different arrangement, or they could contest in court the government's power to establish locations. In light of the decision in *Mohamed v. Government*, litigation did not appear to be a completely promising route.

Not surprisingly, the Indians initially declined to take the postwar government to court on this issue and instead pled their case through political channels and in the court of public opinion. After a protracted and unsuccessful attempt at effecting a compromise, however, the Indians did elect to go to court. Here is Gandhi in January 1904 on the issue of turning to the courts:

> The Indian community . . . has hitherto deliberately refrained from standing on its legal position, hoping that in the end the Government would do it justice; but if the Government would abdicate its function and decline to protect the Indian community, it must invoke the aid of the Supreme Court, and test the question of whether residence includes trade. The Law 3 . . . requires Indians to reside in locations; it says nothing as to trade. . . . [T]hough we still hope that recourse to a law-suit will be unnecessary, if the Government insists on withholding protection to all the existing licence-holders we see no way out of an appeal to the highest tribunal of justice in the Colony.[42]

Two weeks later, he revealed that the decision had been made:

> As a last chance, therefore, the Indians have wisely decided to test . . . the right of the Government to refuse to grant licenses to British Indians to trade outside Locations . . . . It will undoubtedly stand to the credit of the British Indians . . . that they have refrained from bringing the matter before the . . . Court for two years. . . . . They have . . . attempted to come to a reasonable understanding with the white traders and the Government . . . and it is even when this is being denied to them . . . that they must perforce see what they can raise out of the . . . Court.[43]

This preference for negotiation and compromise over litigation was a frequent theme of Gandhi's practice, as well as his politics. Gandhi cited Emerson for the proposition that "the world . . . is governed very largely by the law of compromise."[44] In this instance, however, the route of conciliation failed.

MOTAN V. TRANSVAAL GOVERNMENT

The Indians hired some leading lights of the bar to represent them in their challenge to Law 3, including J. W. Leonard as lead counsel, the principal advocate for the Indians in *Mohamed v. Government*. Gandhi praised these lawyers as possessing "the very best legal talent" and capable of providing the "best legal advice."[45] Why wasn't Gandhi among them? Why did the attorneys from the firm of Lunnon and Nixon act as the instructing attorneys, rather than Gandhi? The case was being litigated just as Gandhi was being admitted to the bar, and so he would not have been admitted to practice for a substantial portion of the case's life. Had he already been licensed as an attorney, he would have been able to instruct the advocates who argued the case, but he would not have been permitted to appear in the Supreme Court to argue it himself. And finally, even if these factors had not been present, Gandhi, a Transvaal newcomer, simply may not have considered himself as possessing the surefootedness that these more experienced hands possessed.

The Indian hires did well. The decision they secured, *Motan v. Government*, decided on May 11, 1904, was not welcome news to the European business community. The Supreme Court of the Transvaal announced that Law 3 did not empower the government to require Indian businesses to operate in locations. The decision stood in high contrast with the 1898 *Mohamed* decision. In that case, which had tested the right of the government to force Indians businesses into locations under Law 3, Justice Morice had said that "the principle of an extensive interpretation in favour of the legislature must be followed, and thus, in case of any doubt or ambiguity, against the person of colour."[46] The *Motan* court adopted a starkly different starting point, stating that when a statute "imposes disabilities upon one section of the community it should be strictly interpreted, and the benefit of any doubt should be given in favour of those affected by it." The Court rejected *Mohamed* and *Suleiman*, both South African Republic decisions, as not binding and found that the text of Law 3 did not support the government's position, saying that if the legislature had intended to force Indian businesses into locations, "some definite provision to that effect would surely have been inserted."[47]

It was a thorough defeat for the government.

For Gandhi, the result may have both dampened thoughts of civil disobedience and revived his hope, previously dashed by the failure of his attack on the DLA, that the courts, with their sense of British fair play, would come to the rescue of the Indians. In victory, however, Gandhi refused to gloat. Rather, he was realistically restrained, as usual, and counseled Indians in the pages of *Indian Opinion* to "make only a moderate use of the right of trading." Fearing a European backlash, Gandhi predicted that if "the people go mad over the victory and begin to apply for licenses to trade here, there and everywhere, a great deal of harm would be done, and [our] detractors would not be slow to use such a state of things as a weapon for dealing further blows."[48] In the weeks afterward, Indians did, in fact, begin to take out licenses in what the Europeans perceived to be large numbers. The European reaction to *Motan*, whether caused by the decision itself or the enthusiastic reaction to it by Indian businesspeople, was just as Gandhi had predicted. The *Rand Daily Mail* reported that "the Asiatic peril ha[d] materialised,"[49] some European colonists began to call for legislative action to counter the court's decision, and soon afterward, members of the Transvaal legislature began to press the imperial government for a legislative solution to the matter.

SACRIFICE

Gandhi's approach to his legal practice and his political work, as illustrated here by his urging restraint on his fellow Indians, was influenced not only by his healthy sense of realism but also by his developing spirituality. For Gandhi, politics, spirituality, and the practice of law were becoming indistinguishable parts of a seamless whole. Tying all these together was Gandhi's evolving understanding of the relationship between sacrifice and suffering, on the one hand, and social change, on the other. The dimensions of this relationship were often explored in the pages of *Indian Opinion* and probed in Gandhi's practice.

In the January 21, 1904, issue of *Indian Opinion* he writes:

> Sacrifice is the law of life. . . . We can do nothing or get nothing without paying a price for it, as it would be said in commercial parlance or, in other words, without sacrifice. It would secure the salvation of the community to which we belong; we must pay for it, that is sacrifice self. Working for the community, we may keep for ourselves only a proportion of what is secured, and no more. And herein lies the sacrifice. At times we have to pay dearly. . . . Christ died on the Cross of Calvary and left Christianity as a glorious heritage. . . . The Americans bled for their independence.[50]

Gandhi then connected this notion to the particular challenge facing the Transvaal Indians. To prevent the colonists from depriving the Indians of their means to a livelihood and from driving them into ghettos, Indians must provide more time, energy, and money to the cause. Moreover, "individual differences must be sunk in the face of common danger. Personal ease and personal gain must be surrendered. To all this must be added patience and self-control."[51]

Left on the dry page, these words are not very instructive. Gandhi, however, brought them to life in the manner in which he reacted to the wealth his practice brought him.

The longer he practiced in the Transvaal, it seemed, the more money he made. There were multiple signs that financial success came very easily to lawyer Gandhi. In a June 1903 letter to a friend, Gandhi wrote that he had "built up a decent practice," one successful enough that he could "afford to pick and choose."[52] For any lawyer to make this assessment a mere two and a half months after being admitted to practice in a new jurisdiction is simply stunning. Much of Gandhi's success was rooted in the voluminous, broad-ranging, and apparently lucrative nature of the office work he performed for his clients during his years practicing in the Transvaal—and to his insatiable appetite for doing it. In just the months between his admission to the bar in mid-April and his June letter, the new attorney found himself assisting his clients with travel permits, handling the payment of promissory notes, rendering advice in the areas of family law and criminal law, and doing a fair amount of work involving the sale and lease of property. Gandhi's Johannesburg practice was so vibrant that he required the assistance of four Indian law clerks, in addition to an articled clerk and a secretary. An important client during this time was one Budree, an Indian merchant and landowner with whom Gandhi was developing what would be a long and profitable professional relationship. Gandhi recounts in his autobiography that it was Budree's money, held in trust by Gandhi, that Gandhi lent to an operator of a vegetarian restaurant in Johannesburg whose business was in distress. The operator quickly lost the money—about £1,000—forcing Gandhi to dip into his own funds to repay Budree. Gandhi's ability to cover the loss is a good indication of the size of his cash flow at this time.[53]

While a great deal of his income was derived from his office practice,[54] Gandhi made regular appearances in lower-level courts when his clients' interests required it. He collected money for his clients in numerous claims concerning promissory notes, rent due, goods sold, wages owed, cash lent, and services rendered. He was successful in representing one plaintiff in an action for ejectment and another in a case against a defendant who had issued a bad check. Gandhi made a rare appearance for a defendant, representing a defendant accused of breaching a contract; Gandhi lost, but got the damages reduced. And he lost two cases for plaintiffs that dealt with wages owed. His overall success rate was quite high, but that was to be expected. Many of these cases involved modest sums and defendants who either represented themselves or simply failed to appear and contest the claims against them.

He valued the role of money, saying: "In the modern world, money is needed at every step; and if it runs short, one has to face disappointment in the end, however great and noble one's hopes and aspirations might be."[55] It should not be a surprise that a man with this mindset accumulated wealth by not being shy about money. He did work very long hours,[56] but at the same time he squeezed the maximum amount of money out of every transaction and relationship. He was never above hounding his clients for his fees, defending his bills, questioning others' bills, beseeching his landlord to lower his rent, arguing that others were cheating him, and pleading poverty to his friends and acquaintances.

At the same time, Gandhi did not forget his reaction to the prosperity he came to know in Durban; he was very sensitive to what riches could do to him. In writing about a fellow Indian who had become a barrister, Gandhi revealed the standard he applied to himself: "He has adopted an honourable profession, but if it is used as a means of amassing wealth, there may be failure staring him in the face. If his attainments are placed at the service of the community, they will grow more and more."[57]

SELF-SUFFERING

Gandhi followed his own advice. While he could have used his income solely to benefit himself, he instead sacrificed a generous measure of his own interests for those of the Indian community. He quietly donated thousands of pounds from his income to help finance *Indian Opinion*, the newspaper he helped establish to be the voice of the Indian cause.[58] Indeed, he would later claim that he invested "the whole of his savings" in the paper.[59] Yet other large portions of his income went into the operation of Phoenix, the communal farm he established in late 1904 and the place to which *Indian Opinion*'s operations were eventually moved. The income from his practice also permitted him to employ his legal skills on behalf of the Indian cause without concern for remuneration. Gandhi's campaign against the corruption of the Asiatic Permit Office is an early example of this. What this example lacks, however, is an emphasis on self-suffering that would soon come to be a distinctive mark of Gandhi's philosophy and strategy of nonviolence, his political work, and his law practice.

The seeds of Gandhi's understanding of the role of self-suffering in politics, law, and social change were planted in another incident that occurred during this time. In early 1903 the police in Heidelberg, just southeast of Johannesburg, conducted an early-morning raid on the municipality's Indian stores, arresting all the employees there preparing for the day's business. They were marched through the streets to the police station, with some being held there without food or drink while the police questioned them one by one as to whether they held the proper permits. Although Gandhi did seek to have an investigation conducted into the behavior of the police, he declined to counsel the Indians to seek either civil damages or criminal penalties. He took this position for a very specific reason. He believed that the patient suffering of the Indians, undergone without thought of retribution, "would create a favourable impression on the minds of the officers immediately concerned."[60] He told his *Indian Opinion* readers in 1903 that "above all else, what is needed in a community which considers itself to be ill-treated at the hands of others is the virtue of love and charity."[61] Gandhi abstained from using the law as a remedy for injustice in this instance, thinking instead that unmerited, willingly accepted suffering would lead to conversion on the part of the oppressor. This is an early expression of a key component of his philosophy of nonviolent civil disobedience. In this instance, Gandhi's approach failed, but the groundwork was being laid for what would develop into a more robust and more effective theory and practice of self-suffering in the years immediately ahead.

Integrally related to this notion of self-suffering is Gandhi's idea of unqualified love for all persons, including—especially including—one's enemies. It is this love that provides, in great part, the foundation for one's ability to take suffering on oneself rather than to project it outward on others. Gandhi understood, too, that self-suffering founded on unqualified love was a superb tactical weapon, causing both the opponent and the public to pause and consider the merits of the sufferer's arguments. This notion began to grow in Gandhi's mind during an incident that was ancillary to the prosecution of Jackson and Walton, the corrupt permit officers. After they had been let go by the Asiatic Permit Office, the municipality of Johannesburg considered them for employment. The word went out, however, that if Mr. Gandhi objected, the municipality would not hire them. Gandhi let it be known that he would not oppose their hiring. He would afterward reflect on this decision, saying that he understood later that his choice not to harm these individuals who had harmed Indians was an essential element of nonviolence. From this incident Gandhi learned that we are all "children of one and the same Creator, and as such the divine powers within us are infinite.

To slight a single human being is to slight those divine powers, and thus to harm not only that being but with him the entire world."[62]

GANDHI'S SPIRITUALITY MEETS HIS PRACTICE

In the early years of his Johannesburg practice Gandhi had no fully formed philosophy that tied his politics, his spirituality, and his practice of law together. Ideas were swirling around in unorganized fashion in his head. He clearly sensed the connections among the various aspects of his life, but was not yet in a position to fully understand how they related to one another. It was a particular challenge for Gandhi to relate the practice of law, with its immense complexities, to his spirituality and his politics.

Gandhi wrote about one such complexity in *Indian Opinion*. There is no more difficult spiritual issue in the law than that created when the representation of a client conflicts with one's own moral beliefs. Gandhi's former Durban colleague R. K. Khan had come under attack when he defended a patently guilty client in a criminal case. Gandhi used the columns of his newspaper to defend Khan's conduct:

> So great an authority as Lord Brougham[63] used to say that an advocate who, although he knew the guilt of his client, declined to take up his case, was unworthy of his profession; and on the principle that every man in the eye of the law is innocent until he is found guilty by a duly constituted court, the doctrine is sound enough. . . . What . . . is the duty of an advocate who finds out in the middle of a case that his client is really guilty? Is he to throw up the brief? If he dare do anything of the kind, we fancy that his conduct would be regarded as highly unprofessional. The matter bristles with difficulty. And we think that it is one for every advocate to determine for himself.[64]

When in the 1920s Gandhi wrote his memoirs covering the first five decades of his life, he focused some of his attention on his practice of law. To illustrate that truth should be the foremost consideration of every lawyer, he recounted his own experience in dealing with an issue similar to that dealt with by Khan:

> On one occasion, whilst I was conducting a case . . . , I discovered that my client had deceived me. I saw him completely break down in the witness box. . . . I asked the magistrate to dismiss the case. The opposing counsel was astonished, and the magistrate was pleased. I rebuked my client for

bringing a false case to me. He knew that I never accepted false cases, and when I brought the thing home to him, he admitted his mistake. . . . At any rate my conduct in the case did not affect my practice for the worse, indeed it made my work easier. I also saw that my devotion to the truth enhanced my reputation amongst the members of the profession.[65]

While there are critical considerations in criminal cases like Khan's that are absent in civil cases like Gandhi's,[66] one cannot help but be overwhelmed with the difference in tone between these two passages that deal with the same broad problem. The first passage is written by a man who is on a journey, the second by one who has arrived. There is no moral absolutism, no moral certainty, in the first passage as there is in the second, later passage.

If there was no certainty in this realm in his early Johannesburg days, could there have been any certainty in Gandhi's mind about the efficacy of the law for creating social change? There could have been nothing but confusion for him here. He had experienced the painful limits of the law as a tool for social change in Natal when his legal attack on the DLA fell short. He was then to experience the potential of the law for transformation when, in the *Motan* case, the Supreme Court of the Transvaal gave an uplifting and unbiased interpretation of Law 3, one that freed Indians, at least temporarily, from some measure of discrimination. In September 1905 the pendulum swung again when Gandhi learned that the Natal Supreme Court had ruled that it was not illegal to deny an Indian a DLA license just because he was Indian—the very question that he and Laughton had declined to take up on appeal in the previous decade.[67] After all this, was the law an ally or just an enemy disguised as a friend?

Gandhi's feelings about the practice of law were equally jumbled. When he founded his Phoenix settlement, he considered, but then rejected, the notion of abandoning his practice altogether in favor of manual labor. When Jackson and Walton, the corrupt permit officials, were acquitted of the bribery of which they were so clearly guilty, Gandhi pronounced himself "disgusted with the legal profession."[68] Yet, at about this very same time, he was reveling in the light that his training in the law cast on his religious thought. In explaining how he came to understand the spiritual notion of detachment from worldly possessions, he wrote:

Was I to give up all I had to follow Him? Straight came the answer: I could not follow Him unless I gave up all I had. My study of . . . law came to my help. Snell's discussion of the maxims of Equity came to my memory. I understood more clearly in the light of the Gita teaching the implication of the word "trustee." My regard for jurisprudence increased, I discovered in it religion. I understood the Gita teaching of non-possession to mean that those who desired salvation should act like the trustee who, though having control over great possessions, regards not an iota of them as his own.[69]

In December of 1905, Gandhi looked back on the year and wrote: "It is not possible to recall anything that may be considered in the light of an achievement. . . . In the Transvaal . . . the position is as indecisive as it was last year."[70]

Here, at the end of 1905, was a man who worked hard and earned great wealth, but consistently emptied himself by giving vast amounts of his money away. Here was a man who believed that a lawyer should take personal responsibility for the causes he represents, but defended a friend who did not take responsibility and a system that encouraged the deflection of responsibility. Here was a man who failed in his use of the courts as an engine of social change in Natal, but experienced their power for good in the Transvaal. Here was a man who practiced law for a living, but was reluctant to take the government to court. Here was a man who urged his fellow Indians to be patient and calm, but also to consider civil disobedience. Here was a man who loved what the law taught him about spirituality, but was beginning to hate the very profession of which he was a part.

Here was a man who confronted a world of profound complexity, but desired no more, and no less, than a life of simple clarity.

FOURTEEN

Disobedience

The law is the will of the people and it is the will of the people
that coloured persons shall not ride with whites in this country.

Transvaal Leader

1906 WOULD BE A YEAR of turning points.

Casting aside his past indecision and finding new resolve, Gandhi would
volunteer to aid the British in the Zulu Rebellion, embrace a life of celibacy,
and undertake a difficult political mission to London. Meanwhile, in a dramatic and historic development, Gandhi and the Transvaal Indian community would openly and solemnly pledge themselves to resist governmental
oppression, by civil disobedience if all else failed.

Amidst all this change—indeed as part of it—Gandhi transformed the
shape and nature of his life as a lawyer. When he had first agreed to stay in
South Africa in 1894, he had done so on the condition that there be a clear
separation between his private legal practice and his public work. That distinction began to break down in Natal in the late 1890s as he and his colleague at the bar Frederic Laughton challenged Natal's Dealers' Licenses Act
in the courts.

In the Transvaal, beginning in 1906, the distinction would collapse
altogether.

TRAMCARS, TEST CASES, AND CIVIL DISOBEDIENCE

A strong sign of a growing unity between Gandhi's two halves—his public
life as a political organizer and his private life as a lawyer—appeared in the
campaign against Johannesburg's restrictions against the use of the city's
tramcars by the Indian population.[1]

After Johannesburg was taken over by the British in the Boer War, the
occupiers dismantled the then-existing horse tram system and comman-

deered the animals for military purposes. The horse-dependent system that was put back into operation in August 1902 was widely recognized as inadequate for the times. With the city's population on the rise, there was a pressing need for efficient, large-scale, and modern transportation technology. Johannesburg, like cities in North America and Europe, decided to take advantage of the development of electricity to install a system of electrical tramcars. The horse-drawn trams that the colonists had long relied upon would rapidly begin to disappear.

But discrimination would not.

With great fanfare, the new electrical tram system began operations on February 14, 1906. Its importance to Johannesburg cannot be exaggerated, but, surprisingly, at the start of operations the city had not come to any conclusions about how it would implement its color prejudices with respect to the system's operations.[2] In mid-February the city's Tramway and Lighting Committee reported its recommendations to the town council. The committee proposal barred all Indians from regular tramcars, except for servants accompanying their masters or mistresses. And even they would have to sit apart from other passengers—in back seats on the top of the car. The committee suggested that the city experiment with colored-only cars for Indians and natives or, should traffic not be sufficient to run them profitably, that further experiments be undertaken to allow Indians to ride either on cars used for hauling parcels or on smaller trailers attached to European cars.[3]

Gandhi and the Indians complained that the proposal was both inadequate and insulting. While they claimed that they were entitled to "the same facilities as any other community"—a claim the *Transvaal Leader* characterized as "absurd"[4]—they also said they were willing to accept segregated cars in which Europeans would be given the main, inner portions and Indians and other non-Europeans would be given the roofs.[5]

After cursorily taking note of the Indians' objections and their alternative proposal, the town council moved straight to a consideration of the committee's recommendation. Two very different camps of councillors opposed the committee's scheme. One camp thought it went too far in disfavoring the Indians, while the other camp thought it did not go far enough. On successive votes, neither was powerful enough to carry the day. The council then adopted the committee's recommendation unchanged, which had the practical effect, as Gandhi then noted, of prohibiting Indians from using the trams.

Gandhi quickly reacted on two fronts. On the public relations front, he moderated the Indian position, arguing only for the right of "well and cleanly dressed" Indians to ride on European cars. He also began to formulate and employ a litigation strategy. He planned to challenge the city by setting up a test case. While Gandhi was plotting this course, the city temporarily suspended its newly adopted restrictions on the Indian use of cars until the system was more fully operational; in the meantime, it would continue to run separate cars for Europeans and "coloureds."[6] It appears that Gandhi wanted an immediate confrontation on the discrimination question, however, because he pushed his test case forward despite the withdrawal of the new restrictions. He arranged for a wealthy Indian merchant, Ebrahim Saleji Coovadia, to board a European tramcar in the company of one of his articled law clerks, William J. MacIntyre.[7]

Thus would begin Gandhi's first foray into civil disobedience. He had written about civil disobedience two years earlier in *Indian Opinion*. Now he meant to try it out. He would send Coovadia out to deliberately breach the color line, hoping that such defiance would land the matter in court. Gandhi envisioned a criminal prosecution, but with a twist. It would not be the activist Coovadia who would be tried, but rather the conductor for refusing to allow Coovadia to board. The city's old traffic bylaws, apparently written without the prospect of segregation in mind, required conductors to take all comers on board.

In their first attempt to ride a European car, Coovadia and MacIntyre received no opposition. Still looking to set up the facts necessary to challenge the segregated system, they boarded a second European car. There they got the opposition they sought. The car's conductor stated that he would allow Coovadia entry only if he was the servant of the white European accompanying him. This was not the case, of course, and consequently, the conductor barred Coovadia from riding. Gandhi had his facts.

Now he needed to engage the legal process. In early March, Gandhi succeeded in forcing the Crown prosecutor to act on a criminal complaint filed by Coovadia. The exact charge leveled by the prosecutor against the conductor is lost to history, but it likely was "contravening the traffic bye-laws."[8] The conductor was summoned to defend his actions. Trial began on March 7, before Assistant Resident Magistrate J. G. Kerr. The prosecution was undertaken by the attorney for the Crown, a Mr. Blaine, while Gandhi was present to brief the prosecutor on behalf of Coovadia. The town council sent an advocate, a Mr. Hile, to defend the conductor. Blaine surprised Gandhi by conducting "the case well without discriminating between the white and the Coloured."[9]

Coovadia's testimony that he was forbidden by the conductor from riding and advised by him to use the trams labeled for "coloureds" went unchallenged. The conductor's defense was that he was simply acting on orders from the city not to allow Indians on European cars unless they were accompanied by their masters or mistresses.

Blaine, the prosecutor, argued for the conductor's guilt by pointing out that the traffic bylaws allowed Indians to ride without restrictions. Hile, for the conductor, conceded this point, but claimed that an old Boer regulation prohibited Indians from riding on European cars. The magistrate agreed with Blaine's response that the Boer provision was no longer in effect and found the conductor guilty. The city immediately announced its intention to appeal to the Supreme Court, but shortly afterward reversed that decision. This left Gandhi and the Indians frustrated. They could not now obtain an authoritative Supreme Court decision upholding the rights they asserted. So Gandhi started over again, sending Coovadia out to board another European car on April 7. He was once again refused permission to board. Another complaint was filed with the Crown prosecutor and trial was set for May 18.

Blaine, the public prosecutor, was once again briefed by Gandhi. To defend John Welch, the conductor, the city brought in Richard Feetham, a Transvaal barrister who earlier had been a powerful local official and who later would sit on several appellate courts in South Africa.[10] The courtroom was crowded with Indians and members of the press. Coovadia recited the by now familiar facts. Welch reprised the conductor's role. He confirmed Coovadia's testimony and stated that he was simply following his instructions not to let "coloureds" on the cars unless they were accompanying their masters or mistresses.

Then Feetham played what he thought was his trump card. He called the city inspector of vehicles to the stand. T. H. R. Jefferson testified that the responsibility for issuing licenses to tramcars resided in his office and that he had, in fact, issued a license for the tramcar in question. Was it an unrestricted license? No. Was it restricted? Indeed, it was. The car was licensed for use by Europeans only. Feetham thought this restriction would fully justify Welch's actions.

Almost before Feetham could sit down, Blaine, with Gandhi at his side, destroyed this defense. The license, they demonstrated, had been issued on April 11, four days after the incident in question. The restrictions imposed by the license were of no effect on the date of the incident, the 7th. These facts constituted a fatal blow to Welch's defense. Feetham was reduced to arguing that without a license the tramcar was not a public vehicle and the conductor could do whatever he wanted. The magistrate, unconvinced by this feeble argument, as well as Feetham's other arguments, found Welch guilty. Feetham's client paid a small fine and went home. Feetham had to read in the next day's papers how Blaine and Gandhi had upstaged and embarrassed the highly regarded barrister.

But the city, with local opinion-makers predicting disaster if the tram system were to be integrated,[11] was not about to be outfoxed.

The prosecutor's charge against Welch was that he had violated the traffic bylaws by refusing Coovadia entry to the tramcar.[12] Because the bylaws required conductors to carry passengers without exception, the conductor's conduct was culpable. The defense had argued that a city regulation, enacted during a time of concern over the spread of smallpox, authorized the city to bar "coloureds" from cars reserved for Europeans.[13] This defense was rejected. The magistrates in the two cases had found the regulation to be ineffective because it had been overridden by the city's more recent bylaws.[14]

So the city took the obvious step—it repealed the bylaws. With nothing to block it, the Boer regulation sprang back into effect, and Indians were once again banned from the cars by force of law. Gandhi was angered but resolute: "This is a clear case of betrayal. This means that we will have to put up a fresh struggle beginning all over again—which will be both very troublesome and costly. But it has to be undertaken if the Indian community does not want to submit to this defeat."[15]

Gandhi recruited another prominent Indian, Abdul Gani, to confront the council. Gani, as chairman of the British Indian Association (BIA), was a natural choice because he had been outspoken about the legal right of all coloured people to ride the trams without restriction. To this assertion the *Transvaal Leader* had replied: "Mr. Gani may talk about law, but the law is the will of the people, and it is the will of the people that coloured persons shall not ride with whites in this country."[16]

To see what the law was, Gani, in the company of the newest associate in Gandhi's office, H. S. L. Polak,[17] boarded a tramcar in May 1906. Gani was promptly informed by its conductor that he could not take a seat. He refused to get off the car. Both the police and a tram inspector were called. All the parties had a polite conversation, the result of which was an agreement that Gani would get off, but be arrested for interfering with the operation of the tramcar. Everything seemed to be in place for another court challenge to the segregation of the cars.

But this challenge was different from that mounted in the Coovadia case. In that instance, Coovadia was the victim of the conductor's violation of the traffic bylaws, thus permitting Gandhi to insist on a prosecution on Coovadia's behalf. In Gani's case, the Indian activist was the one accused of committing an infraction. Gandhi could hardly insist on a prosecution of Gani. The city authorities understood this difference. The town clerk called in Gani and Polak and told them that "the Indians had done enough, and that they should not further harass the Council." The clerk also informed them that the town council was formulating new regulations to govern the trams and that, once they were published, the Indians could challenge them, if they wished.

In short, the city authorities refused to prosecute Gani and give Gandhi the forum he wanted. Had he more experience with civil disobedience, Gandhi might have responded to the city's stratagem with one of his own. He might have sent waves of Indians onto the trams and packed the jails to overflowing. This approach, which would have forced the city's hand and which would later be used by both Gandhi and his spiritual heir Martin Luther King, Jr., simply did not occur to Gandhi in the first half of 1906.[18] His understanding of the power of civil disobedience to change the law was still in its infancy. At this early stage, Gandhi looked at disobedience in a limited way—as a mechanism to get test cases before courts. While he did have a rapidly growing appreciation of the relationship between and among self-suffering, public sympathy, and curative institutional reaction, he did not yet fully understand how to use mass disobedience as a point of leverage for engaging larger social, political, and legal forces. He would learn this soon enough. In the meantime, Gandhi's attack on tramcar segregation, using test-case litigation as his weapon, ended in complete failure.[19] Indians would not be permitted on regular tramcars.

The dogs of European masters, however, would be welcome.

THE ASIATIC LAW AMENDMENT ORDINANCE: REGISTRATION AND RESISTANCE

The fight against tram segregation was but one part of a larger movement of resistance to the Transvaal government.

European retail businesses faced stiff competition from Indian retailers. Just as had been the case in Natal, Indian businesses in the Transvaal were quite good at controlling costs and thus regularly undersold Europeans. As a result, the loyalty of both European and Indian patrons steadily moved from European to Indian establishments. The *Rand Daily Mail* reflected white sentiment when it editorialized that the Indians "seriously limited the market for white enterprise."[20] The European business community reacted by applying enormous pressure on the government to act on its behalf. In response to this and other pressures, the government proposed a number of measures, of which the Asiatic Law Amendment Ordinance provoked the most strident Indian opposition.

Supporters of this new legislation (simply referred to as "the Act" during this time) claimed that a tidal wave of illegal Indian immigration was sweeping over the colony and that, to help control it, it would be necessary to first identify those Indians currently in the country lawfully. To do this, the government proposed an amendment to Law 3 that would require all Indians to register with the government. Indians would be required to carry certificates showing that they had done so. Indians who had not registered would be denied business licenses and ordered out of the colony. While the legislation itself did not explicitly call for fingerprinting, it was broadly understood that, as part of the registration process, Indians would be forced to provide impressions of all ten digits.[21]

The Indians reacted to this proposal with tremendous indignation. They had already been subjected to registration regimes under Law 3 and the Peace Preservation Ordinance of 1903.[22] They saw no need for yet another. They believed, moreover, that the proposed act treated them not with the respect to which British subjects were entitled, but as a class of common criminals. While investigating the proposed act, Gandhi read Edward Henry's book *Classification and Uses of Finger Prints* (1900), from which he concluded that "finger prints are required by law only from criminals."[23]

The day after the text of the Act was published in the August 22, 1906, issue of the *Government Gazette*, Gandhi and other leading Johannesburg Indians laid out their plans for a large protest meeting.[24] Shortly afterward Gandhi prepared the ground for this meeting by proclaiming in the pages of *Indian Opinion* that Indians would choose jail over compliance with the Act::

> If, disregarding our attempts at gentle persuasion, the Government enforces the Ordinance, Indians will not abide by it; they will not register themselves, nor will they pay fines; they will rather go to gaol. We believe that, if . . .

Indians ... firmly stick to this resolution, they will at once be free of their shackles. The gaol will then be a palace to them. . . . And the Government, for its part, will realize that it cannot with impunity go on humiliating Indians. . . . It is our duty to make some sacrifice for the sake of others. We do not realize there is real beauty in this: that it is thus that we please God and do our true duty.[25]

Indians of all social and economic classes had great respect for their countryman who had achieved the lofty status of lawyer. This lawyer was now publicly and unreservedly advising them to break the law. This was not the polite violation of the law in which the lone Coovadia had engaged to help Gandhi set up his court challenge to the segregation of the trams. Rather, this was mass lawbreaking intended to alter the balance of political power between the Indian community and the European colonists. The adoption of such tactics would put the Indians in uncharted territory.

This change in how the Indian community positioned itself was paralleled by a change internal to Gandhi. The day after the early September issue of *Indian Opinion* landed on its readers' doorsteps, Gandhi made a dramatic offer in a speech to the Hamidia Islamic Society:

Let the accusation of breaking the law fall on us. Let us cheerfully suffer imprisonment. There is nothing wrong in that. The distinctive virtue of the British is bravery. If therefore we also unite and offer resistance with courage and firmness, I am sure there is nothing that the Government can do. . . .

I do not want to say more. I would only advise you not to register yourselves again. If the Government sends us to gaol, I shall be the first to court imprisonment. And if any Indian is put to trouble because of his refusal to register afresh in accordance with the Draft Ordinance, I will appear in his case free of charge.[26]

For years Gandhi had used his law license almost exclusively to serve the commercial interests of his clients. With the tram test cases and the DLA cases before those, he gradually transformed himself into a part-time civil rights lawyer. Now he was entering upon a new stage in his understanding of the relationship between his practice of law and his politics.

THE EMPIRE THEATRE MEETING

At the end of his Hamidia Islamic Society speech, Gandhi asked his fellow Indians to attend a protest meeting: "On Tuesday next, we are holding a mass meeting, and I expect you all to close your business on that day and attend it."[27]

And attend they did. On Tuesday, the 11th of September 1906, Indian opposition to the proposed Act reached the boiling point when a huge crowd of Indians pressed into Johannesburg's Empire Theatre, specially rented for the occasion of this protest. The meeting was set for 3 P.M., but Indians from all parts of the Transvaal began arriving at 11 A.M. The doors, not set to open until 2 P.M., had to be flung open at noon. By 1:30 there was not a seat left in the house. Every bit of standing space was taken. Hundreds were turned away. The stage alone was packed with some two hundred Indian leaders. By the time Abdul Gani, as chair, stood up to convene the proceedings, some three thousand people had crammed themselves into the Empire's every nook and cranny.

The theater was cast in semidarkness. There was no artificial illumination, for there would be no electricity available until later in the day. A bright stream of sunlight, however, coursed through one of the theater's windows and fell, auspiciously, upon the chairman's seat and the yellow silk covering that decorated it.

The meeting's organizers had created a lineup of speakers that included some of the most politically active and prominent members of the Indian community. Gani—a partner in the Camrooden firm, head of the BIA, and a Gandhi client—spoke first. He informed the group that a legal opinion had been sought from a distinguished Pretoria lawyer, who concluded that the Act did not, as its sponsors claimed, expand Indian rights, but actually made the condition of the Asiatic "more intolerable than before."[28] Gani then indicated that a resolution to be offered to the group later in the afternoon would have the group pledge to ignore the law and court imprisonment rather than abide by it. Gani's rhetoric reached a peak with these words: "There are moments in the life of a community when resistance . . . becomes a vital necessity and a sacred duty, and I think that such a moment is now at hand for us if we would be called men."[29]

Other speakers included a well-known Indian physician, William Godfrey, whose eloquent speech called for disobedience to the law, and a decorated Indian war veteran, Nawab Khan, who appeared in uniform and gave a dramatic talk in which he argued that the Act treated his service for the British as if it meant nothing.

The afternoon, however, belonged to Haji Habib and H. O. Ally. Habib was a leader in the BIA and a Pretoria merchant. Ally was the founder of the

Hamidia Islamic Society and a Transvaal merchant who had long been active in politics. The two men had played key roles in generating support for the meeting.

Habib spoke first, moving the adoption by the assembly of a jail-going resolution. He roused the crowd by mocking whites, who "were perfect in everything they did, having come down from heaven; while the poor Indians obviously came from the other place, because their skins were black." Indians knew their rights, however. "Will you pledge your word with me to refuse to register and to go to jail instead?" he asked. The reporter for the *Transvaal Leader* described the assembly's reaction to this challenge: "The audience as one man agreed to go to prison rather than apply for a new permit."[30]

As high as emotions were at this point, Ally stoked them even higher. Seconding Habib's motion, Ally contrasted the treatment the Indians were receiving from the Transvaal government with the great traditions that characterized the British Empire. He then took a Union Jack, draped it around his shoulders, and reminded the crowd that the British flag stood for equal rights. He promised the crowd that should the Act become law, he would once again wrap himself in the flag and voluntarily present himself to the police for arrest on the grounds that he would not register. When he challenged his countrymen to do the same, the entire group of three thousand rose and shouted out a resounding "Yes!" Then, in the day's most dramatic moment, each of the three thousand solemnly raised his hand and pledged to go to jail rather than obey the Act.

This was not what Gandhi had expected. As one of the authors of the jail-going resolution, he certainly wanted to see it approved by those in attendance. He had not anticipated, however, that in the process of considering it, the audience would be challenged by the Indian leadership to take a solemn oath to support it. For Gandhi, an oath raised one's commitment to a whole new level. Invoking the name of God, he thought, made the person who does not keep his pledge a sinner. Gandhi feared that the crowd did not understand and appreciate the seriousness of what it was doing. His original intention had been to remain in the background on this day, and consequently he was not on the original roster of speakers. Aware of his role in initially calling for disobedience and sensitive to how the community looked to its lawyer for counsel, however, he sought and received permission to speak. Gandhi rose from his chair on the stage, faced the thousands before him and brought home to them, "in earnest, serious and carefully-chosen language,"[31] the consequences of what they were about to do:

You must understand what is this responsibility, and as an adviser and servant of the community, it is my duty fully to explain it to you. . . .

We may have to go to jail, where we may be insulted. We may have to go hungry and suffer extreme heat or cold. Hard labour may be imposed upon us. We may be flogged by rude warders. We may be fined heavily and our property may be attached and held up to auction if there are only a few resisters left. Opulent today we may be reduced to abject poverty tomorrow. We may be deported. Suffering from starvation and similar hardships in jail, some of us may fall ill and even die. In short, therefore, it is not at all impossible that we may have to endure every hardship that we can imagine, and wisdom lies in pledging ourselves on the understanding that we shall have to suffer all that and worse. If some one asks me when and how the struggle may end, I may say that if the entire community manfully stands the test, the end will be near. If many of us fall back under storm and stress, the struggle will be prolonged. But I can boldly declare, and with certainty, that so long as there is even a handful of men true to their pledge, there can only be one end to the struggle, and that is victory.

A word about my personal responsibility: If I am warning you of the risks attendant upon the pledge, I am at the same time inviting you to pledge yourselves, and I am fully conscious of my responsibility in the matter. It is possible that a majority of those present here may take the pledge in a fit of enthusiasm or indignation but may weaken under the ordeal, and only a handful may be left to face the final test. Even then there is only one course open to some one like me, to die but not to submit to the law.[32]

Perfect silence enveloped the crowd while Gandhi spoke. The lawyer upon whom those in the audience had long relied for advice on the niceties of contracts, promissory notes, and ejectments was now advising them on the consequences attendant on committing civil disobedience. A new relationship between the lawyer and his clients was emerging.

The tension created by Gandhi's sobering remarks was released minutes later when the assembly, giving the jail-going resolution its unanimous approval, burst out in full-throated cheers for what it had done.

EXPERIMENTING WITH DISOBEDIENCE

In his Empire Theatre remarks and elsewhere, Gandhi preached the acceptance of jail as both a consequence of conscientious adherence to principle and, in some vague and undefined way, a pragmatic route to success. It was clear what Gandhi meant when he referred to jail-going as adherence to principle.

In just what way was it a route to success? Did part of the answer depend on how the disobedient positioned himself in court? In particular, should a disobedient Indian bow to the prosecution and quietly accept his punishment in an effort to gain public sympathy? Or, by contrast, should Indian defendants engage in spirited resistance to the government's charges, using the courtroom as a stage to publicize their arguments against registration? And then, if conviction and punishment were, in fact, to follow, could they serve as useful tools in a propaganda campaign? Gandhi would soon have a laboratory, first in the person of a Hindu priest, for his experimentation with these very questions.

Ramsundar Pundit,[33] himself the son of Hindu priests, had emigrated from India in 1898 for the purpose of serving the religious needs of the Hindu community in South Africa. He labored in Natal for seven years, married, and began his family there. Then in 1905, the Germiston Hindu community invited Ramsundar to join it in the Transvaal.[34] The government provided him with a temporary but renewable pass, making it possible for him to move to Germiston. Once there, he gained a reputation for effective leadership. When the campaign against the Asiatic Law Amendment Ordinance began, Ramsundar was quick to speak against the Act and to lead the local effort to picket registration officials.

His opposition to the Act was noted. The government, which had routinely renewed his permit earlier, now refused to do so again. He declined to register under the Act, making his presence in the Transvaal putatively illegal. After he refused to heed the government's advice that he depart the Transvaal, he was arrested on November 8, 1907, and promptly jailed. The charge was for "contravening Act No. 3 of 1907 in residing in Transvaal colony without a permit."[35] Ramsundar refused offers of bail, preferring instead to remain incarcerated pending his trial.

On November 11, Ramsundar appeared in Germiston Police Court with his defender, Mohandas K. Gandhi.[36] The prosecutor sought a postponement so that he could arrange for the presence of a witness. Gandhi did not oppose this and suggested that Ramsundar be released on his own recognizance in the meantime, arguing that Ramsundar had every reason to appear, because he "considered himself innocent . . . and was prepared to fight the case." The court granted Gandhi's application and trial was set for the 14th. Ramsundar left the courthouse to an ovation, cheers, and flowers from the Indian crowd that had gathered to watch the morning's proceedings.

Three days later a much larger crowd of Indians and European colonists took every available seat in the Germiston courtroom. As several hundred more Indians swarmed around the courthouse, Gandhi stood before the magistrate and refused to concede his client's guilt, entering a plea of "not guilty" on his behalf.

The weight of the prosecution's case was carried by the registrar of Asiatics. Montfort Chamney testified that the priest had received a series of temporary permits, the last of which had expired on September 30, 1907. The registrar refused to grant another renewal and had ordered Ramsundar to leave the colony. Gandhi had replied to the registrar, sending along a letter from his client in which Ramsundar stated that he would refuse to leave the colony and pleaded that he was needed by his faithful inasmuch as there was no one to replace him.

The prosecution's case was simple. Ramsundar's previous permit expired and was not renewed. He was ordered out of the colony. He did not leave.

Gandhi saw another dimension to the case. His cross-examination of the registrar demonstrated that the registrar refused to renew Ramsundar's permit only because of Ramsundar's opposition to the Act. When pressed about the source of the information as to Ramsundar's failure of allegiance to the government, Chamney claimed to have received complaints that Ramsundar was preaching about nonreligious matters. In Chamney's mind, this made him an undesirable.

Gandhi asked the registrar if he had warned Ramsundar about the complaints. He had not. Gandhi asked him to state when he had received the complaints. He could not recall. Gandhi asked him if he would produce the complaints. He would not.

Gandhi's hope was to transform the simple factual issue of whether his client possessed a permit into the more complicated political issue of whether the registrar was justified in not renewing the priest's permit. The prosecutor understood exactly what Gandhi was up to. With the registrar on the ropes, he objected to Gandhi's questions as irrelevant. Gandhi's response was that a man who had been virtually accused of sedition should be entitled to know the grounds for the charge, the order to leave the colony, and the "preposterously unjust treatment" accorded him.[37]

The magistrate did not warm to Gandhi's argument, however, stating that the court "could not go outside of the four corners of the law" and that it was his duty to "administer the law as he found it."[38] In other words, he accepted the straightforward paradigm advanced by the prosecution—no permit, no right to be in the colony—and rejected Gandhi's paradigm, which attempted to require the government to offer some justification for the nonrenewal.

In the face of the court's ruling and with the same relentlessness he exhibited in *Adams*, Gandhi asked the court to require the production of the complaints. The court gently refused Gandhi's request.

Gandhi had failed to sink the prosecution's case with his cross-examination of Chamney. With a conviction practically assured, the prosecution rested.

Gandhi called three witnesses in defense of his client. Abdul Kadir, the chairman of the Hamidia Islamic Society, testified that the level of the defendant's opposition to the Act was no greater and no less than that of any other member of the society. He also stated that there was a religious dimension to opposition to the Act. This testimony, in light of the magistrate's interest in only the "four corners of the law," counted for nothing.

Next on the stand was the president of the Hindu congregation to which the defendant ministered. Lal Bahadur Singh claimed that "the accused had never done anything but religious work" and that he had preached against the proposed Act "purely on religious grounds."

Gandhi's third and final witness was the defendant himself. In a dramatic flourish, Gandhi had him complete his testimony by proclaiming that he "would rather suffer imprisonment on account of his religion than leave the Colony" and that he was "quite prepared to die for his religion."[39]

On cross-examination, Ramsundar continued to defend his resistance on religious grounds, arguing that Hindus were prohibited from giving their wives' names, but without referring to any source of this prohibition. From the start of the controversy over the Act, Gandhi and other Indian leaders had claimed there was a religious basis to their opposition. They never succeeded, however, in articulating a compelling explanation of their religious objection.[40] Ramsundar's testimony did not add much clarity to this claim.

In his closing argument, Gandhi forthrightly admitted that conviction was an inevitability, but, in a last attempt to adjust the paradigm by which the court was judging the case, he sought from the magistrate some opinion as to how the law had been administered in Ramsundar's case. The flavor of Gandhi's argument might be learned from a letter he wrote immediately after the conviction to the editor of the *Johannesburg Star*:

> The priest was never given the opportunity of facing his unknown traducers or answering the complaints. . . . [H]e was condemned unheard. I am not aware of any precedent except during war-time, for such high-handed, unjust and tyrannical action. One man [the registrar], who, as he admitted . . ., has not the slightest knowledge of the law, is utterly incapable of weighing evi-

dence, and who can scarcely distinguish between sedition and respectful and manly opposition to a particular law touching on personal liberty, possesses under the Act extreme power over the persons of free and inoffensive British subjects.[41]

The magistrate praised Gandhi's closing argument as "very able," but, nonetheless, declined Gandhi's invitation, stating that the court

> was unable to criticise the law, and had only to administer it as it was placed before the Court. Whether the Registrar . . . had been right or wrong in his reasons for refusing the renewal of the permit did not lie with the Court. The . . . Court was to take the case simply as it was presented in connection with the law . . ., and deal with it in accordance with the evidence.[42]

With that, the court pronounced Ramsundar guilty. The magistrate's sentence, however, was a surprising, barely veiled response to Gandhi's plea for the court to render its opinion of the government's decision to prosecute. He handed the defendant the gentlest and shortest punishment possible—a month in prison without hard labor.

Ramsundar was immediately led from court to jail, but not without first enjoying the vociferous cheering of a large crowd of his countrymen gathered about the courthouse. Gandhi and many other Indian leaders stayed on to address the crowd, now gathered at Market House. During the course of this mass meeting, it was resolved that all Indian businesses would refuse to operate the next day as a show of disapproval of the government's action. And, indeed, not one Indian merchant opened.[43] This demonstration of resolve was preceded by a prophetic resolution, passed by the meeting and stated in the form of a cable to the king:

> Pundit has preferred gaol to sacrifice of principle.
> Thousands ready do likewise.[44]

What were Gandhi's goals in instructing Ramsundar to plead not guilty and in forcing a trial? On the one hand, the lawyer in him sought from the court, if not an acquittal, then an expression of opinion that the prosecution of his client was unjustified and, following from that, the least punitive sentence possible. The political organizer in him, on the other hand, must have desired a suffering hero, a figure to personify to the Indian public the sacrifices necessary for victory to be achieved. His representation of Ramsundar thus exposed the tension between his private role as an advocate for his client and his public role as a political organizer for the Indian cause. Accordingly, the result must have quietly pleased Gandhi in that it gave him everything he wanted: a conviction that made a model of the Indian priest, as well as a sentence that would be served under the most lenient possible conditions and that would free his client from jail in the shortest possible time.

Because the government continued to refuse to compromise with the Indians over registration in the remaining weeks of 1907, it would not be long before Gandhi would be presented with another opportunity to make of the two halves of his life a whole. Before that would occur, however, there was hay to be made in the press from the Ramsundar case. A report in the *Transvaal Leader*, quoting remarks made by Gandhi in late November, is illustrative: "A man perfectly guiltless, and striving to live his life as he best knew how, serving the spiritual needs of his countrymen, had been sent to gaol, and was today in default in Johannesburg simply because of this Asiatic Act.... [A]n Act which had exacted already this heavy price could never be submitted to."[45]

In *Indian Opinion*, Gandhi wrote: "We are convinced that the case against him has done much good to the community. Everyone feels bolder as a result of Pundit's going to gaol. At a time like this, nothing but good can be done by any Indian going to gaol in the course of the struggle against the law."[46]

Indian Opinion also carried an interview by Gandhi with Ramsundar, in which the jailed priest states: "After my release, I shall be prepared to go to gaol again for the sake of the community.... How is it that other Indians have not been arrested, though it is already December? We shall gain our freedom only when that happens."[47]

With Gandhi at his side, Ramsundar was released from jail December 13, 1907. The two men were greeted by about six dozen prominent figures in the Indian community, and then, as they marched to the Fordsburg mosque for a rally, they were joined by several hundred other Indians who garlanded Ramsundar and escorted him to a platform decorated with flowers and canopied with British flags.[48] The press was there to provide ample coverage of Ramsundar's pledge to continue his resistance. The *Transvaal Leader* wrote: "Ram Sundar Pundit ... exhorted his hearers to continue the struggle to the uttermost. If his conduct in going to prison had been an example he hoped it was one which every one of his countrymen would follow.... He was prepared to be arrested and rearrested, but he would not leave the Colony or submit to the demands of the new Registration Law."[49]

His listeners greeted these defiant remarks of Ramsundar, whom they regarded as a martyr, with cheers. As an icon in the fight for Indian rights, Ramsundar Pundit had become by far Gandhi's most celebrated client.

Soon after his release the government threatened him with reimprisonment.

In response, he fled the Transvaal.

FIGURE 1. Gandhi as a law student in London. Courtesy of the Gandhi Sabarmati Ashram and Archive.

FIGURE 2. The Durban Magistrate Court. Courtesy of National Gandhi Museum.

FIGURE 3. Gandhi with his staff, Johannesburg, 1905. Gandhi, center, is flanked by his secretary, Sonja Schlesin, seated on his left, and his associate, Henry S.L. Polak, seated on his right. Courtesy of the Gandhi Sabarmati Ashram and Archive.

FIGURE 4. Gandhi in Johannesburg, 1906. Courtesy of National Gandhi Museum.

FIGURE 5. Jan Christian Smuts. Courtesy of National Gandhi Museum.

FIGURE 6. Albert Cartwright. Courtesy of National Gandhi Museum.

FIGURE 7. Ramsundar Pundit.
Courtesy of National Gandhi
Museum.

FIGURE 8. Sorabji Shapurji.
Courtesy of National Gandhi
Museum.

FIGURE 9. Gandhi, pictured here with his codefendants and clients, moments before being jailed, January 1908. Gandhi is third from left. Courtesy of the Durban Local History Museum.

FIGURE 10.   Gandhi and Indian resisters burn registration papers, Johannesburg, August 16, 1908. Courtesy of National Gandhi Museum.

FIGURE 11. Gandhi in London, 1909. Courtesy of National Gandhi Museum.

FIFTEEN

Courthouse to Jailhouse

We have made up our mind to make this a white man's country, and, however difficult the task before us in this matter, we have put our foot down, and shall keep it there.

COLONIAL SECRETARY JAN SMUTS

True victory will be won only when the entire Indian community courageously marches to the gaol—when the time comes—and stays there as if it were a palace.

GANDHI

THE RAMSUNDAR CASE, WHICH UNFOLDED in the closing months of 1907, foreshadowed the mass arrests of the leaders of the Indian resistance movement that would occur shortly afterward. After threatening action for months, the government moved decisively at the end of 1907 to enforce the Asiatic Law Amendment Ordinance by prosecuting Gandhi and many of his colleagues for their refusal to comply with the Act's registration scheme. To understand how his part in this resistance changed Gandhi's life, some background concerning the Act, and Indian opposition to it, is in order.

GANDHI FOR THE DEFENSE: PRELUDE

The timing of the introduction of the Act in the Transvaal legislature could not have been more insulting to the Indian community. When the Zulu Rebellion erupted in Natal in 1906, Gandhi made the same argument for Indian support of the British and the colonists as he had made when he urged Indian support of the British in the South African War in 1898—and with no better result. Gandhi and other Indians gallantly served in an ambulance corps in mid-1906, and, for their trouble, the Transvaal government enacted the Asiatic Law Amendment Ordinance shortly after the fighting concluded and the corps disbanded. The Act, as described in the preceding chapter, would require Indians to carry registration certificates and was widely understood as also requiring Indians to give all ten of their fingerprints.

After the Act passed, the Indians decided upon a major initiative to block the Act from coming into effect. They committed a large amount of funds to send Gandhi and H. O. Ally to London in an attempt to persuade the British government to disapprove of the colony's legislation. (Because the Transvaal did not yet have responsible government, London wielded substantial authority to veto legislation of which it disapproved.[1]) A one-man whirlwind of activity, the indefatigable Gandhi was masterful in his role as leader of the Indian opposition. Displaying the organizing ability that characterizes excellent lawyers, he fashioned a strong coalition of influential Britons to oppose the legislation. And he applied the force of his personality to the moment. The London correspondent for the *Rand Daily Mail* cabled home: "Mr. Gandhi . . . has, with his intellectual face, his low, intense voice, and his unusual power of concentrating his thought, carried all before him."[2]

And he did meet with great success. The imperial government disallowed the legislation. When the news came, the Indians were overjoyed. In Gandhi's mind, however, this joy had to have been tempered by a realistic concern that the colonists would have the last word.

Prior to the Indian delegation's departure from England, Winston Churchill, then the undersecretary of state for the colonies, predicted to Gandhi that the colonists would simply reenact the legislation when the colony received responsible government status. At that point, Churchill warned Gandhi, there would be little London could do about it.

Churchill was right. The Transvaal received responsible government status on January 1, 1907, held elections in February (from which Indians and natives were, of course, excluded), and convened its legislature in March. The legislature promptly passed legislation virtually identical to the bill London had earlier disallowed, enacting the Asiatic Law Amendment Ordinance in March 1907 by a unanimous vote.[3]

The Transvaal's whites saw the Act as a necessary response to the mortal threat to white society they believed the Indians posed. As the Act's author, Lionel Curtis, articulated the issue: "The question which hangs in the balance is whether the white man in South Africa is to maintain his place for himself and his kindred or to yield it to the Asiatics."[4]

It was not a surprise when the Act received royal assent in early June 1907. The registration scheme was set to become effective on July 1, 1907. Despite Churchill's warning, Gandhi and the Indians were "staggered" by the Act's passage.[5] Gandhi later would write: "I saw nothing in it but hatred.... [It meant] the absolute ruin for the Indians.... I clearly saw that this was a question of life or death for them. I further saw that even in the case of memorials and representations proving fruitless, the community must not sit with folded hands. Better to die than submit to this law."[6]

Throughout the remainder of 1907, the Indians and the government, in the person of Colonial Secretary Jan Smuts, played a cat-and-mouse game. The Indians would state their refusal to register. The government would extend the registration period. The Indians would again state their refusal to register. The government would again extend the registration period. All the while, Gandhi offered to compromise with the government. On numerous occasions, he suggested that Indians be allowed to register voluntarily, with enforcement of the Act reserved for those who failed to do so. The government unwaveringly rejected Gandhi's repeated compromise efforts. In the meantime, he busied himself with motivating Indians to resist, a task at which the *Johannesburg Star* found him proficient: "Mr. M. K. Gandhi, the well-known Indian barrister, is the leader of the passive resistance movement. He has certainly marshalled [*sic*] his forces well, and the Indians as a rule are prepared to follow him to the extreme."[7]

Ample evidence suggests that, during this period of intense public involvement, Gandhi, a glutton for work,[8] did not ignore the needs of his commercial clients, as he continued to regularly represent their private interests in court.[9] And as Gandhi's capacity for work grew, so did his comfort with being a public figure. He appears to have had no difficulty in finding words, whether in speaking before huge audiences—such as the crowd of three thousand who heard him speak on September 11, 1906, or the crowd of two thousand who heard him in Durban in March 1907—or before smaller, more intimate groups such as the fifty or so leaders of the Indian community who heard him speak at a dinner held in his honor (and that of Ally) in January 1907. Of that performance it was written that "Mr. Gandhi, in his calm and expressive tones, held the audience spell-bound whilst he told them of the work they had tried to do in England."[10] Years of public appearances—first in the rough-and-tumble backwaters of Durban's courtrooms and town council chambers, then in the Transvaal's somewhat more sophisticated courts, and finally in the salons of London—taught Gandhi to trust in himself. The tongue-tied youngster so lacking in self-confidence that others had to read his speeches for him had vanished. There now appeared a mature man who spoke with the natural assurance that characterizes the advocate who knows from experience who he is and what he wants. This change in Gandhi developed at the same time he was imposing on himself several self-denial disciplines. During 1906, for example, he decided to permanently refrain from sexual relations with his spouse, Kasturba, and to engage in certain dietary restrictions. All these changes were parts of a larger whole.

By the time of the registration crisis, Gandhi was as comfortable in advocating the Indian position in public as he was in collecting on a promissory note in magistrate court.

And the change, slow in coming, blossomed in Gandhi not any too soon. Indians throughout the Transvaal turned to the man they called "Barrister Gandhi" for guidance in their struggle with the white colonists. The pressure was on him to deliver a singularly clear message—and that he did. In unequivocal terms, he urged his countrymen to refuse to register under the new act and to instead court imprisonment. Over and over, from late 1906 and throughout all of 1907, this lawyer's advice to his community was constant—disobey the law.

> What are we to do in this situation? We have only one answer. We have hailed the refusal of assent to the . . . Ordinance as a victory. But true victory will come only when we show our strength. It is certain that the . . . Ordinance will be introduced. When that happens, there should only be one thought in the mind of every Indian: never to accept such a law. And, if it is enforced, he will rather go to gaol than carry a pass like a Kaffir. True victory will be won only when the entire Indian community courageously marches to the gaol—when the time comes—and stays there as if it were a palace.[11]

To dispel any doubts about his own intentions, Gandhi promised to break the law himself: "I hereby declare my pledge that, should the new law come into force, I will never take out a permit or register under the law but will go to gaol; and even if I am the only one left who has not taken a permit, my pledge shall stand."[12]

The courage to resist the law came more easily for Gandhi than for ordinary Indians who had no experience of courts and jails. Gandhi sought to reassure them by repeatedly guaranteeing that he would personally represent all who defied the law and would do so for free.[13] He publicly made this pledge on several occasions between September 1906 and November 1907.[14] At the start, the pledge was unrealistic on at least three levels. There did not appear to be an effective defense to the charges. Furthermore, if resistance was as widespread as Gandhi hoped it would be, and if the government prosecuted resisters in any numbers at all, Gandhi could not possibly appear everywhere throughout the Transvaal to represent them all. Finally, there was the very real possibility that the government would arrest Gandhi early on—a prospect he recognized—such that the lawyer himself would be imprisoned before his clients were summoned to court.

To make matters worse, the terms of Gandhi's several pledges of aid were unclear, inconsistent, and ill-founded, leading those contemplating resistance to wonder not only whether there was some hope of acquittal but also whether Gandhi would represent them and under what conditions. Gandhi's first offer to represent every Indian who refused to register under the new act appeared to be unconditional. The offer engendered hope among would-be resisters that the purpose of Gandhi's representation would be to effect their discharge. In response, Gandhi attempted to educate his countrymen as to what his approach to their defense would be. It would have two parts. Gandhi would first claim that the resister was only following the advice of his lawyer and the BIA and that therefore the lawyer and BIA leaders, not the resister, should be arrested and convicted. Gandhi's second line of defense, following the lead of his Natal mentor Frederic Laughton, would be to seize upon irregularities in the proceedings, if any, to justify the resister's discharge.

Some of these defenses held no promise. The defense of "on advice of counsel" has never been recognized outside of very limited circumstances. The defense that one acted on the advice of other laypersons (here the BIA) has enjoyed virtually no support in the law. By intending to rely on these defenses, Gandhi exposed his naïveté about the criminal law. Procedural irregularities on the part of the prosecution or court offered somewhat more promise and were, therefore, a more legitimate defense. Although irregularities are always welcomed by defense counsel, they are unpredictable in the frequency of their appearance and, when they do appear, not always strong enough to justify a discharge.

As the months passed from the time of Gandhi's initial offer in September 1906, he began to modify the conditions attached to it. In April 1907 Gandhi announced that he would represent only poor Indians free of charge and, to qualify for this offer, they must hold a permit under the previous registration schemes.[15] In late May 1907 he repeated the offer, dropping the restriction of poverty on the part of the defendant, but adding several new terms, including his refusal, "with or without fees, [to] defend those who do not desire a gaol sentence."[16]

This last-mentioned proviso must have been a wake-up call for those who harbored hopes of acquittal. Indeed, in commenting on his offer, Gandhi warned resisters that his main aim in representing them was to simply "keep up the courage of the accused" and that, in the circumstances resisters would find themselves in, "neither lawyers nor anyone else can help."[17] Yet anyone who had hopes of acquittal could not be faulted for maintaining those hopes in the face of these comments, for Gandhi himself, after discouraging resisters from thinking about any outcome other than jail, repeated the notion that a meritorious defense was possible. The defense he articulated was a variation of the "advice of counsel" and the "advice of others" defenses. Gandhi explained that he would testify that "the Indian community has been bound, by oath and resolution, not to submit to the new law, that the accused has accepted the said resolution, and that, if for such action a sentence has to be passed, it should first be passed on the office-bearers of the Association." The resister would then testify that he was bound by the September 11 resolution not to register. As a result of all this, according to Gandhi, "the accused may be let off."[18] This defense, however, was quite unlikely to find support from the bench. It is difficult to think of a lawyer with any experience at all as actually having confidence in it.

Perhaps Gandhi can be excused for his contradictory statements about the purpose and availability of his services and for not maintaining a firm embrace of his original pledge to represent every nonregistrant. In the months before the government initiated its program of arrests to enforce the Act, he was already engulfed in an increasingly intense blizzard of uncompensated defense work on behalf of Indians resisting the government.[19]

GANDHI FOR THE DEFENSE: FROM COURTHOUSE TO JAILHOUSE

Done with delay, the government, led by colonial secretary and former general Jan Smuts, finally set November 30, 1907, as the last date for registration—and the Indians, led by their lawyer and organizer, Mohandas Gandhi, responded with persistence in their defiance of the law. They would not register. Of the seven to eight thousand Indians in the Transvaal, less than 10 percent—about five hundred—had registered.

There was little conjecture as to whether the government would act against the Indians. Smuts had taken a particularly harsh position on the question, saying that he would "carry out in full the provisions of the . . . Act, and if the resistance of the Indians residing in the country leads to results which they do not seriously face at present they will have only themselves to blame." Gandhi replied in kind, stating that he made "no apology for drawing the General's attention to the solemn declaration of British Indians with reference to the Act."[20]

There was tremendous tension within the Indian community, however, over the question of when and in what manner the government would act. On December 3, 1907, the *Transvaal Leader* reported: "All yesterday afternoon unregistered Indians were enquiring at Mr. Gandhi's office, Court Chambers, as to what was going to be done, and disappointment seemed to be expressed because nothing definite had eventuated."[21]

The question of his own arrest surely was on Gandhi's mind. The enormous demands on his time and talents during December 1907, however, must have provided a measure of distraction from his concerns. The middle two weeks of December are illustrative. He defended some three dozen resisters in Volksrust. He traveled back to Johannesburg, where he defended another resister. He penned letters to the *Johannesburg Star* and *Indian Opinion*. He escorted Ramsundar from jail and spoke at his post-release rally. He wrote eight separate pieces for the *Indian Opinion* of December 14. He wrote two letters to Smuts. Through correspondence with the general manager of the Central South African Railway, he represented the interests of forty workers who had been discharged from their employment for failing to register. He wrote another five articles for the *Indian Opinion* of December 21. And he did all this while continuing to operate his private law practice.

The speculation about when the government would act reached a peak at about the time that the *Transvaal Government Gazette* announced that the king had not disallowed the Immigration Restriction Act (passed earlier in the year by the legislature) and that the act would come into force on the first of the year. Some believed that this act would permit the government to deport those who had not registered.[22] The *Gazette* announcement helped fuel rumors throughout the whole of the Transvaal of impending arrests, causing Gandhi's law office to be besieged by throngs of worried Indians seeking consolation and advice. Finally, two days after Christmas, H. F. Papenfus, the acting commissioner of police for the Transvaal, telephoned Gandhi. Papenfus wanted to know whether Gandhi would meet with him that day. Gandhi agreed to do so. At their meeting at Marlborough House, Papenfus informed Gandhi his arrest had been ordered. He also disclosed to

Gandhi that the arrests of twenty-two other persons had been ordered. Among those to be arrested were Thambi Naidoo, the chief picket in Johannesburg, and M. I. Desai, the chief picket in Pretoria. Three were Chinese allies, including the leader of the Chinese resistance, Leung Quinn. Ramsundar Pundit was to be arrested in Germiston. Gandhi pledged to Papenfus that he and all the other defendants would voluntarily appear in court the next day, December 28.

That night, however, there was a speech to be made at the Hamidia Islamic Society hall, packed to overflowing with a large crowd of six hundred or more anxious Indians.[23] Gandhi minced no words, saying that if "Jesus Christ came to Johannesburg and Pretoria and examined the hearts of ... General Smuts and the others, [Gandhi] thought he would notice something strange, something quite strange to the Christian spirit. . . . [S]ome sections of the Act [were] savage, and he said they were only worthy of an uncivilized Government. . . . He would never be sorry for the advice he had given them. . . . [H]e would give the same advice that he had ventured to give them for the last 15 months."[24]

The next morning, with their spirits fortified by Gandhi's defiant words, the Johannesburg defendants gathered at Gandhi's office. There their spirits were buoyed even further by the presence of a huge crowd of Indians. Shortly before the appointed time of 10 A.M., the ten defendants, accompanied by their supporters, marched off to court to face their accusers. Upon their arrival at the courthouse, Gandhi and the others were asked by Superintendent George Vernon of the Transvaal Town Police, Division B, to display the registration certificates required by the Act. When the defendants did not, they were immediately arrested and put on trial before Magistrate Harry H. Jordan.

The courtroom was filled to overflowing. A large crowd of hundreds of Indians and Europeans who could not squeeze their way into the courtroom milled about on the courthouse grounds. The appearance in court of the well-known English-trained barrister in his role as a defendant rather than as a lawyer was quite the draw.

The case of *Rex v. Mohandas K. Gandhi* was the first to be called. Prosecutor P. J. Schuurman called Superintendent Vernon to testify that Gandhi, an Asiatic over sixteen years of age, had failed to produce his registration when asked to do so that morning. Gandhi, representing all the defendants, including himself, asked no questions. Rather, he pled guilty and stepped into the witness box: "I hope you will allow me to make an explanation. I do not want to make a long explanation, but I think it is necessary, seeing that I am an official of the Court, that I should render an explanation as to why I have not submitted to this Act."

Magistrate Jordan's reaction must have immediately communicated to Gandhi that he had made an unfortunate tactical mistake: "I don't think that has anything to do with the case. The law is the thing, and you have disobeyed it. I don't want any political speeches here, and I won't allow them."

Gandhi agreed: "I don't want to make any political speeches."

Jordan then erected the narrow analytic framework familiar to civil disobedients over the centuries:

> The question is, have you registered or not? If you have not registered there is an end of the case. If you have an explanation to offer *ad misericordiam* [in mitigation] as regards the order I am about to make, that is another story. There is the law, which has been passed by the Transvaal Legislature and sanctioned by the Imperial Government. All I have to do and all I can do is to administer the law as it stands.

Gandhi said that he would decline to give evidence in extenuation. Jordan responded: "All I have to deal with is legal evidence. What you want to say, I suppose, is that you do not approve of the law and you conscientiously resist it."

"That is perfectly true," Gandhi replied. Jordan then gave Gandhi a renewed opening by saying, "I will take the evidence if you say you conscientiously object." When Gandhi resumed his testimony by recounting his arrival in the Transvaal and describing his service as secretary to the BIA, Jordan cut him off: "That does not affect the case." Gandhi acknowledged as much and "asked the indulgence of the court for five minutes."

Jordan turned him down: "I don't think this is a case in which the Court should grant any indulgence. You have defied the law."

Gandhi capitulated: "Very well, sir, then I have nothing more to say."

Numerous observers from the press were present at the trial, ready to provide their papers the copy from which bold headlines are made.[25] By failing to clearly think through his strategy, Gandhi, by far the Indians' preeminent spokesman for passive resistance, had needlessly forfeited his best opportunity to appeal directly to the European public for its understanding and sympathy.

By the time the court turned its attention to the remaining defendants, they found themselves represented by a wiser lawyer than the one who represented Gandhi. "Not guilty!" each of them pled. Unfortunately none of them had Gandhi's capacity for eloquence, as would become evident when Gandhi questioned each defendant as to why he had defied the law. P. K. Naidoo was first. After Superintendent Vernon provided the same testimony against him that he had given earlier, Gandhi examined his co-defendant:

Are you a British subject?

—I am.

Were you in the Transvaal before the war?

—Yes; since 1888.

Did you pay the Dutch government £3?

—I paid nothing.

You have not taken out a registration certificate under this law?

—No, not under any law.

Why not?

—I thought it was not fit for me to do so; it was degrading.

C. M. Pillay testified in a fashion similar to P. K. Naidoo, stating that he did not believe that any self-respecting person should comply with the law. Seeing no irony in his answer, Thambi Naidoo said that to register would have "placed him a grade lower than a Kaffir." Karwa claimed registration was against his religion.[26]

In what amounted to his closing argument, Gandhi directed the court's attention to the fact that all of the defendants had

said something more or less with reference to the finger-print system. He [Gandhi] asked the Court to dismiss from its mind the idea that these men did not know what they were doing. He knew that what he was about to say could not affect the decision of the Court, but he thought it was his duty to himself and his clients to make this explanation. There were certain things in this world which one could not explain, and there were certain things in this world which men felt but could not express, and he left it to the Court to interpret the feelings of the accused with regard to the finger-print system.[27]

Gandhi was correct that this vague defense would have no effect on the decision of the court. After Jordan pronounced himself puzzled by the argument that fingerprinting was against the Indians' religion, he found all the defendants guilty.

The Asiatic Law Amendment Ordinance, along with the Peace Preservation Ordinance and the IRA, equipped the court with the power to order violators out of the country. Schuurman, the prosecutor, took a hard-nosed tack. He pointed out to the court that the defendants had enjoyed a long period of time within which they might have registered and that it was quite plain that they had no intention of registering now. The court should not now give them a long period of time within which to depart the colony. Speaking to Gandhi's case, he urged the court to order him out within forty-eight hours.

Before Gandhi could respond to the prosecutor's position, Jordan openly shared his thoughts, revealing a magistrate who was caught between understanding and intolerance:

> The Government had been extremely lenient . . . yet it appeared that none of these people had registered. . . . He [Jordan] had no wish to be harsh, in the matter; and he did not intend to adopt the suggestion of Mr. Schuurman in regard to 48 hours. He should make reasonable orders. He must give Mr. Gandhi and the others time to collect their goods. . . . He did hope that a little common sense would be shown . . . and that the Asiatic population . . . would realise that they could not trifle and play with the Government. If they did that they would find that when an individual set[s] himself up against the will of the State the State was stronger than the individual, and the individual suffered and not the State.

Gandhi interrupted Jordan. "Make the order for 48 hours," he asked. And if the court could make it for a shorter time, Gandhi continued, he would be even more satisfied. Jordan sarcastically replied: "If that is the case I should be the last person in the world to disappoint you. Leave the Colony within 48 hours is my order."

Jordan gave the remaining defendants forty-eight hours to two weeks to depart the Transvaal. The proceedings closed with Gandhi in command of the courtroom. He stood and thanked "the Court, the Public Prosecutor and the Police for the courtesy which had been shown throughout the trials."[28]

The court's order to quit the Transvaal created even more intense press interest in the "Asiatic question" than had previously existed. Would Gandhi and the others leave? If not, when would the government apprehend them? And, once the nonregistrants were apprehended, would the government attempt to exercise its right to deport them, a right disputed by some? Gandhi would be a free man for at least another forty-eight hours. Making up for the opportunity he had lost in the courtroom, he would use the time to bring home his message to both his supporters and the European colonists. He started quickly; he announced at a rally held immediately after the trial that neither he nor his co-defendants had any intention of leaving the Transvaal and that they were "perfectly resigned to being rearrested."[29] He urged his large audience on Government Square to retain their resolve to go on

> with the struggle, no matter what happened to him or anyone else. He [Gandhi] would certainly not change his views, and he urged the Asiatic communities to strive against the . . . Act even if it meant deportation. . . . He held that it was better to leave the Colony than to lose their self-respect and honour by remaining as slaves. This was a religious struggle, and he gave them the advice he had always given them—to fight to the bitter end.[30]

The next afternoon Gandhi was in Pretoria to address a large Indian crowd that greeted his presence with enthusiastic applause. He took the occasion to announce that Ramsundar had fled rather than face the possibility of a second, and harsher, prison term. "So far as the Indian community was concerned, Pandit was civilly dead." Encouraging his audience to persevere, he stated that if Indians "did their duty it did not matter that the Government of the Transvaal or the might of the whole Empire was against them, he was still certain of victory." Cognizant that his remarks would be read by European readers the next day, he pointedly argued that the Indian struggle was not "against the Europeans as such, but a struggle for self-respect." He concluded by expressing his confidence in the notion that God was on the Indians' side.

On Monday, December 30, Gandhi took full advantage of what was scheduled to be his last day of freedom to write and speak. On that day he composed a striking letter to the *Johannesburg Star*. It contains both Gandhi's harshest and most poetic language to date. Writing about the prospect that deportation would leave the defendants' families "to die of starvation," Gandhi condemned deportation as a disproportionate punishment that strongly savored of barbarism. Speaking with the voice of the lawyer who had counseled his Indian constituency to engage in civil disobedience, he defended both the basis and method of the Indians' resistance to the law: "I claim it to be perfectly honorable . . . to advise my countrymen not to submit to the . . . Act as being derogatory to their manhood and offensive to their religion. And I claim, too, that the method of passive resistance adopted to combat the mischief is the cleanest and the safest, because, if the cause is not true, it is the resisters, and they alone, who suffer." In language worthy of Thoreau, whom Gandhi would later read, he continued: "I refuse to believe in the infallibility of legislatures. . . . It is no part of a citizen's duty to pay blind obedience to the laws imposed on him."

Gandhi saved his most elegant language for the letter's concluding paragraph: "And if my countrymen believe in God and the existence of the soul, then, while they may admit that their bodies belong to the State to be imprisoned and deported, their minds, their wills, and their souls must ever remain free like the birds of the air, and are beyond the reach of the swiftest arrow."[31]

Gandhi also used the day of the 30th to speak before four hundred members of the Chinese Association, to give an interview to Reuters, and to deliver a speech at the Fordsburg mosque. In his speech to the Chinese Association, he made another attempt to explain the religious basis of the resistance and to remind his Chinese allies that if they believed in the rightness of their cause, nothing could stop them.[32] He also referred to the opinion the Indians had secured from Leonard that the government lacked deportation powers. In his Reuters interview, he floated the idea of sending the dispute to the Imperial Conference for resolution. In his Fordsburg speech, he articulated his hope that "after sixteen months' resistance no Indian would now flinch."[33]

The press, the public, and the defendants themselves fully expected the resisters who had been given forty-eight-hour deadlines (Gandhi, P. K. Naidoo, Karwa, Pillay, and Easton, the last a Chinese defendant), having not been arrested on Monday, to be arrested on the morning of Tuesday, December 31. Crowds of Indians buzzed about the police courts and Gandhi's nearby law office on Rissik Street, waiting for the arrest. Gandhi apparently had been told that the defendants should appear in court at 10:00 that morning for the arrest. Word soon began to circulate, however, that the police commissioner had telephoned Gandhi, just as he was about to leave his office for the courtroom, to inform him that the government was not quite ready to have him. The commissioner would send word when the government was, in fact, ready to arrest him. With this news, Gandhi was "almost mobbed" by an elated Indian crowd that then grew to a size so huge and exhibited a tone so defiant that the police moved in to disperse it. Before the police could finish their work, however, Gandhi was able to get in a few words of encouragement. Standing atop a chair, he pleaded with his countrymen to "stand shoulder to shoulder in a strong protest."[34]

Between December 31 and the time when the defendants would be arrested for refusing to obey the court's order to leave, Gandhi would make full use of the intense public interest in the question of when the government would act against him. Ironically, he attracted significant attention on the 1st of January by not speaking. A crowd of some two thousand Indians gathered for a rally that day at the Fordsburg mosque. To demonstrate that the Indians could and would carry on without him, Gandhi, while present, refrained from addressing the crowd. The press made note of this in its coverage of the rally.

The press was also present in force on January 3 to cover Gandhi's defense of Nawab Khan and Sumander Khan, the defendants whose cases had been postponed for lack of an interpreter. Not only was the press present, but also on hand was yet another huge crowd of Indians, estimated to be between 1,000 and 1,500. Those relatively few who could find seats in the courtroom could hear the low hum of the crowd throughout the proceedings.

Vernon testified for the prosecution, as he had in the first case. Gandhi had no questions for him. On direct examination of his clients, Gandhi emphasized their military service, and the injuries they had sustained, as a means of communicating to the public that Indians, their resistance to the Act aside, were actually quite loyal citizens of the empire. This testimony had no effect on Magistrate Jordan. He ordered Nawab Khan out of the colony within fourteen days and then interrupted the proceedings to complain that "he had been approached by both Indians and Chinamen who told him that the question of putting their finger-prints on the permits had nothing to do with their religion—absolutely nothing at all. . . . [T]he truth of the whole thing was that they were frightened to register for fear of being molested by their countrymen."[35]

Hearing this, Gandhi attempted to use Sumander Khan's direct examination to rebut this accusation:

MR. GANDHI: Have you been frightened by anyone?
—No, if they threatened to hang me they could not frighten me. [Laughter.][36]

After inadvertently using his client's own testimony to make the magistrate's point, Gandhi attempted to recover by stating that he was surprised "to hear that some Indians and Chinamen had approached the Magistrate with reference to the registration question. Fortunately or unfortunately the Court had before it two soldiers who were not likely to be frightened, as had been suggested. . . . [T]here was no question of fright. If there was a question of fright the arms of the law were strong enough to protect the King's subjects." Gandhi "thought it was futile," he continued, "to suggest that anyone was frightened into not taking out registration certificates. It was not a question of thumb or finger prints, but this was a thing that touched on their liberty."

At this point, Magistrate Jordan, who had initiated the discussion of this topic, cut Gandhi off, sharply reminding him, much as he had done in the first trial, that if he "wanted to address a meeting he could doubtless do so, but the Court was not the place for such speeches."[37]

Gandhi did not go silent: "The Bench has led the way, otherwise I would have held my peace. I don't wish the public to leave the Court with the impression that the whole of this objection to registration has reference to thumb and finger impressions. It is a religious fight and a fight for liberty."[38]

Magistrate Jordan tried to have the last word, repeating his charge that he had been told by Indians and Chinese that they "were frightened of their lives to register" and ordering Sumander Khan out of the colony in fourteen days.[39] The last word, however, belonged to Gandhi, who had already succeeded in seeing to it that the Transvaal press would carry his message.

Indeed, over the course of the following week, Gandhi carried on a vigorous campaign in the press, highlighted by his response to a much-noticed speech given by General Smuts.[40] On January 5 Smuts broke his silence on the Asiatic question when he returned to the capital from an out-of-town trip to deliver a lengthy speech. In it, he alleged that massive forgeries of permits had taken place and that fingerprinting was now essential. He distinguished the Indian community from its leaders, arguing that resistance to the law was not so much the product of a natural aversion to it on the part of the Indian population as the result of "organized agitation on the part of certain leaders of the Asiatic community." The Asiatics who objected to the law "had been misled by certain of their leaders whom they had trusted."[41] He invited the community, as opposed to its leadership, to confess being misled, plead mistake, and ask for one more chance to register.

Gandhi's response took the form of lengthy interviews with the *Star* and the *Leader*. In the *Star* interview, he rebutted Smuts' charge that there had been a surreptitious influx of thousands of illegal Indians, attacked the fingerprint requirement, called the Act degrading class legislation, called for a judicial inquiry into the question, denied that there had been any intimidation of those attempting to register, and denied that he and the Indian leadership had misled their community. In his interview with the *Leader*, he defined "passive resistance" as a "protest against … degradation and an offence to feeling," expressed an openness to compromise, announced that the Act "can never be accepted by the Indian community, more so as the community is bound by a solemn declaration," and suggested specific legislative actions that would resolve the crisis.[42]

The next day Gandhi gave an interview to Reuters in which he made a very specific compromise offer. If the Act would be suspended, Gandhi would see to it that "every Indian in the country would be registered in one month's time," after which the Act could be repealed. Gandhi emphasized that what the Indians objected to was compulsion.[43]

During the same week that he was giving these interviews he also wrote two entries for *Indian Opinion*. The first and quite lengthy entry is especially notable, for in it he announced his adoption of the term *satyagraha* as a replacement for "passive resistance." He also took the occasion to praise Sonja Schlesin, his young legal secretary who doubled as a pro-Indian activist.[44] The second and shorter entry was dramatically entitled "Last Message to South African Indians." In it Gandhi pleaded with his countrymen "to remain undaunted . . . and be ever mindful of their pledge and keep up their courage." He appealed to Indians outside the Transvaal to send not just their congratulations but their money. And, finally, he appealed to all Indians for Hindu-Muslim unity. Given its title, Gandhi must have expected this to be his last salvo in the press. It was not to be. He had been notified to appear for his arrest in court at 10 A.M. on the 10th of January. He was surprised that day by a visit from Vernon, however, who informed him that his hearing had been postponed until 2 P.M. that day. As was his way, Gandhi jumped into the gap and made it productive. He headed for the Newtown mosque, where a large crowd assembled on short notice to hear him speak one final time before his inevitable incarceration. Gandhi warned his audience that should they bow to the law, they would "lead a dog's life." The community had to continue its resistance after Gandhi was jailed and show the colonists that "they were men." He remained optimistic about the outcome of the resistance. Gandhi

> had not the slightest doubt that General Smuts had sufficient humanity in him to recognize the sincerity of purpose, the real feeling that underlay the community. . . .
>
> He thought the whole of the community would rise and tell General Smuts, if the Colony was convinced they were sincere, willing to suffer for their cause and their country, religion and honour, then the Colonists would tell General Smuts he had not received a mandate to expel these people from the country.[45]

The *Johannesburg Star* reported that Gandhi "was listened to with the greatest intentness. Every eye was fixed upon the slim central figure of

Mr. Gandhi, and the meeting gave an indication of the hold he has upon his countrymen."[46]

A GENTLE RAIN

After the meeting, Gandhi retreated to his office, while a huge crowd of Indians assembled on Government Square in anticipation of the afternoon's proceedings. A quiet, gentle rain fell. At exactly 2 P.M., Gandhi and other members of the leadership made their way onto the square. The crowd may have been there to see Gandhi, but he may not have taken much notice at first. Gandhi, never the one to lose a moment's productivity, had his head buried in the first edition of that afternoon's *Star* as he slowly walked toward court. He had just received word of sentences handed down to his colleagues in Pretoria for their resistance to the Act. Perhaps he was searching this early edition of the *Star* for details that would be relevant in his own hearing.[47] As he did so, he may not have even noticed it was raining, for his supporters had erected a canopy of umbrellas to protect him from the weather. Eventually, however, he had to take cognizance of the assembly and his environment as he and the others were surrounded by well-wishers, many of whom were anxious to shake hands with the defendants.

When the police opened the courthouse doors to the public, the crush of people on the entrance was so great that chaos erupted. The police had to close the entrance on two separate occasions, push back the crowd into the square, arrest some overly enthusiastic people, and set up a line of mounted and regular police before any kind of order in processing would-be spectators could be established. As these events were occurring, the names of the six defendants were called, and the six worked their way through the crowd and into the courthouse.

When they arrived in the courtroom, not only was the public seating section filled, but people were also occupying every bit of the available standing room as well. The magistrate entered and a court official commanded silence. The silence was pierced by the calling of the first case—*Rex v. Gandhi*.

Gandhi stood before the magistrate, his fellow members of the bar, and hundreds of fellow Indians, some of whom he had undoubtedly represented in the very courthouse in which he was now a defendant. Gandhi raised no defense on his behalf. He immediately and without commentary pled guilty to disobeying the court's order to leave the Transvaal.

To make his record, Schuurman, the public prosecutor, called Fred Klette, the court clerk, to the stand. Klette produced the records from Gandhi's December 28 appearance and testified that he personally served the order on Gandhi to remove himself from the colony. Gandhi had no questions for Klette.

Schuurman then called Vernon, who testified that he had seen the defendant in the Transvaal on a number of occasions since the 28th and that he had arrested him earlier that afternoon for defying the court's order. Again, Gandhi had no questions of the witness.

Schuurman rested his case.

Gandhi rose and asked for permission to make a statement. Jordan had prohibited Gandhi from making a statement when Gandhi had pled guilty on the 28th to the charge of not having registered. In a similar vein, he had attempted to discipline Gandhi for comments the court deemed extraneous at the soldiers' trial just the previous week. Now there was Gandhi in front of him again, asking for permission to make a statement. Perhaps sensing the gravity of the moment, Jordan relented.

Gandhi had a most unusual request. He had learned that the resisters in Pretoria had been given sentences of three months' hard labor, plus fines— and if they refused to pay their fines, they had been told, they would be sentenced to an additional three months at hard labor. If these Indians had committed an offense, Gandhi's was greater. The court, therefore, should impose on him the maximum sentence possible. Jordan was incredulous:

MR. JORDAN: You ask for the heaviest penalty which the law authorizes?

MR. GANDHI: Yes, sir.

MR. JORDAN: I must say I do not feel inclined to accede to your request of passing the heaviest sentence, which is six months' hard labour with a fine of £500. That appears to me to be totally out of proportion to the offence. . . . This is more or less a political offence, and if it had not been for the defiance set to the law I should have thought it my duty to pass the lowest sentence which I am authorized by the Act. Under the circumstances, I think a fair sentence to meet the case would be two months' imprisonment without hard labour.[48]

Practically every Indian in Johannesburg was in the crowd outside the courthouse awaiting word of Gandhi's fate and that of the other defendants. When the news of Magistrate Jordan's decision arrived, an ocean of small black flags appeared as if on command. Spontaneous chanting broke out.

Following a very large single black flag hoisted aloft on a long pole, the crowd surged out of the square in a procession that would take it onto the street where Gandhi's office was located and then in the direction of the mosque.

Gandhi, meanwhile, was taken off to a special holding room to await his jailers.

As he sat there, quite alone, Gandhi's mind turned to venues with which he had become so familiar and so comfortable—his home, the law courts where he practiced, the square where he addressed a large public meeting just a short time ago.

Now these were all being taken from him.

The thought shook him.

For the first time in his life, he was going to prison.

SIXTEEN

Malpractice

I do plead guilty. . . . I had too great faith in the statesmanship
of General Smuts, in his honesty, and in his integrity.

GANDHI

AS GANDHI ENTERED THE JOHANNESBURG jail, he did not know that
another troublesome South African lawyer—this one named Nelson
Mandela—would follow his footsteps into that same jail some fifty-four years
later. Nor did he know that a free South Africa would someday honor their
presence there by choosing the site of the jail for its new Constitutional
Court.

What Gandhi did know on January 10, 1908, is that he had to make his
peace with imprisonment. He quickly set about regaining his composure,
and, indeed, he vigorously embraced his jail experience, declaring himself
"content to be in jail" and saying that he actually enjoyed it. Gandhi took
advantage of the opportunity to read and reread a wide variety of materials
—among them the Bible; the Koran; Carlyle's writings on Robert Burns,
Samuel Johnson, and Sir Walter Scott; works by Tolstoy, Ruskin, and Plato;
as well as Bacon's essays on civil and moral counsel. Jail provided this overworked, overextended man with a degree of respite. It was good for him.[1]

His incarceration, however, was not good for the movement. Rather than
inspiring his fellow resisters, it deflated them. Gandhi himself reported that
his followers began to lose courage not long after his jailing. Those who earlier had shown the mettle necessary to go to jail with him "lost their nerve in
a few days, and some hinted that they would not go to jail again." Gandhi's
reaction was clear. "All these things," he wrote shortly afterward, "could not
just be ignored by a person who had been deeply involved in the struggle for
16 months."[2] With fervor for the cause rapidly weakening and under pressure
to strike a quick settlement with the government, Gandhi felt compelled to
act. In doing so, he committed an egregious but, in the end, a productive
error. It would cause the Indian movement in South Africa first to seek help

from the courts and then, out of frustration, to enter into a major campaign of civil disobedience.

WORDS MATTER

When Albert Cartwright, the sympathetic editor of the *Transvaal Leader* and one whom Gandhi considered a friend, visited Gandhi in prison on January 21 with a suggestion on how the dispute could be resolved, Gandhi was ready to listen. He and Cartwright agreed that the settlement should be an exchange of concessions: voluntary registration on the part of the Indians in exchange for repeal of the Act by the government. Cartwright visited Gandhi again on January 28 with a draft of a letter from the resisters to the government.[3] Gandhi believed the letter was inadequate on two points: it failed to indicate that voluntary registrants should be free from the application of the Act, and it failed to address the position of Transvaal Indians then outside the colony's boundaries. Gandhi made changes to the letter that he thought addressed these concerns and signed it.[4] Thambi Naidoo and Leung Quinn, two of the Indian and Chinese leaders in the resistance movement, also signed.

This letter was a key part of the negotiations that would result in a settlement freeing Gandhi and his fellow prisoners from jail at the end of January. Gandhi believed that, starting with this letter, he was piecing together an agreement with Smuts that would embrace the two features he and Cartwright had agreed were vital—repeal of the Act and voluntary registration. A major disagreement between Gandhi and Smuts, however, would erupt over the settlement. Gandhi would claim that Smuts breached the agreement when he later refused to repeal the Act, while Smuts would deny that repeal was ever part of the settlement. The fact is that Gandhi's January 28 letter focuses on the suspension of the operation of the Act—not its repeal. It is possible that what Gandhi *meant* was that the Act would be suspended during voluntary registration and then repealed once voluntary registration was complete. But that is not what the letter *said*.[5]

With the ink from Gandhi's signature barely dry, Cartwright left that same day for Pretoria to present the letter to Smuts. Later that afternoon, Cartwright called Gandhi with the news that Smuts had "accepted the letter."[6]

By the time history brought Smuts and Gandhi together in 1908, they had each undergone a good number of parallel experiences—with a few wrinkles of difference. Both were nearly the same age—born less than a year apart.

Both had been bold enough to venture overseas to study the law at the Inns of Court. Gandhi succeeded at the Inner Temple by dint of discipline and great effort; Smuts won prizes for his brilliant work while studying at the Middle Temple. Both were serious students of philosophy and religion, with Gandhi studying these subjects in the quiet of his room and his jail cell, and Smuts writing about Christ at Cambridge and reading philosophy in Germany. Each had worked in journalism: Smuts had written for the *Cape Times* and Gandhi was then writing for *Indian Opinion*. Gandhi led his people in a nonviolent resistance movement; Smuts became a military leader in the Anglo-Boer War. Both practiced law in the Transvaal. Both men eventually gave up their practices to lead their communities.

Each was a man of deep conviction. Just as Gandhi was determined to overcome white opposition to the assertion of Indian rights, Smuts was determined to maintain the monopoly of political, social, and economic control that whites had over the Transvaal.[7] The failure of the January 28 letter to clearly lay out the terms of the settlement would cause these two strongheaded figures to collide in a test of wills and strategies.

A MIRAGE OF VICTORY

When Smuts saw that the letter brought to him by Cartwright did not explicitly make repeal a condition of the settlement, he must have been pleased. He had been schooled in this question just two months earlier by Lord Selborne, high commissioner for South Africa and governor of the Transvaal. Selborne, in a private letter, had urged Smuts not to make such a concession:

> The Asiatics, through ... Mr. Gandhi, demand ... repeal of the ... Act. This ... ought never to be permitted by Parliament. The Asiatic is a very bad person from whom to run away, and I do not think that any such repeal would be consistent with the self-respect of the Government or the Parliament. But, if the Asiatics are, at the last, prepared to be reasonable, then I would make the way easy for them. The one simple object of the Government is to get them registered so that the Government may control future immigration. I would advise the Government to accept any proposals which the Asiatics may make which *really* would effect this object, even should it require a supplementary Act on this subject.... But the movement must come from the Asiatics to the Government, and it must come in a form which the Asiatics cannot afterwards repudiate. It must be on paper and vouched for by men who undoubtedly represent the Asiatics.[8]

From Smuts' point of view, everything was lining up to meet Selborne's prerequisites. The initiative for settlement came from the Asiatics, the contact was in writing, and Gandhi, Naidoo, and Quinn undoubtedly represented their communities. At noon on January 30, Smuts welcomed Gandhi to a meeting between the two in Pretoria. In reporting on this meeting in *Indian Opinion* a few days later, Gandhi states that Smuts accepted the "demands" contained within the letter.[9] Gandhi makes no mention of Smuts having specifically promised to repeal the Act.[10] In the wake of the meeting, a letter from the acting assistant colonial secretary was handed Gandhi, reflecting the deliberations of Smuts and his cabinet following the meeting. The letter conformed to Selborne's prescription not to repeal the Act but rather to offer some supplementary action by Parliament.[11]

On the same day he met with Smuts, Gandhi had a conversation with Registrar of Asiatics Montfort Chamney—a person for whom Gandhi had almost no respect—which caused him some discomfort about what the parties actually agreed to in the terms of the settlement. As a result, he asked Smuts' secretary for leave to see Smuts again. When he was refused, he put his thoughts into the form of a letter, informing Smuts that Chamney had "harped away on the Asiatic Act" and that Gandhi "gathered that the registration that will now proceed will be legalized under that Act." Gandhi went on to say, "At the interview with you, I did not understand any such thing at all."[12]

In *Indian Opinion*, Gandhi conceded that the letters between himself and Smuts "do not say categorically that the new law would be repealed." He defended the ambiguity this way: "The letters have been so drafted as not to shock the whites."[13] A few months later he made the seemingly baseless argument that repeal was implied in the letters.[14]

Gandhi did succeed in seeing Smuts again on February 3. Gandhi later claimed that several points were agreed upon in this discussion, including the repeal of the Act on the condition that the Indian community register voluntarily.[15] In what would prove to be a highly controversial provision of the settlement, all Indians were to provide their fingerprints during voluntary registration, with the exception of those who were well educated or who owned property.

Thinking this meeting had cleared up any lingering questions about the terms of the settlement, Gandhi declared the success of the Indians' campaign complete.[16]

During the campaign against the Act, so much stress had been laid on the indignity associated with fingerprints that Gandhi had a very difficult time convincing his constituency to accept the settlement.[17] His argument was that the community's real objection had always been to the compulsion inherent in the law and not actually to the giving of fingerprints themselves.[18] This historically accurate but politically ineffective argument contributed to an atmosphere in which Gandhi was widely and bitterly viewed by his compatriots as having betrayed them.

To help counter dissatisfaction with the fingerprinting concession, Gandhi announced he would be the first to register and give his prints. The move backfired. This was more than some of his erstwhile supporters could stomach. In a scene reminiscent of the time Gandhi was beaten after coming ashore in Durban eleven years earlier, he was severely beaten again—but this time by his fellow Indians. Some Pathan members of the Indian community—including a Gandhi client, Mir Alam—violently attacked Gandhi as he was walking to Chamney's office on February 10.[19] Alam and his colleagues struck Gandhi's head from behind with a cudgel, knocked him to the ground, and kicked and hit him repeatedly in the face and ribs until he lost consciousness. If the police had not quickly arrived on the scene and arrested Gandhi's assailants, there is no telling what his fate might have been. In another piece of good timing, a Johannesburg clergyman, Joseph Doke, happened by and spontaneously offered to take Gandhi in. He was carried off to the Dokes' home, where the lacerations to his face were stitched up and his other injuries were looked after by a physician who ordered Gandhi to refrain from speaking until his stitches were removed. The patient then stoically and determinedly returned to the business of the day—registration. When Chamney arrived at the Dokes' home with Gandhi's registration papers in hand, Gandhi silently turned to face him and, in pain, permitted Chamney to take his fingerprints. Gandhi describes what he learned in that moment about the power of self-suffering: "I then saw tears stood in Mr. Chamney's eyes. I had often to write bitterly against him, but this showed me how a man's heart may be softened by events."[20] Gandhi would spend about ten days recuperating under the Dokes' care. While at their home, he would pointedly and repeatedly announce that he wanted no prosecution of his assailants—just as he wanted no prosecution of his attackers in Durban.[21]

With the Indians temporarily weary of resistance and the case for the settlement apparently given an emotional boost by the reaction to Gandhi's beating, registration proceeded apace. At the same time, a semblance of normalcy returned to Gandhi's life. Relieved of the day-to-day pressures of leading the resistance movement, he now had the luxury of resuming his practice for several months. He also shepherded his friend and associate Henry S. L. Polak, through the process of admission to the bar. Polak had taken articles in Gandhi's chambers in 1905, subsequently passed his Transvaal bar examinations, completed his three-year term as an articled clerk under Gandhi, and was enrolled as an attorney before the Supreme Court of the Transvaal on April 6, 1908.[22] Gandhi had originally brought Polak into his practice to help him deal with the demand by Gandhi's commercial clients for legal services—a demand Gandhi could not meet by himself.[23] Little did Polak know that virtually the whole of his immediate career at the bar would now be consumed by his representation of resisters in the movement for Indian rights.[24]

That movement became active about six weeks after Polak's swearing in. By then it had become clear that despite the near-universal compliance of the Indians with the call to voluntarily register, Smuts and his government were not about to repeal the Act. Gandhi and many other Indian resisters were outraged, claiming that Smuts had pledged to repeal the Act upon voluntary registration. They had little, however, by way of convincing proof of Smuts' pledge, pointing only to rhetoric in a speech the colonial secretary had made at Richmond, to their own memories of the negotiations,[25] and to the ambiguous language in the Gandhi-Smuts correspondence.

The settlement collapsed. In an effort to gain what it thought it had already achieved, the resistance movement now had to resurrect itself. Arrests, convictions, jail sentences, bankruptcies, and innumerable other hardships would lie ahead. Gandhi managed to place his community in this unfortunate position because he had not honored a basic principle of law practice. In his January 28 letter to Smuts, Gandhi plainly did not make it clear that repeal was a condition of settlement. In turn, the government's responsive letter of January 30, 1908, made no mention of repeal. Gandhi was left to claim that in their early February meeting Smuts assured him—*orally*—that repeal would be given in exchange for voluntary registration.

Gandhi—the careful lawyer who always monitored the actions of opposing counsel with a microscope, the meticulous lawyer who paid attention to every detail of his own practice, the skeptical and persistent lawyer who was doggedly determined to get a written partnership agreement of his liking with Percy Coakes—this same Gandhi failed to follow the one practical rule of negotiation that every beginning law student knows by instinct: *get it in writing*. Had Gandhi modeled his negotiations with Smuts after his negotiations with Coakes, the parties would have used a document—a single document—to reflect their joint understanding. During the drafting process, this document would have been subject to the inspection and amendments of the parties. It would have been passed back and forth until both parties were satisfied with it. This one controlling document, reflecting the parties' complete proposed agreement, would then be signed by both parties. Only then would the agreement be both complete and final.

At the end of his negotiation with Smuts, what did Gandhi have? A confusing and ambiguous settlement offer from—but not drafted by—him to Smuts, a letter from a lower government official to Gandhi that never once mentioned repeal, and the recollection of a conversation with Smuts—to which only Smuts' ally Chamney was a witness—in which Gandhi claimed Smuts said the government would repeal the Act. This collection of ragtag documents and allegations amounted to something less than compelling and conclusive evidence. Yet repeal of the Act had been the central goal of the movement in the Transvaal for some time. Gandhi's failure to *get Smuts' pledge of repeal in writing* permitted Smuts to later deny that he had ever agreed to repeal the Act.[26]

How could Gandhi make so egregious and so fundamental an error? Perhaps he had confidence in Smuts, a fellow member of the bar, to keep his word.[27] Perhaps his time in prison disoriented him, disconnecting him from the usual practices he employed and the usual sensitivities he displayed everyday as an attorney. Perhaps the involvement of the trusted Cartwright in the negotiations gave Gandhi an unjustified sense that the normal precautions were unnecessary.

All the suffering the Indians had undergone, all the economic sacrifices they had made, and all the organizational work they had performed failed to deliver their most important goal, one they thought had been in their grasp. Now they had to repeat virtually their entire effort.

It was nothing short of a political disaster.

According to Gandhi, "the essence of the compromise [was] that, the under-taking of the Indian community being fulfilled, . . . the Act should be repealed."[28] Smuts, Gandhi surmised, had privately promised repeal in exchange for registration, had succeeded in getting the Indians to register—and then had denied repeal had ever been promised. Gandhi felt that he had been played false. Dedicated in his own life to truthfulness and honest deal-ing, Gandhi was not about to sit still for this.

Despite his many previous disappointments with the judiciary, lawyer Gandhi was still a believer. In 1908, he believed in the power of litigation, he believed in the fairness of the court system, and he believed that the colony's judges were as dedicated to truthfulness and honest dealing as he was. As a consequence, he felt comfortable when he threatened to take Smuts to court in an effort to retrieve the Indians' voluntary registration papers. The courts would rescue the Indians from a dishonest government. Then, with a court ruling in his favor, Gandhi hoped to nullify the volun-tary registrations that had taken place and thus return the power relation-ship between the parties to the state it was in before the settlement. From that position, the Indians would again have leverage on the government by refusing to register.

Gandhi first allowed the government an opportunity to avoid litiga-tion. He wrote to Chamney on May 26, asking for the return of his papers. He reminded Chamney of the agreement he and Smuts had made and Smuts' breach of it. He assumed Chamney would see that the government had "no legal right to the documents" because they were given to Chamney's office "only as a matter of grace, and not in virtue of any law." The naïveté of Gandhi's faith in the courts was rivaled by the seeming naïveté of his confidence in Chamney to act consistently with what Gandhi believed the law to be.[29] He gave Chamney a short deadline for complying: May 29.

Chamney, not surprisingly, ignored the deadline—but evidently passed word of Gandhi's letter to Smuts, who invited Gandhi to meet with him on June 6. Smuts would not commit himself at the meeting to the Act's repeal. After the meeting ended, Gandhi wrote to Smuts and took the position that unless Smuts permitted him to "make a definite statement that the Act is to be repealed," Gandhi would "reluctantly be compelled to fall back upon [his] letter to Mr. Chamney as to withdrawal of the application form." And if

Smuts did not agree that the Government should return the forms? Gandhi threatened "an application . . . to the Supreme Court for an order compelling the return of the documents."[30]

In the week following his unproductive meeting with Smuts, Gandhi brought Charles Ward into the case.[31] Ward agreed with Gandhi that the Indians were entitled as a matter of law to the return of their paperwork. With Ward's reassuring opinion in hand, Gandhi sent a telegram to Smuts citing Ward's opinion to his fellow lawyer and threatening to take the matter to the Supreme Court if no favorable response from Smuts was forthcoming. At the same time, Gandhi began preparing affidavits for use in the case.[32]

Gandhi set the affidavits aside when he received Smuts' call for another meeting on June 13. The two talked about using amendments to the Immigration Act as a way to settle the dispute. Again, Gandhi followed up his meeting with Smuts with a letter written the same day. In his letter, Gandhi carefully reviewed the Indian position, making a point-by-point list of the matters he insisted any new legislation must address. In this letter he is careful and detailed and concerns himself with addressing specific contingencies—all hallmarks of good lawyering—and all characteristics he failed to exhibit when negotiating from jail.

Gandhi and Smuts met again on June 22. At that meeting, Smuts did agree to repeal the Act, but only on the condition that the Immigration Act be amended in several ways that Gandhi found harsh and unacceptable.[33] Disappointed by Smuts' position, Gandhi asked for the return of his voluntary application papers. Smuts refused and challenged Gandhi to go to court to get them. In writing to the press about the failure of this meeting, Gandhi pushed back with an attack on Smuts: "The position of the Asiatics is simple. They must revert to the condition that prevailed in January last in this matter, and they have been advised to withdraw their voluntary application forms. General Smuts has declined to return them. If he had the courage to face the passive resisters, he would return them without much ado."[34]

Gandhi told the *Johannesburg Star* on the same day Smuts challenged him that he would immediately go to court. Gandhi did exactly that. On June 23 the Indians filed a petition with the Transvaal Supreme Court for the return of the application papers of Ebrahim Ismail Aswat, a Transvaal merchant and a one-time BIA officer. Aswat's suit would serve as a test case for the return of all the Indians' voluntary application papers.

Gandhi's petition, which was not a masterpiece of clarity, appears to rest on the notion that the government's refusal to repeal the Act constituted a breach of the settlement agreement and that this breach justified the return of the application paperwork.[35]

When the matter reached the Supreme Court for argument on July 2, Charles Ward argued for the Indian side that the applications were voluntary and that they were tendered "on the understanding that the Act would be repealed." The Act was not repealed and therefore the attempt at registration was, argued Ward, a nullity.

D. De Waal, in arguing for the government, fully accepted Gandhi's legal framework and addressed the breach issue head-on. Aswat, he claimed, had to prove that the government breached the agreement. The government never promised repeal as part of the agreement—thus there was no breach.

In deciding the case, the presiding justice, William H. Solomon, first addressed the question as the parties had framed it: was there a breach of an agreement between the Indians and the government? Solomon considered the two letters (the January 28 letter from Gandhi, Naidoo, and Quinn to Smuts, and the January 30 letter from the government to Gandhi) to constitute the whole of the agreement. After examining the letters, he concluded that "certainly there was no undertaking on the part of the Colonial Secretary to repeal the Act." He then took up Gandhi's allegation that the promise had been made orally by Smuts. Noting that Gandhi's allegation was denied by Smuts and Chamney, Solomon indicated that "in [the] face of their denial I cannot come to the conclusion that any such undertaking was given by the Colonial Secretary."

Solomon then turned to a related question he himself had raised in the course of the oral argument: was the application the property of Aswat or of the government? Solomon announced that it was his opinion that Aswat "intended to part company with the document" when he tendered it to the government. The document was the government's.[36]

For Solomon, the conclusion to all this was inescapable: the Indians were not entitled to their applications back.

It was a thorough defeat for Gandhi. He had not gotten Smuts' agreement to repeal in writing, and now the Indians were paying the price for that blunder. He tried to downplay the loss in the press the next day by characterizing the decision as a "questionable victory gained by General Smuts on a highly technical point of law."[37] It is difficult, if not impossible, to draw the conclusion from the Court's opinion that the Court decided the case on "a highly technical point of law." The result of the case, however, was unquestionable. Gandhi's reliance on the courts did not get him and the movement where they wanted to go—to the state of affairs that existed before the settlement.

But there was another way that would get them there—and it, too, involved the law.

SEVENTEEN

Courtroom as Laboratory

I am doing nothing for the community for the sake of reward or fame. Everything I do is as a matter of duty, and I shall continue to do so in the future. If anyone wants legal advice, my office is always open. And I shall give the best advice I can.

GANDHI

LOOKING BACK FROM THE VANTAGE point of the twenty-first century, it is relatively easy to see how civil disobedience leads to social change. Students of civil disobedience understand the chain reaction a civilly disobedient act has the potential to ignite—disobedience, self-suffering, sympathy from the public, pressure on decision-makers, and curative institutional action. They also understand the power of civil disobedience to cripple and even overthrow governments through the withdrawal of consent. They have the benefit of the lessons taught by the Freedom Rides and the Dandi Salt March. For Gandhi, the Salt March was still ahead of him; the Freedom Rides would occur thirteen years after his passing. In 1908, by contrast, lawyer Gandhi had the greatest understanding of the one purpose with which a lawyer would naturally feel most comfortable—testing the law. In fact, he had used disobedience, unsuccessfully as it turned out, to challenge the lawfulness of Johannesburg's segregated tram system in 1906, and he would again attempt to use the law for testing purposes before the fight in the Transvaal was over.

Gandhi's broader understanding of civil disobedience was developing. In particular, his sense of the relationship between civil disobedience and social change, while incomplete, was growing. He was certainly not a complete stranger to the use of disobedience as a tool for creating change, for he had gotten a taste of it in the period surrounding his own arrest, trial, and imprisonment, when some two hundred other Indians were also imprisoned for defying the Asiatic Law Amendment Ordinance. What did Gandhi learn from this? Surely he read in the press Smuts' extended bemoaning of the colony's inability to deal with this disobedience. Smuts openly admitted two critical points: he could not force the Indians to obey, and, even if he were to arrest all the resisters, the Transvaal's jails could not hold them all.[1] Looking on, Gandhi received a practical lesson in how a government cannot function without the consent of the governed. True, Smuts was saved by the Indians' loss of courage in early 1908. Nonetheless, Smuts' concessions taught Gandhi that immense pressure for change can be brought to bear on a government by a large and dedicated body of disobedients—a luxury he would enjoy when he led the Salt March in India in March, 1930,[2] but was not available to him in the Transvaal in January, 1908.

By the time of his jailing, Gandhi had limited actual experience with civil disobedience—and that experience was rather mixed. While there was much talk of disobedience in 1907, no widespread disobedience took place in the Transvaal until after the expiration of the registration period under the Act—November 30, 1907. Earlier he had used disobedience to stage his unsuccessful attack on Johannesburg's segregated tramways. He had also represented the hero-turned-traitor Ramsundar Pundit in the wake of his disobedience. What is quite remarkable is that despite this limited exposure to disobedience Gandhi possessed a fairly well developed, intuitive sense of the role of self-suffering in creating change. He understood from early on the role self-suffering can play in creating sympathy in the public mind and then pressure upon decision-makers.

He understood that self-suffering, in order to lead to sympathy, must first catch the eye of the public: "Passive resisters depend upon creating public opinion.... It will not be denied that their suffering has at last made some public men in this Colony think."[3] With the attention of onlookers captured, self-suffering can then go about the work of creating sympathy in them. Just before his imprisonment Gandhi said that "he had sufficient faith in human nature to believe that when the Colonists saw husbands torn away from their wives, [and] ... wives ... left to be starved to death ... then the Colonists of the Transvaal themselves would tell General Smuts that he had not received a mandate to treat human beings in that fashion."[4] A few days earlier, he had shared a related sentiment in a letter to a friend: "Passive resistance ... means self-imposed suffering of an acute type, intended to prove the justice of the cause, and thus to bring conviction home to the minds of the Colonists."[5]

These understandings would soon be put to the test. The issue that Gandhi would eventually face before the end of 1908 was whether he could employ these insights about self-suffering to achieve broad social change or whether he would allow his role as a lawyer to overwhelm and suffocate that opportunity.

THE FIRST FRONT: INCINERATION AND INCARCERATION

Of one thing Gandhi was certain—that if he could reignite the fervor his community had shown earlier and if he could thus get his community fully recommitted to jail-going, he would have enormous leverage on Smuts. But first he needed an essential ingredient—an act that defied the law. His initial hope was that the Supreme Court would order the voluntary applications returned so that the Indians could then be restored to their position when the registration period expired—in violation of the mandate to register. Gandhi had great faith in the courts—and it was occasionally justified.[6] It was naïve, however, to think that the Supreme Court, on a question of this magnitude, would turn its back on the very power establishment of which it was a central part. The Court would not be a party to setting up the conditions needed for thousands of dissidents to defy the government.

His frustration with the Supreme Court drove Gandhi from passive resistance to active resistance: "Our object in demanding that the applications be returned was to make certain that we were arrested as soon as possible. We must now achieve the same object by burning the registers."[7]

He was perfectly clear about what the Indians' agenda was when the Court turned down their petition:

There is only one remedy. And that lies in our hands. We should ignore the Government's law and act as follows:

1. When necessary, we should burn the certificates of voluntary registration.
2. We must refuse to affix our finger-impressions or signatures [on any documents] or to give our names when asked for these by the police.
3. We should tender the licence fee, but if the licence is refused, we should carry on trade without one. . . .

We want to go to jail.[8]

Before the Indians began burning their registration certificates, however, Gandhi hoped that the threat of doing so—and thereby filling the jails—would cause Smuts to honor what Gandhi considered to be their original agreement. To make the threat real, the Indians, at a mass meeting held the Sunday following the Court's decision, announced their plans to publicly burn their registration certificates on the following Sunday, July 12, 1908. The Indians did not meet on that date, however, and later in the month Gandhi stated that "the question of burning voluntary registration certificates which were now in the hands of the BIA would not be decided until they knew what legislation the Government intended to introduce."[9]

This deferral proved to be unproductive. For some time, Smuts had insisted that any agreement to repeal the Act had to be accompanied by a complete ban on the entry of Indians into the Transvaal. The Indians sought Smuts' agreement to an exception to the ban that would permit educated Indians to continue to enter—something Gandhi contended the law presently allowed.[10] Smuts refused to budge from his position. At the same time, the secretary was intent on following through with Selborne's recommendation that the voluntary registration the Indians underwent be regularized by supplemental registration. A measure known as the Validation Bill was introduced into Parliament for just this purpose on August 13.

Matters moved quickly after that. Gandhi and the Indians immediately petitioned the Transvaal Parliament against the Validation Bill.[11] Not surprisingly, the Parliament gave no weight to the petition. After some six weeks of threats by the Indians, a day was set for the burning of the certificates. Gandhi wrote one final letter of appeal to Smuts, setting forth the date and seeking a settlement, short of which the Indians would burn their certificates.

Smuts had no interest in Gandhi's proposed settlement. When the appointed day, August 16, arrived, a huge throng of Indians poured into the grounds of the Fordsburg mosque—some three thousand people in all. They had come from all parts of the Transvaal, and they filled every inch of available space as well as the rooftops in the surrounding area. On the stage were representatives from Indian organizations in Durban, Cape Town, and Pretoria. The Indians' Chinese allies were represented by Leung Quin. While civil disobedience was quite the draw, many of those in attendance were not there as mere spectators. Some fifteen hundred registration certificates had been handed in for burning, as well as some five hundred trading licenses.[12]

After the BIA chairman spoke, Gandhi took the stage. He conceived of his role as that of a lawyer who was responsible for giving his client sound advice. Gandhi shared with his audience the careful process he had undergone to come to the counsel he was about to offer. After giving the matter a great deal of thought and prayer, he said, his decision about what advice to give reduced itself to a choice: the Indians could disobey and suffer, or they could obey and accept the indignity of the Validation Act. His choice was for disobedience and suffering. His advice to those present was plain and direct: burn the certificates. With the British flag flapping in the chilly winter wind above, the crowd erupted in protracted applause.

In some of the most eloquent and forceful language used by him in South Africa, Gandhi continued:

> What is this fight that we are engaged upon?
> What is its significance?
> To my mind, its significance did not commence with a demand for the repeal of the Asiatic Act, nor does it end with the repeal of the Asiatic Act. I know full well that it is open to the Government of the Colony to give a repeal of this legislation today, to throw dust into our eyes and then embark upon other legislation, far harsher, far more humiliating, but the lesson that I wanted to learn myself, the lesson I would have my countrymen to learn from this struggle is this: that unenfranchised though we are, unrepresented though we are in the Transvaal, it is open to us to clothe ourselves with an undying franchise, and this consists in recognizing our humanity, in recognizing that we are part and parcel of the great universal whole, that there is the Maker of us all ruling over the destinies of mankind and that our trust should be in Him rather than in earthly kings, and if my countrymen recognize that position I say that no matter what legislation is passed over our heads, if that legislation is in conflict with our ideas of right and wrong, if it is in conflict with our conscience, if it is in conflict with our religion, then we can say we shall not submit to that legislation.[13]

Gandhi then explained how the version of civil disobedience he was promoting was consistent with the rule of law: "We use no physical force, but we accept the sanction that the legislature provides, we accept the penalties that the legislature provides. I refuse to call this defiance, but I consider that it is a perfectly respectful attitude, for a man, for a human being who calls himself man."

After Gandhi spoke, the crowd's attention turned to a huge, black cauldron present for the occasion. It was filled with the offending documents, paraffin was poured into it, and it was lit afire, according to the *Transvaal*

Leader, "amid a scene of the wildest enthusiasm" and, according to the *Johannesburg Star*, amid "indescribable excitement." Hats were hurled into the air. The *Rand Daily Mail*, always hostile to the Indian cause, sarcastically reported: "There was not one Asiatic amidst the huge throng who did not seem to be under the impression that the witnessing of the burning of the certificates, or the actual depositing of his parchment upon the pyre, was the mission of his life."

An Indian who had earlier withheld his support from the cause approached the cauldron, set his registration on fire, and held it up for all to see. When the leaders on the stage tried to address the crowd, there was so much shouting and so many whistles being blown by the exuberant crowd that they could not be heard.

Fifteen hundred registration certificates and five hundred trading licenses were now ashes.

Gandhi had his ticket to jail.

THE SECOND FRONT: THE PENALTY FOR WEARING A BROWN SKIN

When Gandhi realized earlier in the year that Smuts was not about to have the Act repealed, negotiations reopened between the two. Smuts offered repeal, but only on a number of conditions. One of those conditions was that immigration into the colony from India be completely halted. Part of Gandhi's response was to argue that the current law permitted the entry of educated immigrants,[14] and that to now exclude educated Indian immigrants—while continuing to welcome educated immigrants of other racial and ethnic groups—would constitute an unacceptable form of discrimination. Smuts replied that Gandhi was wrong about his view of the law; he claimed that educated Indian immigrants were not entitled to entry under the current law.

The relevant section of the Immigration Restriction Act (IRA) of 1907 barred those who were "unable through deficient education to write out (from dictation or otherwise) and sign in the characters of an European language an application for permission to enter this Colony or other such document as [a duly authorized] officer may require."[15] Under this standard, it was plain that any Indian able to understand and write English would not be barred from entry. Gandhi set out to arrange a test case that would reach that conclusion and prove Smuts wrong.

Gandhi had his client when a Natal store manager and bookkeeper, Sorabji Shapurji, learned of this dispute, communicated with Gandhi, and volunteered to enter the Transvaal to test Smuts' contention. Sorabji had mastered English through years of study and would easily qualify under the IRA. His attempt to enter the Transvaal from Natal at the same time Gandhi was threatening to burn the registration certificates would thus open a second of what would eventually be a total of four civil disobedience fronts in the dispute with Smuts. If Sorabji were denied entry into the Transvaal, Gandhi would have the test case he needed to prove that the law did allow educated Indians into the country.

Before Sorabji presented himself to the border officials, Gandhi notified Chamney of Sorabji's intentions, specifically telling him that Sorabji would attempt to enter, that he had sufficient means, and that he possessed the requisite English skills. Sorabji did in fact appear at the border crossing at Volksrust on June 24, 1908. And then the unexpected happened. He was admitted without challenge. Perhaps sensing that they would be defending an extremely weak legal position, Smuts and Chamney simply were not willing to give Gandhi the forum he wanted.

Sorabji proceeded to Johannesburg, where he was watched by the police, but was left unmolested for more than a week. He was finally arrested on July 4—but not for being a prohibited immigrant. Rather, he was arrested for being in violation of the Act by failing to register. Again, the government would simply not create the issue Gandhi wanted tried.

Four days later, on the afternoon of Wednesday, July 8,[16] Magistrate H. H. Jordan presided over a courtroom filled to capacity for the government's prosecution of Sorabji Shapurji. When Sorabji stood to plead not guilty, Gandhi was at his side. After Prosecutor Schuurman adduced the routine evidence from the police about the defendant's unauthorized presence (under the Act) in the colony, Schuurman called Chamney to the stand to testify that Sorabji had earlier made application for voluntary registration and that Chamney had turned him down because he did not believe Sorabji qualified for voluntary registration under the terms of the compromise.

Under cross-examination by Gandhi, Chamney admitted that the defendant had tendered a number of certificates of good character when he applied. When Gandhi asked Chamney to read them aloud, Schuurman objected. Magistrate Jordan immediately sensed what Gandhi was trying to show with the documents—that Sorabji easily qualified under the IRA for admission into the colony, that Sorabji was being prosecuted under the wrong statute, and that the court should therefore dismiss the charges. The magistrate, however, was of no help to Gandhi. He concluded that because the documents were now the property of the police, he would refuse to require Chamney to involuntarily produce them or read them, despite Gandhi's having earlier served notice on the witness that he wanted them produced.

Undeterred, Gandhi plowed ahead with his cross-examination. Gandhi demonstrated that Chamney's immigration officers had not examined the defendant at the border to see if he qualified under the IRA. Then Gandhi squarely confronted Chamney with the issue, asking Chamney whether he would admit that Sorabji had "sufficient educational attainments" to qualify under the IRA. Chamney said he knew nothing about that. Gandhi asked Chamney whether he would admit that Sorabji had "sufficient means." Chamney said he knew nothing about that, either. When Gandhi asked Chamney why the defendant was allowed to pass through the border crossing, Chamney refused to answer. When Gandhi asked whether Chamney would allow an immigrant to cross if the immigrant could show compliance with the IRA, the witness claimed he would not allow such a person to pass because the person would have been a prohibited immigrant under the Act; under further questioning by Gandhi, however, Chamney admitted that he had allowed what he considered a prohibited immigrant to enter the colony. As a result of Gandhi's skillful questioning, Chamney had painted himself into a corner.

With Jordan appearing unfriendly to Gandhi's argument that the Act was inapplicable to this prosecution, Gandhi turned to a defense—a procedural argument—that would have made his mentor Frederick Laughton proud. Gandhi noted that under the Act unregistered Asiatics were subject to arrest if they were found in the colony "after such a date as may be notified in the [*Government*] *Gazette*." Schuurman, in a fatal mistake, had failed to put this date into evidence before closing his case. Gandhi moved for a discharge on that ground. Admitting that "he knew it was a technical error," Gandhi said it nonetheless "paid the defence to take such action." The magistrate was not pleased, but Gandhi was stubborn about getting his client discharged:

> THE MAGISTRATE: It is this, in short—we must bring the accused up again, and give the Government as much trouble as possible!
> MR. GANDHI: That's the point.[17]

The next morning Jordan announced that he agreed with Gandhi and would discharge Sorabji. Chamney was not through, however. The government immediately re-arrested Sorabji and charged him with the same offense—failing to register under the Act. Two days after being discharged and found not guilty, Sorabji, with Gandhi at his side, found himself back before Jordan on the very same charge. Of the cast of characters, only the prosecutor was different, with A. J. Cramer now representing the government.

The day before, Gandhi had written to Cartwright about the case. His letter is a window into Gandhi's legal strategy, his frank opinion of his opposing counsel, and his equally frank opinion of Chamney:

> Mr. Sorabji, as you know, is not now to be tried under the [IRA] at all. Indeed, to secure conviction under that Act will, in the case of an educated Asiatic, be, I am sure, impossible, without the instrumentality of the Asiatic Act. It just proves my contention. Owing to the stupidity of the Prosecution and the greater stupidity of Mr. Chamney, I was able to take advantage of a flaw in the evidence . . . , and Mr. Sorabji was discharged. To show the vindictiveness on the part of . . . Vernon and . . . Chamney, he was re-arrested immediately. . . . I do not know what will happen tomorrow. I am half inclined to think that there will be a bungle again. If so, I propose to take advantage of it and secure a discharge again. Ultimately, of course, Mr. Sorabji, unless some settlement is arrived at, must pay the penalty for wearing a brown skin and go to gaol.[18]

When court opened the next morning, Cramer called police superintendent Vernon, who recounted his re-arrest of Sorabji and produced notices from the *Government Gazette* that indicated deadlines for registration.[19] Gandhi used his cross-examination of this witness to show that there was virtually no time between Sorabji's discharge on Thursday and his re-arrest the same day.

Chamney testified in the same fashion as he had earlier, but this time he added a twist. Realizing the import of his testimony on Wednesday, Chamney offered an opinion "that, under the Immigrants' Restriction Act, the accused was not eligible to obtain . . . a certificate of registration." Gandhi immediately objected that Chamney was not qualified to give this opinion; the magistrate upheld Gandhi's objection, perhaps recalling Chamney's refusal to answer questions from Gandhi on that very subject in the earlier hearing. On cross-examination, Chamney once more admitted that he had not examined the defendant on his educational qualifications.

With the prosecution's case now complete, Gandhi and the court then engaged in some procedural skirmishing that Gandhi hoped would result in dismissal again. The magistrate in this instance turned his dismissal request down. The silver lining to his ruling was that it permitted the defense to once more make its case under the IRA. Sorabji testified to his educational attainments, causing the magistrate to inquire: "Do you mean to say that any Asiatic who can read and write in a European language can come into this Colony?" To this, Gandhi responded: "I do, Sir, and I am going to try and argue that before the Court, if I get the opportunity."

Gandhi then mounted a substantial argument against conviction, pointing out Sorabji's ability to qualify under the IRA and the inapplicability of the Act to a person in Sorabji's circumstances. The magistrate found Gandhi's arguments "very subtle and very able," but ruled against him one more time. The only important fact for the magistrate was that Sorabji had not registered. He was ordered out of the colony within seven days.[20] On July 20, he was once more brought before Jordan. The charge was failure to obey the order to leave the colony. On the stand, Sorabji freely admitted that he had disobeyed the order and that he had intended to disobey it all along. Gandhi, recognizing that his client was bound for jail, described Sorabji's desires to the court: "The accused wished to suffer for the sake of principle. He had chosen between his conscience and the order of the Court, and he had chosen by his conscience."

For choosing his conscience above the law, Sorabji received a sentence of one month's imprisonment with hard labor.

Sorabji's resistance was helpful to the Indian cause in two ways. First, the government's failure to prosecute him under the IRA was a tacit admission that such a prosecution would be unsuccessful and that Gandhi's interpretation of the IRA was correct.[21] Moreover, the government's prosecution of Sorabji for failure to register gave the Indians multiple opportunities to ventilate Gandhi's IRA interpretation in court and in the press and thus to advance the debate.[22] This was not the outcome Gandhi had sought through this test case; rather, he had sought to use Sorabji's disobedience to create the occasion for a court ruling on the applicability of the IRA. The actual outcome was, however, nearly as effective in making the Indians' point.

The second way Sorabji's resistance was helpful is that it provided the Indians with a heroic figure whose disobedience could serve as an example to others in the movement. Defiant, Sorabji pledged to the Indian community that he would never comply with the law. Indeed, he would refuse to leave the Transvaal as ordered, would continue to refuse to register, and would be jailed again and again. Gandhi would lionize him in the pages of *Indian Opinion*.[23]

Sorabji would make Ramsundar Pundit a faded memory.

The large crowd of Indians that had gathered to observe the proceedings in Sorabji's case quickly reassembled afterward outside Gandhi's Court Chambers law office. There Gandhi announced what he called the next step in the movement. Indians "who possessed licences [would] return them and stand the consequence of being arrested for trading without licences and going to gaol." A number of Indian hawkers promptly surrendered their licenses on the spot so that they might be returned to the authorities. (Hawkers were generally Indians on the lower rungs of the economic scale who made their livings by selling fruits, vegetables, and other items on the streets, often from baskets.) The purpose of this phase of disobedience? According to Gandhi, it was to suffer and thereby to "bring conviction to the minds of the European community that they were fighting for principle."[24] At first blush, one might think that Gandhi's purpose was to create change through self-suffering.[25]

On July 20, the first unlicensed hawkers were arrested. Many more would be arrested in the coming months.[26] In the period running from the time of the first arrests up to early October 1908, Gandhi appeared in court to represent fifty-eight resisters in a total of thirteen known criminal trials. Is there any sign from Gandhi's conduct in these cases that he understood the role they played in achieving one or more of the purposes for civil disobedience described earlier? Let us examine the evidence.

The record discloses how Gandhi pled his clients in eight of the thirteen cases. We know that in four cases he pled his clients not guilty, while in four others he pled them guilty. While the lawyer holds great sway, the client has the ultimate choice in the question of how to plead. These, however, are resistance cases in which resistance prisoners were being represented by the very person leading the resistance effort. Accordingly, while one normally would be reluctant to charge the lawyer with a disproportionate responsibility for the plea, here we can charge Gandhi with a fair degree of influence. Viewing these eight cases together, however, one finds no discernible pattern that explains why some clients were pled guilty and others were not. It does not appear from the pleas entered that Gandhi had a unified and coherent approach to these cases.

What does an examination of the proof brought forward by Gandhi in the entire set of thirteen cases demonstrate? In the great majority of the cases, Gandhi put on evidence to explain to the court (and perhaps to the reading public as well) why the defendants had no licenses. From the witness box the defendants typically described their circumstances. They stated that as a result of the government having broken the terms of the compromise, they resolved not to provide their fingerprints. The accused had applied for their hawking licenses, even tendering the requisite fees, but when the accused refused to provide their thumbprints, they were denied their licenses and were told that no licenses would issue without prints. In some instances it appears that Gandhi put this evidence on in extenuation, but in other instances it appears that this evidence was somehow intended by Gandhi to serve as a complete, substantive defense. On no occasion did the evidence appear to help. Convictions were the result without exception, indicating that when this explanation was used as a defense, the defense failed. The picture with regard to extenuation is somewhat less clear but still fairly indicative of a tactic that had very little, if any, effect. If the sentences for the defendants had varied widely, then perhaps Gandhi's extenuation evidence might be credited for the difference in cases of reduced sentences. But the fact is, the sentences in the thirteen trials fell within a narrow band. Judges gave the defendants their choice: they could pay a fine (ranging from 5 s to £1) or serve a jail sentence of from two to seven days, usually with hard labor.[27] Every defendant chose jail.

It is conceivable that the real purpose of putting on this evidence was not so much to convince the magistrates sitting on the cases as to advance the public debate.[28] The Transvaal newspapers covered these trials with a large degree of faithfulness. By adducing this evidence with reporters present, Gandhi succeeded in explaining his cause many times over to the readership of the colony's most influential media—the *Rand Daily Mail, Transvaal Leader*, and *Johannesburg Star*.

In a very limited number of cases, Gandhi presented defenses based on perceived procedural missteps by the government, thus replicating the defense he had mounted for Sorabji. The reaction of the court to these defenses sent a strong signal to Gandhi: the courts were not concerned with protecting the rights of the defendants as much as they were concerned with protecting the interests of the government. In *Rex v. Bawazeer and Others*, the court inadvertently revealed that the government had given the chief inspector of licenses a list of fourteen individuals who were exempt from the thumb-impression requirement. While the list's existence came as a surprise to Gandhi, he was quick to pounce on it. In closing argument, he contended that "there was absolutely no authority given to the Government to grant exemptions" and urged the court to discharge the defendants rather than "countenance an arbitrary administration of the Act." The court cavalierly ignored this argument, saying that "the charge was admitted and that was all [the Court] had got to do with it." The magistrate offered the defendants a choice between a 10 shilling fine and imprisonment for four days with hard labor.

Gandhi erected the same defense in *Rex v. Ramaswamy and Others*.[29] In that case, Gandhi had Chief Inspector of Licenses L. H. Jefferson on the stand under cross-examination.[30] The way Gandhi's cross-examination unfolded is instructive:

> MR. GANDHI: You have received a list of exemptions?—Fourteen.
>
> MR. GANDHI: Will you produce that list?
>
> The Magistrate and Public Prosecutor both interposed and objected to its production.
>
> MR. CRAMER [the Prosecutor]: I have no objection to Mr. Gandhi asking if the accused's name is on the list.
>
> MR. JEFFERSON: It is not on the list.
>
> MR. GANDHI: Does this mean that I cannot see the document?
>
> THE MAGISTRATE (to MR. JEFFERSON): Are you permitted to show the document?
>
> —No, Sir.
>
> MR. GANDHI: But it must be a public document. Have you been prevented by the authorities?
>
> THE MAGISTRATE (interrupting): I'm not going to allow it, Mr. Gandhi; that is final.
>
> MR. GANDHI: Have you been prevented by the authorities?
>
> THE MAGISTRATE: Mr. Gandhi, for the last time, I will not allow this.[31]

Gandhi, ever stubborn, went on to make his point to the magistrate in closing argument. The *Transvaal Leader* was there to capture Gandhi's closing: "Mr. Gandhi said that he held it was a most curious position that here they had a list which applied to the whole community, and which could not be produced. He thought it was very remarkable that they were not allowed to see it. . . . He thought it within the jurisdiction of the Court to say whether Mr. Jefferson should produce the document."[32]

The magistrate continued to oppose Gandhi's position and imposed a fine of £1 or seven days in jail with hard labor. There could hardly be a clearer example of the failure of judicial independence than the magistrate's refusal to order Jefferson, a government official, to divulge the government's list of exempt Indians. The magistrate simply bowed to the government's wishes without entertaining argument on the point and without explanation of the decision. It was this essential, bedrock characteristic of ultimate deference by the Transvaal courts to the government—despite a few aberrational decisions to the contrary—that helped drive Gandhi away from litigation and into civil disobedience.[33]

Gandhi had resisted convictions in these cases on procedural grounds and lost each time. It is difficult to see what purpose of civil disobedience could be achieved by disobedience that resulted in a courtroom defense that primarily rested on a technicality having nothing to do with the merits of the controversy.

Finally, there were two cases in which Gandhi mounted no defense and presented no mitigation evidence at all. We have very little information about one of these.[34]

The other such case was quite telling. It demonstrates how Gandhi's understanding of civil disobedience and its purposes was incomplete, but evolving. A group of six Indians charged with hawking without licenses came before Magistrate P. C. Dalmahoy on July 28. All the defendants pled guilty. Gandhi announced that he intended to call no witnesses. He did have a statement to make, however. He said that he had conducted a long conference with the accused during the course of which the prisoners had instructed him to seek the severest penalty possible for them. This was so, Gandhi indicated, because the defendants had acted "with deliberation."[35]

The magistrate sentenced five members of the group to a fine of £1 or seven days in prison. The sixth member of the group—Thambi Naidoo—received a double sentence of a £2 fine or fourteen days in jail because of his previous convictions.

A few days after the conclusion of this trial, Gandhi wrote to his *Indian Opinion* readers about his representation of these disobedients:

> [T]hose who are prepared for imprisonment should go to gaol without depending upon a lawyer or myself. That is not to say that I go back on my promise of defending Indian satyagrahis[36] arrested in connection with the campaign against the law. I shall go wherever I find my presence is needed. But the best way is to have no lawyer and go to gaol straight away and undergo whatever sentence is passed.[37]

For those who wanted to resist jail, Gandhi would act as a traditional lawyer by mounting defenses, adducing evidence in extenuation, and throwing procedural roadblocks in the prosecution's path. For those who held themselves to a higher standard, standing mute was best. In all of this, Gandhi was experimenting with self-suffering in civil disobedience and with his role as a lawyer for the disobedient.

In the case before Magistrate Dalmahoy, Gandhi had essentially stood silent. An important reason for his doing so was the identity of the one of the five defendants receiving the £1/seven days sentence—Harilal Gandhi, the defense lawyer's eldest son, who had been arrested for unlicensed hawking.[38]

Harilal's father believed that the purest act of disobedience involved the most self-sacrificial suffering.[39] He himself was not available to court arrest because, as he put it, he was "enrolled as an attorney."[40] Did he mean that his role as an attorney for the unlicensed hawkers was indispensable? Or did he mean that it was somehow unseemly or disreputable for an attorney to hawk? It is not clear what Gandhi meant. What is clear is that he was using Harilal as a stand-in for himself—and that the Gandhis would hold themselves to the highest forms of self-sacrificial suffering while refraining from clouding the public's picture of their disobedience with distracting legal maneuvers in court.[41]

Gandhi believed that the manner in which he and Harilal had acted in Harilal's case—by not fighting the prosecution, but simply accepting punishment—set the standard. He explained this approach as an experiment:

> When I go to defend those who have been arrested, I do not, strictly speaking, defend them but only send them to gaol. If we have acquired real courage, there should be no need for me to present myself in Court. I thought it only proper that I should make this experiment in the first instance with my son. Accordingly, no arrangements were made for him at Volksrust, and he was left to fall back on his own strength. Since there were others with him in Johannesburg, I attended the Court, but asked for the maximum penalty for him and for his associates. It was their misfortune that they did not get it.[42]

For most ordinary disobedients, Gandhi would appear in court and act like a defense lawyer. He would explain the reasons for the disobedients' actions, he would try to get the charges dismissed on procedural grounds, and he would make as much trouble as possible for the prosecution. For his son and other idealistic, self-sacrificing disobedients, however, he would stand mute, just as they would stand mute. Silent acceptance of the punishment would allow the public to see the suffering of the disobedient without interference, on clear lines, in clear terms. If the public could see the suffering clearly, the public might well sympathize with the disobedient. Such sympathy could lead to pressure on decision-makers, which in turn could lead to change in the form of curative, institutional reaction.

One of Gandhi's quintessential features was that his understanding of the world never came to a rest. It was always under development. In regard to civil disobedience and its purposes, he was determined in 1908 to advance his understanding through experimentation—even if it meant sitting down, being silent, and surrendering his role as a lawyer in his own son's case.

THE FOURTH FRONT: CROSSING THE BORDER

While he had surprisingly perceptive insights into self-suffering, Gandhi's understanding in 1908 of its role in civil disobedience campaigns was nonetheless limited and in an early stage of development. Judging from his speeches and writings during this period, he did understand the immense power of self-suffering to generate the sympathy and help of onlookers—one of the major uses for civil disobedience. There was an important reality, however, he did not grasp. He did not understand how easily this power could be disrupted and diminished by the legal process—and, in particular, by lawyers. This limitation in Gandhi's understanding is evident in the manner in which he and his associates, acting as the disobedients' lawyers, shaped the fourth civil disobedience front between July and early October 1908.

In July Gandhi publicly and defiantly urged Indians to "fill the jails."[43] What was his purpose in rendering this advice? Gandhi articulated three different goals for Indian disobedience to the registration requirements. The first was to win a war of attrition with the Smuts administration. By sending forth wave after wave of disobedients for the government to prosecute and imprison, Gandhi hoped to "tire out the government" and thus force it into capitulation.[44] The Indians' disobedience would, in a sense, be a limited withdrawal of consent to be governed by the Smuts regime. In addition to this goal, Gandhi was open about his interest in using the Indians' disobedience, and the self-suffering that would accompany it, to attract the attention and sympathy of London—a development that might lead, in turn, to intervention in South Africa by the British on behalf of the Indians. With respect to

London, the hope was that the Indians' disobedience could both advance the debate and create political change.

In aid of these three goals—withdrawing consent, advancing the debate, and creating political change—Gandhi would send prominent Indians into the Transvaal from Natal for the purpose of challenging the government's interpretation of the IRA that educated Indians and prewar residents of the Transvaal were not entitled to entry. When at the border, these volunteer disobedients would be asked to produce registration papers that, of course, they did not possess. As a consequence, the government's registration requirements would also be challenged. Much of Sorabji's disobedience was centered on these same objectives. The twist now was to send prominent Indians to the border and to send them repeatedly.[45]

The Indians would have had to look hard to find a more prominent disobedient than one whose name was Gandhi. When Harilal Gandhi presented himself at the Transvaal-Natal border in July, the authorities refused to play Mohandas Gandhi's game. They let Harilal pass unchallenged. After displaying prolonged forbearance in refusing to arrest him, the government's decision to finally move against him on August 10 for failure to register under the Act can best be explained by the quite public nature of Harilal's defiance.[46]

When Harilal was tried that very afternoon before Magistrate H. H. Jordan, Mohandas Gandhi reprised the role he had played in Harilal's earlier trial for hawking without a license. He pled Harilal guilty and refrained from asking any questions of Superintendent Vernon, the prosecution's usual witness. Gandhi then asked the magistrate to order Harilal out of the colony within twenty-four hours, rather than the standard seven days, so that Harilal could begin his jail time with other young Indians who had also defied the law. The magistrate declined to accede to the senior Gandhi's request and gave Harilal seven days to leave.

When Harilal refused to obey the order to leave, he was brought before the magistrate on that charge on August 19, with *Indian Opinion* reporting that he "appeared quite cheerful in the dock."[47] With the elder Gandhi away in Pretoria negotiating with Smuts, George Godfrey, a recently arrived Indian lawyer, volunteered to represent Harilal—and did so consistently with Mohandas' representation of him earlier. Godfrey offered no defense, presented no evidence in extenuation, and declined to make any statement. Accepting the defendant's guilty plea, the magistrate sentenced Harilal to a one-month term with hard labor.

Gandhi also represented other prominent disobedients in August who had either presented themselves at the border without registration papers or were recent and prominent intracolony transplants who lacked registration papers. The contrast between Gandhi's response to these prosecutions and that of Harilal could not have been greater. A week before Harilal's arrest, a leading member of the BIA who had previously been arrested for unlicensed hawking was taken into custody for having earlier entered the Transvaal without a registration certificate. In contrast to the course he had taken in Harilal's trial, Gandhi did not pass up the opportunity to cross-examine the prosecution's chief witness or to produce evidence in extenuation.[48] Two weeks later, the government sent out instructions to arrest another prominent Indian for failing to register, as a result of which Gandhi found himself before Magistrate Jordan again. Gandhi pled his client not guilty. Gandhi then argued without avail for a dismissal of the charges—a move he would never have made for Harilal.[49]

In an effort to provoke the government, other Indians—many of them with high profiles in the Transvaal or Natal—openly courted arrest during August, September, and October for refusing to register. Although it was not necessarily in its best interest, the government reacted to these provocations by arresting the Indians as they deliberately tried to cross into the Transvaal from Natal without registration papers. These Indians claimed a right of entry as educated immigrants, as prewar residents, or because they held permits under the Peace Preservation Ordinance. Many of these disobedients were represented by Gandhi's friend, protégé, and office associate, H. S. L. Polak.[50] In the ensuing trials, neither Polak nor his clients stood by silently in the face of prosecution.

In addition to simply wearing out the prosecution, it is likely that Gandhi and Polak's aim was to show the reading public, especially those in London, the injustice of making the Indians comply with yet another registration regime—all in aid of Gandhi's goal of encouraging the intervention of the imperial government on this issue.[51]

In a disobedience campaign designed to "tire the government out," it makes good sense to resist prosecution every step of the way and to erect as many obstacles to conviction and sentencing as possible. The same tactics might also serve the purpose of advancing the debate; the newspapers would be filled with the Indians' arguments against the Act. A disobedience campaign designed to secure the sympathy of onlookers in London and elsewhere would be far better served, however, by different tactics—namely, the refusal to mount legal arguments and the quiet, brave acceptance of punishment and self-suffering. Standing mute is effective in garnering sympathy because it engages the emotions of the audience. Looking upon willingly accepted self-suffering, the public naturally becomes inquisitive about the motives of disobedients: "Why are these people undergoing voluntary suffering? What is the injustice that moves them?" Suffering voluntarily accepted leads to these questions—and to sympathy. Sympathy leads to pressure on decision-makers—and pressure on decision-makers leads to change. The erection of legal defenses and the tendering of mitigating evidence, by contrast, are too readily seen by the public as efforts to escape or diminish punishment, thus interfering with the image of a self-suffering disobedient completely willing to accept the full consequences of his actions and thus short-circuiting the chain reaction that otherwise would be initiated by silent self-suffering and would eventually result in change.[52] To purchase the possible benefit of showcasing the Indians' argument that it was unjust to subject them to multiple registration regimes, Gandhi had to forgo a very different kind of public sympathy that may have resulted from standing mute, as he had done in Harilal's cases.

When a defendant resists prosecution at trial and mounts arguments against conviction, the public's attention is invariably drawn to the disobedient's particular arguments for acquittal. Such an approach may engage the intellect of the audience, but not its emotions. It is true that if the disobedient can win a debate on the legal merits, then, perhaps, the disobedient can make an appeal for the audience's subsequent sympathy. By that stage, however, sympathy is much harder to come by. Moreover, the sympathy available at that time is an intellectual sympathy in reaction to a logic problem, not an emotional sympathy in reaction to a gross injustice.

None of this is to say that Gandhi and his clients were unaware of the self-suffering the Indians would have to undergo by reason of their jail sentences. They were quite aware of that hardship.[53] They might not have fully appreciated, however, the differences in how the public perceived them and their disobedience. They could be seen either as humbly and courageously accepting their punishment and willingly undergoing suffering, or as determinedly resisting conviction and reluctantly undergoing suffering. These images send very different political messages—a distinction Gandhi did not capitalize upon, in part because he did not yet fully understand it. His and his colleagues' insistence on erecting defenses and presenting evidence in extenuation interfered with the most productive use of the Indians' disobedience.

The Indians' 1908 resistance did produce a modicum of attention in London and can be said, therefore, to have succeeded in advancing the debate. With respect to the far more important goals of withdrawing consent and creating political change, however, the movement failed. The border-crossing resistance carried out in August and September—like the burning of registration certificates, Sorabji's disobedience, and hawking without licenses—had produced neither Smuts' capitulation nor London's intervention.

Another approach was needed.

ROLE-DIFFERENTIATED BEHAVIOR

The government was not unaware of the dynamics of civil disobedience. Accordingly, it was cautious about conducting an unlimited campaign of arrests against the Indians for their failure to register; Smuts and his government realized that they simply could not house and feed too large a number of disobedients. Moreover, there certainly had to be some measure of political sensitivity on the government's part to the danger that mass prosecutions would hand Gandhi exactly what he wanted.

In a final attempt to get the reaction he sought, Gandhi found he had one card left to play—his own arrest. It would be a risky gambit; his last jailing had deflated the movement. Gandhi nonetheless boldly challenged Smuts to arrest him, saying that while he was the one who had encouraged his countrymen to defy the law—as a result of which they had been imprisoned—he was "still at large." He even taunted Smuts: "Is it courageous to leave me alone and harass poor Indians?"[54]

When Gandhi failed to draw a reaction from Smuts and when London failed to intervene, Gandhi put in motion a plan that would make it practically impossible for Smuts not to arrest him. Gandhi would travel south to Natal, ostensibly to offer legal counsel to some Indians there, but knowing of course that he had to cross the Natal-Transvaal border on his journey back to Johannesburg. He knew that, when he did so, the authorities would be confronted with the most prominent Indian in all of South Africa—a person who had no registration papers and who would resist being fingerprinted.

When Gandhi presented himself at the Volksrust border crossing on October 7, he did in fact refuse to comply with requests for him to produce registration papers and to allow his thumb impression to be taken. He was promptly taken into custody by the Transvaal authorities, along with a number of his companions. After some period of confusion over what the exact charges should be, word came from Pretoria that he was to be charged with violating the Act by reason of his failure to provide his thumb impression for identification. Gandhi refused bail and remained in the Volksrust jail until his trial on October 14.

The prosecution chose to try him along with seventeen other Indian resisters. Gandhi represented not only himself but all the other defendants as well. His performance on this day is a microcosm of his legal work during this period—and the fundamental problem it created.

For fourteen of the seventeen defendants, the record discloses how Gandhi handled the defense. In three remaining instances it does not. In the fourteen cases about which we do have information, Gandhi chose to mount legal defenses for every one of the defendants rather than to quietly accept the punishment.[55]

For every one of these defendants, Gandhi found it impossible to remain silent and to counsel his clients to accept their punishment and silently suffer—despite his knowledge of the salutary effects of self-suffering on the public. He raised defenses instead of accepting punishment. He felt compelled to present evidence, cross-examine witnesses, and make arguments for his clients' innocence. As he stood in the courtroom, facing a hostile magistrate and a prosecutor determined to punish Indian defendants, he could not help but be a lawyer. And the lawyer desirous of playing the lawyer's role overcame the nonviolent strategist who possessed a remarkably sophisticated understanding of the power of self-suffering.

He had been practicing law in South Africa for more than fifteen years. His identity was that of Barrister Gandhi, Advocate Gandhi, Solicitor Gandhi.[56] This was who he was. If he was in court, he was going to use his standing there to speak and act. This is what lawyers do for their clients.

Earlier Gandhi had managed to give himself and Harilal an exemption from this self-treatment. And he would give himself an exemption again on Wednesday, October 14, 1908. He would mount no defense for himself. Rather, when his own case was finally called, Gandhi pled guilty. In a brief statement to the court, he made three points. First, the Act offended the consciences of South Africa's Indians. Second, in light of this affront, he advised his fellow Indians to defy the Act. Third, their disobedience notwithstanding, Indian resisters believed in the rule of law and accepted the sanctions imposed by the law for their disobedience.

His statement made, Gandhi concluded: "I am now before the Court to suffer any penalty that may be inflicted on me. I wish to thank the prosecution and the public for having extended to me the ordinary courtesies."

Even the magistrate—who was openly hostile to Gandhi, but who, in a moment, would impose a sentence significantly less severe than that sought by the prosecutor—recognized the power in Gandhi's nonresistance to punishment. While he disagreed with Gandhi's point of view, he conceded that he did understand that Gandhi was suffering for his country.

This was the sort of performance that could open ears to the Indians' cries.

Gandhi's inability to bring this same powerful, entrancing, and moving approach to the cases of others whom he represented harmed the movement. By pleading his clients not guilty and by mounting defenses, he obscured their suffering from view, thus sapping the sacrifices of many jail-going Indians of the capacity to generate sympathy and create change.

Gandhi's role as a lawyer—as he conceived that role—was interfering with his role as a political organizer and civil disobedient.

Something had to give.

EIGHTEEN

Closing Arguments

We shall have to consider how we can realize the self and how
serve our country.

GANDHI

BY THE TIME GANDHI ENTERED the Volksrust jail on October 14,
1908—twelve days after his thirty-ninth birthday—he had spent more than
half his life in the study and practice of law. In some ways the law had been
very good to Gandhi, his family, and the movement for Indian rights in
South Africa. Gandhi's status as a lawyer had given him credibility with the
authorities and with his own community. His practice had provided his
immediate family and, at times, his extended family, too, with income.
Indeed, Gandhi's practice was so financially successful that he was able to
funnel huge sums of money into the Indian movement's operations.[1]

But in an arena more important than money, the law was not good to
Gandhi and his movement. Gandhi's many encounters with litigation as a
tool of social change told another story altogether. His attack against Law 3
of 1885 was rebuffed, first by a noted jurist in an absurd arbitration decision
and then predictably by the High Court of the South African Republic. He
suffered the painful recognition, when fighting the DLA in Durban, that the
Natal judiciary lacked the political independence necessary to invalidate the
deliberately discriminatory application of this piece of legislation. His arguments on behalf of Indian property rights were rejected by the judges of the
Transvaal Supreme Court. After building an airtight case against the officials
of the Asiatic Permit Office and handing it off to the prosecutor, Gandhi was
left to stand by helplessly as a white jury acquitted the obviously corrupt
defendants. He was stopped cold in his effort to use the courts to integrate
Johannesburg's segregated tram system. When the passive resistance movement sought the return of registration applications, the Transvaal Supreme
Court backed Jan Christian Smuts and his repressive government rather
than Gandhi and the Indians. And it was the court system that imprisoned

Thambi Naidoo and Harilal Gandhi and Sorabji Shapurji and hundreds of other sincere and conscientious Indians whose only crime was to ask for a small measure of human equality.

With his confidence in the courts slowly but ineluctably disappearing, Gandhi experimented with civil disobedience in 1908. He found that when it came to working with his fellow disobedients, he could not relate to them except as a traditional courtroom lawyer—pleading them not guilty, mounting defenses, and challenging the prosecution—all at a time when he knew from experience that such tactics were more often than not fruitless. Their use only infrequently produced acquittals. More significantly, they failed to lead to social change. And they were even less effective for the simpler goal of garnering attention for the cause of Indian rights than were standing mute and willingly accepting the suffering inflicted by the courts—a response to prosecution that he allowed for himself and that not only got attention but had some potential for moving the feelings of others.

Over the course of his professional career, Gandhi intermittently expressed a desire to abandon the practice of law. Aware of the substantial advantages his practice had brought him and his community, he turned his back on that notion every time he considered it. As he did so, however, the movement's accumulated failures in the courts remained a weight on him and persistently goaded him to return to the question of quitting the profession. Should he remain a lawyer? Or should he instead embrace the life of a full-time resister and civil disobedient? Even with the solitude and perspective afforded him by two months in jail in late 1908, Gandhi could not come to a decision.

He needed a public stage on which to rehearse his answers to both sides of the question, experiment with them, and finally settle the argument he was having with himself.

THE ARGUMENT FOR SACRIFICE, SUFFERING, AND CIVIL DISOBEDIENCE

After a term of two months and ten days, Gandhi was released from the Volksrust jail on December 12. Not able to contain it within himself a moment longer, the argument for civil disobedience over litigation came pouring out of him that same day in a speech to his supporters in Johannesburg:

In a country where people suffer injustice and oppression and are denied their ... rights, their real duty lies in suffering imprisonment.... This, I think, is the true meaning of religion for those who have faith in God.

... [T]he outcome of our campaign does not depend upon whether we win or lose in the Supreme Court. We should rather, if need be, bear separation from our families, sacrifice our property for the sake of truth, endure whatever other hardships we may encounter and thus make the voice of truth heard in the Divine Court. When the echoes of that voice strike the ears of General Smuts, his conscience will be stirred and he will acknowledge our rights, will see that we invite suffering in order to secure them, that we have suffered more than enough. It is then that we shall get what we have been demanding. It is not the Imperial Government that will secure you your rights; you will get them only from God. If you fight truthfully with Him as your witness, your bonds will be loosened....

... God is present everywhere; He sees and hears everything. I am sure that we shall be free when that God stirs ... [our opponents'] conscience. We do not sacrifice as much as we should. The moment we do so, our fetters will fall away.[2]

There is no more explicit explanation of Gandhi's argument for civil disobedience over litigation than this tribute to suffering's ability to create change.[3] In an argument in which Gandhi's faith in civil disobedience appears inseparable from his faith in God, he maintains that undeserved suffering will move both God and the consciences of the Indians' opponents. Once moved, God will grant the Indians their freedom. Once moved, Smuts will recognize their rights.

In this process of change, human courts would make no contribution.[4]

COULD THE LEGAL SYSTEM YET BE MADE TO WORK?

As powerful a rejection of the courts as this speech was, Gandhi remained less than fully convinced. In mid-December he fell back upon litigation and his professional role, experimenting with the representation of a large group of Indians who had been arrested while picketing the Johannesburg registration office. As if to give the legal system another chance to make its case, there was lawyer Gandhi—barely a week removed from his Johannesburg speech—in front of the magistrate, pleading his clients not guilty, conducting the defense, and trying a new approach to making the courts work for the Indian cause.[5]

During the time Gandhi was in jail, Polak had begun mounting a novel defense. On behalf of Indians charged with a failure to register, he claimed that registration could not be required of the Indians, because the government had not properly appointed a registrar of Asiatics to take their registration applications. This was a clever defense, but one that could serve no useful civil disobedience purpose. It could not advance the public debate on any substantive or determinative issue, it could not lead to the withdrawal of consent, it could not do honor to the defendants' consciences, and it could not bring the Indians sympathy. It might test the law, but not on an issue of relevance. It was a purely technical defense designed to do nothing other than force an acquittal of the defendants—a handy defense if the Indians were ordinary criminal defendants, but not so useful for defendants out to make a political point.

Gandhi was nonetheless determined to try out the defense Polak had invented when he represented the pickets. To Gandhi's undoubted disappointment, the magistrate scoffed at it and convicted the defendants. Another not-guilty plea, another defense, another conviction, another missed opportunity. Gandhi simply did not understand that his courtroom tactics were interfering with the effectiveness of the very disobedience he was encouraging. To the extent the disobedience of his clients could have drawn attention to their cause, his tactics clouded over the substantive issues by diverting attention to a defense that had nothing to do with the merits of the debate. To the extent the disobedience of his clients could have made an appeal to consciences in London and Johannesburg through the quiet acceptance of undeserved suffering, his tactics destroyed this possibility by painting a picture of defendants stoutly resisting suffering.

The failure of the "no registrar" defense did not end this round of experimentation. In fact, jail had given Gandhi the opportunity to think about yet another form of experimentation with the legal system, one that did elevate the role of suffering, to a fault. The courts in the Transvaal observed that jail sentences were not discouraging Indian merchants from disobeying the licensing laws governing hawking. Accordingly, magistrates began to hand out stiff monetary penalties to the merchants, with no alternative of a jail sentence. The magistrates' aim was to substantially hurt the businesses of Indian merchants. Gandhi's goal in January 1909 was to outflank the courts by encouraging convicted Indian businessmen to voluntarily surrender their goods to the European wholesalers from whom they had taken the goods on credit. There would then be nothing for the government to seize upon the merchants' refusal to pay the civil penalties assessed by the courts. The tactic combined an appeal for sympathy with an attempt at coercion. It would encourage sympathy by showing the willingness of the merchants to suffer large losses. (Indeed, this tactic was emphatically Gandhian in that it called for a commitment on the part of Indian merchants to what could be a huge amount of self-suffering.) It would also threaten economic harm to the European wholesalers with whom the Indian retailers did business and owed money; if the Europeans refused an Indian retailer's offer, the retailer might become insolvent upon the government's seizure of the goods, and there would be insufficient assets remaining after liquidation to fully pay all the wholesalers whose goods the Indian retailer had in his store on credit.[6] Gandhi hoped the wholesalers would foresee this outcome and avoid it by running the stores themselves, using the Indian owners as their managers. In this way, Gandhi surmised, Indians might be allowed in some fashion to stay in business.

Gandhi's threatened tactic got the attention of the European community—but not its sympathy. Rather, European backs stiffened. The executive committee of the Johannesburg Chamber of Commerce, after an emergency meeting, warned the Indians against such a move. The *Rand Daily Mail* predicted that Gandhi's tactics would "destroy the last shred of sympathy with the Asiatic cause."[7] The *Johannesburg Star* referred to any who might follow Gandhi on this course as "deluded faddists."[8]

The chairman of the BIA, the merchant Adam Mahomed Cachalia, had agreed to lead the way. Gandhi represented him in a meeting with his creditors at which Gandhi suggested the creditors take over Cachalia's business. Cachalia's European creditors were not about to capitulate, however, and were willing to take some losses for principle. They declined to assume control of the business and instead demanded a cash payment. Cachalia refused to pay. The next week, when the merchants took the initiative by moving a Transvaal court to put Cachalia in full-fledged bankruptcy and to liquidate his business, his lawyer, Mohandas K. Gandhi, was powerless to stop the process.[9] Gandhi's creative but unrealistic experiment with the bankruptcy system had backfired on his client. Not surprisingly, no other Indian merchants followed Cachalia's example.[10]

At the same time as this failure, there was bad news from the Supreme Court in a resistance test case. The Court dismissed the appeal of an Indian claiming the right to enter the colony as a lawful immigrant. This case was followed up in the next several weeks by two more significant Supreme Court cases—one on the question of whether the alleged improper appointment of the registrar of Asiatics invalidated convictions for failure to register (Polak's argument, but not Polak's case),[11] and the other on the definition of "prohibited immigrant."[12] The Indians lost both cases.

These defeats added to the palpable sense of the Indian community that its cause was hopeless. That sense was reflected in a steep drop in the number of Indians keeping faith with the resistance movement. By early 1909 almost all Indians had registered under the 1908 act. Gandhi had little popular support for active opposition to the government beyond a small band of hard-core resisters—and most of those were in jail. He himself conceded that "many Indians have given in."[13] The *Rand Daily Mail* gloated: "The back of the passive resistance campaign has been broken. In asking the traders to take a step which means the sequestration [bankruptcy] of their estates, the leaders of the British Indians have gone further than their fellow-countrymen are prepared to follow."[14]

Gandhi's most recent experiments with invoking the processes of the legal system had failed. With a stunning rapidity, he once again swung away from the courts and toward the alternative remedy of suffering and civil disobedience of which he had eloquently spoken on his release from jail in December. He would challenge the government to arrest him yet again. In mid-January he traveled back to Natal, entered the Transvaal, was arrested for not having registered, was quickly deported to Natal, returned immediately, and was re-arrested and released on bail. He was allowed to attend to his ailing wife for a period of several weeks before being tried on February 25, 1909. By the time of his trial his movement was almost in full retreat. Nonetheless, in his statement to the court he remained faithful to his previous discipline—he mounted no defense and accepted, indeed invited, punishment:

> I am quite aware that my offence is deliberate and wilful. . . . I maintain the conclusion that, . . . as a citizen of the State and as a man who respects conscience above everything, I must continue to incur the penalties so long as justice, as I conceive it, has not been rendered by the State to a portion of its citizens. I consider myself the greatest offender in the Asiatic struggle, if the conduct that I am pursuing is held to be reprehensible. I, therefore, regret that I am being tried under a clause which does not enable me to ask for a penalty which some of my fellow objectors received, but I ask you to impose on me the highest penalty.[15]

After Gandhi thanked the court and the prosecutor for having delayed the trial so that he could attend to his wife, the magistrate sentenced him to a fine of £50 or three months' imprisonment with hard labor.

Gandhi brought this round of experimentation to a close. He chose jail.

LONDON AGAIN

When Gandhi was released from jail in late May 1909, South Africa's European colonists were in dialogue with London about the formation of the Union of South Africa, a federation of the Cape, the Transvaal, Natal, and the Orange Free State. Believing that their interests also should be represented, the Indian community decided to send a delegation to the United Kingdom. Although Gandhi's popularity was at a low point at this time, he was chosen as one of the delegates—thanks to a series of serendipitous events that allowed him to survive a strong challenge to his leadership.[16] He had no confidence, however, in the ability of the delegation to do any good, claiming that "passive resisters depend upon their sufferings for relief and not upon the appeal of any deputation."[17] On the other hand, while Gandhi "did not want a deputation to London . . . he evidently did not want to be bypassed if there were one."[18] So, on June 21, 1909, he went—as did Smuts. Gandhi spent about four months in London, during which time all efforts by the Colonial Office to mediate a settlement between the two leaders failed miserably. Gandhi's time in England, however, was not uneventful— it brought him into contact with a number of Indian nationalists there who subscribed to anarchism as a philosophy. Gandhi felt challenged to "meet their arguments as well as to solve the difficulties of Indians in South Africa who held similar views." He would have a period of uninterrupted solitude to do just that—and "to demonstrate the sublimity of Satyagraha"—while he was on board the SS *Kildonan Castle*, the steamer that would carry him home to South Africa.[19]

Gandhi's effort would take the form of writing done by hand on 271 pages of ship stationery at a furious pace over the period November 13–22, 1909.[20] The resulting booklet was, as Gandhi described it, "an attempt to see beauty in voluntary simplicity, poverty and slowness."[21] He called it *Hind Swarajya* (later to be changed by Gandhi to its more familiar title, *Hind Swaraj*) and published it in his native Gujarati in two installments of *Indian Opinion* on his return home in December.[22] Soon afterward, he would translate it into English, call it *Indian Home Rule*, and print that version in March 1910.

Hind Swaraj is not written as a cohesive, unified treatise. Rather, it is a series of questions and answers between an editor and a reader in somewhat the fashion of a Socratic dialogue. It addresses an array of topics from the influence of Giuseppe Mazzini on Italy to the meaning of swaraj.[23] The analysis is usually quite brief—most of its twenty chapters are just a few pages long. At the work's core is Gandhi's denunciation of Western civilization.[24] Gandhi sharply criticizes its manifestations in parliaments, newspapers, machinery, manufacturing, railways, and educational systems. He argues that the West's choice to emphasize material goods—while ignoring morality and religion—is so wrong-headed that the end of Western civilization will come about as an act of self-destruction.

Gandhi's feelings about the matter were quite pronounced and welled up from the deepest parts of him: "The more I observe, the greater is the dissatisfaction with modern life. I see nothing good in it. . . . The fact is that we are all bound to do what we feel is right. And with me I feel that the modern life is *not* right."[25]

Nor was the law, as a part of modern life, right. Gandhi devotes an entire chapter of *Hind Swaraj* to a blistering assault on the legal system to which he had belonged for two decades. In conducting this assault, Gandhi articulates—and, in fact, broadens—his argument for leaving the profession. One might expect Gandhi to identify the failure of the court system to bring justice to his people as a fundamental basis of his argument. He does not disappoint. While he is speaking of India, he reflects the hard lesson he has learned from his frustrating attempts to use the South African legal system: "Do you think that it would be possible for the English to carry on their Government without law courts? It is wrong to consider that courts are established for the benefit of the people. Those who want to perpetuate their power do so through the courts."

Gandhi has little more to say about the law as a system. Instead, he uses the occasion of *Hind Swaraj* to give vent to feelings about his fellow practitioners that must have been building in him for some time. He expresses an "abhorrence for the profession" in large part because of the character and behavior of those persons who become lawyers. In Gandhi's estimation, people who take up the law are lazy. Moreover, they are interested only in enriching themselves, not in serving others.[26] They rejoice when people engage in disputes, because it means business for them. Indeed, Gandhi says, lawyers actually stir up disputes to serve their self-interest.

People who seek to go to court to settle their disputes are blameworthy, too. Men who use courts become "unmanly and cowardly."[27] Gandhi goes so far as to say that "men were less unmanly when they settled their disputes either by fighting or by asking their relatives to decide upon them." He argues that resolving a dispute by using a third party is as much a sign of savagery as is settling a dispute by fighting. The basis for this position appears to reside in Gandhi's stated belief that those who resolve disputes for others in courts are not infallible and that the parties themselves, possessed of a unique knowledge of the right, are better equipped to resolve the dispute by themselves. While one might question whether the resort to a courtroom is a "sign of savagery," one must certainly admit that this notion that parties should resolve disputes on their own is consistent with the larger emphasis in *Hind Swaraj* on self-rule as self-control and with a growing emphasis by Gandhi on personal morality of which *Hind Swaraj* is itself a notable part.[28]

So intense is Gandhi's criticism of lawyers and the legal profession that his emphasis on individual personal morality does not preclude him from faulting lawyers for their collective political effect. While conceding that some lawyers have attended to the public interest, he claims they have done so "as men rather than as lawyers." The larger effect of the profession is to tighten "the English grip." If lawyers were to cease their work, "English rule would break up in a day."

Perhaps the harshest and most important of all the harsh points Gandhi makes in his argument against the profession is that it "teaches immorality." Lawyers are obligated by professional duty "to side with their clients, and to find out ways and arguments in favour of the clients to which they (the clients) are often strangers." In other words, Gandhi is arguing that it is in the very nature of the lawyer's job to focus on and magnify disputes—rather than repress them—by creating from whole cloth purely utilitarian arguments where none existed before. A better way, says Gandhi, is for clients to refrain from going to lawyers, to admit that fault lies on both sides of every dispute, and to just stop quarreling.

One must wonder whether Gandhi was thinking of himself when he mounted this attack. Was he thinking of his advocacy of the no-registrar defense? Or his successful use of purely technical defenses in the initial Sorabji case?

Those were arguments to which his clients surely were strangers.

To understand Gandhi's argument that society would be better off without lawyers, one must see it in the context of his overall mission in *Hind Swaraj*. Gandhi was interested in not merely rejecting the trappings of Western civilization, but in embracing a more authentic and historic Indian way of life—a life that was simpler, was centered in small communities, and was based on a universal observance of morality. It was in such a setting that Gandhi imagined that each person would master self-control, making possible a society free of lawyers, courts, and the regulatory machinery of modern life.[29] Lawyers would simply be unnecessary.

What were the intellectual and experiential roots that gave rise to this thinking? They were many. In his introduction, Gandhi confesses that the ideas in *Hind Swaraj* were not original with him. Indeed, for the broad framework of his thought Gandhi took inspiration from a wide range of thinkers and activists and from Christian, Muslim, and Hindu scripture.[30] Of all these, Sir Henry Sumner Maine's *Village-Communities in the East and West* may have had the greatest effect on what Gandhi wrote regarding the legal system. As Anthony Parel, in his review of the influences Gandhi cites, explains:

> It was Maine's contention that villages in traditional India were representative institutions, and that the ancient village council had enjoyed both quasi-judicial and quasi-legislative powers. The introduction of the new utilitarian state, with its new adversarial court system, led to the ruin of the villages as the ultimate unit of national life, shifting . . . their quasi-judicial and quasi-legislative powers to the new breed of lawyers condemned in . . . *Hind Swaraj*. As far as Gandhi was concerned, this was one of the worst consequences of the introduction of modern civilisation into India. The life of the Indian peasant had become a veritable hell. He had become prey for the greedy urban middle class.[31]

While Gandhi's reading of Maine and others was enormously important to the development of the ideas he expressed in *Hind Swaraj*, so too was his experience in South Africa's justice system. Oliver Wendell Holmes once famously wrote, "The life of the law has not been logic; it has been experience."[32] Never was the role of experience more important than in the case of Mohandas K. Gandhi's transformation from lawyer to civil disobedient. Over the course of his professional career, Gandhi had repeatedly cried out to the court system for justice—and had been rarely heard. Had the court system responded favorably to his pleas, Gandhi would likely have never written chapter 11. But it did respond unfavorably, Gandhi did write chapter 11, and he was thinking—aloud—about turning his back on the profession.

A month before he wrote *Hind Swaraj*, he had shared his frustrations with his confidant and colleague Henry Polak. He wrote: "The railways, telegraphs, hospitals, lawyers, doctors, and such like have all to go, and the so-called upper classes have to learn to live conscientiously and religiously and deliberately the simple peasant life, knowing it to be a life giving true happiness."[33]

This was Gandhi's dream, not just for Indian society, but for himself.

Hind Swaraj was an opportunity to see if he could convince himself that he was right.

UNDERLINING *HIND SWARAJ*: THE ARGUMENT IN PRACTICE

With *Hind Swaraj*, Gandhi had expressed his frustrations with the law in writing. As if to validate his theoretical disposition against the law, he would now pair this expression with the actual experience of frustration.

In late December 1909, three Indian merchants were tried for refusing to produce their registration certificates and for being, as a result, prohibited immigrants. Gandhi appeared for the merchants and argued that because his clients had voluntarily registered, they could be guilty only of the first charge and not the second. The magistrate rejected Gandhi's argument and found all three merchants guilty on both charges.[34]

After this loss, Gandhi would never represent a civil disobedient again. We do not know if this was a conscious decision. We do know that the loss in the merchants' case came just days after Gandhi published *Hind Swaraj*. We also know that his behavior in the merchants' case was consistent with his previous practice. During his entire South African period, he never did allow his community to benefit from the power that would have come from allowing his disobedient clients to suffer silently without raising legal defenses—defenses, notably, that usually failed. Silent suffering was a tactic reserved for defendants named Gandhi.[35]

Indian merchants in the Krugersdorp location were not interested in silent suffering. In early 1910 the municipal government was attempting to force them out against their will. The municipality was disturbed by the location's proximity to white areas—and appeared to be using objections to the condition of the Indians' buildings as a pretext for its position that the Indians should be relocated. Krugersdorp had no hand in the creation of the location— it had been created by the colonial government years earlier over the municipality's objection—and now it wanted the Indians out. The Indians did not want to move, because they had made substantial property investments. To determine whether removal of the Indians to a new location was desirable and practical, Krugersdorp established a "Committee of Inquiry into the Krugersdorp Indian Locations." Gandhi appeared at the committee's hearing on February 17, 1910, to represent the interests of the Indian residents of the location.

Gandhi was allowed to examine Krugersdorp's mayor. His goal was to get him to admit that, if the Indians were to address all the alleged deficiencies through the repair of their buildings, the municipality would have no objection to the location remaining where it was. The mayor refused to agree, however, claiming that what was in order was total demolition and rebuilding. When Gandhi asked if it would satisfy the municipality if the Indians did just that, the mayor conceded it would, but only from a sanitary point of view—and that, he made clear, was not the municipality's ultimate concern.

Gandhi had not succeeded in winning his point, but had succeeded in making the municipality's racial motivations clear. That, of course, was no embarrassment in South Africa in 1910 and certainly not enough to stop the committee from recommending that the Indians be forced into a new location.[36] The committee, on which his nemesis Montfort Chamney sat, gave Gandhi a cold reminder of the argument for quitting practice: legal skills were an unreliable mechanism for stopping mass injustice in a system controlled by his opponents.[37]

By early 1910, with the lessons of these cases and *Hind Swaraj* behind him, Gandhi faced two powerful arguments for the abandonment of the practice of law. The first was the failure of the courts to serve as an instrument for social change. The second was that the profession led its practitioners into immorality. Gandhi's last cases would form a response to these arguments.

COUNTERARGUMENT: VIRTUE IN THE ORDINARY
PRACTICE OF LAW

The final two cases in which Gandhi would be involved had a common characteristic: each involved innocent people who were not themselves resisters, but who were caught up in the resistance movement and needed help. The first was Mahomed Chotabhai, the sixteen-year-old son of the merchant A. E. Chotabhai.

One Indian complaint about the Act of 1907 had been that it called for the direct registration of minors. The Act of 1908 addressed this concern by providing for the transfer of the "registration of such children to their parents' certificates."[38] In 1910, the Asiatic Department recognized a flaw in the 1908 act that the department claimed allowed it to deport children of lawful residents (who had been earlier transferred to their parents' registration certificates) on the grounds that the children, upon turning sixteen, became prohibited immigrants—a paradigmatic instance of following the letter of the law rather than its spirit.

When Gandhi learned of the government's attempt to deport young Mahomed, he was appalled. His commentary on the case as it moved from initial decision to final resolution is a window into the thinking of a man who found himself caught between two poles—his desire to have nothing more to do with the practice of law, on the one hand, and, on the other, his particularized knowledge from years of practice that litigation could help individuals in trouble. He let this internal conflict show in the pages of *Indian Opinion* as the case was starting to make its way through the judicial system: "This move of the . . . Government has . . . a deeper meaning. It shows that the sheet-anchor of our hope lies not in the uncertainty of law suits but in the certainty of passive resistance."[39]

After the Appellate Division of the Supreme Court of the newly formed Union of South Africa had ruled in Chotabhai's favor, Gandhi took a completely contradictory position, stating that "the community is . . . justified in attaching great importance to the Court's judgment."[40]

The second case that occupied Gandhi as 1910 drew to a close involved another nonresister caught up in the movement, Rambhabai Sodha. She was the wife of a resister—Ratanshi Sodha, who by the end of 1910 had spent a year and a half in Transvaal jails. Because the family had no means of support with Ratanshi in jail, Gandhi resolved to bring Rambhabai and her children from Natal to the Transvaal, where the community could help support them. This meant Rambhabai had to cross the border without having registered. Gandhi thought that the Transvaal would permit Rambhabai to enter, because the government had shown a steady disinclination to arrest Indian women. Gandhi had even alerted the authorities to Rambhabai's intentions, confident they would let her pass without trouble.

They did not. The government arrested her for being a prohibited immigrant. When she was tried, Gandhi argued that she simply was not guilty of the charge brought against her. The law, he maintained, squarely held that if Rambhabai's husband was not a prohibited immigrant, neither was she. Gandhi called her husband, Ratanshi, to the stand and demonstrated that he had passed the education test when he had entered the country. He was, accordingly, clearly not a prohibited immigrant. It was true he had been arrested, but for refusing to register, not for being a prohibited immigrant. The difference was crucial. If Rambhabai's husband was not a prohibited immigrant, neither could Rambhabai be a prohibited immigrant. The common law was consistent with this understanding, for it bestowed on women the right to follow their husbands.

Gandhi's last argument as a lawyer was as sound an argument as he had ever made.

In a decision that had to signal once again to Gandhi that the South African courts would never serve as a dependable defender of Indian civil rights, the magistrate rejected Gandhi's argument, pronounced his client guilty, and sentenced her to a fine of £10 *and* a one-month prison term.[41] On appeal to the Transvaal Provincial Division of the Supreme Court, the court upheld the conviction, but altered the sentence by providing Rambhabai a choice between a fine and a jail term. She appealed once more and lost. Gandhi would not rest. After Rambhabai let it be known that she would not pay the fine, even to the point of suffering a jail term, Gandhi successfully negotiated directly with Smuts on her behalf, persuading him to pledge that under no circumstances would she be sent to prison.[42] Gandhi thus effectively ended the government's pursuit of Rambhabai.

Gandhi received no compensation for his work in this his last case, except for the inconvenient lesson that the lawyering skills he condemned in *Hind Swaraj* were not worthless. They could sometimes be put to use to help blameless people in trouble—like Mahomed Chotabhai and Rambhabai Sodha.

A LAST INDIAN DEFEAT—AND A LAST LESSON LEARNED

The Chotabhai and Sodha cases reminded Gandhi that the profession was not without its redeeming qualities.[43] Innocents could be helped. Good could be done. There could be virtue in the ordinary practice of law. Helping individuals, however, was not sufficient; Gandhi's interest was in large-scale change. Whatever flicker of hope he may have harbored about the court system's capacity to bring about such change, however, had to have been emphatically extinguished by a remarkably emblematic case that seized the attention of both Gandhi and South Africa in October 1910.

Twenty-one resisters who had been deported from the Transvaal to India had returned, but had been denied permission to land at a series of ports. Finally, they came to Durban. Frederick Laughton, Gandhi's Natal mentor, sought an order from the Natal Division of the Supreme Court restraining the authorities at the Durban port from deporting the Indians and ordering that they be allowed to land. Surprisingly, the Court issued just such an order and immediately telegraphed it to Durban. The Durban immigration officer defied the Court's order. He refused to allow the Indians to land, claiming that they could not meet his demand that they post security first. The Indians' ship, the SS *Gertrude Woermann*, retreated up the coast to Delagoa Bay.

Laughton rushed back to the Court to ask it to hold the officer in contempt for having disobeyed its order. During oral argument, the Court asked the government's lawyer whether he was prepared to admit that the officer had acted contrary to the Court's order and, moreover, whether the government was prepared to arrange for the Indians' return passage to Durban. His response was astonishing for what it revealed about the power relationship between the Court and the government. He boldly told the Court that "the Government was not prepared to assent to the course requested by the Court."

Faced with ordering the government to do something it plainly would refuse to do, the Court instead chose to back down and save face by adopting the government's narrative that there had been a "misunderstanding" on the officer's part. Then the Court made a frank admission: it "would make no comment on the action of the Government in the matter, and felt that it could not order the Government to do anything." If the Indians wanted to return at their own expense, the Court held, they were free to do so—provided that when they arrived in Durban they posted the nearly impossible £100 bond insisted upon by the officer who had earlier "misunderstood" the Court's order.

This was a dramatic capitulation by the Court to the government. Gandhi watched it with great interest—and not simply because of Laughton's involvement. He understood the magnitude of what had just happened. The rule of law depends, in large part, on the good faith of all parties in honoring an implicit compact that binds all to obey the rulings of the courts, regardless of what the relative political strengths of each party may be in any particular circumstance. Such an arrangement offers hope of both stability and orderly change. When the government in the deportees' case openly defied the Court, it committed a blatant breach of this compact and signaled its willingness to go to any length to drive the Indians out of the continent.

The court system rarely sided with the Indians. Now, on this rare occasion when it initially did, it proved impotent. With the Government's unchecked arrogance staring him in the face, Gandhi would have been foolish to continue to look to the courts for the vindication of Indian rights.

Gandhi also understood the very human dimension of the government's defiance. The men on the *Woermann*, including a resister named Narayansamy, had spent weeks outdoors on deck as their vessel, looking for refuge, was denied entry in port after port. During this time, they were subjected to the harshness of the elements without sufficient clothes, having earlier been robbed of them.[44] With Laughton waiting to help, there must have been real hope among these desperate men for relief in Durban. On October 14, however, the immigration officer defied the Court's order and prevented the *Woermann* from discharging its passengers. The extended time on deck proved too much for Narayansamy. He died two days later.

Gandhi condemned the government's action as "legalized murder": "The Officer, acting under instructions from the Minister of the Interior . . . gave a meaning to the order of the Court which no common sense man would give, and in indecent haste sent these men to Delagoa Bay with the result that . . . Narayansamy is no more."[45]

And also "no more" was Gandhi's long-held faith in litigation as a tool for social justice. The argument against practice from the deportees' case was unmistakably clear—and an echo of *Hind Swaraj*. The courts could not be counted on to join the attack on basic, underlying norms and on the power establishment of which they themselves were a part.

LEAVING THE PRACTICE, TO OTHERS

In 1911, three realities loomed large in Gandhi's life. The first was the maturation of his understanding of the limitations of South Africa's court system as an instrument of social change. The deportees' case closed the book for

Gandhi on the argument that litigation could be used for this type of change. His insight into this reality had deepened and taken a final and firm hold of him.

The second was his expectation that the new Union government would come to a settlement with him and his community over the question of Indian rights to immigrate and travel throughout the new country. While these hopes would eventually be dashed and a final settlement not reached until 1914,[46] Gandhi was quite optimistic that 1911 would bring an end to the struggle.

The third was the move Gandhi had made just a few months earlier to Tolstoy Farm to take up a life more focused on manual labor.[47]

All this meant that the time had arrived to make a final break with the profession to which he had dedicated most of his life. The opportunity to do so presented itself in the person of Lewis W. Ritch. Ritch had articled in 1903 in Gandhi's Johannesburg office before being sent by Gandhi to London, where he both served as the animator of the South African British Indian Committee (SABIC) and had an opportunity to complete his legal training. Now Gandhi's former clerk was on his way back to South Africa from his SABIC post in London. He had two items on his agenda—continuing to aid the Indian cause and providing for his family. When he arrived in Cape Town, he assumed the role of the Indians' official representative to the new Union government in the settlement talks. Gandhi remained in Johannesburg, instructing Ritch by telegram and letter. Smuts, however, eventually refused to deal with Ritch.[48] As a result, Gandhi and Ritch switched places, with Ritch moving to Johannesburg and Gandhi taking up Ritch's mission in Cape Town.

With Ritch in need of income to support his family and Gandhi in need of someone to take over what remained of his practice, Gandhi's route out of the profession was clear. In April of 1911, Ritch opened his law practice in Gandhi's office, 21–24 Court Chambers, Rissik Street, Johannesburg.[49] Putting the attention on Ritch rather than himself, Gandhi made the announcement to the community in the pages of *Indian Opinion*: "Mr. Ritch has started legal practice in Johannesburg. . . . Now that he has started practice, it is . . . the community's duty to extend to him their patronage. We trust all those who need the services of a lawyer will engage Mr. Ritch and so show their readiness to encourage him."[50]

With Ritch installed in his office,[51] Gandhi gave vent to his feelings. On May 8, 1911, he wrote to a friend that "I can make at least £200 if I forget all else and only practise. But I am resolved not to have anything to do with that."[52]

By the South African fall of 1911, Gandhi had made his decision. He was resolved to be done with litigation and resolved to be done with practice.

He was not, however, resolved to be done with the law. The lesson that Gandhi learned in South Africa was that he had to break the law, and accept the punishment of the law, if he wanted to achieve justice under the law. While it would not do so in the manner he originally expected it would, the law would thus help liberate Gandhi and his people.

TRANSFORMATION AND FREEDOM

In the end, Gandhi realized that he had to choose between two fundamentally different futures for himself.

The first was to continue in a world of legal practice controlled by those who were no friends to the Indian cause. It would be a world in which disappointment would ordinarily be encountered, a world in which victories would almost never be won, a world in which progress, if it were to come at all, would always be incremental and slow. This would be a world that Gandhi understood most men and women to populate—including those concerned with the public good, such as Lewis Ritch and, indeed, the Gandhi of the previous two decades. It would be a world of compromises where aspirations were limited by hard realities: self-interest as a powerful motivation for behavior, the constrictions of time and place on the ordinary person's vision, and the limitations of all imperfect human institutions—the court system included—to create the good. It would also be a world where even the most self-sacrificing, well-intentioned lawyers would be distracted from their true mission by the prestige, respect, and access to wealth and power the profession enjoys. It would be a world where the signposts were up, the path was well trod, and the journey safe and predictable. At the end would await a numbing and ultimately unfulfilling sense of right order for those who dutifully respond to the world's expectations.

The second was to walk through the door opened by civil disobedience, a door leading to an entirely different and challenging world. This would be a world of unlimited possibilities, of a vision beyond the horizon, of aspirations confined only by imagination. It would be a world where the perfect, while never achieved, would be striven after and where saintliness, while never reached, would be prized—a world, in short, where the community might be saved and the law might be faithful to its ideal of equal justice.

When Gandhi first stood before the court in South Africa to plead guilty and accept his punishment, defendant Gandhi abandoned lawyer Gandhi, declaring instead his faith in the world—and the law—as they should be. He would go to prison twice in 1908, once in 1909, once again in 1913, and then, taking what he had learned in South Africa with him, several more times during the struggle for independence in India. On every occasion that he was prosecuted, he bowed to the penalty imposed by the court. By his willing acceptance of punishment, he demonstrated to the world that individuals could rise above their own immediate interests for the good of the community of which they were a part. By his resolute refusal to raise defenses for himself, he kept the focus squarely on the ideal of equal justice. And by his civil disobedience, he became a beacon of hope.

So it was that Gandhi's experiences in the law helped transform one man's life—and free, a continent away, the lives of three hundred million others.

MOHANDAS K. GANDHI CHRONOLOGY

An asterisk marks events about whose dates the sources differ.

1869	Gandhi born, Porbandar, India
1882	Marries Kasturba*
1885	Father, Karamchand, passes away*
1888	Son, Harilal, born Sails for London to start law studies, leaving Kasturba in India
1889–1891	Reads *The Song Celestial* Reads the New Testament, including the Sermon on the Mount Encounters theosophy, vegetarianism
1891	Called to the bar; returns to India Attempts to establish practice
1892	Son Manilal born
1893	Accepts offer to work in South Africa; leaves family in India Refuses to remove turban, ejected from Durban courtroom Train incident in Pietermaritzburg en route to Pretoria
1894	Reads Tolstoy's *The Kingdom of God Is Within You* Natal Legislature considers disenfranchising Indians Decides to remain in South Africa to fight disenfranchisement Natal Indian Congress established Partners with Coakes Admitted to the Natal bar
1896	Travels to India; publishes *The Grievances of the British Indians in South Africa: An Appeal to the Indian Public* (the "Green Pamphlet"); returns with his family
1897	Assaulted in Durban Son Ramdas born

	Takes up the fight against the Dealers' Licenses Act and other anti-Indian legislation in Natal
1899	Organizes Indian Ambulance Corps to serve in Boer War
1900	Petitions against segregated Durban rickshaws Son Devdas born
1901	Departs South Africa for India
1902	Establishes practice first in Rajkot, then in Mumbai Called back to South Africa
1903	Admitted to the Transvaal bar Establishes practice in Johannesburg *Indian Opinion* publishes first issue
1904	Suggests civil disobedience in *Indian Opinion* Reads Ruskin's *Unto This Last* Establishes Phoenix Settlement in Natal Kasturba and sons join Gandhi in South Africa
1906	Organizes civil disobedience to set up tram car test cases Serves in Indian Ambulance Corps in Zulu Rebellion Embraces celibacy Empire Theatre speech Sails to London as part of Indian deputation
1907	Represents Ramsundar Pundit, Indian disobedient Arrested, tried, and convicted for refusing to register with the Transvaal government
1908	Adopts term "satyagraha" in place of "passive resistance" Jailed in January; reaches settlement with Smuts and is released Attacked by Mir Alam Settlement with Smuts collapses Burning of registration papers Arrested and jailed Released
1909	Arrested and jailed Released On diplomatic mission to London Begins correspondence with Leo Tolstoy Writes *Hind Swaraj*
1910	Establishes Tolstoy Farm
1911	Abandons the practice of law
1913	March across Transvaal border; mass arrests Arrested and jailed Released

1914	Settlement with Smuts Permanently departs South Africa; sails for England
1915	Arrives in India from England Establishes Kochrab Ashram in Ahmedabad, predecessor of Sabarmati Ashram
1917	Assists indigo workers in Champaran Founds Sabarmati Ashram
1918	Kaira campaign Mill workers' campaign in Ahmedabad
1919	Satyagraha campaign against Rowlatt Bills Arrested and shortly thereafter released Amritsar/Jallianwala Bagh massacre
1920	Noncooperation campaign
1921	Mass civil disobedience
1922	Chauri Chaura incident; suspends campaign Arrested, tried, sentenced, and imprisoned for sedition
1924	Released
1925	Begins writing his autobiography
1928	Publishes *Satyagraha in South Africa* Bardoli tax satyagraha
1929	Indian National Congress declares complete independence as its goal
1930	Leaves Sabarmati Ashram and begins Salt Campaign Arrested and jailed
1931	Released Gandhi-Irwin Pact Attends London Round Table Conference
1932	Civil disobedience resumes Arrested, tried, convicted, imprisoned
1933	Released; individual civil disobedience begins Arrested and jailed Released
1934	Indian National Congress abandons civil disobedience
1936	Moves to Sevagram from Wardha to continue village work
1940	Begins campaign of individual civil disobedience
1941	Ends individual civil disobedience campaign
1942	Mounts Quit India campaign Arrested; jailed at Aga Khan Palace

1944	Kasturba passes away in prison
	Released from incarceration
	Negotiations with Jinnah fail
1946	Communal violence
1947	Walking tour for communal peace
	Indian independence, with Pakistan a separate country
	Fasts in Calcutta against communal violence
1948	Fasts in New Delhi against communal violence
	Assassinated, New Delhi

ABBREVIATIONS

Autobiography	Mohandas K. Gandhi, *An Autobiography: The Story of My Experiments with Truth*
BSP	British Sessional Papers, Papers Relating to the Grievances of Her Majesty's Indian Subjects in the South African Republic
CWMG	*The Collected Works of Mahatma Gandhi* (The *Collected Works* consists of one hundred volumes published over a long period of time with some volumes having gone through more than one edition. Accordingly, there is no one publication date for the *CWMG*; rather, each edition of each volume of the *CWMG* has its own publication date. To specify the edition of each volume cited, this work provides each volume's year of publication at that volume's first citation.)
IO	*Indian Opinion*
JS	*Johannesburg Star*
NA	*Natal Advertiser*
NLR	*Natal Law Reports*
NM	*Natal Mercury*
NW	*Natal Witness*
RDM	*Rand Daily Mail*
Satyagraha	Mohandas K. Gandhi, *Satyagraha in South Africa*

SN	Gandhi Smarak Sangrahalaya, Sabarmati Ashram, Ahmedabad, and the documents housed there by serial number
TL	*Transvaal Leader*
TP	*The Press*
TSCR	*Transvaal Supreme Court Reports*

NOTES

The following notes reflect only a portion of the research undertaken to support this book. A full set of endnotes can be found at disalvo.law.wvu.edu. The interested reader may also find other materials at that site, including a description of resistance cases litigated by Gandhi in 1907.

INTRODUCTION

Epigraph, page xi: King, *The Papers of Martin Luther King, Jr.*, Vol. 5, *Threshold of a New Decade* (Berkeley: University of California Press, 2005), 126.

1. "Our goal . . . is not primarily to have an effect. It is . . . to be faithful." Resister Greg Boertje-Obed, quoted in Nepstad, *Religion and War Resistance in the Plowshares Movement* (Cambridge: Cambridge University Press, 2008), 65.

2. *Brown et al. v. Louisiana*, 383 U.S. 131 (1965).

3. See Stanton, Anthony, and Gage (eds.), *The History of Woman Suffrage* (New York: National American Woman Suffrage Association, 1881), 2:691.

4. Stanley Wolpert addresses suffering in Gandhi's life in *Gandhi's Passion* (New York: Oxford University Press, 2001).

5. Branch, *Parting the Waters: America in the King Years, 1954–1963* (New York: Simon & Schuster, 1988).

6. "The social view of power sees rulers and other command systems, despite appearances, to be dependent on the population's . . . support. . . . Power always depends for its strength and existence upon a replenishment of its sources by the cooperation of numerous institutions and people—cooperation that does not have to continue." Sharp, *Waging Nonviolent Struggle: 20th Century Practice and 21st Century Potential* (Boston: Porter Sargent, 2005), 28.

7. Kirkpatrick and Sanger, "A Tunisian-Egyptian Link That Shook Arab History," *New York Times*, February 13, 2011, http://www.nytimes.com/2011/02/14/world/middleeast/14egypt-tunisia-protests.html?pagewanted=all&_r=0.

8. When first created, these universities did not offer courses. Rather, they set courses of study at affiliated institutions and examined their students.

9. Seal, *The Emergence of Indian Nationalism: Competition and Collaboration in the Later Nineteenth Century* (Cambridge: Cambridge University Press, 1968), 148, quoted in Copland, *India, 1885–1947: The Unmaking of an Empire* (Harlow, UK: Longman, 2001).

10. *Satyagraha*, 109.

11. As Thomas Weber has shown, the tax had long concerned Gandhi and his mentor Gopal Krishna Gokhale. Weber, *On the Salt March: The Historiography of Mahatma Gandhi's March to Dandi* (New Delhi: Rupa & Co., 2009) is the definitive work on the Salt March.

12. Brown, *Gandhi and Civil Disobedience: The Mahatma in Indian Politics, 1928–1934* (Cambridge: Cambridge University Press, 1977), 94.

13. Thomas Weber, having traversed the route himself, provides this number in *On the Salt March*, 548.

14. Ibid., 531.

15. Brown, *Gandhi: Prisoner of Hope* (New Haven: Yale University Press, 1989), 339.

16. King, *Papers*, 5:136.

17. See Chenoweth and Stephan, *Why Civil Resistance Works* (New York: Columbia University Press, 2011).

18. Kirkpatrick and Sanger, "A Tunisian-Egyptian Link."

CHAPTER ONE

Epigraph, page 1: Ball, *The Student's Guide to the Bar* (London: Macmillan, 1879), 7.

1. James Hunt demonstrates in *Gandhi in London* (New Delhi: Promilla, 1978), 8, that most Gandhi biographers get the time and place of arrival wrong. He makes a compelling case for September 29 and Tilbury Station.

2. An earlier pregnancy ended with the death of the child very soon after its birth. Tendulkar, *Mahatma: Life of Mohandas Karamchand Gandhi* (New Delhi: Government of India, 1951), 1:27.

3. For Gandhi's family tree, see Pyarelal, *Mahatma Gandhi—The Early Phase* (Ahmedabad, India: Navijivan, 1965), 184.

4. "Interview with *The Vegetarian*," *CWMG* 1 (1969 edition): 42.

5. Pearce, *A History of the Inns of Court and Chancery* (London: Bentley, 1848), 50.

6. "It was only the call to the bar of the Inn which could confer" the right "to plead in court." Holdsworth, *A History of the English Law* (London: Methuen & Co., 1923), 506. At the time of Gandhi's enrollment, women were excluded from the bar. Ringrose, *The Inns of Court* (London: Paul Musson, 1909), 142.

7. Quoted in Barton, Benham and Watt, *The Story of the Inns of Court* (Boston: Houghton Mifflin, 1924), 58. For a less cynical view, see W. C. Richardson, *A History of the Inns of Court* (Baton Rouge: Claitor, 1975).

8. Benchers were members of the bar governing the Inn. Ball, *Student's Guide*, 11.

9. Alexander, *The Temple of the Nineties* (London: Hodge & Co., 1938), 29.

10. It appears that shortly after Gandhi's time, the practice of attending lectures may have changed somewhat. *CWMG* 1:66.

11. Ball, *Student's Guide*, 23, 24.

12. Ibid., 25. Gandhi, having worked without a university education, intimates that more time be spent. *CWMG* 1:66.

13. Napier and Stephenson, *A Practical Guide to the Bar* (London: H. Cox, 1888), 35.

14. Ibid., 37, 35.

15. Ball, *Student's Guide*, 42.

16. Gandhi paid costs exceeding £40 in November 1888 to the Inner Temple. SN 7910. He paid an additional £100 deposit to the Inner Temple that December. SN 7908.

17. Gandhi would have been mistaken. The Middle Temple hosted the most Indians. Napier and Stephenson, *Practical Guide*, 19.

18. See Hunt, *Gandhi in London*, 16. Another theory is age-based. Gandhi arrived in London at eighteen. Napier and Stephenson state that "there is . . . no limit of age at the Inner Temple, which, in this respect, differs from all the other Inns." Napier and Stephenson, *Practical Guide*, 22.

19. Abel, *The Legal Profession in England and Wales* (London: Basil Blackwell, 1988), 47. Gandhi left Samaldas College after one year.

20. *Autobiography*, 53.

21. Ibid., 54.

22. Ibid., 55.

23. James Hunt theorizes that a "lack of seriousness in getting down to his legal studies" or Gandhi's "weakness in Latin" might also explain the delay. Hunt, *Gandhi in London*, 18.

24. Gandhi's study of Roman law "was not without its value later on in South Africa, where Roman Dutch is the common law." *Autobiography*, 80.

25. Ibid.

26. Ibid.

27. I am indebted to James Hunt for the full titles of these works. Hunt, *Gandhi in London*, 19.

28. *Autobiography*, 80. Although Gandhi is to be given credit for reading books while others used notes, it must be noted that he did not read all the texts recommended, a feat undoubtedly accomplished by very few.

29. Gandhi's recollection of the difficulty of the examinations is off base. "The percentage of passes in the Roman law examination used to be 95 to 99 and of those in the final examination 75 or even more. They could not be felt as a difficulty." *Autobiography*, 79. The actual percentages were lower: 86.9% passed the Roman law examination while only 70.6 passed the English law examination.

30. Napier and Stephenson, *Practical Guide*, 51.

31. "When we go [to England] . . . , we ought to do there everything that would make of us good Barristers and not indulge in luxuries or pleasures." *CWMG* 1:102.

32. *Autobiography*, 50. See also Fischer, *The Life of Mahatma Gandhi* (New York: Harper and Row, 1983), 24, quoting correspondence with a Gandhi contemporary during his London student years, who points out that the Inner Temple was thought by Indians to be "the most aristocratic."

33. A more immediate motivation should also be noted. After Gandhi embarrassed a friend by exhibiting his vegetarianism at a posh restaurant where meat was de rigueur, Gandhi resolved to try to become "an English gentleman." *Autobiography*, 50.

34. Farquhar, *Modern Religious Movements in India* (Norwood, MA: J. S. Cushing Co., 1915), 211. Blavatsky's character is discussed in Braden, *These Also Believe: A Study of Modern American Cults and Religious Movements* (New York: Macmillan, 1953), 222.

35. Besant, *The Ancient Wisdom* (London: Theosophical Publishing, 1897), 2, 3. Besant was a prominent theosophical figure toward the end of the nineteenth century.

36. According to Pyarelal, theosophy's appeal for brotherhood attracted Gandhi, whereas he had no use for communication with spirits through mediums. See Pyarelal, *Gandhi—The Early Phase*, 259, quoting Gandhi in *Young India*, September 12, 1929. Another theosophical theme, truth, would later be echoed by Gandhi. In her 1888 book, *The Secret Doctrine*, Blavatsky begins and ends with the declaration "There is no religion higher than truth."

37. Farquhar, *Modern Religious Movements*, 267. Besant published numerous books on theosophy and eventually served as president of the Theosophical Society. She also served as president of the INC in 1917.

38. "Message on Annie Besant's Birthday," October 1, 1919, *CWMG* 16:201.

39. *Autobiography*, 68. There is some evidence that Gandhi actually joined the Theosophical Society, but it is unpersuasive. Gandhi indicates he declined at least one invitation to join. Ibid., 68.

40. Ibid., 42.

41. Ibid., 46.

42. Ibid., 47.

43. Ibid., 48.

44. Ibid.

45. *CWMG* 1:120.

46. Hunt, *Gandhi in London*, 27.

47. *Autobiography*, 58.

CHAPTER TWO

Epigraph, page 17: *Autobiography*, 92.

1. This expectation was actually ingrained in traditional Indian law: "The earnings of a professional man, educated at joint family expense, were joint family

property." Gledhill, *The Republic of India: The Development of Its Law and Constitution* (Westport: Stevens and Sons, 1964), 265.

2. *Autobiography*, 90.

3. Ibid., 90, 81.

4. A native practitioner with less training and prestige than an English-schooled barrister. For a description of the profession's evolution, see Schmitthener, "A Sketch of the Development of the Legal Profession in India," 3 *Law and Society Review* 339 (1968–1969), 350, n. 87. See also Dutt-Majumdar, *Conduct of Advocates and Legal Profession* (Kolkata, India: Eastern Law House, 1974), 21.

5. *Autobiography*, 92.

6. Ibid., 94.

7. Ibid., 96.

8. The court likely was the Small Cause Court for Bombay, established under the Presidency Small Cause Courts Act of 1882. See Jois, *Legal and Constitutional History of India*, Vol. 2 (Bombay: Fred B. Rothman, 1984), 215–216.

9. *Autobiography*, 39.

10. Ibid., 42.

11. Ibid., 47.

12. Ibid., 60.

13. Ibid., 61.

14. Ibid.

15. 24 & 25 Vict. C. 104. See Jois, *Legal and Constitutional History*, 2:199; and Bhansali, *Legal System in India* (Jaipur, India: University Book House, 1992), 13–14.

16. Fawcett, *The First Century of British Justice in India* (1934), quoted in Schmitthener, "Development of the Legal Profession," 57.

17. Schmitthener, "Development of the Legal Profession," 358, 363. See also Paul, *Legal Profession in Colonial South India* (Bombay: Oxford University Press, 1991), 13.

18. Barristers' fees in 1862 were as much as seven times those charged in England. Their practices during this period and afterward were very lucrative. Schmitthener, "Development of the Legal Profession," 345–346, 370.

19. Ibid., 345.

20. Gandhi understood this dynamic. "Barristers," he observed, "are at a discount." *CWMG* 1:101.

21. Washbrook, "Law, State and Agrarian Society in Colonial India," 15 *Modern Asian Studies* 649 (1981), 650.

22. Ibid., 692–693.

23. Schmitthener, "Development of the Legal Profession," 367–368.

24. *Autobiography*, 89.

25. Ibid., 95.

26. Ibid.

27. Gandhi was aware of the mismatch between his personality and his profession, wondering whether he "should be able even to earn a living by the profession."

Comparing himself to Mehta, "a lion in the law courts," he felt quite inadequate. *Autobiography*, 81.

28. Touting was considered "underhanded and unprofessional" and in violation of professional rules. Paul, "Vakils of Madras" (Ph.D. dissertation, University of Wisconsin–Madison, 1986), 147, 331.

29. *Autobiography*, 97.

30. Ibid., 98.

31. Ibid.

32. Ibid., 99.

33. Ibid.

34. Ibid.

35. Ibid., 101.

36. Ibid., 102.

37. Ibid.

38. Ibid.

CHAPTER THREE

Epigraph, page 31: J. F. Hofmeyr (a member of the Economic Research Unit of the University of Natal), quoted in Brookes and Webb, *A History of Natal* (Pietermaritzburg, South Africa: University of Natal Press, 1965), 85.

1. "A certain vagueness . . . is associated with the Republic of Natalia. Its beginning may well be dated before 1840." Brookes and Webb, *History of Natal*, 35–36.

2. Hattersley, *The British Settlement of Natal* (Cambridge: Cambridge University Press, 1950), 224.

3. Brookes and Webb, *History of Natal*, 179. The responsible government model has the executive immediately responsible to the parliament rather than the Crown.

4. Hattersley, *British Settlement of Natal*, 235. Tea was also grown; see "The Curse of Natal," *RDM*, March 9, 1910.

5. A bold governmental official, Theophilus Shepstone, helped protect natives from exploitation. Palmer, *The History of the Indians in the Natal* (Cape Town: Oxford University Press, 1957), 11.

6. *NM*, June 6, 1855.

7. Calpin, *Indians in South Africa* (Pietermaritzburg, South Africa: Shuter & Shooter, 1949), 3.

8. Gandhi would call indentured servitude "slavery-tainted labour." *CWMG* 10 (1963 edition): 145.

9. Calpin, *Indians in South Africa*, 6. Maureen Swan, in *Gandhi: The South African Experience* (Johannesburg: Ravan Press, 1985), 1, notes that the land offer expired in 1890. By the time Gandhi set up his Durban practice in 1894, the period of indenture had grown to five years.

10. Palmer, *History of the Indians in the Natal*, 20. Palmer argues that the depression was the real cause for immigration's suspension.

11. Quoted in Calpin, *Indians in South Africa*, 7.

12. By 1894, conditions of indenture had changed little. Report of the Natal Indian Commission, "The Indian Commission," *NW*, April 20, 1894.

13. Konczacki, *Public Finance and Economic Development of Natal, 1893–1910* (Durham, NC: Duke University Press, 1967), 4 (citing Natal Blue Books, Statistical Year Books, and Census Reports of 1891 and 1904); Fair, *The Distribution of Population in Natal* (Cape Town: Oxford University Press for University of Natal, 1955), 11–12.

14. Many Indians found it easy to enter market-gardening after their indentured servitude. Fair, *Distribution of Population in Natal*, 17.

15. Palmer, *History of the Indians in the Natal*, 43, 46.

16. Konczacki, *Public Finance and Economic Development of Natal*, 198.

17. Swan, *South African Experience*, 26 (citations omitted).

CHAPTER FOUR

Epigraph, page 36: *Autobiography*, 121.

1. *NM*, May 26, 1893; *Autobiography*, 106.

2. *NA*, June 9, 1893.

3. *NA*, May 9, 1893.

4. *NM*, May 26, 1893.

5. *NM*, May 27, 1893.

6. *Autobiography*, 105.

7. *NM*, May 30, 1893.

8. *Autobiography*, 109.

9. *Autobiography*, 111–117. For Gandhi's other recountings of the incident, see *CWMG* 68 (1977 edition): 165 and *Satyagraha*, 42–43.

10. The £4,000 figure is cited in "An Indian Case," *TP*, June 9, 1894.

11. *Autobiography*, 119.

12. Given the modern ethical stricture against communicating with a represented opponent, few lawyers today would feel comfortable with Gandhi's seeking out, and collaborating with, Mohamed.

13. *Autobiography*, 125–127.

14. Baker was conducting these services in the midst of his *Abdulla* work. "Local and General: Cape General Mission," *TP*, May 7, 1894.

15. "Mr. Attorney Baker's Arrest," *NA*, June 11, 1894.

16. "A Big Arbitration Case," *TP*, May 16, 1894.

17. *Autobiography*, 132–133.

18. Gandhi's memory is imprecise. This was the purchase price, not the sum owed. "Natal: A Pretoria Case," *TP*, January 9, 1894.

19. *Autobiography*, 133–134.

20. Swan, *South African Experience*, 48.

21. Ibid., 41 (quoting sources).

CHAPTER FIVE

1. "The Asiatic Franchise Question," *NM*, September 15, 1894.

2. With fewer than three hundred Indian voters enrolled at the time of the Franchise Amendment Bill, the "real significance of the franchise question lay in the fact that it reflected the hostility of the ruling white minority towards Indians." Swan, *South African Experience*, 45.

3. The other chamber was the Legislative Council.

4. *CWMG* 1:105.

5. *Autobiography*, 143. Citing Colonial Office records, Swan puts this figure at "some 9,000." Swan, *South African Experience*, 61, n. 103.

6. *Autobiography*, 142–143.

7. The home government eventually took the position that it would agree to a bill only if it did not mention Asiatics (as colonists then called Indians) and if the legislation did not disenfranchise the few current Indian voters. Finding this acceptable, the Natal legislature passed a revised bill that accomplished the same end as the previous bill. The Colonial Office approved the bill in the summer of 1896. *See* Swan, *South African Experience*, 67.

8. *Autobiography*, 143.

9. Ibid., 144.

10. Ibid., 145.

11. Ibid., 144, 162.

12. I am indebted to Burnett Britton for Paul's full name.

13. While Coakes advocated as an lawyer for the Indian community, he was not prepared to be politically identified with the movement. *CWMG*, Supplementary Vol. 1 (1989), p. 11.

14. See "Advocates of the Supreme Court (Corrected to 31st December, 1894)" and "Attorneys of the Supreme Court (Corrected to 31st December, 1894)," XV *NLR*, following p. 375 (1894).

15. "Durban Circuit Court," *NM*, October 11, 1894.

16. *CWMG*, Supplementary Vol. 1, p. 7.

17. *Autobiography*, 145. Escombe was indebted to the Indians. Prior to the Franchise Bill, Indian merchants had registered to vote to help Escombe win election. Ibid., 139.

18. On July 21, 1894. *CWMG*, Supplementary Vol. 1, p. 6. The Durban Circuit Court clerk also expressed support. Ibid., p. 10.

19. Gandhi did so sometime between August 7 and 17. "An Indian Barrister," *NM*, August 7, 1894; "Indian Barrister," *NM*, August 18, 1894. On August 16, the Supreme Court posted this notice: "Notice is hereby given that application will be made on behalf of Mohandas Karamchorra [*sic*] Gandhi, on the first day of September, 1894, for admission as an advo[ca]te of the Supreme Court, and that all objections in respect thereof must be lodged . . . before that date." "A Novel Application," *NW*, August 17, 1894.

20. Whites feared Gandhi was the first of a "tide" of Indian barristers. "Indians in Natal," *NM*, September 26, 1894. Gandhi would, in fact, later call for more Indian barristers. "The Natal Indian Congress," *NA*, October 2, 1895.

21. Editorial, *NW*, September 5, 1894. The *Natal Mercury* had a different view: "We question if the Natal Law Society would have troubled itself . . . if Mr. Ghandi [*sic*] had been . . . European." "An Indian Barrister," *NM*, September 6, 1894.

22. Gandhi recognized the subterfuge. "One of their objections was that the original English certificate was not attached to my application. But the main objection was that, when the regulations regarding admission . . . were made, the possibility of a coloured man applying could not have been contemplated." *Autobiography*, 146.

23. Ibid., 365.

24. Dold and Joubert, *The Union of South Africa: The Development of its Laws and Constitution* (London: Stevens & Sons Ltd., 1955), 190.

25. "In . . . Roman law the division of legal practitioners into advocates and attorneys . . . was recognized . . . early . . . and this division persisted in the Roman-Dutch law." Ibid., 189.

26. *Satyagraha*, 45.

27. Gandhi's admission was scheduled for September 1 but was postponed because of Escombe's absence. "Supreme Court.—Saturday," *NA*, September 3, 1894; "New Advocates," *NW*, September 3, 1894. At this first hearing Gandhi learned of objections to his application. "An Indian Advocate," *NA*, September 4, 1894.

28. "Indian Advocate of the Supreme Court," *NM*, September 3, 1894.

29. Gandhi was familiar with the *Rules. CWMG*, Supplementary Vol. 1, pp. 7, 12.

30. "An Indian Barrister," *NM*, August 7, 1894; "The Indian Barrister," *NA*, August 7, 1894. See also *CWMG*, Supplementary Vol. 1, p. 12.

31. The *Natal Witness* stated that "the Law Society endeavoured to make it appear that it was the chance of informalities creeping in that raised the opposition, but the public is not to be taken in by such . . . pretences." Editorial, *NW*, September 5, 1894.

32. "An Indian Advocate," *NA*, September 4, 1894.

33. *Autobiography*, 147–148; "Indian Advocate of the Supreme Court," *NM*, September 5, 1894; *In re Gandhi*, XV *NLR* 263 (September 3, 1894). Gandhi later wrote, "I wanted to reserve my strength for fighting bigger battles." *Autobiography*, 147.

34. Bird, *Annals of Natal*, 2:470, quoted in Roberts, "Natal, 1830–1909," in Mellet, Scott, and van Warmelo (eds.), *Our Legal Heritage* (Durban, South Africa: Butterworth, 1982), 79.

35. "Roman-Dutch law is the . . . system which applied in Holland during the seventeenth and eighteenth centuries. It was the product of . . . two elements: medieval Dutch law . . . and the Roman law of Justinian." Hahlo and Kahn, *The South African Legal System and Its Background* (Cape Town: Juta & Co., 1968), 329.

36. Professor Ellison Kahn provides several reasons for the turn to British law, including the fact that "the expansion of economic activity in the late nineteenth

and early twentieth centuries could not be met by the Roman-Dutch legal system that had died long before in the land of its birth." Kahn, "The Development of South African Substantive Law," in Mellet, Scott, and van Warmelo, *Our Legal Heritage*, 117.

37. Spiller, *A History of the District and Supreme Courts of Natal (1846–1910)* (Durban, South Africa: Butterworth, 1986), 56.

38. Morice, *English and Roman-Dutch Law: Being a Statement of the Differences Between the Law of England and the Roman-Dutch Law as Prevailing in South Africa and Some Other of the British Colonies* (Grahamstown, South Africa: African Book Company, 1905), 2.

39. Spiller, *History of the District and Supreme Courts*, 57 (citing XIV *NLR* 20 [1893]).

40. Women were not admitted to practice.

41. As late as 1895 the *Natal Advertiser* editorialized that "the calibre of the Natal lawyer is not as a rule very high." *NA*, March 30, 1895. The quality of the bench was no better. Hahlo and Kahn, *The Union of South Africa: The Development of Its Laws and Constitution* (London: Stevens & Sons, 1960), 222.

42. Editorial, *NW*, September 5, 1894.

43. "An Unpleasant Atmosphere," *NW*, August 14, 1894.

44. "Durban Circuit Court," *NA*, October 13, 1894. Shortly after Gandhi's admission, the Law Society moved to correct this deficiency. See "Natal Law Society," *NM*, September 5, 1894.

45. "Civil Court Witnesses," *NA*, June 9, 1893. See also "The Indian in Natal," *NW*, December 29, 1894; "Indians," *NM*, January 22, 1895.

46. *CWMG*, Supplementary Vol. 1, pp. 5–9.

47. The case was first with Coakes before he passed it to Gandhi. *CWMG*, Supplementary Vol. 1, p. 13.

48. "The Indian Barrister," *NA*, September 14, 1894; "The Indian Barrister," *NM*, September 15, 1894. Gandhi mistakenly records that he won the case on September 19. *CWMG* Supplementary Vol. 1, p. 15.

49. *Autobiography*, 81.

50. Ibid., 153–154.

51. "More Recognition," *NM*, June 5, 1896.

CHAPTER SIX

Epigraph, page 67: *CWMG* 1:266.

1. He wore a notary's hat, too, as well as others. See "Trust Transfer of 1895," SN 709 (1895).

2. "Death of Deacon Coakes," *NM*, October 1, 1894. Coakes's father died on September 29; he buried him that afternoon with hardly a word to anyone.

3. "*Ex parte* Russell, *In re* Coakes," XVI *NLR* 98 (March 26, 1895). See also "Supreme Court—Tuesday, An Attorney Suspended," *NW*, March 27, 1895.

4. The defendant had borrowed £10 from Coakes. Is this connection how Gandhi came to represent him? "Alleged Theft," *NM*, February 14, 1895.

5. "*In re* Intestate Estate of Hassan Dawjee," XVI *NLR* 95 (March 21, 1895).

6. "One for Mr. Ghandhi [*sic*]," *NW*, March 22, 1895.

7. Wragg was known to be vindictive. When a court employee accidentally spilled water from a window on Wragg and his silk hat below, Wragg imprisoned him in one of the court's rooms for an afternoon. "The Judge and His Hat," *NA*, August 14, 1895.

8. *CWMG* 1:193.

9. The auctioneer would testify that the clothing was taken as security for the debt. "Sequel to a Market Dispute," *NA*, March 28, 1895.

10. "Action against Constable Tuohy," *NM*, March 27, 1895. Three other Indians corroborated Ismail's story.

11. "Action against the Market Constable," *NM*, April 6, 1895. An *Advertiser* columnist editorialized on a similar case Gandhi brought in July 1895, revealing the popular anti-Indian sentiment in such cases and validating Gandhi's judgment in settling the Tuohy case: "It is to be hoped that the experience of the plaintiff . . . will put a stop to the assumptions of . . . these Indians. . . . [I]f only one were to recover damages the time of the court . . . would be occupied with nothing else." "City Notes," *NA*, July 24, 1895.

12. See *CWMG* 1:199–222, 229–244.

13. "The Indian Drum," *NM*, July 26, 1895.

14. Gandhi's client wanted a divorce on desertion grounds. To receive a divorce on this basis, the parties were required to first live apart for twelve months. When the magistrate pointed this out, Gandhi was forced to withdraw his petition; the parties had, as the magistrate also had to point out to him, not been married even a year. "Application for Divorce," *NM*, September 14, 1895.

15. Swan, *South African Experience*, 27.

16. "Coolies Thrash Police," *NA*, May 20, 1895.

17. *CWMG* 1:228–229; "The Railway Indians," *NA*, May 22, 1895.

18. It is believed that the Congress took a leading role in this case; it claimed the litigation as one of its significant 1895 activities. *CWMG* 1:245, 249. The Congress, whose purpose was to work for Indian rights, was founded in August 1894. Gandhi almost surely was instrumental in its founding. Swan, *South African Experience*, 49.

19. Cases of this nature could be brought in the Supreme Court. Spiller, *History of the District and Supreme Courts*, 78. Little documentation exists to tell us what happened when the case was tried before the full bench of the Court. *Cassim Abdulla v. Bennett*, XVI *NLR* 159 (July 16, 1895); "'Injury of Body and Mind,'" *NW*, July 17, 1895.

20. *CWMG* 1:245, 249.

21. *In re Regina v. Camroodeen*, XV *NLR* 335–336 (November 8, 1894).

22. *CWMG* 1:245, 249.

23. Because of the European view that Indian witnesses were untruthful, it was difficult for Indians to prevail in fact-based disputes with Europeans.

24. *CWMG* 1:262.

25. "Rungasamy Padiachy v. The Clerk of the Peace, Durban," XVI *NLR* 244 (November 25, 1895).

26. *CWMG* 1:261. As with *Padiachy*, Lucas's decision in *Poonsamy* was overturned by the Supreme Court.

27. Britton, *Gandhi Arrives in South Africa* (Canton: Greenleaf Books, 1999), provides a detailed description of *Padiachy*.

28. *NA*, October 1, 1895.

29. "S.M. Bedat v. S.M. Akoom," *NA*, December 11, 1895.

30. "S.M. Bedat v. S.M. Akoom: A Difficulty," *NM*, December 12, 1895.

31. Ibid.

32. Ibid.; "S.M. Bedat v. S.M. Akoom," *NA*, December 11, 1895.

33. "Mr. Ghandhi [*sic*] as Translator," *NW*, January 24, 1896.

34. *CWMG* 1:297, n. 2.

35. A washerman.

36. "Indians and Passes," *NM*, February 29, 1896.

37. "Indians and the Curfew," *NW*, February 22, 1896.

38. "Out After Hours," *NM*, February 21, 1896.

39. *CWMG* 1:297–300.

CHAPTER SEVEN

Epigraph, page 84: *Autobiography*, 504.

1. *Autobiography*, 165.

2. *CWMG* 3 (1960 edition): 101.

3. *Autobiography*, 148.

4. The company was upset with Adams for mishandling correspondence to have been delivered in Mozambique and for failing to adequately deal with a consignment of salt. A company employee reported that the captain got drunk at Delagoa Bay. Finally, the company believed Adams boarded unticketed passengers and moved second-class passengers into first-class without justification and without charging them.

5. The most likely explanation for Adams' refusal to settle in Bombay is that between the time he submitted his bill in Bombay and the time he refused payment there, he realized he could do better by submitting the bill in pounds in Durban.

6. Inferior courts were not empowered to grant such commissions. "Evidence by Commission," *NA*, April 15, 1896.

7. Gandhi had gone to Frederick Laughton, an experienced lawyer friendly to the Indians and an expert in procedure, to obtain Laughton's advice as to whether Abdulla could successfully appeal Gallwey's decision. Laughton opined not only that there were adequate grounds for the Supreme Court to take the appeal but that the Court had the power to grant Gandhi's application, as well. "Opinion Letter from F. A. Laughton to M. K. Gandhi," SN 870 (April 15, 1896).

8. "The Courland Shipping Case," *NA*, April 16, 1896.

9. Ibid. A counterclaim was then known as a "claim in reconvention."

10. Ibid.

11. Ibid.

12. The clerk, Bissessur, had boarded the *Courland* with instructions to watch Adams. Bissessur testified that Adams, among other things, defied the company's order that he not board his family.

13. "The Courland Shipping Case," *NA*, April 20, 1896.

14. "The 'Courland' Shipping Case," *NM*, April 23, 1896.

15. "The Courland Shipping Case," *NM*, April 24, 1896.

16. In a move not calculated to endear his client to the court or the public, Gandhi defiantly stated that, in regard to passenger lodging, it should not be the business of the plaintiff or the court "whether the *Courland* was a floating palace or a pig stye." "The Courland Shipping Case," *NA*, April 24, 1896.

17. Gandhi was largely unsuccessful with his counterclaim. Waller did rule for the company on some minor matters of damages. Considering that at one point in the case Gandhi had offered to drop his counterclaim entirely, this ruling was not a bad result. Costs, however, were assessed against Dada Abdulla and Company. "The Courland Shipping Case," *NA*, May 15, 1896, and "The 'Courland' Shipping Case," *NM*, May 16, 1896.

18. "Mr. Gandhi's Departure," *NA*, June 5, 1896.

19. *Autobiography*, 503–504.

CHAPTER EIGHT

Second epigraph, page 95: *Satyagraha*, 58.

1. An approximation of the speech can be found in *CWMG* 2 (1976 edition): 50.

2. *CWMG* 2:103.

3. Gandhi gave other speeches in India, including one at Madras that he was apparently able to read himself. *Autobiography*, 179.

4. "Mr. Gandhi Ashore: Mobbed.—Stoned and Kicked," *NA*, January 14, 1897. Gandhi's later recollection was that he had taken a month to write the pamphlet in India. *Autobiography*, 169.

5. Reproduced in *CWMG* 2:2.

6. According to Reuters, Gandhi claimed Indians "are treated like beasts." *CWMG* 2:142.

7. "Passengers Interviewed: How Mr. Gandhi Views the Agitation," *NM*, January 12, 1897; "The Asiatic Invasion: Events of Yesterday—Return of the Deputation," *NA*, January 12, 1897. Gandhi estimated one hundred were newcomers. "Mr. Gandhi Ashore: Mobbed.—Stoned and Kicked," *NA*, January 14, 1897.

8. *CWMG* 2:199.

9. "The Asiatic Invasion," *NM*, January 8, 1897.

10. *CWMG* 2:129, 159.

11. Spiller, *District and Supreme Courts of Natal*, 60, 122–123. Laughton was a member of Goodricke, Laughton, and Cooke, a firm with which Gandhi had earlier come into professional contact. During the quarantine crisis, the firm sought relief from various government officials. *CWMG* 2:146–150, 156.

12. *Satyagraha*, 57. Gandhi writes that Laughton was "an old and well-known advocate of Durban.... I used to consult with him in difficult cases and often to engage him as my senior. He was a brave . . . man." Ibid.

13. "In Support of Mr. Gandhi," *NM*, January 16, 1897.

14. "Mr. Gandhi Comes Ashore," *NM*, January 14, 1897.

15. "Mr. Gandhi and the Lady," *NM*, January 18, 1897; "Mr. Gandhi Ashore: Mobbed.—Stoned and Kicked," *NA*, January 14, 1897. *Satyagraha*, 58.

16. *Autobiography*, 191–194; "Mr. Gandhi Comes Ashore," *NM*, January 14, 1897; "Asiatic Invasion—How Gandhi Got Away," *NW*, January 16, 1897. Gandhi reports the crowd numbered in the thousands, and those milling outside the house threatened to burn it. *Satyagraha*, 59. The press accounts do not support his crowd estimate, but do support his report of the threat to burn the building.

17. The Alexanders urged Gandhi to forgive his attackers and to "forget the past," a course Gandhi adopted. "Letter from R. Alexander to M. K. Gandhi" (January 22, 1897), SN 1938; "Letter from J. Alexander to M. K. Gandhi" (January 22, 1897), SN 1939.

18. *CWMG* 2:241.

19. "Pars about People," *NA*, January 20, 1897.

20. *NM*, December 30, 1896, quoted in *CWMG* 2:163.

21. *CWMG* 2:13.

22. *CWMG* 2:118.

23. *Autobiography*, 195.

24. Ibid.

25. "Letter to the Natal Mercury," *NM*, April 16, 1897.

26. *Autobiography*, 196.

27. "Mr. Gandhi Comes Ashore," *NM*, January 14, 1897.

28. Laughton quoted in "In Support of Mr. Gandhi," *NM*, January 16, 1897.

CHAPTER NINE

Second epigraph, page 104: *CWMG* 3:121.

1. *CWMG* 2:161; *CWMG* 2:152.

2. *NA*, February 26, 1897, cited in *CWMG* 2:267; *The Star*, May 10, 1897, cited in *CWMG* 2:267–268.

3. *CWMG* 2:272.

4. *CWMG* 2:260.

5. The act used the British spelling "licences." Newspapers of the era used both "licences" and "licenses."

6. For a history of the £3 tax, see Swan, *South African Experience*, 45–46. Proposals were also entertained to have a servant's indenture end in India. *CWMG* 2:140.

7. *CWMG* 2:260.

8. Ibid.

9. Ibid.

10. Ibid.

11. "Restrictions on Immigration," *NW*, April 1, 1897.

12. "The big merchants ... were unable to expand by opening a new branch, to break a partnership into ... elements, or to pass ... a business to an heir. . . . [T]hose with property ... were ... affected ... if persons leasing ... from them were refused renewal of licence, and those with debtors among the petty traders stood to lose if their debtors were forced to shut up shop." Swan, *South African Experience*, 68–69.

13. Gandhi's faith in reason is almost naïve. Referring to the IRA, he would write in late 1897, "If the Act is to be ever removed, it can only be done by persuasion." "Letter to the Editor," *NM*, November 13, 1897.

In petitioning against the IRA, Gandhi wrote that the act restricted the immigration of Indians while never mentioning them. "Such a mode of procedure," he argued, "is un-British, and, therefore, it should not receive countenance in a Colony which is supposed to be the most British in South Africa." "The Asiatic Question: Indians Petition against the Bills," *NM*, March 30, 1897.

14. *CWMG* 2:140.

15. Ibid.

16. Ibid.

17. *CWMG* 2:243.

18. *CWMG* 2:231.

19. "Letter to the Natal Mercury," *NM*, April 16, 1897.

20. *CWMG* 2:260.

21. *CWMG* 2:281.

22. "Undesirables at Dundee," *NM*, September 21, 1897.

23. *CWMG* 2:290.

24. "Undesirables at Dundee," *NM*, September 21, 1897.

25. "The New Licensing Act," *NA*, October 28, 1897.

26. Spiller, *District and Supreme Courts of Natal*, 94.

27. Coakes had presented much the same argument earlier. Coakes won at the magistrate level; there was no appeal. "Are They Retail Shops?" *NM*, February 26, 1897; "Not a Retail Shop," *NM*, February 27, 1897.

28. "Selling in Passages," *NM*, December 10, 1897.

29. *Musa v. Dyer*, XIX *NLR* 26 (1898).

30. Ibid.

31. "Letter to M. K. Gandhi," SN 2893 (December 26, 1898).

32. Law 39 of 1896, Section 8.

33. "The Dealers' Licences Act," *NA*, January 31, 1898.

34. *Vanda v. Newcastle*, XIX *NLR* 28 (1898). Case records show the correct name as "Vauda." See, e.g., "Costs, Charges and Expenses relating to the Appeal of Suliman Ebrohim Vauda," SN 2879 (undated).

35. "Traders' Licences," *NA*, March 3, 1898.

36. Ibid.

37. Ibid.

38. Ibid.

39. Ibid.

40. *Vanda* would not permit a conventional appeal to the Court. To avoid this problem, Laughton and Gandhi postured the case as one for a writ of mandamus.

41. "What is the use of allowing an appeal to the Town Council, and then declining to grant the applicant a copy of the record?" "Licensing Appeals," *NA*, March 3, 1898. "Dealers' Licences Act—A Durban Indian's Case—Mr. Gandhi Eloquently Appeals," *NW*, March 3, 1898.

A columnist for the *Natal Witness* also referred to Gandhi's "eloquent appeal" but then went on to opine that it was not "improbable that had the Indian seeker after a licence taken the precaution to have himself represented by someone other than Mr. Gandhi, the Council might not have been quite so unanimous in upholding the Licensing Officer's decision." "Talk of the Town," *NW*, March 5, 1898. This same columnist would later join in the criticism of the Durban Town Council. "Topics of the Town," *NW*, April 2, 1898.

42. Spiller, *District and Supreme Courts of Natal*, 121. All levels of professionals could then perform all functions of solicitors, attorneys, and advocates.

43. *Solnath v. Durban Corporation*, XIX *NLR* 70 (1898).

44. Ibid.

45. Ibid.

46. "Licensing Appeals," *NA*, June 7, 1898.

47. Ibid. The *Natal Mercury* stated that Gandhi had "demolished" the officer's reason. "The Licence Appeals," *NM*, June 8, 1898.

48. "Licensing Appeals," *NA*, June 7, 1898.

49. "Retail Licensing Appeals," *NM*, June 7, 1898.

50. "Licensing Appeals," *NA*, June 7, 1898. The council also denied the appeal of a third Gandhi client, who, it was revealed at the hearing, also did not know English. "Retail Licensing Appeals," *NM*, June 7, 1898.

51. *CWMG* 3:17.

52. "Licensing Appeal—Anti-Asiatic Feeling—Attitude of the Town Council," *NA*, September 15, 1898.

53. *CWMG* 3:17.

54. "Licensing Appeal—Anti-Asiatic Feeling—Attitude of the Town Council," *NA*, September 15, 1898.

55. Ibid.

56. Ibid.

57. "Licences to Asiatics," *NA*, September 15, 1898. "There was ... no other objection to the ... licence than that the applicant was an Indian." "Town Council and Indian Licences," *NM*, September 16, 1898.

58. On December 22, 1898, Gandhi drafted a brief in which he sought an opinion regarding this very question. *CWMG* 3:24. In response, Labistour opined that excluding Indians was an unlawful exercise of discretion. "Preliminary Opinion re Indian Licences," SN 3114 (March 12, 1899). Laughton differed, stating that if the licensing officer's decision did not stem from "corrupt motives," he could exercise his discretion in any fashion whatsoever. "The Act," Laughton held, "was the injustice[,] not refusing licenses to Indians under it." "Opinion of F. A. Laughton," SN 3134 (March 14, 1899). Labistour retorted that the attack on the DLA "had so far been fairly bungled." "Letter to M. K. Gandhi," SN 3165 (March 31, 1899).

CHAPTER TEN

Epigraph, page 126: *Autobiography*, 219.

1. *Vauda [sic] v. Mayor and Councillors of New Castle*, December 10, 1898, Judicial Committee of the Privy Council, 1899 *Law Reports* 246; LXXIX *The Law Times Reports* 600; XX *NLR* 1 (December 10, 1898); "Indian Appeal Case," *NA*, December 12, 1898.

2. Gandhi considered the decision "a calamity." Untitled document, SN 4036 (undated).

3. *Autobiography*, 202.

4. See, for example, "Letter to Gandhi from O. J. Askew," SN 3919 (January 24, 1896); and "Letter to W. Lehman from M. K. Gandhi," SN 3812 (April 17, 1901). For a less typical example, because it deals with a less typical client—the Congress—see "Letter to Gandhi from William Edward Pitcher," SN 2605–2 (November 22, 1897).

5. See, for example, "Letter to Gandhi from William Morcom," SN 2891 (December 23, 1898).

6. See, for example, "Statement of Bennett Expenses due to Hawthorn and Mason," SN 2969 (July 30, 1895); "Letter to Gandhi from G. B. Cooke," SN 405 (July 22, 1895).

7. "Supreme Court—Tuesday: An Indian Advocate," *NW*, July 12, 1899.

8. *CWMG* 3:283.

9. *In re: M. C. Camrooden & Co.*, XX *NLR* 171 (September 1, 1899).

10. Ibid.; "The Supreme Court—In Re M. C. Camrooden & Co.," *NM*, September 2, 1899; "A Big Security," *NM*, September 4, 1899.

11. See *CWMG* 5 (1961 edition): 37.

12. Thompson, *A History of South Africa* (New Haven: Yale University Press, 1990), summarizes the war's causes, the conduct of the war, and postwar developments.

13. *CWMG* 3:113–114.

14. For a description of the corps's work, see *Satyagraha*, 76–78.

15. *CWMG* 3:160.

16. *CWMG* 3:183.

17. Gandhi stated in 1899 that he had had "some little experience" of law governing indentured servants. *CWMG* 3:72. Whatever it was, it does not appear to have been experience of representing significant numbers of servants in court. Gandhi did represent Balasundaram and appears to have represented another indentured servant during 1896 or earlier. See *Satyagraha*, 53.

18. "Absent from Roll Call," *NA*, August 16, 1900; "Durban District Circuit Court: Civil Business—Monkeys and the Roll Call," *NM*, August 17, 1900; "Durban Circuit Court: Another Roll Call Episode," *NA*, August 17, 1900; "Indians and Witnesses," *NM*, December 14, 1900; "Transfer of Indians," *NA*, December 14, 1900; "A Review," *NM*, December 14, 1900; *Chelligadu v. G. Wilkinson*, XXII *NLR* 24 (January 15, 1901); *CWMG* 3:173.

19. In 1898 Gandhi floated the Congress a £300 loan. *CWMG* 3:7. By comparison, Natal's attorney general's yearly salary was £800. "The Boer Republics: Their Financial Resources," *NM*, January 26, 1900. Gandhi spearheaded a relief effort, donating generously himself. "Indian Famine Relief Fund," *NM*, August 23, 1900. See also SNs 2091–0001 et seq. He also may have been supporting his extended family in India; see *CWMG* 3:50.

20. "Durban Civil Court," *NA*, January 4, 1901.

21. *CWMG* 2:100.

22. While it is impossible to say what Gandhi's income was at this time, a sense of its magnitude can be gained from a partnership proposal he made two years earlier to an Indian lawyer. Gandhi estimated that, working together, they could earn as much as £150 per month. *CWMG* 2:67.

23. "Indian Famine Fund: Meeting of Indians," *NW*, August 9, 1900.

24. *CWMG* 3:108.

25. *CWMG* 3:165–166.

26. *NM*, July 12, 1900.

27. *CWMG* 3:171.

28. Ibid.

29. In 1901 Gandhi refers to the fight against the DLA as "a sealed book." *CWMG* 3:213.

30. *CWMG* 2:67.

31. *Autobiography*, 212.

32. Ibid.

33. *Autobiography*, 212. Khan appeared to be fulfilling both functions when he succeeded in convincing the Supreme Court to overturn the conviction of an indentured servant who had been found guilty of desertion. *Duyall v. G. A. Riches*, XXIII *NLR* 94 (April 15, 1902). Nazar, who would later edit *Indian Opinion*, succeeded Gandhi as court translator. *In re M. H. Nazar*, XXII *NLR* 369 (November 19, 1901).

34. Gandhi started a trust with the gifts, indicating it was a trust for the community's benefit. *Autobiography*, 221. The trust instrument dedicates the use of the trust to the Congress. *CWMG* 3:208.

CHAPTER ELEVEN

Epigraph, page 138: *Autobiography*, 250–251.
  1. Swan, *South African Experience*, 90.
  2. *CWMG* 3:227.
  3. *Autobiography*, 222–223.
  4. Ibid., 228.
  5. *CWMG* 3:216.
  6. *Autobiography*, 231.
  7. *CWMG* 3:246.
  8. *CWMG* 3:255.
  9. *Autobiography*, 243.
  10. Ibid., 243–244.
  11. Ibid., 245.
  12. Ibid.
  13. *CWMG* 3:260.
  14. *CWMG* 3:261.
  15. Ibid. "The solicitors who were preponderantly British ... preferred to take business to their countrymen." J. S. Gandhi, *Lawyers and Touts: A Study in the Sociology of the Legal Profession* (Delhi: Hindustan Publishing, 1982), 31.
  16. *CWMG* 3:261.
  17. *CWMG* 3:262.
  18. *Autobiography*, 219.
  19. *CWMG* 3:236.
  20. Ibid.
  21. *CWMG* 3:262.
  22. Gandhi saw this as an opportunity to redeem his failure to prevent Natal's anti-Indian legislation. If Britain could be convinced to discard the Boer anti-Indian legislation, Natal's anti-Indian legislation simply could not stand. Swan, *South African Experience*, 92–93.
  23. *CWMG* 3:263.

CHAPTER TWELVE

First epigraph, page 146: Quoted in Pillay, *British Indians in the Transvaal: Trade, Politics and Imperial Relations, 1885–1906* (London: Longman, 1976), 46–47.
Second epigraph, page 146: *CWMG* 1:222.

1. See Richardson, *Chinese Mine Labour in the Transvaal* (London: Macmillan, 1982).

2. *Satyagraha*, 25.

3. Beck, *The History of South Africa* (Westport, CT: Greenwood Press, 2000), 91.

4. "Law respecting Coolies, Arabs, and other Asiatics (No. 3, 1885)," Appendix A, BSP, C-7911, p. 438 (1895).

5. Pillay, *British Indians in the Transvaal*, provides an excellent history of the act.

6. "Article XIV of the Convention of London, 1884," Appendix A, BSP, C-7911, p. 434 (1895).

7. "Law respecting Coolies, Arabs, and other Asiatics (No. 3, 1885)," as amended, *Staats Courant*, No. 621, November 23, 1898 (emphasis supplied).

8. Pillay, *British Indians in the Transvaal*, 25.

9. "Law respecting Coolies, Arabs, and other Asiatics (No. 3, 1885)," as amended, Appendix A, BSP, C-7911, p. 440 (1895) (emphasis supplied).

10. *Ismail Suleiman & Co. vs. Landdrost of Middelburg*, II *Reports of Cases Decided in the Supreme Court of the South African Republic* (Transvaal) 244 (August 14, 1888) (hereinafter *Suleiman*).

11. Ibid.

12. Pillay, *British Indians in the Transvaal*, 25.

13. In arbitration, parties voluntarily submit to the authority of a neutral third party, who decides the case. Arbitration is binding when parties agree that the arbitrator's decision is final and cannot be appealed.

14. *CWMG* 1:210.

15. Pillay, *British Indians in the Transvaal*, 36.

16. "Explanation of the so-called Coolie Question now pending between Her Majesty's Government and the Government of the South African Republic," BSP, C-7911, pp. 393, 392 (1895).

17. See "Affidavit of Ibrahim Mahomed Patel," BSP, C-7911, pp. 417–418 (1895).

18. "Case to be submitted to the Arbitrator on behalf of Her Majesty's Government," BSP, C-7911, pp. 391, 390 (1895).

19. "Bloemfontein Award," BSP, C-7911, p. 398 (1895).

20. "Reasons of the Arbitrator for his Award," BSP, C-7911, p. 409 (1895).

21. "Bloemfontein Award," BSP, C-7911, p. 412 (1895).

22. Ibid., p. 413.

23. *CWMG* 3:68.

24. Gandhi calls this petition a "memorial." *CWMG* 1:197–198.

25. *CWMG* 1:201.

26. *CWMG* 1:208.

27. *CWMG* 1 (1969 edition): 212. "Kaffir" is a pejorative term for a native person. Gandhi later repeats the odious comparison of Indians to natives in a petition to Lord Elgin, viceroy and governor-general of India; see *CWMG* 1:219.

28. The *Collected Works* attributes this sentiment to Gandhi. *CWMG* 3:76.

29. *CWMG* 3:68.

30. *CWMG* 2:50.

31. See Brown, *Prisoner of Hope*, 205 et seq.; *Autobiography*, 397 et seq.

32. Of nonviolence, King said: "Christ furnished the spirit and motivation, while Gandhi furnished the method." Washington (ed.), *A Testament of Hope: The Essential Writings of Martin Luther King, Jr.*, (Harper & Row: San Francisco, 1986), 17.

33. Pillay, *British Indians in the Transvaal*, 59 et seq.

34. *CWMG* 1:254.

35. *CWMG* 3:86.

36. Pillay, *British Indians in the Transvaal*, 63–64.

37. "Law respecting Coolies, Arabs and other Asiatics," Enclosure 2 in No. 6, Appendix A," BSP, C-7911, p. 441 (1895).

38. *CWMG* 3:8.

39. See Hahlo and Kahn, *The Union of South Africa*; and Chanock, *The Making of South African Legal Culture, 1902–1936: Fear, Favour and Prejudice* (Cambridge: Cambridge University Press, 2001).

40. *Marbury v. Madison*, 1 Cranch 137, 2 *L. Ed.* 60 (1803).

41. *Tayob Hajee Khan Mohamed v. The Government of the South African Republic (F. W. Reitz, N.O.)*, V *Reports of the Cases Decided in the High Court of the South African Republic* 168 (1898) (hereinafter *Mohamed v. Government*).

42. Pillay, *British Indians in the Transvaal*, 77.

43. *Mohamed v. Government*.

CHAPTER THIRTEEN

First epigraph, page 159: "Transvaal Legislative Council: Asiatic Bazaar Question," *IO*, December 31, 1903.
Second epigraph, page 159: *CWMG* 4 (1960 edition): 123.

1. Of this time, Donald Denoon has written that there is "an unusually great temptation to interpret Transvaal affairs in terms of personalities." Denoon, *The Grand Illusion* (London: Longman, 1973), xiii.

2. *CWMG* 3:271.

3. Pillay, *British Indians in the Transvaal*, 77.

4. *CWMG* 3:271.

5. *CWMG* 3:292.

6. *CWMG* 3:278.

7. *CWMG* 3:282.

8. *Autobiography*, 261.

9. *CWMG* 4:282.

10. See Chanock, *The Making of South African Legal Culture*, 222–224.

11. *Autobiography*, 365.

12. Ibid., 261.

13. Order of Court, Supreme Court of the Transvaal, *Ex Parte Gandhi*, April 14, 1903, on file with the Incorporated Law Society of the Transvaal.

14. Council of the Incorporated Law Society of the Transvaal, minutes of April 14, 1903, meeting.

15. "Meeting of Legal Practitioners: This Afternoon, a Strong Protest against the Annual Tax," *JS*, April 29, 1903.

16. "The Banns," *TL*, September 5, 1906.

17. "Debating Society: An Indian Gentleman Admitted," *RDM*, July 7, 1903.

18. The conventional and political aspects of Gandhi's practice would not be neatly separable, in part because discrimination was omnipresent, even in Gandhi's property practice. See, for example, "Opinion Letter from Gregorowski to Gandhi," SN 4069 (July 24, 1903).

19. *Autobiography*, 256.

20. *CWMG* 3:283.

21. "Asiatic Permits," *JS*, September 22, 1903. The office determined who received permits to enter the colony. *CWMG* 3:272.

22. One defendant testified that the funds he received came from selling a horse to an Indian permit applicant. "Asiatic Permit Case," *JS*, November 25, 1903.

23. *Autobiography*, 274–275; *CWMG* 5:383.

24. *Autobiography*, 274–275.

25. *CWMG* 3:372.

26. "Opinion of Seward Brice," SN 3784 (October 9, 1902). Brice's opinion appears to have been found in Gandhi's files.

27. At least one other case in which Gandhi was involved raised the same question. See "Letter of Dumat & Davis to Gandhi," SN 4079 (September 2, 1903); "Letter of Dumat & Davis to Gandhi," SN 4081 (September 3, 1903); and "Letter of Dumat & Davis to Gandhi," SN 4082 (September 5, 1903). The case was settled without trial. "Letter of Gandhi to Dumat and Davis," SN 4087 (September 19, 1903).

28. 1905 *Transvaal Law Reports* 239 (May 8, 1905), 245.

29. "In the Nature of a Test Case," *IO*, May 27, 1905, cited in *CWMG* 4:450.

30. "Transvaal Legislative Council: Asiatic Bazaar Question," *IO*, December 31, 1903.

31. "Asiatic Traders," *TL*, December 22, 1903.

32. "Transvaal Legislative Council: Asiatic Bazaar Question," *IO*, December 31, 1903.

33. CWMG 4:143.

34. "The Capital: Pretoria Day By Day—Asiatic Traders' Commission," March 15, 1904, *TL*.

35. "Asiatic Traders: Why Was the Commission Appointed? Most of the Claims Withdrawn," *RDM*, March 18, 1904.

36. Ibid.

37. *CWMG* 4:157.

38. "Asiatic Traders," *TL*, March 25, 1904.

39. *CWMG* 4:143–144, 195–196. See also "Asiatic Traders' Commission," *TL*, March 18, 1904.

40. "Asiatic Traders: Why Was the Commission Appointed? Most of the Claims Withdrawn," *RDM*, March 18, 1904.

41. "A New Year's Gift," *IO*, January 14, 1904.

42. Ibid.

43. *CWMG* 4:117. See also *CWMG* 4:183.

44. *CWMG* 4:67.

45. *CWMG* 4:182.

46. *Mohamed v. Government.*

47. *Motan v. Government.*

48. *CWMG* 4:190.

49. "Asiatic Trading," *RDM*, June 8, 1904.

50. "Self-Sacrifice," *IO*, January 21, 1904.

51. Ibid.

52. *CWMG* 3:352.

53. Gandhi had his client's permission to make the loan. *Autobiography*, 267–268. In March 1905 Gandhi drew up a bond securing a loan from Budree ("Badri" in the *Autobiography*) to the restaurateur. "Notarial Bond," SN 4225 (March 4, 1904). The restaurant failed a few months later. See *CWMG* 5:33.

54. Gandhi's work for Budree is illustrative. He performed wide-ranging work for him, much of it appearing to be property-related. The Sabarmati Ashram archive contains evidence of this aspect of Gandhi's practice. See, for example, "Letter of Budree to M. K. Gandhi," SN 4318a (January 24, 1905). There is also evidence of Gandhi's continuing, extensive work for Budree in the *Collected Works*. See, for example, *CWMG* 9 (1963 edition): 485.

55. *CWMG* 4:363.

56. With respect to the burden of his public work and his private practice, Gandhi wrote that "at present, I have to work from nearly a quarter of nine in the morning to ten o'clock at night, with intervals for meals and a short walk." *CWMG* 4:352.

57. *CWMG* 5:75.

58. *CWMG* 4:332. In his autobiography Gandhi states that at one point he was contributing £75 a month, "practically sinking all [his] savings in it." *Autobiography*, 286.

59. *CWMG* 6 (1961 edition): 196.

60. *CWMG* 3:298.

61. *CWMG* 3:411.

62. *Autobiography*, 275–276.

63. A nineteenth-century British lawyer, politician, and reformer.

64. "An Opportunity for the Indians," *IO*, October 2, 1903.

65. *Autobiography*, 365–366.

66. The representation of a factually guilty defendant is justified with the argument that forcing the prosecution to prove guilt safeguards the liberties of all. This rationale does not exist in civil cases.

67. *CWMG* 5:72.

68. *Autobiography*, 275.

69. Ibid., 265. Gandhi refers here to Snell, *The Principles of Equity Intended for the Use of Students and Practitioners*, 6th ed. (London: Stevens & Haynes, 1882).

70. *CWMG* 5:167.

CHAPTER FOURTEEN

Epigraph, page 180: "The Colour Question," *TL*, February 16, 1906.

1. Trams resemble trolleys on fixed tracks.

2. The system first opened in 1891 with no regulations in place. Spit and Patton, *Johannesburg Tramways: A History of the Tramways of the City of Johannesburg* (London: Light Railway Transport League, 1976), 11.

3. "Town Council," *TL*, February 15, 1906.

4. "The Colour Question," *TL*, February 16, 1906.

5. "Letter to Town Clerk," February 10, 1906, *CWMG* 5 (1961 edition): 186. The Indians became aware of the committee's recommendations in advance through the tram's manager.

6. *CWMG* 5:206.

7. Ibid. MacIntyre, a Scot, was a theosophist whom Gandhi had taken into his office. *Autobiography*, 306; *CWMG* 6:67. MacIntyre also identified himself as a bookkeeper for Gandhi. *CWMG* 8 (1962 edition): 416. Coovadia was treasurer of the British Indian Association at this time. "Traffic By-Laws," *TL*, May 19, 1906.

8. See "Indians on Trams," *RDM*, May 19, 1906.

9. *CWMG* 5:230.

10. Musiker and Musiker, *Historical Dictionary of Greater Johannesburg* (Lanham, MD: Scarecrow Press, 1999), 130.

11. "Unless the ... cars are kept exclusively for white[s] ... the ... system will be boycotted by them and be a colossal failure." "Indians on Tram Cars," *TL*, May 19, 1906.

12. "A Tram Car Case," *JS*, May 18, 1906.

13. The regulation stated that "no coloured person shall be allowed to be conveyed in any hired vehicle designated for white persons, and the conveyance of coloured passengers shall be allowed only in trams and omnibuses specially and exclusively licensed therefor." See "A Tram Car Case," *JS*, May 18, 1906.

14. Magistrate Graham Cross appears to have reasoned in the second case not only that the Boer rule had been displaced but that Coovadia was not the type of "coloured" person contemplated by the rule. See "Indians on Trams," *RDM*, May 19, 1906.

15. *CWMG* 5:322.

16. *TL* cited in "Johannesburg Trams and Coloured People," *IO*, February 24, 1906.

17. Polak had recently passed his law certificate examination. See "Facts and Comments," *IO*, February 3, 1906. Polak would later serve as acting secretary of the BIA while Gandhi was in London lobbying against the Asiatic Law Amendment Ordinance. "A Noteworthy Appointment," *IO*, October 6, 1906.

18. The approach would later be contemplated by Gandhi in the matter of the railway workers' strike.

19. In May 1907 the government published regulations firmly establishing a segregated system. See *CWMG* 6:495. The new order would restrict Indians to separate cars. See "A Reply," *IO*, July 6, 1907.

20. "Asiatic Policy," *RDM*, September 11, 1906.

21. See "Legislative Council: Further Rebukes to Mr Hull: Asiatic Ordinance Passed," *JS*, March 22, 1906.

22. Law 38 of 1902. The Peace Preservation Ordinance prevented certain persons from entering or residing in the Transvaal without a permit.

23. *Satyagraha*, 101. Gandhi took the position later that it was not so much the fingerprints that the Indians resented but forced registration. See *CWMG* 7:279.

24. *Satyagraha*, 101.

25. *CWMG* 5:414.

26. *CWMG* 5:418.

27. Ibid.

28. "British Indians: A Mass Meeting," *JS*, September 11, 1906.

29. "British Indian Protest," *RDM*, September 12, 1906.

30. "British Indians," *TL*, September 12, 1906.

31. "Some Notes on the Meeting," *IO*, September 22, 1906.

32. *Satyagraha*, 104–107.

33. *Indian Opinion* gives his name as Ramsundar Pandit and Ram Sundar Pundit. Gandhi writes it as Pandit Rama Sundara. When he himself writes to the *Rand Daily Mail*, he uses Ramsundar Pundit. The English word "pundit" is derived from the Hindu word for learned person, *pandit*.

34. Germiston is a Johannesburg suburb.

35. "Asiatic Registration: Well-Known Indian Arrested," *RDM*, November 9, 1907.

36. "Asiatic Question: The Germiston Test Case," *JS*, November 11, 1907.

37. "Indians Protest: Stores to Be Closed Today," *RDM*, November 15, 1907.

38. Ibid.

39. "Asiatic Law: The Germiston Case—Hindu Priest in Court," *TL*, November 15, 1907; "Ram Sundar Pundit," *IO*, November 23, 1907.

40. As Gandhi explained it: "It took away the personal liberty of every Asiatic coming within . . . the Act. . . . [I]nstead of his being the creature of God only, he became the creature of any official appointed under the Act, and a man believing in God would never even dream of submitting to an Act which really enslaved him." "Ram Sundar Pandit Interviewed," *IO*, November 16, 1907.

41. "Asiatic Registration: Ram Sundar Pundit's Trial," *JS*, November 16, 1907.

42. "Asiatic Law: The Germiston Case—Hindu Priest in Court," *TL*, November 15, 1907; "Ram Sundar Pundit," *IO*, November 23, 1907.

43. "Asiatic Registration," *TL*, November 16, 1907.

44. "Asiatic Law: The Germiston Case—Hindu Priest in Court," *TL*, November 15, 1907; "Ram Sundar Pundit," *IO*, November 23, 1907; "Indians Protest: Stores to Be Closed Today," *RDM*, November 15, 1907.

45. "The Asiatic Law," *TL*, November 28, 1907.

46. "Ram Sundar Pundit," *IO* [translated from the Gujarati], December 7, 1907.

47. "Johannesburg Letter: Message from Ram Sundar Pundit," *IO*, December 7, 1907.

48. "The Asiatics," *TL*, December 14, 1907; "Release of Indian Priest," *RDM*, December 14, 1907.

49. "The Asiatics," *TL*, December 14, 1907; "Release of Indian Priest," *RDM*, December 14, 1907.

CHAPTER FIFTEEN

First epigraph, page 197: *CWMG* 7 (1962 edition): 285.

Second epigraph, page 197: *CWMG* 7:306.

1. With a grant of responsible government status, a colony enjoyed a relationship with London that offered almost total freedom of action. See, for example, "Our Asiatics," *TL*, August 31, 1907.

2. Cited in "Letter from Gandhi and Ally to London Press," *IO*, December 29, 1906. Earlier the *Rand Daily Mail* stated that "Mr. Gandhi's marshalling [*sic*] of the facts and his submission of them in printed form betrayed a skilled as well as a determined hand." *RDM* cited in "The Deputation Again," *IO*, December 8, 1906.

3. "The Indian Peril," *JS*, April 29, 1907.

4. "The Asiatic Act," *JS*, May 4, 1907.

5. "Asiatic Bill," *RDM*, March 26, 1907.

6. *Satyagraha*, 99.

7. "Asiatic Registration," *JS*, August 12, 1907.

8. To his brother he complained, "I am so hard pressed for time that I scarcely know what to do." *CWMG* 5:334. He confided to Chhaganlal Gandhi that he did not get "a moment's respite." *CWMG* 6:303.

9. Gandhi's court appearances were as numerous as ever. See, for example, the entries labeled "Civil Judgments" in the *Rand Daily Mail* in 1906 (March 8, April 12, May 4, June 2, July 14, August 21, September 4, October 27) and 1907 (January 8, February 2, March 8, April 19, May 3, June 25, August 10, September 12, October 11) and in the *Johannesburg Star* (February 3, 1906; August 14, 1907; December 28, 1907). See also *Rama and Another v. Rex*, 1907 *TSCR* 949 (October 21, 1907). He even instructed a criminal defense advocate. "Illicit Liquor Traffic," *TL*, August 15, 1907.

He also made time to frequent Phoenix, the large rural outpost some fourteen miles from Durban that he had purchased in 1904 and where he had gathered his devotees to publish *Indian Opinion*. "My original idea had been gradually to retire from practice, go and live in the Settlement, earn my livelihood by manual work there, and find the joy of service in the fulfillment of Phoenix. But it was not to be." *Autobiography*, 304.

10. "Durban Notes," *IO*, January 12, 1907.

11. *CWMG* 6:306. See also *CWMG* 5:412, 6:332, 6:378, 6:383, 6:393, 6:420, 6:456, 6:468, 7:139, and 7:142; "British Indian Association," *TL*, May 14, 1907.

12. *CWMG* 6:448.

13. *CWMG* 5:418.

14. See, for example, *CWMG* 6:440, 7:129, and 7:387.

15. *CWMG* 6:440.

16. *CWMG* 6:495. These conditions attached to Gandhi's offer to represent nonregistrants. He also offered to represent nonviolent picketers. *CWMG* 7:283.

17. *CWMG* 7:9; *CWMG* 7:89.

18. *CWMG* 7:129.

19. From February 1907 to December 1907, Gandhi defended fifty-five resisters in court. Details about these cases, as well as a complete set of endnotes, can be found at disalvo.law.wvu.edu.

20. "Asiatic Law: Mr. Gandhi's Proposals," *JS*, August 19, 1907.

21. "Passive Resisters,", *TL*, December 3, 1907.

22. Gandhi had secured a different opinion from Leonard, who believed that no colony possessed power to act beyond its borders. "Opinion of J. W. Leonard and Arthur Hume," SN 4780 (December 30, 1907).

23. "Bitter-Enders: Mass Meeting of Indians," *RDM*, December 28, 1907. *Indian Opinion* estimated that there were "at least 1,000 people present." "A Meeting at Vreedorp," *IO*, January 4, 1908.

24. *CWMG* 7:449. See also "A Johannesburg Demonstration," *TL*, December 28, 1907.

25. The *Johannesburg Star's* afternoon headline was "Asiatic Question: Ringleaders in Court—48 Hours Notice to Leave—New Phase of the Struggle."

26. Karwa's full name is not available. Three Chinese defendants also testified. The cases of Nawab Khan and Sumander Khan were postponed until January 3 to arrange for the presence of translators; neither spoke English.

27. "The Registration Law: Simultaneous Arrests in Johannesburg Pretoria and Pietersburg—Mr. Gandhi Ordered to Leave the Transvaal—Within 48 Hours," *IO*, January 4, 1908.

28. "Asiatic Question: Ringleaders in Court—48 Hours Notice to Leave—New Phase of the Struggle," *JS*, December 28, 1907; "The Asiatic Question: Leaders before the Court—Ordered to Leave Colony," *TL*, December 30, 1907; "The Asiatics: Law Enforced—Leaders in Court—Ordered to Leave the Colony," *RDM*, December 30, 1907; "The Registration Law: Simultaneous Arrests in Johannesburg Pretoria and Pietersburg—Mr. Gandhi Ordered to Leave the Transvaal—Within 48 Hours," *IO*, January 4, 1908.

29. "Meeting on the Square: Ringleaders Refuse to Leave," *JS*, December 28, 1907.

30. "Speech in Government Square," *IO*, January 1, 1908.

31. "Method of Deportation," *JS*, December 30, 1907.

32. "Every religion taught that if a man did anything that degraded his manhood, there was no religion in him." *CWMG* 7:471.

33. "Strong Speaking," *RDM*, December 31, 1907. See also "At the Mosque," *JS*, December 31, 1907, and "At the Mosque: Shaking Empire's Foundations," *TL*, December 31, 1907.

34. "The Passive Resisters: To-Day's Developments," *JS*, December 31, 1907; "Meeting This Morning: The Police Intervene," *JS*, December 31, 1907; untitled entry, *IO*, January 4, 1908. *Indian Opinion* estimated the crowd to number at least one thousand.

35. "Another Prosecution," *RDM*, January 4, 1908.

36. "The Asiatics: Cases in the Courts," *TL*, January 4, 1908.

37. "Another Prosecution," *RDM*, January 4, 1908.

38. "The Asiatics: Cases in the Courts," *TL*, January 4, 1908.

39. "Another Prosecution," *RDM*, January 4, 1908.

40. Gandhi's campaign might be said to have begun with his letter to the *Johannesburg Star* of January 4. "The Religious Aspect: A Reply from Mr. Gandhi," *JS*, January 4, 1908. There Gandhi makes an unpersuasive case for the religious basis of the resistance. One comes away feeling he painted himself into a corner on this issue and never managed to find a way out.

41. "Asiatic Question," *JS*, January 6, 1908.

42. "Mr. Gandhi Interviewed: Reply to General Smuts," *TL*, January 7, 1908.

43. "Interview to Reuter [*sic*]," January 8, 1908, CWMG 8 (1962 edition): 19.

44. *CWMG* 8: 22. For more on Schlesin, see Weber, *Going Native: Gandhi's Relationship with Western Women* (New Delhi: Lotus, 2011).

45. *CWMG* 8:33.

46. "Asiatic Question: Ringleaders, Sentenced—Mr. Gandhi's Valediction, Appeal to His Followers," *JS*, January 10, 1908.

47. They would not appear until the 4:45 P.M. edition.

48. "Asiatic Question: Ringleaders, Sentenced—Mr. Gandhi's Valediction, Appeal to His Followers," *JS*, January 10, 1908.

CHAPTER SIXTEEN

Epigraph, page 216: *CWMG* 8:319.

1. It was not a complete vacation. He addressed office work during Polak's visits. *CWMG* 8:158.

2. *CWMG* 8:113.

3. In February and March, Gandhi stated that the letter was drafted by Cartwright. *CWMG* 8:113; *CWMG*, Supplementary Vol. 1, p. 67. In 1928, Gandhi stated that the letter was "drafted or approved of by General Smuts." *Satyagraha*, 154.

4. Gandhi would later claim that his amendment made it clear that repeal was intended. *Satyagraha*, 155. An examination of the document simply does not support this characterization. Indeed, this was not Gandhi's position in February, when he wrote that the letters between himself and Smuts "do not say categorically that the new law would be repealed." "Johannesburg Letter," *IO*, February 8, 1908.

5. The letter was poorly drafted. It failed to unequivocally make repeal a condition of the settlement.

6. *CWMG* 8:65.

7. Smuts and the colony's whites were also concerned with the demonstration effect of the Indians' resistance on natives. "The Asiatic Deadlock," *JS*, January 27, 1908.

8. "Letter of Selborne to Smuts," November 30, 1907, quoted in Hancock, *Smuts: The Sanguine Years, 1870–1919* (Cambridge: Cambridge University Press, 1962).

9. "Johannesburg Letter," *IO*, February 8, 1908.

10. Gandhi would claim that Smuts pledged to repeal the Act at this, and at a subsequent, meeting. "Asiatic Question," *JS*, June 26, 1908.

11. *CWMG* 8:65.

12. CWMG 8:49. On January 31 Smuts stated that repealing the Act was "a preposterous proposal, and now the Indians have dropped it." "Mr. Smuts Interviewed," *JS*, January 31, 1908. Either Gandhi did not read this—an unlikely occurrence—or he ignored it.

13. *CWMG* 8:65.

14. *CWMG* 8:283.

15. *CWMG* 8:65.

16. "A Dialogue on the Compromise," *IO*, February 15, 1908.

17. See, for example, "A Fresh Development," *TL*, January 29, 1908.

18. *CWMG* 8:44.

19. "Asiatic Question: Mr. Gandhi Injured," *JS*, February 10, 1908. Gandhi's one-time Pathan supporters also participated in a Durban mass meeting, where some started a disturbance to protest Gandhi. A shot was fired, missing Gandhi. "Indians at Durban," *JS*, March 6, 1908.

20. *Satyagraha*, 170.

21. *CWMG* 8:75. Gandhi also wrote to the attorney general, indicating he did not want his assailants prosecuted. *Satyagraha*, 168. Two were nonetheless prosecuted. "Assault on Mr. Gandhi," *JS*, February 20, 1908. As Swan shows, Gandhi, with a change of conditions, had altered his views somewhat by May when he urged Smuts to deport "the most violent member of the Pathan community . . . who ha[d] been an active agent" in having the assaults against Gandhi and others committed. Swan, *South African Experience*, 163; *CWMG* 8:253.

22. *CWMG* 8:182. According to the *Transvaal Leader* of April 10, 1908, Polak was admitted to the bar on April 6 and took the requisite oaths on April 8.

23. *Autobiography*, 305.

24. Polak would put his own impression on representing disobedients by defending them on the basis of their "conscientious objection" to the law. See, for example, "The Florida Case," *TL*, July 31, 1908; and "Hawkers Sentenced," *TL*, August 1, 1908. Gandhi adopted this theme. See "Letters to the Editor," *TL*, August 10, 1908.

25. "The Asiatic Situation," *RDM*, June 25, 1908; "Asiatic Agitation," *JS*, July 8, 1908.

26. "Asiatic Question," *JS*, May 29, 1908.

27. Gandhi states that he "had too great faith in the statesmanship of . . . Smuts, in his honesty, and in his integrity." *CWMG* 8:319. In describing his January 30 meeting with Smuts, Gandhi recalled him saying, "You know I too am a barrister." *Satyagraha*, 156.

28. *CWMG* 8:231.

29. Gandhi may also have thought a court would not entertain a lawsuit without this request having first been made.

30. *CWMG* 8:277.

31. "[Ward] had a thorough knowledge of English case law." Nathan, *Not Heaven Itself: An Autobiography* (1944), 218–219, quoted in Kahn, *Law, Life and Laughter*, 335. Gandhi had attempted to retain Leonard, who was preoccupied. Gandhi described Ward as a "very able barrister, though not of the same calibre as . . . Leonard." *CWMG* 8:297.

32. *CWMG* 8:297.

33. *CWMG* 8:308.

34. *CWMG* 8:306.

35. It is likely that Gandhi wrote this unclear petition "after consulting Barrister Ward." *CWMG* 8:311, n. 2.

36. Solomon reasoned that the application was like "a letter written by one person to another," with ownership passing to the recipient. *Aswat v. Registrar of Asiatics*, 1908 *TSCR* 568 (July 2, 1908).

37. "Letter from Mr. Gandhi," *RDM*, July 3, 1908.

CHAPTER SEVENTEEN

Epigraph, page 227: *CWMG* 8:55.

1. "Mr. Smuts at Richmond," *JS*, February 6, 1908.

2. Weber, *On the Salt March*; Brown, *Gandhi and Civil Disobedience*. The Gandhi-led 1913 South African workers' strike and march (see Swan, *South African Experience*, 245–256) and the 1895 railway workers strikes in Natal (see chapter 6) provide other, though somewhat less clear, examples.

3. "Letter to the Editor," *JS*, December 31, 1907.

4. "Meeting of Chinese: Mr. Gandhi's Exhortation," *JS*, December 31, 1907.

5. *CWMG* 8:399.

6. "When I talk of equality of treatment in the eye of the law the idea is jeered at. . . . To my mind, it is the only thing that binds the Empire together." *CWMG* 9:30.

7. *CWMG* 8:347.

8. *CWMG* 8:329.

9. "The Asiatics: Mr. Gandhi on the Position—Determined to Hold Out," *TL*, July 24, 1908.

10. "The Asiatic Question," *JS*, July 17, 1908; "Mr. Gandhi Again Explains," *JS*, August 13, 1908. Gandhi and the Indians also wanted the government to honor the right to return of Indians who had formerly lawfully lived in the Transvaal.

11. "The Asiatic Problem," *JS*, August 14, 1908.

12. The leadership had thirteen hundred certificates in hand. Two hundred were surrendered during the event. "The Asiatic Question: Prominent Indians Charged," *TL*, August 18, 1908.

13. *CWMG* 8:456. (The paragraphing here has been slightly changed for clarity.) In reporting on the rally, the *Rand Daily Mail* stated that Gandhi "seemed to be suffering from mental stress." "Gaol Before Indignity: Asiatics Burn Certificates," *RDM*, August 17, 1908.

14. "Educated Indians," *TL*, August 14, 1908.

15. *CWMG* 8:487.

16. In 1908 there was often little time between arrest and trial.

17. "Law and Police: Law and Asiatics—The Registration Problem—Test Case From Charlestown," *JS*, July 9, 1908.

18. *CWMG* 8:352.

19. Gandhi argued that the case should be dismissed because the defendant was previously acquitted. The magistrate overruled Gandhi.

20. "Law and Police: Parsee and Permit—Shapurjee Again Charged—Ordered to Leave This Time," *TL*, July 11 1908; "Rand Police Courts: Ordered to Leave—Indian Immigration Case—Government Defied," *RDM*, July 11, 1908; *CWMG* 8:357.

21. "A Dilemma," *TL*, July 18, 1908.

22. "A Test Case," *RDM*, July 6, 1908. See also "The Sorabji Case," *JS*, July 15, 1908; "The Asiatic Question" *JS*, July 17, 1908.

23. *CWMG* 8:367, 8:387, 8:398.

24. *CWMG* 8:378.

25. This front had actually opened five days earlier, when BIA chair Essop Mia announced that the BIA leadership would hawk—without licenses. "The Asiatic Question" (letter to the editor from Essop Mia, Chair, British Indian Association), *JS*, July 17, 1908.

26. By August 15 approximately one hundred Indians had gone to jail. "The Asiatics," *TL*, August 15, 1908. Many were petty hawkers to whom Gandhi turned when merchant support declined. Swan, *South African Experience*, 167.

27. Some differences existed in whether the courts gave hard labor sentences (see "The Asiatics: Government and the Hawkers," *TL*, July 31, 1908), but these differences are explained by geography. Johannesburg judges imposed hard labor, while judges in outlying areas were more forgiving.

28. Gandhi was not ignorant of this civil disobedience function: "The self-suffering which the community has undergone . . . has been undertaken . . . to draw public attention to a grievance." "Indian Passive Resisters," *RDM*, August 6, 1910.

29. "Hawkers Go to Gaol: Mr. Gandhi and Exemptions," *TL*, July 28, 1908; "Hawkers Fined," *RDM*, July 28, 1908.

30. Identified elsewhere as T. H. Jefferson and Thomas H. Jefferson. See, for example, "Law and Police: Asiatics Sentenced—Leaders in the Dock—A New Feature," *TL*, July 23, 1908; "Hawkers Fined," *RDM*, July 28, 1908.

31. "Hawkers Go to Gaol: Mr. Gandhi and Exemptions," *TL*, July 28, 1908.

32. Ibid.

33. Gandhi also raised a procedural defense in *Rex v. V. M. Bagas and Others*. In that case the magistrate overruled Gandhi on a critical point, after which Gandhi refrained from calling witnesses. The defendants received fines of 5 shillings or three days' imprisonment with hard labor. "Trial of V. M. Bagas and Others," *IO*, September 15, 1908.

34. *Rex v. Ghila, Deva, and Bhachar*, a prosecution for hawking without licenses. The defendants pled guilty, Gandhi indicated that the defendants would not tender evidence, and the magistrate promptly pronounced a sentence of £1 or seven days' imprisonment with hard labor. "Stubborn Asiatics," *RDM*, July 31, 1908.

35. "The Asiatics: 'Hawkers' Go To Prison—Young Gandhi Sentenced—Naidoo's Third Conviction," *TL*, July 29, 1908.

36. One engaged in satyagraha.

37. *CWMG* 8:432.

38. "The Asiatics: Harilal Gandhi Arrested," *TL*, July 28, 1908.

39. "Satyagraha always calls for sacrifice of self." *CWMG* 8:335. "Those who wish to serve India must give up all thought of serving their own interests." *CWMG* 8:429.

40. *CWMG* 8:432.

41. Ibid.

42. Ibid.

43. *CWMG* 8:380–381.

44. *CWMG* 8:1.

45. As many as 120 resisters were engaged in this practice as of October. "A Heavy Sentence," *JS*, October 13, 1908.

46. "The Indian Agitation," *JS*, August 10, 1908.

47. "The Indian Struggle in the Transvaal: Harilal Gandhi Gets a Month," *IO*, August 22, 1908.

48. When the magistrate ordered Gandhi's client out of the colony within seven days, Gandhi announced that this "sort of thing would go on until the struggle was over." "The Asiatic Agitation," *JS*, August 4, 1908; *CWMG* 8:421; "Asiatics Again," *RDM*, August 5, 1908; "Indian Question," *TL*, August 5, 1908.

49. *CWMG* 8:479; "The Asiatic Problem: Another Phase," *JS*, August 26, 1908.

50. Godfrey also represented some defendants. See, for example, "Heavy Sentences," *JS*, October 13, 1908.

51. "Indian Problem: Volksrust Sentences," *JS*, September 9, 1908. *The Times* of London did give some attention to Indian disobedience. See, for example, "Indians in the Transvaal: Active Resistance to the Law," September 11, 1908; "Indians in the Transvaal," October 5, 1908; and "Indians in the Transvaal," October 15, 1908.

52. Thomas Weber addresses the Gandhian approach to conflict resolution (including its emphasis on self-suffering) in "Gandhian Philosophy, Conflict Resolution Theory and Practical Approaches to Negotiation," *Journal of Peace Research*, Vol. 38, No. 4 (July 2001): 493–513. Weber correctly points out that there is some debate as to whether the dynamic I describe universally applies. The understanding I offer of the relationship among civil disobedience, self-suffering, and change is, in fact, not the only understanding of the dynamic. For an exploration of the relationship, including alternative views, see Pelton, *The Psychology of Nonviolence* (Elmsford, NY: Pergamon Press, 1974).

53. "The Asiatics: Volksrust Trials—Indians in the Dock; 'Prepared to Suffer,'" *TL*, August 19, 1908.

54. *CWMG* 8:384.

55. Dawjee Amod had entered the colony without having registered. Gandhi pled Amod not guilty to being a prohibited immigrant, argued that he did not violate the immigration act, and cross-examined the government's witness. Amod was found guilty.

Next, a group of nine was accused of the same crime as Amod. It appears Gandhi pled them all not guilty. He again argued that they were not in the colony unlawfully and conducted a second, identical cross-examination of the government's witness. He added, perhaps by way of extenuation, that the accused had been advised by him to enter the colony. All were found guilty.

Four Indians were then brought forward to also face charges of being prohibited immigrants. Gandhi pled them, too, not guilty and argued that they were qualified to enter as educated immigrants or as prewar residents. Gandhi himself testified that he had advised these defendants to enter the Transvaal and had assisted them in doing so. All were found guilty. "Cost of Defying the Law," *RDM*, October 15, 1908; "Indian Problem," *JS*, October 14, 1908; "Trial of Dawjee Amod and Others," *IO*, October 17, 1908.

56. Gandhi had been admitted to practice as a barrister and was known as such during his brief practice periods in India. In Natal, his formal title was advocate and in the Transvaal, solicitor.

CHAPTER EIGHTEEN

Epigraph, page 249: *CWMG* 10:70.

1. *CWMG* 10:229.

2. *CWMG* 9:107.

3. Gandhi made the case for suffering repeatedly during this period. For example, in July 1909, he says that he "can think of no course so wonderfully effective as voluntary suffering. . . . Suffering is bound to bring redress." *CWMG* 9:312. Later, he states: "Every white who hears of our gaol-going is struck with admiration. Voluntary submission to suffering cannot but have a powerful effect." *CWMG* 9:317.

4. Gandhi echoed this argument a short time later. See *CWMG* 9:188.

5. At about this same time, Gandhi was advising people to consult lawyers to vindicate their rights. *CWMG* 9:139.

6. "The Asiatic Side: Mr. Gandhi Interviewed," *RDM*, January 22, 1909. Gandhi less than convincingly denied any attempt at coercion. See "Letter from Mr. Gandhi," *RDM*, January 23, 1909.

7. "Passive Resistance?" *RDM*, January 22, 1909.

8. "The Asiatic Question," *JS*, January 23, 1909.

9. "Indians and Their Licenses," *JS*, January 26, 1909; "Law Reports," *RDM*, January 27, 1909.

10. One other merchant proclaimed that he intended to follow Cachalia's example (see "Indian Agitation," *JS*, January 23, 1909; *CWMG* 9:166, 176), and there was talk of others. See "Indian Merchants: Forty to Surrender Their Estates," *RDM*, January 26, 1909. There is no clear evidence, however, that anyone followed Cachalia's example. (Gandhi later refers in *Indian Opinion* to "Mr. Rustomjee and Mr. Cachalia" as having "lost their all." *CWMG* 10:175. It appears, however, that Rustomjee sacrificed his assets in a different form of resistance.)

11. "The Asiatic Question: Naidoo Appeal Fails," *JS*, January 23, 1909; *Naidoo and Others v. Rex*, 1909 *TSCR* 43 (January 22, 1909).

12. *Randeria v. Rex*, 1909 *TSCR* 65 (February 4 and 5, 1909).

13. *CWMG* 9:198.

14. "The Resisters Fail," *RDM*, February 4, 1909.

15. *CWMG* 9:197.

16. Ally and Habib attempted to establish a moderate group to negotiate a settlement with the Transvaal government and send a deputation to London. This effort collapsed when key Ally-Habib supporters, faced with having to oppose Gandhi's desire for an all-resister deputation, withdrew their support. See Swan, *South African Experience*, 175–176. See also Hunt, *Gandhi in London* (New Delhi: Promilla & Co., 1978).

17. "The Deputation," *IO*, June 26, 1909.

18. Swan, *South African Experience*, 176.

19. *Satyagraha*, 231–232.

20. In addition to the 271 pages, Gandhi wrote a 5-page introduction. Suresh Sharma and Tridip Suhrud (eds.), *MK Gandhi's "Hind Swaraj": A Critical Edition* (New Delhi: Orient BlackSwan, 2010), p. xi. Anthony Parel puts Gandhi's writing of *Hind Swaraj* in context:

> [Gandhi] came into contact with a very important segment of the newly emerging Indian middle class, the expatriate Indians living abroad. These were the new converts to modern civilisation, and it is their uncritical acceptance of their newly found secular faith that really bothered Gandhi. . . . They were attracted to . . . revolutionary movements . . . [and were not opposed to violence]. . . . Gandhi had this group very much in mind when he wrote *Hind Swaraj*.

Parel (ed.), *"Hind Swaraj" and Other Writings* (Cambridge: Cambridge University Press, 1997), xxiv–xxv. I am greatly indebted to Professor Parel for much of what follows in this chapter with respect to *Hind Swaraj*.

21. *CWMG* 70 (1977 edition): 241.

22. For the original Gujarati, see Sharma and Suhrud, *MK Gandhi's "Hind Swaraj."*

23. "*Swa* refers to 'self' as an individual and as a collective; 'raj' refers to rule or control." Ibid., xv.

24. Professor Parel points out that Gandhi's position on Western civilization is not absolute:

> A glimpse into Gandhi's Western intellectual sources should go a long way towards correcting the view held by some that the Mahatma was opposed to Western civilisation as such. Such a view is so simple as to be false. As Sir Ernest Barker puts it, he was a 'bridge and a reconciler.' The breadth and depth of his knowledge of Western intellectual sources suggest that his attack was limited to certain unhealthy tendencies of modern Western civilisation.... On the contrary, in *Hind Swaraj* he joins forces with many concerned Western thinkers in defence of true civilisation values everywhere, East and West.

Parel, *"Hind Swaraj" and Other Writings*, xlvii.

25. *CWMG* 10:127.

26. Almost contemporaneously with *Hind Swaraj*, Gandhi writes: "If a lawyer would boast of his altruism or spirituality, let him earn his livelihood through physical labour and carry on his legal practice without charging anything for it." *CWMG* 10:203.

27. "Men" is Gandhi's term.

28. See, generally, Swan, *South African Experience.*

29. Lloyd Rudolph and Susanne Hoeber Rudolph locate *Hind Swaraj* against modernity in *Postmodern Gandhi and Other Essays* (Chicago: University of Chicago Press, 2006).

30. While Buddhism and Jainism had a mild influence on Gandhi, Christianity's influence on him was strong. Parel, *"Hind Swaraj" and Other Writings*, 10, n. 8.

31. Ibid., xlii.

32. Holmes, *The Common Law* (Boston: Little, Brown & Company, 1881), 1.

33. *CWMG* 9:477.

34. "Asiatic Registration," *RDM*, December 29, 1909; "West Rand," *RDM*, December 31, 1909; *CWMG* 10:108.

35. Erik H. Erikson claims that Gandhi defined himself as the "only one" capable of particular important missions. Erikson, *Gandhi's Truth* (New York: W. W. Norton, 1969), 170, 393.

36. "Asiatic Report," *RDM*, August 12, 1910.

37. Shortly after the hearing, Gandhi wrote: "We shall obtain no justice by going to courts of law. We must fight on, relying on our own strength." *CWMG* 10:196.

38. *CWMG* 10:298.

39. Ibid.

40. *CWMG* 10:404.

41. *CWMG* 10:392. It was rare for a magistrate to order a resister to both pay a fine and serve a jail sentence.

42. Undoubtedly remembering his earlier dispute with Smuts, Gandhi wrote a detailed account of the meeting. *CWMG* 11 (1963 edition): 31. See also *CWMG* 11:29.

43. Gandhi would later clarify that "under swaraj . . . I do not dream . . . of . . . no laws and no law courts. On the contrary . . . [t]here will be law and law-courts . . ., but they will be custodians of the people's liberty." *CWMG* 23 (1967 edition): 29.

44. *CWMG* 10:334.

45. *CWMG* 10:324.

46. For a description of the settlement and the events preceding it, see Swan, *South African Experience*.

47. Gandhi commuted from the farm to Johannesburg two or three times weekly. At first he would allow himself to go only twice weekly. *CWMG* 10:272. Later he increased this to three times weekly. *CWMG* 10:384.

Gandhi had been thinking about manual labor for some time. From his reading of Ruskin's *Unto This Last*—essays on political economy Polak had given him—he had learned "that a lawyer's work has the same value as the barber's." *Autobiography*, 299. Inspired by Ruskin, Gandhi had established Phoenix settlement in 1904, a land-based commune in Natal intended to improve its residents' lives and provide *Indian Opinion* a home. Gandhi deferred his goal of living on the land himself. He began living at Tolstoy Farm in June 1910.

48. "British Indian Association's Action," *IO*, March 18, 1911. Smuts' basis for rejecting Ritch is unknown.

49. "Mr. L. W. Ritch, who arrived in Johannesburg on the 5th inst., has commenced practice as a solicitor at Nos. 21–24, Court Chambers, Rissik Street, Johannesburg." "Transvaal Notes," *IO*, April 15, 1911. *The Johannesburg Star* reported that Gandhi "has already arranged for his legal practice to be taken over by Mr. Ritch." *CWMG* 11:44.

50. *CWMG* 11:25. Earlier he had alerted the community to Ritch's coming: "He [Ritch] will start practice shortly. If the community helps him, he will earn enough for a living." *CWMG* 10:453.

51. Ritch was not the only associate whom Gandhi encouraged to practice law. He also encouraged Schlesin (see "Ladies as Attorneys," *JS*, April 23, 1909; *Schlesin v. Incorporated Law Society*, 1909 *TSCR* 363 [April 23, 1909]; and Paxton, *Sonja Schlesin: Gandhi's South African Secretary* [Glasgow: Pax Books, 2006]), Chhaganlal Gandhi (see *CWMG* 9:438), and Sorabji (see *CWMG* 11:5, n. 1; *Satyagraha*, 212–213).

52. *CWMG* 11:64.

SOURCES

PAPERS

British Sessional Papers. *Papers Relating to the Grievances of Her Majesty's Indian Subjects in the South African Republic.* C-7911 (1895).

NEWSPAPERS

For citations to the newspaper stories on which the author relied, please see the author's complete endnotes at disalvo.law.wvu.edu.

Indian Opinion
Johannesburg Star
Natal Advertiser
Natal Mercury
Natal Witness
The Press
Rand Daily Mail
Times of London
Transvaal Government Gazette
Transvaal Leader

DOCUMENTS: GANDHI SMARAK SANGRAHALAYA, SABARMATI ASHRAM, AHMEDABAD

"Bank deposit receipts and other famine relief records." SNs 2091–0001 et seq.
"Correspondence from William Edward Pitcher to M. K. Gandhi" (November 30, 1897 and December 1, 1897). SNs 2609 and 2612.

"Costs, Charges and Expenses relating to the Appeal of Suliman Ebrohim Vauda." SN 2879 (undated).

"Fee Statement from E. Howard Langston to Gandhi." SN 3855 (June 26, 1901).

"Letter from C. Bird to Dada Abdoola and Company." SN 1958 (January 25, 1897).

"Letter from Dumat and Davis to Gandhi." SN 4082 (September 5, 1903).

"Letter from G. A. De R. Labistour to M. K. Gandhi." SN 2901 (January 4, 1899).

"Letter from Gregorowski to Gandhi." SN 4069 (July 24, 1903).

"Letter from J. Alexander to M. K. Gandhi." SN 1939 (January 22,1897).

"Letter from Master of the Transvaal Supreme Court to M. K. Gandhi." SN 4071 (August 6, 1903).

"Letter from Parsee Rustomjee to M. K. Gandhi." SN 32371 (October 19, 1901).

"Letter from R. Alexander to M. K. Gandhi." SN 1938 (January 22, 1897).

"Letter from R. Gregorowski to M. K. Gandhi." SN 4110 (December 18, 1903).

"Letter from William Morcom to M. K. Gandhi." SN 2891 (December 23, 1898).

"Letter of Budree to M. K. Gandhi." SN 4318a (January 24, 1905).

"Letter of Dumat & Davis to Gandhi." SN 4079 (September 2, 1903).

"Letter of Dumat & Davis to Gandhi." SN 4081 (September 3, 1903).

"Letter of Dumat & Davis to Gandhi." SN 4082 (September 5, 1903).

"Letter of F. A. Laughton to Gandhi." SN 2764 (June 24, 1898).

"Letter of F. A. Laughton to Gandhi." SN 3263 (August 4, 1899).

"Letter of G. B. Cooke, Solicitor, to M. K. Gandhi." SN 405–0001 (July 22, 1895).

"Letter of Gandhi to Dumat and Davis." SN 4087 (September 19, 1903).

"Letter of George Goodricke to M. K. Gandhi." SN 4354a (April 10, 1906).

"Letter of Goordeen Ahir to M. K. Gandhi." SN 4318b (February 22, 1906).

"Letter of M. K. Gandhi to Assistant Master of the Supreme Court." SN 4219 (January 5, 1905).

"Letter of M. K. Gandhi to Goordeen Ahir." SN 4318c (March 6, 1906).

"Letter of M. K. Gandhi to Hillier & Co." unknown SN (April 22, 1906).

"Letter of Oswald Askew to M. K. Gandhi." SN 3638 (January 8, 1897).

"Letter of R. K. Khan to M. K. Gandhi." SN 4320 (June 4, 1908).

"Letter of Reuben Beningfield & Son to M. K. Gandhi." SN 4712a (August 12, 1909).

"Letter to Abdoolla Carim" (*sic*). SN 3661 (March 30, 1897).

"Letter to Abdoolla Carim" (*sic*). SN 3662 (March 30, 1897).

"Letter to D. B. Shukla." SN 233944 (undated).

"Letter to Gandhi from F. A. Laughton." SN 3262 (August 4, 1899).

"Letter to Gandhi from F. A. Laughton." SN 3413 (March 22, 1900).

"Letter to Gandhi from G. B. Cooke." SN 405 (July 22, 1895).

"Letter to Gandhi from Gustave Labistour." SN 3114 (March 12, 1899).

"Letter to Gandhi from Khan." SN 2758 (June 1898).

"Letter to Gandhi from O. J. Askew." SN 3919 (January 24, 1896).

"Letter to Gandhi from William Edward Pitcher." SN 2605–2 (November 22, 1897).

"Letter to Gandhi from William Morcom." SN 2891 (December 23, 1898).
"Letter to Indian Merchants." SN 2182–0001 (March 30, 1897).
"Letter to M. K. Gandhi." SN 2893 (December 26, 1898).
"Letter to M. K. Gandhi." SN 3165 (March 31, 1899).
"Letter to M. K. Gandhi from William Morcom." SN 3915 (October 3, 1901).
"Letter to W. Lehman from M. K. Gandhi." SN 3812 (April 17, 1901).
"Memorandum of Agreement among Sheik Ameer, Budrea and others." SN 4323 (March 1906).
"Memorandum of Frederick Laughton analyzing the merits of Gandhi's exceptions to the complaint in *Meter v. Meter.*" SN 560 (October 12, 1895).
"Notarial Bond." SN 4225 (March 4, 1905).
"Opinion Letter from F. A. Laughton to M. K. Gandhi." SN 870 (April 15, 1896).
"Opinion Letters from F. A. Laughton to M. K. Gandhi." SNs 3757 (January 18, 1901) and 3759 (January 21, 1901).
"Opinion Letter from Renaud and Robinson." SN 2900 (December 31, 1898).
"Opinion Letter of R. Gregorowski." SN 4247 (August 5, 1905).
"Opinion Letter of William Morcom." SN 2054 (February 19, 1897).
"Opinion of F. A. Laughton." SN 3134 (March 14, 1899).
"Opinion of J. W. Leonard and Arthur Hume." SN 4780 (December 30, 1907).
"Opinion of Seward Brice." SN 3784 (October 9, 1902).
"Pleadings of June 17, 1898." SNs 2755 and 2757 (Moosa Hajee Adam v. Hassim Juma [Durban Circuit Court]).
"Preliminary Opinion of Gustave A. de Roquefeuil Labistour re Indian Licences." SN 3114 (March 12, 1899).
"Statement of Bennett Expenses due to Hawthorn and Mason." SN 2969 (July 30, 1895).
"Trust Transfer of 1895." SN 709 (1895).
Untitled item. SN 2091–0016 (June 6, 1896).
Untitled item. SN 3750C.
Untitled item. SN 4036.
Untitled item. SN 7908.
Untitled item. SN 7910.

STATUTES, PROCLAMATIONS, REGULATIONS, RULES

Natal

General Rules for the Admission of Advocates or Attorneys and Candidate Attorneys to the Supreme Court of Natal (1893).
Government Notice No. 517 of 1897.
Law 39 of 1896, Section 8.
Law No. 19 of 1872.

South African Republic

Law 30 of 1896.

Law respecting Coolies, Arabs, and other Asiatics (No. 3, 1885), as amended, Staats Courant, No. 621, November 23, 1898.

Transvaal

Law 38 of 1902.

Transvaal Proclamation No. 14 of 1902.

CASE REPORTS

Natal Law Reports

Advocates of the Supreme Court (Corrected to 31st December, 1894) and *Attorneys of the Supreme Court (Corrected to 31st December, 1894).* XV *Natal Law Reports* (1894).

Advocates of the Supreme Court (Corrected to 31st December, 1895) and *Attorneys of the Supreme Court (Corrected to 31st December, 1895).* XVI *Natal Law Reports* (1895).

Advocates of the Supreme Court (Corrected to 31st December, 1896) and *Attorneys of the Supreme Court (Corrected to 31st December, 1896).* XVII *Natal Law Reports* (1896).

Cassim Abdulla v. Bennett. XVI *Natal Law Reports* 159 (1895).

Chelligadu v. G. Wilkinson. XXI *Natal Law Reports* 24 (1900).

Coakes v. Ismail Dawjee. XV *Natal Law Reports* 369 (1894).

Duyall v. G. A. Riches. XXIII *Natal Law Reports* 94 (1902).

Ebrahim v. Jennings. XIX *Natal Law Reports* 93 (1898).

Ex parte Coakes. XVI *Natal Law Reports* 106 (1895).

Ex parte Russell, In re Coakes XVI *Natal Law Reports* 98 (1895).

In re Gandhi. XV *Natal Law Reports* 263 (1894).

In re: Intestate Estate of Hassan Dawjee. XV *Natal Law Reports* 211 (1894).

In re Intestate Estate of Hassan Dawjee. XVI *Natal Law Reports* 95 (1895).

In re K. B. Ratanji. XXIII *Natal Law Reports* 41 (1902).

In Re: M. C. Camrooden & Co. XX *Natal Law Reports* 171 (1899).

In re M. H. Nazar. XXII *Natal Law Reports* 369 (1901).

In re Regina v. Camroodeen. XV *Natal Law Reports* 335–336 (1894).

In re Russell v. Mackenzie. XVI *Natal Law Reports* 45 (1895).

In re Stephenson. XII *Natal Law Reports* 169 (1891).

Laughton v. Griffin & Others. XV *Natal Law Reports* 369 (1894).

Mahomed Amod Kajee v. Mapumulo Licensing Board. XXII *Natal Law Reports* 92 (1901).

Moosa Hoosen v. Clerk of the Peace. XX *Natal Law Reports* 212 (1899).

Moosajee v. Randles Brother and Hudson. XV *Natal Law Reports* 223 (1894).

Musa v. Dyer. XIX *Natal Law Reports* 26 (1898).

P. D. Desai v. Alum. XXI *Natal Law Reports* 278 (1900) ("P. D." appears to be a typographical error.)

P. B. Desai v. Alum. XXII *Natal Law Reports* 3 (1901).

Randles Bros. & Hudson v. M. S. Coovadia. XXI *Natal Law Reports* 31 (1900).

Robinson & Son v. Durban Corporation. XV *Natal Law Reports* 360 (1894).

Rungasamy Padiachy v. The Clerk of the Peace, Durban. XVI *Natal Reports* 244 (1895).

Solnath v. Durban Corporation. XIX *Natal Law Reports* 70 (1898).

Vanda v. Newcastle. XIX *Natal Law Reports* 28 (1898).

Vauda [sic] v. Mayor and Councillors of New Castle. Judicial Committee of the Privy Council. 1899 *Law Reports* 246 (1898); LXXIX *The Law Times Reports* 600 (1899); XX *Natal Law Reports* 1 (1898).

South African Republic Case Reports

Brown v. Leyds N.O. IV *Official Reports of the High Court of the South African Republic* 17 (1897).

Ismail Suleiman & Co. vs. Landdrost of Middelburg. II *Reports of Cases Decided in the Supreme Court of the South African Republic (Transvaal)* 244 (1888).

Tayob Hajee Khan Mohamed v. The Government of the South African Republic (F. W. Reitz, N.O.), V *Reports of Cases Decided in the High Court of the South African Republic* 168 (1898).

Transvaal Case Reports

African Political Organisation and The British Indian Association v. Johannesburg City Council. 1906 *Transvaal Law Reports* 962 (1906).

Aswat v. Registrar of Asiatics. 1908 *Transvaal Supreme Court Reports* 568 (1908).

Habib Motan v. Transvaal Government. 1904 *Transvaal Law Reports* 404 (1904).

Lucas' Trustee v. Ismail and Amod. 1905 *Transvaal Law Reports* 239 (1905).

Mangena v. Law Society. 1910 *Transvaal Provincial Division* 649 (1910).

Naidoo and Others v. Rex. 1909 *Transvaal Supreme Court Reports* 43 (1909).

Rama and Another v. Rex. 1907 *Transvaal Supreme Court Reports* 949 (1907).

Randeria v. Rex. 1909 *Transvaal Supreme Court Reports* 65 (1909).

Schlesin v. Incorporated Law Society. 1909 *Transvaal Supreme Court Reports* 363 (1909).

Union of South Africa Case Reports

Chotabhai v. Minister of Justice and Another. 1910 *South African Law Reports (Transvaal Provincial Division)* 1151 (1910).

Chotabhai v. Union Government (Minister of Justice) and Registrar of Asiatics, 1911 *South African Law Reports (Appellate Division)* 13 (1911).

Council of the Incorporated Law Society of the Transvaal, Minutes of the Meeting of April 14, 1903.

"The Petition of Mohandas Karamchand Gandhi of Johannesburg in this Colony[,] Barrister at Law." March 27, 1903, on file with the Incorporated Law Society of the Transvaal.

BOOKS, JOURNAL ARTICLES, AND WEBSITES

Abel, Richard. *The Legal Profession in England and Wales.* London: Basil Blackwell, 1988.

Alexander, Gilchrist. *The Temple of the Nineties.* London: Hodge & Co., 1938.

Baker, A. W. *Grace Triumphant: The Life Story of a Carpenter, Lawyer and Missionary in South Africa from 1856 to 1939.* London: Pickering & Inglis, Ltd., 1939.

Baker, J. H. *The Legal Profession and the Common Law.* London: Hambledon Press, 1986.

Ball, W. W. Rouse. *The Student's Guide to the Bar.* London: Macmillan, 1879.

Barton, D. Plunkett, Charles Benham, and Francis Watt. *The Story of the Inns of Court.* Boston: Houghton Mifflin, 1924.

Beck, Roger. *The History of South Africa.* Westport, CT: Greenwood Press, 2000.

Besant, Annie. *The Ancient Wisdom.* London: Theosophical Publishing, 1897.

Bhansali, S. R. *Legal System in India.* Jaipur, India: University Book House, 1992.

Blavatsky, H. P. *The Key to Theosophy.* London: Theosophical Publishing Company, 1889.

———. *The Secret Doctrine.* London: Theosophical Publishing Company, 1888.

Bondurant, Joan V. *Conquest of Violence: The Gandhian Philosophy of Conflict.* Berkeley: University of California Press, 1969.

Braden, Charles. *These Also Believe: A Study of Modern American Cults and Religious Movements.* New York: Macmillan, 1953.

Branch, Taylor. *Parting the Waters: America in the King Years, 1954–1963.* New York: Simon & Schuster, 1988.

Britton, Burnett. *Gandhi Arrives in South Africa.* Canton, ME: Greenleaf Books, 1999.

Brookes, Edgar, and Colin Webb. *A History of Natal.* Pietermaritzburg, South Africa: University of Natal Press, 1965.

Brown, Judith M. *Gandhi and Civil Disobedience: The Mahatma in Indian Politics, 1928–1934.* Cambridge: Cambridge University Press, 1977.

———. *Gandhi: Prisoner of Hope.* New Haven: Yale University Press, 1989.

———. *Gandhi's Rise to Power: Indian Politics, 1915–1922.* Cambridge: Cambridge University Press, 1972.

Calpin, G. H. *Indians in South Africa*. Pietermaritzburg, South Africa: Shuter & Shooter, 1949.

Chanock, Martin. *The Making of South African Legal Culture, 1902–1936: Fear, Favour and Prejudice*. Cambridge: Cambridge University Press, 2001.

Chenoweth, Erica, and Maria J. Stephan. *Why Civil Resistance Works*. New York: Columbia University Press, 2011.

Copland, Ian. *India, 1885–1947: The Unmaking of an Empire*. Harlow, UK: Longman, 2001.

Davenport, Rodney, and Christopher Saunders. *South Africa: A Modern History*. New York: St. Martin's Press, 2000.

De Kock, W. J., and D. W. Kruger (eds.). *Dictionary of South African Biography*. Cape Town and Johannesburg: Human Sciences Research Council, 1972.

DeMello, F. M. *The Indian National Congress*. London: Oxford University Press, 1934.

Denoon, David. *The Grand Illusion*. London: Longman, 1973.

Doke, Joseph J. *M. K. Gandhi: An Indian Patriot in South Africa*. 1909. Reprinted, Faridabad: Government of India Press, 1967.

Dold, G. W. F., and C. P. Joubert. *The Union of South Africa: The Development of Its Laws and Constitution*. London: Stevens & Sons, Ltd., 1955.

Dutt-Majumdar, Nirmalendu. *Conduct of Advocates and Legal Profession: Short History*. Kolkata, India: Eastern Law House, 1974.

Embree, Ainslie. *Indian's Search for National Identity*. New York: Alfred A. Knopf, 1972.

Erikson, Erik H. *Gandhi's Truth*. New York: W. W. Norton, 1969.

Fair, T. J. D. *The Distribution of Population in Natal*. Natal Regional Survey, Vol. 3. Cape Town: Oxford University Press for University of Natal, 1955.

Farquhar, J. N. *Modern Religious Movements in India*. Norwood, MA: J. S. Cushing Co., 1915.

Ferguson-Davie, C. J. *The Early History of Indians in Natal*. Johannesburg: South African Institute of Race Relations, 1977.

Fischer, Lewis. *The Life of Mahatma Gandhi*. New York: Harper & Row, 1983.

Gandhi, J. S. *Lawyers and Touts: A Study in the Sociology of the Legal Profession*. Delhi: Hindustan Publishing, 1982.

Gandhi, Mohandas K. *An Autobiography: My Experiments with Truth*. Boston: Beacon Press, 1957.

———. *Collected Works of Mahatma Gandhi*. 100 vols. New Delhi: Publications Division.

———. *Satyagraha in South Africa*. Translated by V. G. Desai. Stanford, CA: Academic Reprints, 1954.

Gledhill, Alan. *The Republic of India: The Development of Its Law and Constitution*. Westport, CT: Stevens & Sons, 1964.

Hahlo, H. R., and Ellison Kahn. *The South African Legal System and Its Background*. Cape Town: Juta & Co., 1968.

———. *The Union of South Africa: The Development of Its Laws and Constitution*. London: Stevens & Sons, 1960.

Hancock, W. K. *Smuts: The Sanguine Years, 1870–1919*. Cambridge: Cambridge University Press, 1962.

Hattersley, Alan F. *The British Settlement of Natal*. Cambridge: Cambridge University Press, 1950.

Hayman, J. "Smuts as a Lawyer: An Intimate Study, By One of His Pupils." 67 *South African Law Journal* 339 (1950).

Headlam, Cecil, and Gordon Home. *The Inns of Court*. London: A & C Black, 1909.

Holdsworth, W. S., II. *A History of the English Law*. London: Methuen & Co., 1923.

Hunt, James D. *Gandhi in London*. New Delhi: Promilla & Co., 1978.

Hutchins, Francis G. *The Illusion of Permanence: British Imperialism in India*. Princeton: Princeton University Press, 1967.

Itzkin, Eric. *Gandhi's Johannesburg*. Johannesburg: Witwatersrand University Press, 2000.

Iyer, Raghavan. *The Moral and Political Thought of Mahatma Gandhi*. New York: Oxford University Press, 1973.

Jois, M. Rama. *Legal and Constitutional History of India*. Vol. 2. Bombay: Fred B. Rothman, 1984.

Judd, Denis. *The Lion and the Tiger: The Rise and Fall of the British Raj, 1600–1947*. Oxford: Oxford University Press, 2004.

Kahn, Ellison. "The Development of South African Substantive Law." In H. F. Mellet, Susan Scott, and Paul van Warmelo (eds.). *Our Legal Heritage*. Durban, South Africa: Buttersworth, 1982.

———. *Law, Life and Laughter: Legal Anecdotes and Portraits*. Cape Town: Juta & Co., 1991.

King, Martin Luther, Jr. *The Papers of Martin Luther King, Jr.*, Vol. 5, *Threshold of a New Decade*. Berkeley: University of California Press, 2005.

Konczacki, Zbigniew A. *Public Finance and Economic Development of Natal, 1893–1910*. Durham, NC: Duke University Press, 1967.

Kruger, D. W., et al. (eds.). *Dictionary of South African Biography*. Pretoria: National Council for Social Research, 1968; Cape Town: Tafelberg-Uitgewers, Ltd., 1977.

Kumar, R. *Essays on Gandhian Politics: The Rowlatt Satyagraha of 1919*. London: Oxford University Press, 1971.

Lemming, David. "Blackstone and Law Reform by Education: Preparation for the Bar and Lawyerly Culture in Eighteenth-Century England." 16 *Law and History Review* 211 (Summer 1998).

Loftie, W. J. *The Inns of Court and Chancery*. London: Seeley & Co. Limited, 1893.

Mandela, Nelson. "Gandhi, the Prisoner: A Comparison." In B. R. Nanda (ed.), *Mahatma Gandhi: 125 Years*. New Delhi: Indian Council for Cultural Relations, 1995.

Marais, J. S. *The Fall of Kruger's Republic*. London: Oxford at the Clarendon Press, 1961.

Martin, Briton. *New India, 1885*. Berkeley: University of California Press, 1969.

McLane, John R. *Indian Nationalism and the Early Congress*. Princeton: Princeton University Press, 1977.

Morice, George T. *English and Roman-Dutch Law: Being a Statement of the Differences Between the Law of England and the Roman-Dutch Law as Prevailing in South Africa and Some Other of the British Colonies.* Grahamstown, South Africa: African Book Company, 1905.

Mukherjee, Mithi. *India in the Shadows of Empire: A Legal and Political History, 1774–1950.* New Delhi: Oxford University Press, 2010.

Munshi, K. M. *Bombay High Court: Half a Century of Reminiscences.* Bombay: Bharatiya Vidya Bhavan, 1963.

Musiker, Naomi, and Reuben Musiker. *Historical Dictionary of Greater Johannesburg.* Lanham, MD: Scarecrow Press, 1999.

Nanda, B. R. *Three Statesmen: Gokhale, Gandhi, and Nehru.* New Delhi: Oxford University Press, 2004.

Napier, T. B., and R. M. Stephenson. *A Practical Guide to the Bar.* London: H. Cox, 1888.

Nepstad, Sharon Erickson. *Religion and War Resistance in the Plowshares Movement.* Cambridge: Cambridge University Press, 2008.

Noble, T. C. *Memorials of the Temple Bar.* London: Diprose & Bateman, 1869.

Nordau, Max. *The Conventional Lies of Our Civilization.* Chicago: L. Schick, 1884.

Pabst, Martin. *Tram and Trolley in Africa.* Krefeld, Germany: Rohr Verlag, 1989.

Palmer, Mabel. *The History of the Indians in Natal.* Natal Regional Survey, Vol. 10. Cape Town: Oxford University Press, 1957.

Pandey, B. N. *The Indian Nationalist Movement, 1885–1947: Select Documents.* London: Macmillan, 1979.

Parel, Anthony J. (ed.). *"Hind Swaraj" and Other Writings.* Cambridge: Cambridge University Press, 1997.

Paul, John J. *The Legal Profession in Colonial South India.* Bombay: Oxford University Press, 1991.

———. "Vakils of Madras: The Rise of the Modern Legal Profession in South India." Ph.D. dissertation, University of Wisconsin–Madison, 1986.

Paxton, George. *Sonja Schlesin: Gandhi's South African Secretary.* Glasgow: Pax Books, 2006.

Payne, Robert. *The Life and Death of Mahatma Gandhi.* New York: E. P. Dutton & Co., 1969.

Pearce, Robert E. *A History of the Inns of Court and Chancery.* London: Bentley, 1848.

Pelton, Leroy H. *The Psychology of Nonviolence.* Elmsford, NY: Pergamon Press, 1974.

Pillay, Bala. *British Indians in the Transvaal: Trade, Politics and Imperial Relations, 1885–1906.* London: Longman, 1976.

Polak, H. S. L., H. N. Brailsford, and Lord Pethwick-Lawrence. *Mahatma Gandhi.* London: Odhams Press, Ltd., 1948.

Prasad, Nageshwar (ed.). *"Hind Swaraj": A Fresh Look.* New Delhi: Gandhi Peace Foundation, 1985.

Pyarelal. *Mahatma Gandhi: The Early Phase.* Ahmedabad: Navijivan, 1965.

Ransom, Josephine. *A Short History of the Theosophical Society*. Adyar, India: Theosophical Publishing Company, 1938.

Richardson, Peter. *Chinese Mine Labour in the Transvaal*. London: Macmillan, 1982.

Richardson, W. C. *A History of the Inns of Court*. Baton Rouge: Claitor, 1975.

Ringrose, Hyacinthe. *The Inns of Court*. London: Paul Musson, 1909.

Roberts, S. N. "Natal, 1830–1909." In H. F. Mellet, Susan Scott, and Paul van Warmelo (eds.). *Our Legal Heritage*. Durban, South Africa: Butterworth, 1982.

Rudolph, Lloyd, and Susanne Hoeber Rudolph. *Postmodern Gandhi and Other Essays*. Chicago: University of Chicago Press, 2006.

Saunders, Christopher, and Nicholas Southey. *Historical Dictionary of South Africa*. Lanham, MD: Scarecrow Press, 2000.

Schmitthener, Samuel. "A Sketch of the Development of the Legal Profession in India." 3 *Law and Society Review* 339 (1968–1969).

Selvan, R. L. *Early Days at the Johannesburg Bar*. http://www.johannesburgbar.co.za/earlydays.html.

Sharma, Suresh, and Tridip Suhrud (eds.). *MK Gandhi's "Hind Swaraj": A Critical Edition*. New Delhi: Orient BlackSwan, 2010.

Sharp, Gene. *Waging Nonviolent Struggle: 20th Century Practice and 21st Century Potential*. Boston: Porter Sargent, 2005.

Snell, Edmund H. T. *The Principles of Equity Intended for the Use of Students and Practitioners*. 6th ed. London: Stevens & Haynes, 1882.

Spear, Percival (ed.). *The Oxford History of India*. New Delhi: Oxford University Press, 1981.

Spiller, Peter. *A History of the District and Supreme Courts of Natal (1846–1910)*. Durban, South Africa: Butterworth, 1986.

Spit, Tony, and Brian Patton. *Johannesburg Tramways: A History of the Tramways of the City of Johannesburg*. London: Light Railway Transport League, 1976.

Stanton, Elizabeth Cady, Susan B. Anthony, and Matilda Joslyn Gage (eds.). *The History of Woman Suffrage*. New York: National American Woman Suffrage Association, 1881.

Swan, Maureen. *Gandhi: The South African Experience*. Johannesburg: Ravan Press, 1985.

Tendulkar, D. G. *Mahatma: Life of Mohandas Karamchand Gandhi*. New Delhi: Government of India, 1951.

Thompson, Leonard. *A History of South Africa*. New Haven: Yale University Press, 1990.

VerSteeg, Russ. *The Essentials of Greek and Roman Law*. Durham, NC: Carolina Academic Press, 2010.

Warmelo, Paul van. "Roman-Dutch Law." In H. F. Mellet, Susan Scott, and Paul van Warmelo (eds.), *Our Legal Heritage*. Durban, South Africa: Buttersworth, 1982.

Washbrook, D. A. "Law, State and Agrarian Society in Colonial India." 15 *Modern Asian Studies* 649 (1981).

Washington, James M. (ed.). *A Testament of Hope: The Essential Writings of Martin Luther King, Jr.* San Francisco: Harper & Row, 1986.

Weber, Thomas. "Gandhian Philosophy, Conflict Resolution Theory and Practical Approaches to Negotiation." *Journal of Peace Research*, Vol. 38, No. 4 (July 2001): 493–513.

———. *Going Native: Gandhi's Relationship with Western Women.* New Delhi: Lotus, 2011.

———. *On the Salt March: The Historiography of Gandhi's March to Dandi.* New Delhi: Rupa & Co., 2009.

Welsh, Frank. *A History of South Africa.* London: HarperCollins, 2000.

Wolpert, Stanley A. *Gandhi's Passion.* New York: Oxford University Press, 2001.

———. *Tilak and Gokhale.* Berkeley: University of California Press, 1962.

ACKNOWLEDGMENTS

I consider myself very fortunate to have had the help of many kind and generous people over the many years during which this book was written. I will start by thanking my research assistants, who helped me sift through more than ten thousand issues of South African newspapers. Without their assistance this book would not have been possible. I enjoyed the camaraderie and benefited from the analytic skills of Professors Tom Carney and Nameeta Mathur, who, as young history doctoral students at West Virginia University, served as my first researchers. They were followed by a long line of talented and dedicated students, almost all of them law students from West Virginia University: William Adams, Molly Aderholt, Amanda Alderman, John-Mark Atkinson, Matthew Becker, Sara Bird, Emily Bish, Phillip Cantrell (history, WVU), Amber Cook, Natalie Crites, Maura DiSalvo (history, Minnesota; law, Aberystwyth), Leslie Dillon, James Domzalski (law, Duke), Brad Dorsey, Matthew Elshiaty, Elizabeth Fayette, Jenny Flanigan, Sallie Godfrey, Sara Beth Harkless, Matthew Hickman, Philip Isner, Justin Jack, Heather Laick, Cassandra Means, Leslie Miller-Stover, Daniel Minardi, Leckta Poling, Christopher Prezioso, Wendy Radcliff, Steve Rao, Molly Russell, Jacob Shaffer, Stephanie Shepherd, Amy Skinner, Amanda Steiner, Woodrow Turner, Jason Wandling, and Tamara Williamson.

The staff of the College of Law Library at West Virginia University, under the leadership of Camille Riley and Susan Wolford, was endlessly patient with my requests for assistance. I have also been privileged to work with the most cooperative and helpful secretaries, assistants, budget officers, and IT specialists. Those who have sat in the Dean's chair at the West Virginia University College of Law gave me, year in and year out, the support I needed to complete this project: Teree Foster, John Fisher, and Joyce McConnell. I have Dean Carl Selinger to thank for nominating me to the professorship I hold; the research and travel assistance made possible by the Woodrow A. Potesta Professorship was key to this work.

Professor Jonathan Klaaren of the University of the Witwatersrand was kind enough to put me in touch with one of his very capable law students, Joel Kimutai, for the purpose of unearthing the records of the Transvaal Law Society. Mary Bruce of the Kwa-Zulu Natal Law Society was enormously helpful in finding documents relating to the practice of law in Natal during Gandhi's time. I am grateful to Burnett Britton, Judith Brown, Margaret Chatterjee, E. S. Reddy, and Peter Spiller for generously lending their expertise along the way. Thanks to Sailaja Gullapalli of Gandhi Smriti & Darshan Samiti, Eric Itzkin, then Curator of Museum Africa, Rebecca Naidoo of the Durban Local History Museum, Antoinette Pieterse of the National Library of South Africa, Julie Preston of University College London, and Anupama Srivastava of the National Gandhi Museum for their assistance.

For my introduction to the community of Gandhi scholars, I am in the debt of Professors Debjani Ganguly of the Australian National University and Tara Sethia of California State Polytechnic University at Pomona for inviting me to speak at Gandhi conferences at their respective institutions. It was at Cal-Poly Pomona that I met Professors Anthony Parel and Lloyd Rudolph, whose encouragement I have much appreciated. And it was at ANU that I met Tridip Suhrud, now the director of the Gandhi Sabarmati Ashram in Ahmedabad, India. Professor Suhrud was very kind in arranging my research stay at Sabarmati, where Amrut Modi, Kinnari Bhatt, and the very accommodating staff made me feel at home. Dr. V. K. Raju, ever thoughtful, and Dr. Tejas Shah provided me with logistical help for my visit.

My West Virginia University colleagues graciously lent their substantive expertise, critical eyes, and moral support. I am most appreciative of our faculty and staff; they are like a second family.

For their comments on the manuscript, I thank Robert Bastress, Forest Bowman, Allan Karlin, Paul Kellogg, George Record, John Rosenberg, Emily Spieler, and Renee Wolf.

I owe an enormous debt of gratitude to the distinguished Gandhi scholar Thomas Weber, recently retired from his post at LaTrobe University in Melbourne, Australia. From early on, he has been unstintingly generous in offering both wise advice and much-appreciated encouragement. I cannot thank him adequately. Any mistakes in the manuscript should be attributed to my failure to consult Tom on an issue or to listen to him carefully enough when I did.

Thanks go to Professor Michael Blumenthal for introducing me to Nat Sobel, to Nat for believing in the book, and to Nat's associates Julie Stevenson and Adia Wright and co-agent Arabella Stein for their help. I am grateful to UCP's Reed Malcolm for his enthusiasm for the manuscript and to Steven Baker, Stacy Eisenstark, Elena McAnespie, and Jessica Moll for their good work.

To my children, Clare, Maura, and Phil, I say thank you for so graciously allowing me to bring Gandhi home to dinner every night as you were growing up. Had he been present in body as well as spirit, I think he would have enjoyed discussing the law, politics, and morality with you as much as I did.

To my good fortune and with one exception, there are many other family members and friends who are truly too numerous to thank individually. The exception is Kathleen Kennedy.

She is the best in-house editor a spouse could have—sharp eyes and a warm, generous, and caring spirit. This book is hers as much as it is mine.

Abdulla, Cassim, 75–77, 285n19

Abdulla, Dada, 29, 36–48, 77, 155; character reference from, 56; and Escombe, 54; farewell party for Gandhi, 48; and Gandhi as "white elephant," 38–39, 48; as Gandhi's client, 61–62, 66, 284nn47–48; strong backer of Gandhi, 52

Abdulla v. Mohamed, 39, 41–47, 155; and accounts, 39, 41–42, 281n10; and arbitration, 42, 44–47, 281n12; award paid in installments, 46–47, 281n18; documents seized, 44–45, 47; facts of case, 45–46; Gandhi's reflections on, 45–47

Academy of Change (Egypt), xxviii

acquittals: and resistance to registration, 194, 201–2, 234–35, 245, 250, 252, 305n19; and Sorabji case, 234–35, 305n19

Adam, Abdulla Hajee, 44

Adam, Ismail Hajee, 72, 285nn9–11

Adam, Moosa Hajee, 56, 114–16

Adams, James Matthew, 85–93, 286nn4–5, 287n12

Adams case, 85–94, 286nn4–7, 287n12, 287nn16–17; rupees and pounds, 86, 91–92; and trust, 91

adoption, 18

adversary system, xv–xvi, 258, 260; and adversarial speech, 26

advocates, 54–55, 59, 283n25, 307n56; and criminal prosecutions, 177; and dual practice, 55, 59, 162; Leonard as, 166; licenses for, 54, 282n19; and "right of

audience," 162; in Transvaal, 161–62, 166. *See also* barristers

affidavits, 153, 224; and *Adams* case, 87–88; and Gandhi's admission to bar, 56–57

African Americans, xvii, 154

Africans. *See* native Africans

Afrikaners, 146–150, 157, 159–160, 164. *See also* Boers

agricultural lands: in India, 24; in Natal, 31–35, 37–38, 51, 106

Ahmedabad Ashram, xi, xxiii, 297n54

Alam, Mir, 220

Alexander, Jane, 100, 288n17

Alexander, Richard, 81–83, 100–101, 288n17

Allahabad, 97

Allinson, Thomas R., 21

Ally, H. O., 188–89, 198–99, 308n16

Amod, Dawjee, 307n55

anarchism, 255

Anderson, Hugh, 112

Anthony, Susan B., xvii

anti-Indian law (Transvaal), 129–130, 139, 293n22; and Asiatic Department, xv, 160–61, 164–65, 175, 261; and Asiatic Trading Commission, 167–170; and Bazaar Notice (Government Notice 356), 160, 167; IRA (Immigration Restriction Act), 203, 206–7, 224, 232–33, 289n13; Law 3 (1885), 148–158, 160, 166–173, 293n22. *See also* Asiatic Act

anti-Indian legislation (Natal), 104–26, 285n7; IRA (Immigration Restriction Act), 105–6, 112–13; litigation against,

anti-Indian legislation *(continued)*
112–126; losing battle against, 126–28,
131, 135, 178, 292n29, 293n22; petitions
against, 107–10, 119, 126, 289n13; Quarantine Act, 105–6, 113; as "un-British,"
109, 111, 118–19, 289n13; Uncovenanted
Indians Act, 105–6, 109, 113. *See also*
DLA (Dealers' Licenses Act)
anti-Indian mob, 97–103; and beating of
Gandhi, 100–102, 288n16; concessions
to, 116; fears about plague, 97–98;
Gandhi's refusal to prosecute, 101–3,
288n17
April 6 Movement, xxviii
Arab Spring, xviii, xxvii–xxviii
arbitration: and *Abdulla v. Mohamed*, 42,
44–47, 281n12; and Camrooden partnership case, 132–33; and Law 3 (1885),
150–53, 294n13; in Natal, 127, 132–33; in
Transvaal, 42, 44–47, 150, 281n12
architects, European, 128
Arnold, Edwin, Sir, 13
Arookian, 69–70, 75, 285n4
arranged marriage, 2–3, 5
arrests: of Baker, 44, 47; of Christian
Indians, 81–82; of Gandhi, xxiii–xxiv,
47, 201, 203–4, 209, 212, 214, 246–47,
255; of Gandhi, Harilal, 243; of Gandhi's assailants, 220; of Gani, 184; of
indentured Indians, 105–6; in India,
xxiii–xxiv; of Indian workers, 74–75; in
Natal, 60, 74–75, 81–82; of Ramsundar,
191; of Ratanshi Sodha, 262; and resistance to registration, 189, 191, 201–4,
209, 212–14, 221, 229, 233–35, 237, 244,
246–47, 251, 255, 305n16; and Salt
Campaign, xxiii–xxiv; and Sorabji case,
233–35, 305n16; and tramcars, 184;
wrongful arrests, 105–6
artisans, 97, 130
Asiatic Act (Asiatic Law Amendment
Ordinance), 186–248; arbitrary administration of, 238–39; and border-crossing
resistance, 242–46, 261, 306n45,
306n48, 307n55; and burning of registration certificates, 229–233, 305nn12–
13; and children, 261; and compromise,
199, 211–12, 223, 233, 238; and deporta-

tion, 190, 203, 207–11, 213–14, 301n22;
as derogatory to manhood, 208, 212, 231,
301n32; and educated Indians, 219, 230,
232, 234–36; and Empire Theatre meeting, 186–190; enforcement of, 199–215;
and fingerprinting, 186, 206, 210–11,
219–220, 229, 238–240, 246–47,
299n23; and Gandhi's London trip
(1906), 180, 198, 298n17, 300n2; and
Gandhi's pledge to defend resisters,
200–203, 301n16, 301n19; and immigration ban, 230, 232; and Indian pickets,
251–52; and intimidation by countrymen, 210–11; and jail-going resolutions/
pledges, 189–190, 200, 202, 212; and
jailings, 186–87, 189–191, 194–96,
200–202, 208, 212, 214–18, 221–22, 224,
227–29, 232, 235–243, 249–251, 254–55,
261–62, 302n1, 305n26, 309n41; letters
concerning, 217–19, 221, 224–25,
302nn3–4, 303n5; and list of exempt
Indians, 238–240; as offensive to religion, 193, 206, 208–11, 299n40, 301n32,
301n40; petitions against, 224–25, 229,
304n35; and property owners, 219; and
Ramsundar case, 191–96, 299n33,
299n40; and registration deadlines,
234–35; and registration period, 199,
207, 228–29; repeal of, 212, 217–19,
221–25, 230–32, 302n4, 303n5, 303n10,
303n12; and resistance as religious
struggle, 193, 206, 208–11, 231, 251,
299n40, 301n32, 301n40; and return of
application papers, 223–25, 229, 249,
303nn35–36; and right of return,
305n10; and settlement, 216–223, 225–
26, 230; and Sorabji case, 233–35; and
supplemental registration, 230; suspension of, 212, 217; and trading without
licenses cases, 237–242, 252–53,
305nn25–26, 306nn33–34, 308n6; and
Validation Act, 230–31; and voluntary
registration, 199, 212, 217, 219, 221,
223–25, 229–230, 233, 254, 259
"Asiatic question," 96, 105, 207, 211
Askew, Oswald, 65, 79
assault, 28, 61, 72, 77
Aswat, Ebrahim Ismail, 224–25

Attenborough, Richard, 1
attorneys, 53–55, 59, 283n25; and dual
    practice, 55, 59, 162; Gandhi as, 162,
    300n9; instructing attorneys, 166,
    171–72, 300n9; Polak as, 221; in Trans-
    vaal, 161–62, 166, 171–72, 300n9. *See
    also* solicitors; *names of attorneys*
auctioneers, 72, 285nn9–11
automobiles, 134

Bacon, Francis, 216
bail, 191; for Baker, 44; for Dundee Indi-
    ans, 112–13; for Gandhi, 247, 254
Baker, Albert Weir, 42–45, 47, 55, 99,
    281n14
Balasundaram, 63–67, 79, 112, 292n17
Bale, Henry, 68, 76, 107, 135
Ball, William, 7, 10
bankruptcy, 46, 60, 73, 135; of Cachalia,
    253; death preferred to, 46; and *Lucas'
    Trustee v. Ismail and Amod,* 166–67;
    and resistance to registration, 221,
    253–54, 308n10; and Scheurmann, 66
bar, 5–7; admission to in Natal, 52, 54–61,
    70, 282n18, 283nn20–22, 283n27,
    283n31, 284n40; admission to in Trans-
    vaal, 43, 156, 161–63, 171–72, 221,
    303n22; and apprenticeships, 7, 11, 16, 18,
    278n31; being called to bar, 5, 7–8, 11–12,
    17, 26, 52, 56, 128, 162, 276n6; elitist
    traditions of, 5–7; European, 39, 48, 54;
    examinations for, 5, 7–11, 13, 15–16, 55,
    59, 221, 277nn23–24, 277n29; in India,
    18; joint bar for attorneys/advocates,
    54–55; and partnerships, 52–54; women
    excluded from, 276n6, 284n40
Barker, Ernest, Sir, 309n24
barristers: and apprenticeships, 7, 11, 16, 18,
    278n31; encouraged by Gandhi to
    immigrate, 84, 101, 139, 144; fees of, 23,
    28–29, 54, 61, 133, 279n18; Gandhi as,
    xiv–xv, 3, 12, 16–20, 24–25, 27–29, 36,
    38, 50, 52–55, 64, 94, 96, 283n20,
    307n56; in India, 22–25, 27–29, 84, 101,
    139, 144, 279n18, 279n20; Indian, 24, 37,
    53–55, 64, 94, 96, 101, 283n20; and Inns
    of Court, 5–6, 8, 11, 50; Khan as, 128; in
    Natal, 36–38, 52–56, 60, 64, 94, 283n20;

privileged status of, 12; in South Africa,
    xiv–xv, 29–30; in Transvaal, 42, 162,
    183–84; unseemly to perform transla-
    tion work, 80
baskets, 237
Bawazeer and Others, Rex v., 238
beatings, xxv; of Balasundaram, 63, 65; of
    Gandhi, xv, 40–41, 43, 99–102, 220–21,
    288n16, 303n19; threats of, 77
Becharji Swami, 4
Bechuanaland, 147
Bedat v. Akoom, 79–80
Bennett, Thomas, 75–76
Besant, Annie, 13, 278n35, 278n37
Bhagavad Gita, 13, 178–79
Bhavnagar, 2
BIA (British Indian Association), 184,
    188, 298n7, 298n17; and "on advice of
    counsel" defense, 201–2; and Aswat,
    224; and border-crossing resistance,
    244; and burning of registration
    certificates, 230–31; Gandhi's role in,
    205; and trading without licenses, 253,
    305n25
Bible, 216
Birdwood, George, Sir, 49
birth control, 21
black flags, 214
Blavatsky, Helena Petrovna, 12–13, 278n36
Bloemfontein Award, 154
Boers, xiii, 111, 128, 130, 139, 146. *See also*
    Afrikaners
Boer War, 130–33, 139, 147–48, 157, 160,
    291n12; and Camrooden partnership
    case, 129; and Indian Ambulance
    Corps, 130–31, 133, 197; Indian loyalty
    to Britain during, 130–31, 197; and
    Smuts, 218
Bombay, xx, 3–4, 47, 143; and *Adams* case,
    85–92, 286n5; Aga Khan building, 143;
    Gandhi's 1896 visit to, 95–96, 103;
    Gandhi's departure from, 35; Gandhi's
    home in, 144; Gandhi's law practice in,
    18–19, 22–26, 52, 55, 138, 141–45; High
    Court, 18–19, 22–23, 55–56, 143, 162;
    high school teaching position in, 26;
    Small Cause Court, 19–20, 279n8
Bombay University matriculation exam, 2, 8

bookkeeping, 39; and DLA, 106, 113, 116, 290n50; required to be in English, 106, 113, 118, 121, 123, 290n50
border-crossing resistance, 242–46, 306n45, 306n48, 307n55; and Ramb-habai, 261
boycotts, xxiv
bribery, 164–65, 178
Brice, Seward, 166
Brighton, 10
Britain: and common law, 8, 10, 58–59, 262, 277n24, 283n36; and fair play, xiii, xxi, 60, 107, 172, 289n13; High Court, 17; House of Commons, xxiii; Parliament, 62; Union Jack, 189, 195, 231; and upper-class mores, 12. *See also entries beginning with* British colonial government
British colonial government, xiii, xix–xx; and Boer War, 129–133, 139, 147–48, 157, 160, 180, 291n12; Colonial Office, 32, 34, 108–10, 147, 255; and *Hind Swaraj,* 256; Imperial Conference, 209; Privy Council Judicial Committee, 117, 126, 291n2; Protector of Immigrants, 63–65, 73–74; Queen's Counsel, 57; Queen's Proclamation (1858), 111; secretary of state for colonies, 50–51, 78, 84, 101, 108–12, 123–24, 139, 144, 147, 152, 167, 199; undersecretary of state for colonies, 198; and Union of South Africa, 255. *See also entries beginning with* British colonial government; *names of British officials*
British colonial government (India), xix–xxv, 11, 18, 22, 24, 28–29
British colonial government (Natal): and anti-Indian legislation, 108–12, 117–19, 123–24, 126, 291n2; and indentured Indians, 31–34; and Indian Ambulance Corps, 130; and Indian franchise, 50–51; and legal system, 58–59; and responsible government model, 32–34, 105, 280n3; and rickshaws, 135; and Zulu Rebellion, 180, 193
British colonial government (Transvaal), 43, 129–130, 139, 146–47, 293n22; and Asiatic Act, 186–248; and Asiatic Department, xv, 160–61, 164–65, 175, 261; and Asiatic Trading Commission,

167–170; and Law 3 (1885), 148–158, 160, 164, 167, 173, 293n22; Registrar of Asiatics, xv, 192, 219, 251–54; and resistance to registration, 186–89, 194–95, 197–98, 206, 231, 242–44, 246, 251–52, 306n51; and responsible government model, 198, 300n1
British Indian Association. *See* BIA
British Indians, xxi, 73, 111, 151, 170, 186, 203, 254
Britton, Burnett, 282n12
Brougham, Lord, 177, 297n63
Brown, Judith, xxiii, xxvi
"brown skin," 235
Buddhism, 309n30
Budree, 174, 297nn53–54
Burma, 141
Burns, Robert, 216

Cachalia, Adam Mahomed, 253, 308n10
Cadir, Abdul, 123
Cairo (Egypt), xxviii
Calcutta, 139–140; High Court, 22
Caliphate movement (1920s), xxii
Cambridge, 218
Camroodeen, In Re Regina v., 76–77
Camroodeen, Mohamed, 77
Camrooden and Company, 129, 132–33, 135, 188; dunning of, 141
Camrooden partnership case, 129, 132–33, 135; and *curator bonis* (guardian of property), 129; dissolution of, 129, 133, 135
Cape Colony, 31–32, 59, 129, 146–47, 255; Rhodes as prime minister of, 147
Cape of Good Hope, 32, 58; Colonial Office, 32, 34
Cape Times, 153, 218
Cape Town, 230, 265
capitalism: and India, 24; and Natal, 32–33
Carlyle, Thomas, 216
Cartwright, Albert, 217–18, 222, 235, 302n3
Cassim Abdulla v. Bennett, 75–77, 285n19
castes, 4–5, 50; elections held in, 50; Gandhi as outcast, 4–5
celibacy, 180, 200
Central South African Railway, 203

certificates: for admission to bar, 55–57, 283n22; of admission to Inner Temple, 55–57, 162, 283n22; and border-crossing resistance, 243–46; burning of, 229–233, 305nn12–13; of good character, 55–56, 233–34; from Natal Supreme Court, 161–62; original certificates, 55–57; proof of good standing, 161–62; registration certificates, 186, 189, 191, 204, 206, 210, 229–233, 243–46. *See also* licenses; permits

Chamberlain, Joseph: and anti-Indian legislation, 108–12, 123–24, 139, 154–55; and beating of Gandhi, 101–2; and Boer War, 147–48; and Indian franchise, 84; visit to South Africa, 144, 159, 161, 165

Chamney, Montfort, xv, 192, 219–220, 222–23, 225; and Krugersdorp case, 260; and Sorabji case, 233–35

Charlestown, 39–40, 75

Chinese, 32, 147, 165; and DLA, 114; and resistance to registration, 204, 209–11, 217, 230, 301n26

Chinese Association, 209

Chotabhai, A. E., 261

Chotabhai, Mahomed, 261–62

Christians: being faithful to gospel, xvi–xvii; and Christ, 173; Christian Indians, 81–83; encouraging Gandhi to convert, 43–44; and *Hind Swaraj,* 258, 309n30; in Pretoria, 43–44; and resistance to registration, 204

Churchill, Winston, 198

civil disobedience, xii–xviii, xxii–xxviii, 1, 266–67; advancing debate, xvii, 242–44, 246, 252, 305n28; berating in court for, 80; and border-crossing resistance, 242–48, 307n55; burning of registration certificates, 229–233, 305nn12–13; and "conscientious objection," 303n24; experimenting with, 190–96, 250–54; failure of during World War II, xxvi; in India, xxii–xxv, xxii–xxvii; and Indian workers in Natal, 74–75; and jail-going resolutions/pledges, 189–190, 200, 202; and location restrictions, 169–172, 176; narrow analytic framework for, 205;

and resistance to registration, 180, 189–190, 205, 216–17, 227–28, 230–38, 240–48, 250–54; as route to success, 190–91; and Salt Campaign, xxii–xxvi, 276n11; and Sorabji case, 233–38, 243, 246, 250, 257; and trading without licenses cases, 237–242, 252–54, 305nn25–26, 306nn33–34, 308n6, 308n10; and tramcars, 182, 185, 228

civil liberties in India, xxii, xxiv–xxv

civil rights, Indian, xiii–xv, 139, 262; and Boer War, 130; in Natal, 75–77, 80, 84, 94, 126, 128, 130, 133; in Transvaal, 161

civil rights lawyers, 164, 187

class, social: and Asiatic Act, 211; and discrimination, 153–54, 294nn27–28; in Transvaal, 153–54, 211, 294nn27–28

Classification and Uses of Finger Prints (Henry), 186

closing arguments: and *Adams* case, 90–91; and adversarial speech, 26; and *Arookian* case, 69; and resistance to registration, 206; and trading without licenses cases, 239

Clyde, SS, 1, 4–5, 13–14, 20, 276n1

Coakes, Percy Evans, 52–54, 60–62, 282n13; and DLA, 289n27; ethical troubles of, 60, 67–68, 70–71, 93–94; father of, 68, 284n2; money-lending practices of, 60, 68, 285n4; negotiating with, 53–54, 61, 222; as notary, 284n1; partnership with Gandhi, 52–54, 60–62, 64, 67–68, 284nn47–48; resumption of practice, 79

coal, 73–74

coercion, 252–53, 308n6

coffee, 32

Coke, Lord, 8

The Collected Works of Mahatma Gandhi, 45, 108, 127

common law: Inner Temple focused on, 8, 10; and Rambhabai, 262; and Roman-Dutch law tradition, 58–59, 277n24, 283n36

complaint: and Balasundaram, 63–64; and Indian law, 18; and Indian workers, 74; petition much like, 49; and tramcars, 182–83 compromise, 132, 171, 266; and Asiatic Act, 199, 211–12, 223, 233

confidence, xiv–xv; and *Abdulla* case, 46–47; and Bombay law practice, 141–43; and Indian franchise, 49; and Mamibai case, 19; and negotiations, 53; and partnership with Coakes, 53; and petitions, 49; and public speaking, 96; and Transvaal law practice, 161

conflicts of interest, 79–80

conscience: acting in concert with, xvi–xvii, xviii, 231; and Natal, 36, 50, 67–68; passive resistance based on, xxi; and Sorabji case, 236; and Transvaal, 231, 236, 247, 252, 254

consent of governed, xviii, xxv, xxvii, 246, 252; and resistance to registration, 227–28, 242–43, 275n6

contracts, 55, 135, 166, 174, 190

conversion, 43–44; of Christian Indians, 81–82

conveyances, 7, 16, 127

convicts, 32

"coolies," 148–49, 156

Coovadia, Ebrahim Saleji, 182–84, 187, 298n7, 298n14

corruption: in Asiatic Permit Office, 164–65, 175–76, 249, 296n22; in Indian legal system, 27, 29

cotton, 32

Council of the Incorporated Law Society of the Transvaal, 163

counterclaims, 85, 87–88, 92, 287n17; as "claim in reconvention," 87, 287n9

courage, xiv, 21, 96–97; of Baker, 47; of Gandhi's refusal to prosecute attackers, 102–3; of Indian workers, 74; and resistance to registration, 187, 200, 202, 212, 216, 228, 241; in taking on judges, 71, 78

Courland, SS: and *Adams* case, 85–91, 287n12, 287n16; Gandhi's family aboard, 98–99; and petitions, 108–9; provisions for, 86–89, 91–92; and quarantine crisis, 98, 101–2, 104, 287n7

Cramer, A. J., 235, 239

creditors and debtors, 60, 63, 73; and trading without licenses cases, 252–53

criminal prosecutions, xv–xvi; and Coakes, 60; Gandhi's refusal to prosecute attackers, 101–3, 220, 288n17, 303n21; and guilty defendants, 69–70, 177–78, 297n66; in India, 25; and Indian workers, 75; in Natal, 60, 62–63, 67, 69–70, 75, 77, 128, 177–78; to test law, xvii, 43, 182; for trading without licenses, 237–240, 306nn33–34; and tramcars, 182; in Transvaal, 174, 176–78, 182, 201, 237–241, 251–52, 306nn33–34; and witness intimidation, 77

cross-examination: and adversarial speech, 26; and border-crossing resistance, 244, 247, 307n55; of Christian Indians, 81–82; first rule of, 69; in Mamibai's case, 20–21; and irrelevant testimony, 77, 192–93; and Ramsundar case, 192–93; and Sorabji case, 233–35; and trading without licenses cases, 239

curator bonis (guardian of property), 129

Curtis, Lionel, 198

customs regulations, 44

Dada, Haji, 56

Dada Abdulla and Company, 29–30, 38–39, 41, 45, 66; and *Adams* case, 85–87, 89, 91, 286n4, 287n12, 287n17; and DLA, 128–29; and Laughton, 99

da Gama, Vasco, 31

Dalmahoy, P. C., 240–41

Dandi, xxiii–xxiv, 227

Danish population in World War II, xviii

Dave, Kevalram Mavji, 2, 142–43

Dawje, Hassan, 70

Dealers' Licenses Act. *See* DLA

DeBeers Consolidated, 147

decision-makers, pressure on, xiv, 227–28, 242, 245

Delagoa Bay, 89–90, 263–64, 286n4

demonstration effect, 165, 303n7

Denoon, Donald, 295n1

deportation orders, 190, 208–11; and border-crossing resistance, 243, 306n48; and children, 261; and Gandhi, 207, 213–14, 254; and Gandhi, Harilal, 243; and Gandhi's assailants, 303n21; and IRA, 203; and Khan, Nawab, 210; and

Khan, Sumander, 211; Leonard's views on, 209, 301n22; and resisters denied permission to land, 263–65; and Sorabji, 236

Desai, M. I., 204

de Villiers, Melius, 150–52, 154

De Waal, D., 225

Dharasana Salt Works, xxiv

dhoby (washerman), 81, 286n35

diamond production, 147

dignity, 90, 103, 170

Dillon, James Francis, 62, 72–74

discrimination: and Freedom Riders, xviii; in Louisiana public library, xvii; in Natal, 107, 123–24, 126, 134–35; and native Africans, 153–54, 294nn27–28; and rickshaws, 134–35; in South African Republic, 147–49, 153–54, 156, 159–160; and tramcars, 181–85; in Transvaal, 147–49, 153–54, 156, 159–160, 164, 178, 181–85, 232, 296n18; in U.S., xvii–xviii. *See also* prejudice; race relations/racism

divorce law, 73, 285n14

DLA (Dealers' Licenses Act), 105–11, 113–125, 249, 289n12; appeals barred by, 107, 109, 111, 113–126, 290n50; arbitrary denials permitted by, 106, 113–125, 178, 291n58; bookkeeping in English required by, 106, 113, 116, 121, 123, 290n50; designed to put Indians out of business, 107; and "desirability," 122–24; and licensing officers, 106–7, 109, 113–125, 291n58; litigation against, 113–125, 172; losing battle against, 126–28, 131, 135, 178, 292n29, 293n22; petitions against, 108–11; and sanitary conditions, 106, 110, 113, 117, 122–24; and town councils, 106–7, 113–14, 116–122, 126, 290n41, 290n50, 291n57

Doke, Joseph, 220

Douglas, W. M., Rev. and Mrs., 69

drafting work, 7, 26–27, 30, 55, 61, 142–43

drums, 73

due process, 107, 111, 120–22, 125

Dundee Indians, 112–13

Durban, 31, 36–40, 47; and *Adams* case, 85–92, 286n5; anti-Indian mob in, 97–101; Beach Grove Villa, 52, 61, 93, 98; Circuit Court, 66, 79, 86, 132; Congress Hall, 93; Criminal Court, 62; and curfew passes, 81–82; fruit auction, 72; German Cafe, 66; Indian Committee, 48; and interpreters, 37–38, 52; lacking a law library, 60, 284n44; mayor of, 114, 118, 122; mosque in, 114–15; Pine Street, 62; port of, 98, 263–64; and rickshaws, 100, 134; Stanger Street, 100; Town Council, 114, 117–125, 134–35, 290n41, 290n50, 291n57; Town Hall, 122; town solicitor, 119–120, 290n42; West Street, 81, 100, 114–15

Dutch, xiii, 31–32, 44, 58, 146, 280n1

Dyer, W. H., 115, 118, 120–21

East India Company, 22

Ebrahim, Mahomed, 129

economic life: in India, 24; in Natal, 33–34, 51–52, 54, 57; in Transvaal, 152, 164; and working class, 97

education: and educated Indians, 230, 232, 234–36, 243–44, 262, 307n55; in India, xx–xxi, 276n8

Egypt, xviii, xxvii–xxviii; Academy of Change, xxviii; April 6 Movement, xxvii–xxviii; and Arab Spring, xviii, xxvii–xxviii

electricity, 181, 188

elites: "commercial elite," 34; elitist traditions of bar, 5–7, 12; in India, xx–xxi, 24; landed elites, 24; in Natal, 34–35, 52

Emerson, Ralph Waldo, 171

Empire Theatre meeting, 186–190

England: and abstention from wine/meat/women, 4, 12–15, 22, 278n33; legal education in, xiii–xiv, xx–xxi, 2–11, 277n10, 277n12, 277nn16–18; life and customs of, 8–15, 17; steamer to, 1, 4–5, 13–14, 20, 276n1

English language, 8–9, 20, 29; and DLA, 106, 113, 116, 121, 123, 290n50; Gandhi's fear of speaking, 14, 16; *Hind Swaraj* translated into, 255; and IRA, 106, 232–33; and Maharaj, 121; in Natal, 62–63; and Osman, 123

entrepreneurs, Indian, 34, 37; and DLA, 105, 107, 289n12; in Transvaal, 155

Erikson, Erik H., 309n35

Escombe, Harry, 54, 56–57, 61, 282n17, 283n27; and anti-Indian mob, 98–102, 104; and Boer War, 130

Esselen, Ewald, 150

Estcourt, 75–76

evidence, 26; and *Abdulla* case, 76; and *Adams* case, 86–90, 286n6; and *Arookian* case, 69; and Asiatic Department, 165; and border-crossing resistance, 243–44, 247, 307n55; and de Villiers' arbitration, 151; and DLA, 120; in extenuation, 205, 238, 241, 243–45, 307n55; and *Gandhi, Rex v.*, 205; Indian Evidence Act, 18, 142; and Jamnagar case, 142; Mehta's mastery of evidence law, 18, 142; in Natal, 55, 59, 64, 69, 76, 86–90; and Ramsundar case, 193–94; and Sorabji case, 233–35; and trading without licenses cases, 237–38; in Transvaal, 151, 165, 193–94, 205, 233–35, 237–38, 243–45

exchange rate, 86, 91

facts of case, 45–46, 89, 123; and *Gandhi, Rex v.*, 205; and Ramsundar case, 192–93; and Sorabji case, 236; and tramcars, 182

fair play, xiii, xxi, 60, 107, 172, 289n13

famine, Indian, 133, 292n19

Farman, Ernest: and *Adams* case, 85, 87–92; and Coakes, 68; on Durban Town Council, 121

farms, communal, 175, 178, 265, 300n9, 310n47

Feetham, Richard, 183–84

fines: and DLA, 115; and Indian workers, 74; and *Moosa* case, 115; in Natal, 62, 74, 115; and Rambhabai, 262, 309n41; and Salt Campaign, xxiv; for trading without licenses, 238–240, 252, 306n33; and tramcars, 184; in Transvaal, 170, 184, 186, 190, 194, 214, 238–240, 252, 254, 306n33

fingerprinting, 186, 206, 210–11, 219–220, 229, 246–47, 299n23; list of exemptions from, 238–240; and thumb-impression requirement, 238–39, 247

Finnemore (Justice), 116–17, 120

firewood, 73–74

"The Foods of India" (Gandhi speech), 15

Fordsburg mosque, 195, 209–10, 230

forgeries, 211

formative experiences, 31, 67–83, 85

Fortescue, John, Sir, 5–6

forum for test cases, xvii; and Sorabji case, 233; and tramcars, 185

franchise, Indian: and Coakes, 53, 60, 282n13; in India, 51; letters concerning, 50; in Natal, 34, 48–51, 53, 60, 84, 282n2; petitions against Franchise Law Amendment Bill, 49–51, 282n5, 282n7; questions concerning, 50

freedom, 267; in India, xxiii, 80; and resistance to registration, 186–87, 194–95, 207–9, 211

Freedom Riders, xxvi

free Indians: coming out of indenture, 33–34, 105–6, 108, 111, 119, 126, 130–31, 147, 281n14; and Indian Ambulance Corps, 130; tax on, 106; in Transvaal, 147; and Uncovenanted Indians Act, 105–6

French language, 9, 133

From Dictatorship to Democracy (Sharp), xxvii–xxviii

Gallwey, Michael: and *Abdulla* case, 76; and *Adams* case, 86, 286n7; and anti-Indian legislation, 116; and Coakes' ethical troubles, 68; and Gandhi as translator, 80; and Gandhi's admission to bar, 57, 59; and Islamic law, 70

Gandhi (film), 1

Gandhi, Chhaganlal (nephew), 161, 300n8

Gandhi, Harilal (son), 241–45, 247, 250

Gandhi, Karamchand (father), 2–5, 142

Gandhi, Kasturba (wife), 2–4; and celibacy, 180, 200; health of, 254; moving to Natal, 84; "pangs of parting" from, 30; parents of, 3–4; pregnancies of, 3–4, 276n2

Gandhi, Lakshmidas (brother), 2–4, 17, 23, 25–29, 38; as vakil, 23, 27–28

Gandhi, Mohandas K., xii–xvi, xviii–xxii, xxviii, 300n9; abandoning practice of

law, 250, 256–261, 263–67; arranged
marriage of, 2–3, 5; arrests of, xxiii–xxiv,
47, 201, 203–4, 209, 214, 246–47, 255; as
ascetic, xi–xii, 1; as "Barrister Gandhi,"
200, 247; beatings of, 99–102, 220–21,
288n16, 303n19; biographies of, xii,
xxviii, 37, 276n1; caring for sick in
hospital, 127, 131; caste of, 4–5; and
celibacy, 180, 200; and choice of career,
xiii, 2–3; as civil disobedient, xii, xxiii–
xxv, 228, 246–48, 250, 258; as civil rights
lawyer, xiii–xiv, 164, 187, 240–42, 248,
250, 252, 255, 259, 262; clothing of, 12,
36–38, 40–41; death of, xxv, 227; and
dietary restrictions, 200; as dignitary,
133; encouraging immigration to South
Africa, 84, 101, 139, 144; as "English
gentleman," 8–9, 41, 278n33; faith in
law, xiii–xiv, 169–170, 172, 178, 223, 226,
229, 266–67, 304n6; family of, 2–5, 9,
12, 84, 95, 98–99, 101, 141, 144, 241–45,
247, 249–250, 254, 276n2; father of,
2–5, 142; fear of practicing law, 62–63;
fear of public speaking, 14, 16, 20–22,
26, 30, 43, 96, 103, 139–140, 199; financial assistance to others, 133, 174–75,
179, 193n34, 249, 292n19, 297nn53–54;
health of, 2, 138–39, 141–42, 144; image
of, xi–xii, 1; jailing of, 201, 212, 214–18,
222, 224, 228, 232, 249–251, 254–55,
302n1; last case of, 262; Laughton as
mentor, 131–32, 201, 234, 263; learning
English ways, 8–15, 17; and leper, 127;
London trip concerning Asiatic Act
(1906), 180, 199, 298n17, 300n2; London
trip concerning Union of South Africa
(1909), 255, 308n16; as "person of color,"
158; photograph of, xi–xii; playing
wealthy barrister, 12, 19, 36–37, 61,
278n32; pledge to return to Natal if
needed, 143–45; professional identity of,
xiv–xvi; reading in jail, 216, 218; registration of, 220; religious explorations of,
10, 12–13, 43–45, 178–79, 218; reputation of, 29, 38, 70–71, 94, 102; responsible for family, 2–3, 12, 17, 30, 133, 141,
278n1, 292n19; return to India (1901),
136–39, 142–44; as shy and timid,

20–22, 26, 107–8, 115, 199; significance
of today, xxv–xxviii; son of, 241–45,
247, 250; and Tolstoy Farm, 265,
310n47; trip to India (1896), 65, 84, 93,
95–99; use of racial argument, 153–55;
volunteering at hospital, 127; writing
talents of, 15, 71, 96–97, 108, 155, 203, 255
Gandhi, Mohandas K., works: *The Col-
lected Works of Mahatma Gandhi,* 45,
108, 127; *The Grievances of the British
Indians in South Africa,* 97, 287n4,
287n6; *Hind Swaraj,* 255–59, 308n20;
The Law and Lawyers, xii; *My Experi-
ments with Truth,* 45, 93
Gandhi, Putli Ba (mother), 4, 14; Gandhi's
pledge to, 4, 11–15, 22
Gandhi, Rex v., 204–7, 213
Gandhi-Irwin Pact, xv, xxiv
Gani, Abdul, 184–85, 188
Garlicke, Thomas, 119–120
*General Rules for Admission . . . to the
Supreme Court of Natal,* 57, 283n29
German Cafe, 66
Germany, 218; German influences, 58;
German occupation of Denmark, xviii
Germiston, 41, 191–93, 204; courtroom,
191–92; Hindu community, 191–93;
Police Court, 191
Gertrude Woermann, SS, 263–64
Ghila, Deva, and Bhachar, Rex v., 306n34
Ghonim, Wael, xviii
gifts: at farewell ceremony in Natal, 136,
293n34; and Indian law, 18
Godfrey, George, 243, 306n50
Godfrey, William, 188
Gokhale, Gopal Krishna, 139–141, 161,
276n11
gold mining, 147
Goodricke, Laughton, and Cooke, 288n11
Gopee, Maharaj, 61
Government Gazette, 110, 186, 203, 234
Greene, Edward Mackenzie, 56–57, 76
Green Pamphlet (Gandhi), 97, 287n4,
287n6
*The Grievances of the British Indians in
South Africa* (Gandhi), 97, 287n4,
287n6
guardianship, 18

Gujarati language, 34, 39, 42, 79–80; Gandhi as licensed translator of, 80; as Gandhi's native tongue, 39, 42, 79–80; and *Hind Swaraj,* 255

Habib, Haji, 188–89, 308n16
"habitation," 149–152
Hamidia Islamic Society, 187–89, 193, 204
Hammond, Alfie, 74–75
hard labor, 106, 194, 214; and Gandhi, 214, 254; and Gandhi, Harilal, 243; and IRA, 106, 236; in Johannesburg, 305n27; and Ramsundar, 194; and Sorabji, 236; for trading without licenses, 238–39, 306nn33–34
Hathorn, Kenneth, 115
hawkers, 252; Gandhi's son as, 241; in Natal, 33–34; in Transvaal, 237–241, 305nn25–26, 306nn33–34
Heidelberg, 176
Hely-Hutchinson, Walter, Sir, 50
Henry, Edward, 186
Hills, Arnold F., 21
Hind Swaraj, 255–260, 308n20, 309n24; argument in practice, 259–260, 264
Hind Swarajya, 255. *See also Hind Swaraj*
Hindu-Muslim discord, xxii–xxiii, xxv, 42
Hindus, xxii, 1, 4; Gandhi as Hindu, xxii, 1, 4, 13, 43, 70; and *Hind Swaraj,* 258; Hindu-Muslim unity, 212; Hindu priests, 190–96; in India, 18; in Natal, 38; and theosophy, 13; in Transvaal, 42–43, 190–96; and turbans, 38
Holland, 58, 283n35
Holmes, Oliver Wendell, 258
Honey, J. W., 168
hospitals: and lepers, 127; volunteering at, 127, 131
Hunt, James, 276n1, 277n23, 277n27

ICS (Indian Civil Service), xix
immigration, Indian: and Asiatic Act, 230, 232; and educated Indians, 230, 232; "illegal," 186, 211; and Natal, 32–34, 37–38, 73, 280n10; and Quarantine Act, 105; and Ramsundar, 191; resumption of, 33–34; suspension of, 32, 280n10; and Transvaal, 154, 186, 191, 203, 218, 230, 232; and women, 33, 35; working class protests against, 97–98. *See also* IRA
Immigration Restriction Act. *See* IRA
INC (Indian National Congress), xxii–xxiv; and Besant, 278n37; disorganization of, 140; and Gandhi, 138–141; resolution in support of South African Indians, 139–140
indentured Indians, 32–35, 51, 280nn8–10, 281n12; anti-Indian protests against, 97–98; Arookian as, 69; Balasundaram as, 63–67, 79, 112, 292n17; becoming free, 33–34, 106, 108, 111, 119, 126, 131, 147, 281n14; and Boer War, 130–31; and DLA, 119, 126; father of Christian Indian as, 81; as Gandhi's clients, 63–67, 131–32, 292n17; in Indian Ambulance Corps, 130–31; and IRA, 106, 108; Maharaj as, 119; suspension of importation of, 109, 111; transfer to new master, 64–65; and Uncovenanted Indians Act, 105–6
India, xiv–xv, xix–xxvi; boycott in, xxiv; and British rule, xv, xix–xxv, 139; Caliphate movement (1920s), xxii; and constitutional reform, xxiv; and Dominion status, xxii–xxiii; Gandhi's return to (1901), 136–39, 142–44; Gandhi's touring of (1902), 141; Gandhi's visit to (1896), 65, 84, 93, 95–99; and independence, xix, xxii–xxiii, xxv; infrastructure of, xix–xx; local self-government in, 50; and Natal, 32–34; and parliamentary democracy, xix; partition of, xxv; and plague, 97–98; and representative government, 50, 84; and Round Table Conference, xxii–xxiii; and Salt Campaign, xxii–xxvi, 227–28, 276n11; Tamil-speaking area of, 63; university system in, xx–xxi, 276n8; and "untouchables," 154
Indian Ambulance Corps, 130–31, 133, 197
Indian Home Rule, 255
Indian independence movement, xiii, xxi–xxv; Dominion status vs. complete independence, xxii–xxiii; moderates vs.

extremists in, xxi; and Salt Campaign, xxii–xxvi, 276n11

Indian Law (Mayne), 18

Indian legal system, 11, 18–22; and applications, 26–27, 30; and barristers, 22–25; Bombay High Court, 18–19, 22–23, 55–56, 143, 162; British control of, 11, 18, 22, 24, 28–29; Calcutta High Court, 22; Civil Procedure Code, 18; and commissions, 27; and complaints, 18; corruption in, 27, 29; "fashionable to doze" in High Court, 19; and Gandhi, 1, 8, 11–12, 18–23; Indian Evidence Act, 18, 142; Indian High Courts Act (1861), 22, 24; Madras High Court, 22; and Mamibai case, 19–21, 25; and memorials, 25–26; and native practitioners, 22–23, 26, 279n4; and petitions, 27, 30; and referrals, 24–25, 27; Small Cause Court, 19–20, 279n8; and solicitors, 23–24, 143, 293n15; and touts, 25, 280n28; and vakils, 18, 23, 27–28

Indian movements: in Natal, 51–52; in Transvaal, 216–17, 221–22. *See also* BIA (British Indian Association); NIC (Natal Indian Congress)

Indian National Congress. *See* INC

Indian Ocean, xix

Indian Opinion, 186–87, 203, 212, 218–19; and Asiatic Trading Commission, 169–170; and border-crossing resistance, 243; and children as prohibited immigrants, 261; and civil disobedience, 176, 182, 187, 240–41; Gandhi's financing of, 175, 297n58; and *Hind Swaraj,* 255; "Last Message to South African Indians," 212; and *Motan v. Transvaal Government,* 172; and Phoenix settlement, 175, 300n9; and Ramsundar case, 195, 299n33; and Ritch, 265; and sacrifice, 173; and Sorabji case, 236; and spirituality, 177; and trading without licenses cases, 240–41

indigo, 32

Indus River, xix

inheritance, 18, 126

Inner Temple, 7–11, 218, 277n16, 277n18; certificate of admission to, 55–57,

283n22; and common law, 8, 10; and contacts in Pretoria, 43; as most expensive/prestigious, 8, 278n32

Innes (Justice), 167

Inns of Court, 5–12, 276n6, 277nn16–18; age requirements for, 7, 277n18; and "benchers," 6, 277n8; and bolts and moots (mock exercises), 6; Easter term, 11; and English law examination, 7–10, 277n29; Gray's Inn, 8; Hilary term, 11; and Indian students, 8, 277n17, 278n32; Inner Temple, 7–11, 55–57, 218, 277n16–18, 278n32, 283n22; and Kahn, 128; and keeping terms (dinner requirement), 6–12; and lectures, 7, 277n10; libraries of, 7; Lincoln's Inn, 8, 128; Michaelmas term, 10; Middle Temple, 8, 218, 277n17; and Natal, 55–57, 59; and reading in chambers, 6–8; and recommended textbooks vs. notes, 10, 277nn27–28; and Roman law examination, 7–10, 277n23, 277n24, 277n29; and Smuts, 218; and social status, 5–7, 12, 278n32; special admission examination for, 8–9; Trinity term, 10–11; and university vs. nonuniversity students, 6–8, 10, 277n12

insider's game, 36, 41

interpreters/translators, 13, 37–39, 42, 52, 61, 79–80; Gandhi as, 13, 39, 42, 61, 79–80, 102; licenses for, 80; Nazar as, 292n33; and resistance to registration, 210, 301n26

intimidation trial, 77–78

IRA (Immigration Restriction Act): amendments to, 224; and border-crossing resistance, 243; and Dundee Indians, 112–13; and educated Indians, 230, 232, 234–36, 243–44, 262, 307n55; European language proficiency requirement for, 106, 232–38; illegal immigration punishable by hard labor, 106; ineffective and highly unpopular, 113; in Natal, 105–6, 112–13; paupers prohibited from immigrating, 106, 124, 233–34; and petitions, 289n13; and prewar residents, 243–44, 307n55; and prohibited immigrants, 233–34, 254, 259, 261–62, 307n55; and right of return,

IRA (continued)
305n10; and Sorabji case, 233–38; tax on
free Indians who remained, 106; in
Transvaal, 203, 206–7, 224, 232–38,
243, 289n13
Irwin, Viceroy, xxii–xxiv; negotiating with,
xv, xxiii–xxiv
Islamic law, 70–71
Ismail Suleiman and Company, 149–150
Italy, 256

Jackson, Cecil, 165, 176, 178
jailings: of Arookian, 69; and border-crossing resistance, 242–43; of Dundee
Indians, 112–13; of Gandhi, 201, 212,
214–18, 222, 224, 227–28, 232, 249–251,
254–55, 302n1; of Gandhi, Harilal,
241–43; and hard labor, 194, 214, 236,
238–39, 243, 254, 305n27, 306nn33–34;
of Indian workers in Natal, 74–75; and
jail-going resolutions/pledges, 189–190,
200; of Rambhabai, 262, 309n41; of
Ramsundar, 191, 194–96, 203, 208; of
Ratanshi Sodha, 261; and resistance to
registration, 186–87, 189–191, 194–96,
200–202, 208, 212, 214–18, 221–22, 224,
227–29, 232, 235–243, 245, 249–250,
254, 302n1; and Salt Campaign, xxiv; of
Sorabji, 235–36; for trading without
licenses, 237–38, 240–41, 305nn25–26,
306nn33–34; and tramcars, 185
Jainism, 309n30; Jain monks, 4
Jameson, Leander, 147
Jamnagar, 142
Jefferson, L. H., 239–240. See also T.H.R.
Jefferson
Jefferson, T. H. R., 183. See also L.H.
Jefferson
Jews (as license applicants), 114
Jhaveri, Sheth Abdul Karim, 29
Johannesburg, xi–xii, 37, 39–41, 146, 148,
150–51; Chamber of Commerce, 253;
Constitutional Court, 216; Empire
Theatre, 186–190; Exploration Building,
163; Fordsburg mosque, 195, 209–10, 230;
Government Square, 208, 213; hard labor
imposed in, 305n27; jail in, 216–17; law
office in, 164–65, 174, 176–77, 203, 209,

213–14, 237, 265; Market House, 194;
Marlborough House, 203–4; meetings of
law society in, 163–64; Parliamentary
Debating Society, 163–64; and resistance
to registration, 186–190, 203–15, 230,
250–51; rights of British Indians in, 73,
128; Rissik Street, 164, 209, 265; and
Sorabji case, 233; Town Council, 181–82,
185; and tramcars, 180–85, 187, 249,
298n11, 298nn1–2, 298n5, 298nn13–14,
299n19; Tramway and Lighting Committee, 181; vegetarian restaurant in, 174
Johannesburg Star, 199, 203, 212–13, 224,
301n47; and burning of registration
certificates, 232; Gandhi's reading of,
213; interviews in, 211–12; letters to,
208–9, 302n40; and Ramsundar case,
193–94; and trading without licenses
cases, 238, 253
Johnson, Samuel, 216
Jordan, Harry H., 204–7, 210–11, 214,
233–36, 243–44
Jorissen, Mr. Justice, 44–45
judges. See magistrates
judicial immunity, 76
judicial independence, failure of, 239–240,
249, 263–64
juries, xv, 69, 165, 249
justice, xiii–xvi, xxi, 36, 266; and Hind
Swaraj, 256, 258; in Natal, 60, 264;
social justice, 264; in Transvaal, 165,
170–71, 228, 254

Kadir, Abdul, 193
Kaffir, 153, 200, 206, 294n27, 294nn27–28
Kahn, Ellison, 283n36
Karim, Abdulla, 89
Karwa, 206, 209, 301n26
Kate Hillary v. T.B. MacKenzie, 68
Kathiawad, 27, 29–30, 142
Kennedy, Robert F., xviii
Kerr, J.G., 182
The Key to Theosophy (Blavatsky), 13
Khan, Nawab, 188, 210, 301n26
Khan, Rahim Karim, 128, 133, 135, 292n33;
and Boer War, 130; and criminal pros-
ecutions, 177–78; letters to, 141, 144;
practice turned over to, 136

Khan, Sumander, 210–11, 301n26
Kher, S. B., xii
Kildonan Castle, SS, 255
King, Martin Luther, Jr., xxvi, xxviii, 134; Gandhi's influence on, xxvi, 154, 185, 295n32
The Kingdom of God Is Within You (Tolstoy), 43
Klette, Fred, 214
Konczacki, Zbigniew, 34
Koran, 216
Kotze, John, 150
Krause, Albert, 43
Kruger, Paul, 148, 157
Krugersdorp, 259–260, 309n37; mayor of, 260

Labistour, Gustave Aristide de Roquefeuil, 55–56; and DLA, 124–25, 291n58; as friend to Indian cause, 56
landlords, 60, 77, 114, 123, 128–29, 174–75
Latin, 9, 277n23
latrines, 140
Laughton, Frederick: and *Adams* case, 286n7; and anti-Indian legislation, 116–17, 119–120, 125–28, 164, 180, 290n40, 291n58; and beating of Gandhi, 99–100, 102–3, 288nn11–12; and Boer War, 130; and Camrooden partnership case, 129, 132; and law of procedure, 116–17, 125, 131–32, 135, 152, 201, 234; as mentor, 131–32, 201, 234, 263; and resisters denied permission to land, 263–64
law, xii–xiv, xx, xxii–xxv; and anti-Indian legislation, 107; Gandhi's faith in, xiii–xiv, 169–170, 172, 178, 223, 226, 229, 266–67, 304n6; and *Hind Swaraj,* 256; as insider's game, 36, 41; and Natal, 36, 52; salt laws in India, xxii–xxv; and spirituality, 177; in Transvaal, 73, 175–77, 185; and truth, 45–47; as vocation, 1, 145
Law 3 (1885), 148–158, 160, 166–173, 293n22; and arbitration, 150–53, 249, 294n13; and Asiatic Act, 186–248; and discrimination against native Africans, 153–54; implausibility of Gandhi's argument

against, 156–57; litigation against, 154–58, 166–67, 169–173; and location restrictions, 148–49, 151–54, 157, 160, 166–173, 259–260, 309n37; test cases as challenge to, 154–58, 166–67, 169–173, 178
The Law and Lawyers (Gandhi), xii
law practices (Gandhi): abandoning, 250, 256–261, 263–67; and articled clerks, 174, 182, 221; in Bombay, 18–19, 22–26, 52, 55, 138, 141–45; and bookkeepers, 182, 298n7; and criminal prosecutions, 177–78; financial aspects of, 127–28, 133, 136–37, 141–43, 145, 161, 173–75, 179, 249, 265–66, 292n19, 292n22, 297nn53–54; Gandhi's pledge to defend resisters, 200–203, 301n16, 301n19; and Khan as associate, 128, 130, 133, 135–36, 292n33; and law clerks, 174; and long work hours, 176, 199, 203, 216, 297n56, 300n8; in Natal, 39, 52, 61–93, 112–125, 127–137, 280n9, 292n19, 292n22; partnership with Askew, 79; partnership with Coakes, 52–54, 60–62, 64, 67–68, 70–71, 93–94, 284nn47–48; and pro bono work, 25, 175, 262; in Rajkot, 26–29, 138, 141–43; retainer fees from merchants, 52, 61, 79; and Ritch, 265; and secretaries, xi, 174, 212; suspension of during Boer War, 130; in Transvaal, xi–xii, xv, 131, 146, 148, 158, 160–69, 173–79, 200–203, 221, 296n18, 297n56
Lawson, James, xxvi
lawyers, xii–xvi; civil rights lawyers, 164, 187, 240–42, 248, 250, 252, 255, 259, 262; European, xiv–xv, 37–39, 42–47, 53–54, 112–13, 115, 156; fees of, 46–47, 59–60; and *Hind Swaraj,* 256–58, 309n26; Indian, xiv–xv, 55–56, 128; Mandela as, 216; as public persons, 19, 26, 95, 199, 279n27; and role-differentiated behavior, xv–xvi, 246–48. *See also* barristers; solicitors; *names of lawyers*
legal education, xiii–xiv, xx, 2–11, 277n23; and apprenticeships, 7, 11, 16, 18, 278n31; dismal state of in England, 5–8; finances for, 3, 8–9, 11, 17, 23, 141, 277n16, 278n1; and Inns of Court, 5–12, 276n6, 277n8,

legal education *(continued)*
277n12, 277nn16–18, 277nn27–29;
obstacles to, 3–5
legal philosophy, 43, 51, 93
Lely, Frederick, 3
Leonard, Charles, 150
Leonard, James Weston, 156–57, 166, 171,
304n31; views on deportation, 209,
301n22
lepers, 127
licenses: for advocates, 54, 282n19; for
attorneys, 150, 163, 172; and DLA,
106–7, 109, 113–125, 289n12; fees for,
229, 238; for Indian merchants, 149,
165, 167–68, 170, 172–73, 176, 186,
229–230, 237–242, 305n25; licensing
tax on attorneys, 163; in Natal, 80,
106–7, 109, 113–125, 134, 288n5, 289n12;
for rickshaws, 134; trading without,
237–242, 252–54, 259, 305nn25–26,
306nn33–34, 308n6, 308n10; for tramcars, 183–84; for translators, 80; in
Transvaal, 128, 149–150, 163, 165,
167–68, 170, 172–73, 176, 183–84,
229–230, 237–242, 305n25; and Uncovenanted Indians Act, 105–6, 288n5;
variant spellings of, 288n5. *See also*
certificates; permits
licensing officers: appeals of decisions
barred, 107, 109, 113–126, 290n50;
arbitrary denials by, 106, 113–125, 178,
291n58; and DLA, 106–7, 109, 113–125;
employment by council creating impermissible bias, 119–120; requests for
reports of, 118, 120–22, 290n41
"Lion of Bombay". *See* Mehta, Pherozeshah,
Sir
Livingstone, John, 44–45
Lloyd George, David, xix
London: Gandhi's arrival in, 1, 4–5, 7–9,
12–13, 276n1; Gandhi's departure from,
17, 21; Gandhi's trip to (1906), 180,
198–99, 298n17; Holborn restaurant, 21;
Inns of Court, 5–12, 128, 276n6,
277nn16–18; SABIC, 265; West Kensington, 14, 20
London Convention of 1884, 148–49, 151;
Article 14, 149, 151

love: conquering hatred by, 140; and Satya-
graha, xxi; self-suffering based on,
176–77
Lucas, Gould, 62, 74–75, 77–78, 286n26
Lucas' Trustee v. Ismail and Amod, 166–67
Lunnon and Nixon law firm, 171
LVS (London Vegetarian Society), 15–16,
21; Executive Committee, 15, 21

MacIntyre, William J., 182, 298n7
Madras High Court, 22
magistrates, xiii–xv; and *Adams* case,
85–92, 94, 286n7; and adversarial
speech, 26; and Balasundaram, 64–65;
and Dundee Indians, 112–13; and *Gan-
dhi, Rex v.*, 204–7, 213; and guilty
defendants, 177–78; in India, 19, 24, 28.
See also names of judges and magistrates
Maharaj, Gopee, 61–62, 284nn47–48
Maharaj, Somnath, 117–122
Mahomed, Dowd, 77
Mahomed Cassim and Company, 123
Mahomed Majam and Company, 121–22
Maine, Henry Sumner, Sir, 49, 258
Majam case, 121–22
Makanji, Seth Gokaldas, 3–4
Malays, 32
Mamibai case, 19–21, 25
mandamus, writ of, 119, 290n40
Mandela, Nelson, 216
manhood: and Asiatic Act, 208, 212, 231,
301n32; and *Hind Swaraj,* 257, 309n27
manners: Gandhi's experimentation with,
8–9, 12; and Inns of Court, 5–7
manual labor, 149, 178, 265, 309n26
Maritzburg, 107, 116, 119–120
market-gardeners, 33–34, 281n14
Mason (Justice), 80, 116–17, 119–120
Mazmudar, Tryambakrai, 20–21
Mazzini, Giuseppe, 256
McWilliam, Alexander, 123
meat: abstention from, 4, 12–15, 278n33; in
England, 4, 12–13, 278n33
media: and *Adams* case, 86, 94; for advancing debate, xvii, 238; and anti-Indian
legislation, 125; and anti-Indian mob,
99, 288n16; and border-crossing resistance, 244, 306n51; and Coovadia case,

183; and *Gandhi, Rex v.*, 205, 207; and
   Gandhi as mediator, 132; in India, xxiii,
   95–97; and Indian Ambulance Corps,
   130; and Ramsundar case, 195; and
   resistance to registration, 205, 207,
   209–12, 224, 236–39, 244, 306n51; and
   Sorabji case, 236; and trading without
   licenses cases, 237–39; and vagrancy
   case, 81–83. *See also names of newspapers*
medicine: caring for sick in hospital, 127,
   131; study of, xiii, xx, 2–3
Meghjibhai (cousin), 3
Mehta, Pherozeshah, Sir, 18, 63, 95–96, 139,
   142; mastery of evidence law, 18, 142;
   "no power in our own land," 139
Mehta, Pranjivan, 14, 28, 139
merchants, European: in Natal, 32–33,
   55–56, 114, 123; in Transvaal, 149–151,
   153, 160, 252–53
merchants, Indian: and bankruptcy, 253–
   54, 308n10; distinguished from natives,
   153–54; and DLA, 106–7, 113–14, 117–
   126, 289n12, 290n42, 290n50, 291n57; as
   Gandhi's clients in Natal, 34–35, 51–53,
   60–61, 66, 78–79, 106–7, 117–126,
   128–132, 290n42, 290n50, 291n57; as
   Gandhi's clients in Transvaal, 164,
   166–69, 174, 188; as Hindus, 42; and
   Indian Ambulance Corps, 130; Kasturba as daughter of, 3; in Krugersdorp,
   259–260, 309n37; and Law 3 (1885),
   148–158, 160, 166–173, 178, 293n22; and
   location restrictions, 148–49, 151–54,
   157, 160, 166–173, 259–260, 309n37; as
   Muslims, 42; in Natal, 32–35, 39–40,
   48, 51–53, 55–56, 60–61, 66, 78–79, 93,
   106–7, 113–14, 117–125, 128–132, 282n17,
   290n42, 290n50, 291n57; prewar trading of, 167–170; prohibited from owning property, 166–67; trading without
   licenses, 237–242, 252–54, 259,
   305nn25–26, 306nn33–34, 308n6,
   308n10; and tramcars, 182; in Transvaal,
   42, 46–47, 147–158, 160, 164, 166–173,
   176, 182, 185–190, 194, 224, 230, 237–
   242, 252–54, 259, 261. *See also names of
   merchants*
Mia, Essop, 305n25

Middelburg district, 149
Middle Temple, 8; Indian students in, 8,
   277n17; and Smuts, 218
Millar, Alfred, 77
Miller, Webb, xxiv
Milner, Alfred, 147–48, 155
Milosevic, Slobodan, xxvii
missionaries: Baker as, 44; and Hinduism,
   13
modernity, 256–58
Mohamed, Tayob Hajee Khan: and
   Abdulla v. Mohamed, 39, 41–42, 44–47,
   155, 281n12; and *Mohamed v. Government,* 155–58, 170, 172
Mohamed and Company, 39, 41, 45
Mohamed v. Government, 155–58, 170, 172
money-lending practices, 60, 68–69, 285n4
moots, 6, 143
morality, personal: and adversary system,
   xv–xvi, 260; and guilty defendants,
   xv–xvi, 67, 177–78, 297n66; and *Hind
   Swaraj,* 256–58; in Natal, 67–68, 85;
   and nonviolent resistance, xxvi–xxviii;
   in Transvaal, 177, 179, 260
Morcom, R. F., 115–16
Morice, George, 149, 157–58, 172
mortgage bonds, 128
mosques, 114–15, 195, 209–10, 212–14, 230
Motan v. Transvaal Government, 171–73,
   178
Muller, Max, 49
Mumbai. *See* Bombay
Munro, Thomas, Sir, 49
Muslim-Hindu discord, xxii–xxiii, xxv, 42
Muslims, xxii; as "Arabs," 34, 53; encourag-
   ing Gandhi to convert, 43; and *Hind
   Swaraj,* 258; Hindu-Muslim unity, 212;
   in India, xxii–xxiii, 18; Khan as, 128; in
   Natal, 34, 39, 70–71; Pakistan as Mus-
   lim state, xxv; in Pretoria, 42–43. *See
   also names of Muslims*
My Experiments with Truth (Gandhi), 45,
   93
Mysore, 50

Naderi, SS, 98–99, 104; and petitions,
   108–9; and quarantine crisis, 98,
   101–2

Naidoo, Thambi, 204, 206, 209, 217, 219, 225, 240, 249–250

naïveté, xxi, 21, 48, 50, 201, 223, 229, 289n13; in defending reputation of Natal Indian Congress, 78; in defending resistance to registration, 201–2, 223, 229, 304n6, 304n29; and petitions, 107, 289n13

Napier, T. B., 7, 10–11

Narayansamy, 264

Natal, 31–138; and anti-Indian legislation, 104–25, 178, 289n13, 292n29, 293n22; DLA (Dealers' Licenses Act), 105–11, 113–125, 249, 289n12; economic depression in, 32, 280n10; farewell ceremony for Gandhi, 136–37; Franchise Law Amendment Bill, 49–50, 84, 282n2, 282n7, 282n17; Gandhi's arrival in, 29–30, 36–37; Gandhi's pledge to return if needed, 143–45; governor of, 50, 134; and home rule, 58; indentured Indians in, 32–35, 51, 63–65, 69, 79, 81, 97–98, 105–6, 108–9, 111, 119, 126, 280nn8–10, 281n12, 281n14; and Indian franchise, 34, 48–51, 53, 60, 84, 282n2, 282n7, 282n17; Indian population in, 33–34, 49, 51, 60, 82, 111; IRA (Immigration Restriction Act), 105–6, 112–13; and native Africans, 31–32, 60–63, 134, 280n5; premier of, 50; Quarantine Act, 105–6, 113; and Ramsundar, 191; and responsible government model, 32–34, 105, 280n3; Uncovenanted Indians Act, 105–6, 109, 113; and Union of South Africa, 255; and Zulu Rebellion, 180, 197. See also Natal legal system; Natal Parliament

Natal Advertiser, 37–38, 78–79, 284n41; and anti-Indian legislation, 119, 290n41; and anti-Indian mob, 99, 103; and beating of Gandhi, 103; and gifts at farewell ceremony, 136; letters to, 38, 74; and Tuohy case, 285n11; and vagrancy case, 81–82

Natal Government Railway, 73–75, 83

Natal Indian Congress. See NIC

Natal Law Society, 55–57, 60, 68, 283n21, 283n31

Natal legal system: attorney general, 55–56, 60, 99, 107; and credentials, 38; and

Gandhi's admission to bar, 43, 52, 54–61, 70, 282n18, 283nn20–22, 283n27, 283n31; and Gandhi's law practice, 39, 52, 61–93, 112–125, 127–137, 280n9; and Khan's admission to bar, 128; Ordinance 3 (1850), 115; and Roman-Dutch law tradition, 55, 58–59, 283n25, 283nn35–36; Section 8 of Law 39 (1896), 116–17; Section 75 of Law Number 19 (1892), 135. See also Natal Supreme Court

Natal Mercury, 32, 38, 53, 71, 82, 283n21; and beating of Gandhi, 101, 103; and Dundee Indians, 113; letters to, 82, 110

Natal Parliament, 48–49, 98–99, 109–10, 115–16, 124, 282n3; Indian Immigration Law Amendment Bill, 73; Legislative Assembly, 49–50, 58, 73, 84, 104–5, 107–10, 125; Legislative Council, 109, 282n3; Supreme Court Act (1896), 58

Natal Supreme Court: and Abdulla case, 76, 285n19; and Adams case, 86, 286n7; and Camrooden partnership case, 129, 132; and Coakes, 60, 68; and DLA, 115–17, 119–121, 125–26, 178; and farewell ceremony, 135–36; and Gandhi's admission to bar, 56–58, 76; and Islamic law, 70, 83; and Khan, 292n33; and Poonsamy case, 78, 286n26; and resisters denied permission to land, 263–64; and translator's licenses, 80. See also names of justices

Natal Witness, 54, 60, 70, 119, 283n31, 290n41

nationalism in India, xiii, xx–xxv, 138, 140–41, 145; and Gokhale, 140–41; and Mehta, 95–96. See also INC

native Africans: discrimination against, 153–54, 294nn27–28; farms of, 147; as "Kaffir," 153, 200, 206, 294nn27–28; in Natal, 31–32, 60–63, 134, 280n5; and tramcars, 181; in Transvaal, 147, 149, 151, 153–54, 160, 294nn27–28, 303n7

native practitioners, 22–23, 26, 279n4. See also vakils

Navajivan Publishing House, xxvii

Nazar, Mansukhlal, 136, 141, 144, 292n33

negotiations, xv, xxiii–xxiv; and Adams case, 86–87; for Balasundaram, 64–65;

with Coakes, 53–54, 61, 222; for Durban
villa, 61; and Law 3 (1885), 171; with
Smuts, 217–19, 221–25, 232, 262, 265,
302nn3–4, 303n7, 303n10, 303n12,
304n27
Newcastle, 116–17; Town Council, 116–17,
126; *Vanda v. Newcastle,* 116, 120, 126,
290n40
Newtown mosque, 212–13
NIC (Natal Indian Congress), 75–79, 84,
285n18; and Askew, 79; and Congress
Hall, 93; and DLA, 117–18, 122–23; and
Gandhi, 75–78, 112, 117–18, 138, 141,
193n34, 292n19; and Karim, 89; reputation of, 77–78; request for money from,
141; and Rustomji, 65
nonviolence, xiii, xxi–xxii, xxv–xxviii; and
anti-Indian mob, 102, 104; in India, xxi,
xxiv–xxvii; and King, xxvi, xxviii, 154,
295n32; and power of self-suffering, xiv,
xvii–xviii, 175–77, 185; and satyagraha,
xxi–xxii, 212; in Serbia, xxvii–xxviii;
successful only in controlled situations,
xxvi–xxvii; in Transvaal, 154, 176, 218,
301n16
notaries, 284n1
nuclear weapons, xvi–xvii

Olcott, Henry, 12
Oldfield, Josiah, 15–16
oppressors: changing mind of, xiv, 251; and
nonviolent discipline, xxvi–xxviii; and
power of self-suffering, 176
Orange Free State, 59, 111, 129, 147, 150, 255
Osman, Dada, 122–25
Otpor (Resistance), xxvii–xxviii

Padiachy, Rangasamy, 77–78, 286n26
Pakistan, xix, xxv
Papenfus, H. F., 203–4
paralegals, 26, 47
Pardekoph, 40–41
Parekh, Devchand, 144
Parel, Anthony, 258, 308n20, 309n24
Parmanandbhai (cousin), 3
partnerships: dissolution of, 129, 133, 135;
and DLA, 114, 126; law partnership
with Askew, 79; law partnership with

Coakes, 52–54, 60–62, 64, 67–68,
70–71, 93–94, 284nn47–48; and M. C.
Camrooden and Company, 129, 132–33;
premiums for, 53; share of profits, 53–54
passive resistance, xxi, 199, 205, 208, 211,
224, 228–29, 254, 261; "satyagraha" as
replacement term for, xxi–xxii, 212. *See
also* civil disobedience
Pathan community, 220, 303n19, 303n21
Pather, Poonsamy, 77–78
Paul, Louis, 52–54, 282n12
Peace Preservation Ordinance (1903), 186,
206–7, 244, 299n22
Pearce, F. A., 72
Pearce, Robert, 5
perjury, 57
permits: and Asiatic Permit Office, 165, 176,
178, 249, 296n22; and Asiatic Trading
Commission, 167, 170; forgeries of, 211;
Indians required to register for, 176, 186,
189, 191–94, 200–201, 210–11; and Peace
Preservation Ordinance (1903), 186,
244, 299n22; and Ramsundar case,
191–94; and Receiver of Revenue, 170;
travel permits, 174. *See also* certificates;
licenses
petitions, xxi; against anti-Indian legislation, 107–12, 119, 126, 289n13; cover
letters for, 109–11; end of, 110–12;
against franchise restrictions, 49–51,
109, 282n5, 282n7; in India, 27, 30; and
Law 3 (1885), 152–53, 294n24; as "memorials," 294n24; in Natal, 49–51, 107–12,
134–35, 282n5; for return of application
papers, 224–25, 229, 304n35; and rickshaws, 134–35; in Transvaal, 152–53,
224–25, 229–230, 304n35; against
Validation Bill, 230
Phoenix settlement, 175, 178, 300n9
physicians, European, 153
physicians, Indian, 100, 188
Pietermaritzburg, 78; railway station, 39–41
Pillay, C. M., 206, 209
Pillay, Moroogasa, 77
Pincott, Frederick, 49, 62–63
The Pioneer (newspaper), 97
plague, 97–98, 113, 288n17
Plato, 216

Plea for Vegetarianism (Salt), 15

Plowshares civil disobedience movement, xvi–xvii, 275n1

Polak, Henry S. L.: admission to bar, 221, 298n17, 303n22; and BIA, 298n17; and border-crossing resistance, 244; and "conscientious objection," 303n24; and *Hind Swaraj,* 259; photograph of, xi; and Registrar of Asiastics, 251–54; and tramcars, 184–85

police: and anti-Indian mob, 100–101; and Asiatic Department, 165; and beatings of Gandhi, 100–101, 103, 220, 288n17; in India, xxiv; in Natal, 62–63, 71–74, 81–83, 105–6, 285nn9–11; police brutality, xxiv, 43; police superintendent, 81–83, 100–101, 288n17; and registration of Indians, 189, 191; and resistance to registration, 189, 191, 203–4, 207, 209, 213, 229, 233–35; and rickshaws, 134; and Sorabji case, 233–35; and tramcars, 184; in Transvaal, 43, 165, 176, 184, 189, 191, 203–4, 207, 209, 213, 233–35; and Uncovenanted Indians Act, 105–6

political change, xiv, xvii–xviii, xxv–xxvi, 243, 246

political organizing, 51, 78–79, 126, 180, 248; and Ramsundar case, 194–95

politics: and *Abdulla* case, 76; and anti-Indian legislation, 107, 112, 115, 126–27; and anti-Indian mob, 98, 102; and Asiatic Act, 187–89, 192, 205, 211, 220, 222; and Balasundaram, 112; and Boer War, 130; in India, xxi–xxii, 27, 138, 145; in Natal, 33–34, 48, 50–52, 61, 76, 98, 102, 107; petty politics, 27; and resistance to registration, 187–89, 192, 205, 211, 214, 220, 222; and spirituality, xvi; in Transvaal, 148, 164, 170–71, 173, 175–77, 180, 185, 187–89, 192, 205, 211, 214, 220, 222, 296n18

Poonsamy Pather and Three Others, Regina v., 77–78, 286n26

poor/poverty: and Islamic law, 70–71; in Natal, 34–35, 65–66, 70–71, 131; and resistance to registration, 201; in Transvaal, 201

Porbandar, 2–3, 27; and Abdulla, 29, 36; British administrator of, 3; and Gujarati language, 34, 39; and Mohamed, 46

Portuguese, 31

A Practical Guide to the Bar (Napier and Stephenson), 7, 10–11

prayer, 44, 231

precedent, 36, 58

prejudice: and DLA, 107, 109–11; in Natal, 37, 53, 60, 107, 109–11; toward native Africans, 154; in Transvaal, 154, 156, 163, 181. *See also* discrimination; race relations/racism

preparation, xv; for bar examinations, 5–6, 10; failure of, 88, 94; Gandhi known for meticulous preparation, 51, 142; and shipping law, 88, 94; sometimes Gandhi's strong suit, 113

press. *See* media; *names of newspapers*

The Press (Pretoria), 45

Pretoria, 39–47, 162; and *Abdulla v. Mohamed,* 41–47; and curfew passes, 43; Indian life in, 42–43; and Law 3 (1885), 148–49, 151–52, 154–55, 168; open-air church services in, 44; Pretoria Convention (1881), 148–49; religious exploration in, 43–45; and resistance to registration, 204, 208, 213–14, 217, 219, 230, 243; rights of British Indians in, 73; Royal Courts of Justice, 168

principled action, 51, 190

The Principles of Equity (Snell), 10, 179

Principles of the Law of Real Property (Williams), 10

Privy Council Judicial Committee, 117, 126, 291n2

procedure, law of: and adversarial speech, 26; and appellate judges, 132; Civil Procedure Code, 18; as defense for resistance, 125; and DLA, 115–120, 125; and Laughton, 116–17, 125, 131–32, 135, 152, 201, 234; and Law 3 (1885), 152; in Natal, 59, 115–120, 125, 135; and rickshaws, 135; and Sorabji case, 234–35; and trading without licenses cases, 238, 306n33; in Transvaal, 152, 201, 234–35, 238, 241

produce stands, 114–16, 128–29, 289n27

professional ethics: and commissions, 27, 29–30; in India, 25, 27–30; in Natal, 60, 67–68, 85; and touts, 25, 280n28; and undue influence, 27–28

prohibited immigrants, 233–34, 254, 259, 261–62, 307n55; and children, 261; and Rambhabai, 262

promissory notes, 39, 41, 61, 128, 174, 190, 200

public interest/pressure, xiv, xvii–xviii, xxiii–xxvi; and Arab Spring, xviii; and border-crossing resistance, 244–45, 247–48, 306n51; in Denmark, xviii; in Egypt, xviii; in India, xxiii–xxv; international, xxiii–xxv; and Natal Indian Congress, 77; and Ramsundar case, 191, 194–95; and Salt Campaign, xxiii–xxv; and Sorabji case, 236; and trading without licenses cases, 237–38, 241; and tramcars, 181–82, 185, 242; in Transvaal, 170, 176, 181–82, 185, 191, 194–95, 205, 209–10, 227–28, 236–38, 241–42, 244–48, 305n28, 306n51

public persons, 19, 26, 95, 199, 279n27

public speaking, 30; and adversarial speech, 26; on *Clyde, SS,* 14, 20; in Durban, 93, 96, 133, 199; fear of, 14, 16, 20–22, 26, 30, 43, 96, 103, 139–140, 199; in India, 20, 93, 95–96, 139–140, 153, 287n3; in London, 16, 20–22; petitions contrasted to, 108; in Rajkot, 20; in Transvaal, 42–43, 162, 187, 189–190, 199–200, 204, 209, 212–13, 250–51

punishment, xiii–xiv, 191, 266–67; and castes, 4; and Indian workers, 74; and resistance to registration, 184, 208, 241, 245, 247–48, 254. *See also* deportation orders; fines; jailings

Quarantine Act, 105–6, 113

quarantine crisis, 98, 101–2, 288n11; no lawsuit for damages, 102–3

Quinn, Leung, 204, 217, 219, 225, 230

"Quit India" movement, xxii

race relations/racism, xv; and *Adams* case, 90; and anti-Indian mob, 98–103; in Natal, 37–38, 53–57, 60, 72–73, 81–83, 105–7, 109, 113–14, 119, 133–34, 285nn9–11; and native Africans, 153–54, 294nn27–28; and railway system, 39–41; and rickshaws, 134–35; and stage coaches, 40; and tramcars, 181–85; in Transvaal, 43, 148, 151, 153–57, 161–64, 181–85, 260, 294nn27–29; in U.S., xvii–xviii, 154. *See also* anti-Indian law (Transvaal); anti-Indian legislation (Natal); discrimination; prejudice

railway systems: and first-class tickets, 39–40; in India, xix–xx, 139; in Natal, 39–41, 73–75, 299n18, 304n2; and racism, 39–41; and reserved berth and bedding tickets, 40; and strikes, 74, 299n18, 304n2; in Transvaal, 40–41, 203

rain, 213

Rajkot, 2, 4, 17–18, 20; Gandhi's law practice in, 26–29, 138, 141–43

Ramaswamy and Others, Rex v., 239

Ramsundar Pundit, 191–96, 203–4, 228, 299n33, 299n40; as faded memory, 236; fleeing from Transvaal, 196, 208; jailing of, 191, 194–96, 203; religious grounds for resistance of, 193, 299n40; wife of, 193

Rand Daily Mail: and Asiatic Act, 186; and Asiatic Trading Commission, 169; and burning of registration certificates, 232, 305n13; and Gandhi's London trip (1906), 198, 300n2; and *Motan v. Transvaal Government,* 173; and Ramsundar case, 299n33; and trading without licenses cases, 238, 253–54

Ravishankar (cook), 19

reform, curative/institutional, xvii–xviii, xxv, 185, 227, 242. *See also* political change; social change

refugees, Indian, 164–65

Registrar of Asiatics, xv, 192, 219, 251–54

registration regimes: Peace Preservation Ordinance (1903), 186, 244, 299n22. *See also* Asiatic Act

religious explorations, 10, 12–13; and *Hind Swaraj,* 256; in Transvaal, 43–45, 178–79, 218

religious struggle, 193, 206, 208–11, 231, 251, 299n40, 301n32, 301n40

Renaud, Eugene, 63
Republic of Natalia, 31–32, 58, 280n1
resistance to registration. *See* Asiatic Act
responsible government model: and Natal, 32–34, 105, 280n3; and Transvaal, 198, 300n1
retail dealers, 106, 110, 115, 125, 289n27; in Transvaal, 185–86, 252–53, 308n10. *See also* merchants, European; merchants, Indian
Reuters, 97, 209, 287n6; and interview, 212
revolution: in Egypt, xviii; handbook for, xxvii–xxviii; nonviolent, xxvii–xxviii
Rhodes, Cecil, 147
Richards, Samuel, 81–82, 85, 100
rickshaws, 100, 134–35; losing battle against, 135; and separate-but-equal by-law, 134–35
ridicule, 18, 71, 136; and *Adams* case, 85, 87–89, 92
Riebeeck, Jan van, 58
Ripon, Lord, xx, 50–51, 108–9, 152
Ritch, Lewis W., 265–66, 310nn48–51
Roberts, John Lutchman, 81–82, 85, 100
Robinson, John, Sir, 78
role-differentiated behavior, xv–xvi, 246–48
Roman-Dutch law tradition, 55, 58–59, 277n24, 283n25, 283nn35–36; examinations for, 55; and M. C. Camrooden and Company, 129
Roman law, 58, 283n25; examinations for, 7–10, 277n23, 277n24, 277n29
Roosevelt, Theodore, 135
Round Table Conference, xxii–xxiii
Rubie, J. F., 169
rule of law, 231, 247, 263–64
rupees and pounds, 86, 91–92
Ruskin, John, 216
Rustomji, Parsi, 65, 100, 288n16, 308n10

Sabarmati Ashram (Ahmedabad), xi, xxiii, 297n54
SABIC (South African British Indian Committee), 265
sacrifice, xxii, 173, 187, 194, 242, 251, 266, 306n39
Safari, SS, 35–36

Salt, Henry, 15
Salt Campaign, xxii–xxvi, 227–28, 276n11; and march to sea, xxiii–xxiv
Samaldas College, 2
"Sami," 40
sanitary conditions: and DLA, 106, 110, 113, 117, 122–24; in India, 140; and Indians, 42, 110, 117, 134, 149, 153, 260; and Law 3 (1885), 149, 153, 260; in Natal, 106, 110, 113, 117, 122–24, 134; and rickshaws, 134; and tramcars, 181–82; in Transvaal, 42, 149, 153, 181–82, 260
satyagraha, xxi–xxii, 212, 255, 306n39
scavengers, 140
Scheurmann, Max, 66–67
Schlesin, Sonja, xi, 212, 310n51
Schmitthener, Samuel, 24
schoolteachers, 81–82
Schuurman, P. J., 204, 207, 214, 233–34
Scott, Walter, Sir, 216
Searle, Malcolm W., 150
sedition, 192–94
segregation: and Freedom Riders, xviii, xxvi; in Louisiana public library, xvii; and tramcars, 181–85, 187, 228, 249, 298n11, 298nn13–14, 299n19; in Transvaal, 128, 181–85, 187, 228, 298n11, 298nn13–14, 299n19; in U.S., xvii–xviii, xxvi
Selborne, Lord, 218–19, 230
Serbia, xxvii–xxviii
servants, Indian, 181–84
settlements, xv; and Balasundaram, 65; and Indian workers, 74–75; of Salt Campaign, xxiii–xxiv; and Tuohy case, 72, 285n11; and willingness to compromise, 132
Shapurji, Sorabji, 233–38, 243, 246, 250, 257; as heroic figure, 236. *See also* Sorabji case
Sharp, Gene, xxvii–xxviii, 275n6
Shepstone, Theophilus, 280n5
shipping law, 88, 94
Shukla, Dalpatram, 14, 143–44
Singh, Lal Bahadur, 193
smallpox, 184
Smith, Albert, 112
Smuts, Jan Christian, xv, 199, 202–4, 211–12, 227–230, 242, 246, 249, 251;

London trip concerning Union of South Africa (1909), 255; negotiations with, 217–19, 221–25, 232, 243, 262, 265, 302nn3–4, 303n7, 303n10, 303n12, 304n27, 309n41; and Rambhabai, 262, 309n41; and Ritch, 265; and Sorabji case, 233

social change, xiv, xvii–xviii, xxv–xxvi, 1, 249–250; and failure of courts, 260, 264–65; in Natal, 36, 74, 178–79; and resisters denied permission to land, 264–65; in Transvaal, 173, 175–76, 178, 185, 227–28, 237, 242, 245, 307n52

Sodha, Rambhabai, 261–62, 309n41

Sodha, Ratanshi, 261–62

solicitors, 55–56; in Durban, 119–120, 290n42; in India, 23–24, 143, 293n15; in Transvaal, 162, 293n15, 307n56

Solomon, William H., 225, 304n36

Somnath case, 117–122

The Song Celestial (Arnold), 13

Sorabji case, 233–38, 243, 246, 250, 257; and acquittal, 234–35, 305n19

South Africa, xiii–xvi, xviii–xix, xxi–xxii, xxviii; map of, ix; railway system in, 39–41. *See also* Cape Colony; Natal; Orange Free State; Transvaal

South African Republic, 73, 146–154, 172; and discrimination, 147–49, 153–54, 156, 159–160; High Court, 41–42, 45, 149–150, 152, 154, 156–57, 160, 249; Volksraad, 149, 157. *See also* Law 3 (1885)

South African War. *See* Boer War

Sparks, Harry, 99

Spiller, Peter, 59

spirituality, xxviii; and Baker, 44; and detachment from worldly possessions, 178–79; and politics, xvi, 173, 177; and theosophy, 12–13; in Transvaal, 173, 177–79

stage coaches, 40

Standerton, 40

stands, removable, 114–16, 128–29, 289n27

steamship lines, 85–87, 98, 101–2, 104; and Quarantine Act, 105; and quarantine crisis, 98, 101–2. *See also Courland,* SS

Stephenson, R. M., 7, 10–11

storekeepers, Indian, 62–63, 72, 75

The Student's Guide to the Bar (Ball), 7

suffering, xvii–xviii, xxii, xxiv–xxvi; from beating, 103, 220; and border-crossing resistance, 242, 245, 247–48; power of self-suffering, xiv, xvii–xviii, 175–77, 185, 220, 227–29, 237, 240–42, 245, 247, 305n28, 307n52, 307n3, 309n35; and Rambhabai, 262; and Salt Campaign, xxii, xxv–xxvi; in silence, 80, 240–42, 245, 247, 250, 259; and trading without licenses cases, 237, 240–42; in Transvaal, 173, 175–76, 185, 212, 220, 222, 227–28, 231, 237, 240–42, 245, 250–52, 254, 259, 262, 307n3

sugar, 32

Suleiman, Ismail, 149–150

Suleiman case, 149–150, 152, 172

Swan, Maureen, 34–35, 48, 73, 147, 153–54, 282n5, 303n21

"swaraj," 256, 309n23, 310n43

sympathy, xxv–xxvi, 191, 205, 227–28, 244–45, 252–53

Tatham, Fredric, 70–71

taxes: in Egypt, xviii; salt tax in India, xxiii, 276n11

Taylor, Daniel, 114, 119, 122, 124–25

tenants, 60, 77, 117, 123, 174–75

test cases, xvii–xviii, xxii–xxv, 43, 227; Aswat suit, 223–25, 303nn35–36; Coovadia case, 182–85; and DLA, 115; and Law 3 (1885), 154–58, 166–67, 169–173, 178; *Lucas' Trustee v. Ismail and Amod,* 166–67; *Mohamed v. Government,* 155–58, 170, 172; *Motan v. Transvaal Government,* 171–73, 178; Sorabji case, 233–38, 243, 246, 250, 257; and tramcars, 182–85, 227; in Transvaal, 150, 154–58, 166–67, 169–173, 182–85, 224–25, 232, 253

theft, 69, 285n4

Theosophical Society, 12–13, 278n37, 278n39

theosophy, 12–13, 278nn35–37, 278n39; in Johannesburg, 164, 298n7

Thoreau, Henry David, 208

Tilbury Station, 1, 276n1

The Times of London, 306n51

tobacco, 32

Tolstoy, Leo, 43, 216
Tolstoy Farm, 265, 310n47
touts, 25, 164–65, 280n28
town councils: and DLA, 106–7, 113–14,
116–125; in Durban, 114, 117–125,
134–35, 290n41, 290n50, 291n57;
employment of licensing officers, 119–
120; in Johannesburg, 181–82, 185; and
law of procedure, 132; in Newcastle,
116–17, 126; recessing to discuss cases in
private, 118–120; refusing requests for
information, 118, 120–22, 290n41; and
rickshaws, 134–35; and tramcars, 181–
82, 185
tradesmen. *See* merchants, European;
merchants, Indian
tramcars, 180–85, 187, 298n11, 298nn1–2,
298n5, 298nn13–14, 299n19; all Indians
barred from but servants, 181–84;
conductors on, 182–85; electrical, 181;
and horse tram system, 180–81; and
native Africans, 181; and sanitary
conditions, 181–82; and segregation,
181–85, 187, 249, 298n11, 298nn13–14,
299n19
Transvaal, 36, 39–45, 59, 111, 146–255,
295n1; and *Abdulla v. Mohamed,* 41–45,
155; Administration of Justice Proclamation (1902), 162; Asiatic Act (Asiatic
Law Amendment Ordinance), 186–248;
Asiatic Department, xv, 160–61, 164–
65, 175, 261; Asiatic Permit Office,
164–65, 175–76, 178, 249, 296n22;
Asiatic Trading Commission, 167–170;
Bazaar Notice (Government Notice
356), 160, 167; and Boer War, 129–133,
139, 147–48, 157, 160, 291n12; British
annexation of (1877), 146; citizenship
rights in, 148–49; deportation from,
190, 203, 207–11, 213–14, 301n22; and
diamond production, 147; and Dundee
Indians, 112–13; and Empire Theatre
meeting, 186–190; Europeans in, 42–43,
81, 147, 149–151, 157, 166–67, 172–73,
182–85, 187, 191, 198, 204, 207–8, 218,
237; failure of judicial independence in,
239–240; Gandhi's departure from
(1914), 48; Gandhi's law practice in,

xi–xii, xv, 131, 146, 148, 158, 160–69,
173–79, 221, 296n18, 297n56; and gold
mining, 147; governor of, 218; and
Indian franchise, 198, 231; Indian population in, 149; and Indian refugees,
164–65; IRA (Immigration Restriction
Act), 203, 206–7, 224, 232–33, 289n13;
landdrost, 149; and Law 3 (1885), 148–
158, 160, 166–173, 178, 293n22, 296n27;
Legislative Council, 167, 169, 173;
mineral resources in, 146–47; and
native Africans, 147, 149, 151, 153–54,
160; president of, 43; public prosecutor,
128; railway system in, 40–41; Receiver
of Revenue, 170; and registration of
Indians, 186–248, 299n23; and responsible government model, 198, 300n1; and
sidewalks/public transportation restrictions, 154; and Union of South Africa,
255; war for Afrikaner independence
(1880), 146–48
Transvaal Leader, 181, 184, 189, 195, 203;
and burning of registration certificates,
231–32; editor of, 217; interviews in, 211;
and trading without licenses cases,
238–39
Transvaal Parliament, 218–19, 230–31
Transvaal Supreme Court, 249, 251; and
Coovadia case, 183; and Gandhi's application for admission, 161–63; and Law 3
(1885), 166–67, 171–73, 178; and *Lucas'
Trustee v. Ismail and Amod,* 166–67;
and *Motan v. Transvaal Government,*
171–73, 178; and Polak's application for
admission, 221, 303n24; and prohibited
immigrants, 254; and Rambhabai, 262;
and registrar of Asiatics, 253–54; and
return of application papers, 224–26,
229, 303nn35–36
"trustee," 178–79
truth: and *Adams* case, 88, 93–94; and
Arookian, 70; and Indian merchants,
42; and Law 3 (1885), 155; and practice of
law, 45–47, 177–78; and Satyagraha,
xxi; and theosophy, 12–13, 278n36; and
vegetarianism, 15
Tunisia, xviii, xxvii
Tuohy (police constable), 72, 285nn9–11

turbans: of Abdulla, 75; of Balasundaram, 64; demands for removal of, 38, 58, 75, 283n33; of Gandhi, 38, 58, 100

Turnbull, John, 57

uitlanders, 147

Uncovenanted Indians Act, 105–6, 109, 113; as nuisance, 113; and pass system, 105–6; petitions against, 109

Union Jack, 189, 195, 231

Union of South Africa, 255, 261–62, 265; settlement with, 265; Supreme Court, 261

United States: civil rights movement, xvii–xviii, xxvi–xxviii, 154, 227; Freedom Riders, xviii, 227; Interstate Commerce Commission, xviii; Louisiana public library, xvii; race relations/racism in, xvii–xviii, 154; struggle for independence, 173; Supreme Court, xvii, 157; and woman's suffrage, xvii

University of London matriculation examination, 9–10

"untouchables," 154

Vaal River, 146

vagrancy case, 81–83, 85, 100

vakils, 18, 23, 27–29; in Bombay, 142; Lakshmidas as, 23, 27–28; in Rajkot, 142; in South Africa, 29. See also native practitioners

Valee, Joosub Hajee, 168–69

Validation Act, 230–31

Vanda v. Newcastle, 116, 120, 126, 290n40

Vankaner, 2

The Vegetarian (journal), 15

vegetarianism, 12–16, 21, 278n33; books on, 15; conference about, 15, 21; farewell vegetarian dinner, 21; Gandhi's articles /speeches on, 15–16, 21; in India, 15, 19; in Transvaal, 174, 297nn53–54; vegetarian restaurants, 14–15, 174, 297nn53–54

Vegetarian Messenger (Manchester publication), 15

Ventnor, 21

Vernon, George, 204, 206, 210, 212, 214, 235, 243

Verulam, 79–80

Victoria, Queen, 133

Victoria Hotel, 14

Village-Communities in the East and West (Maine), 258

village life, ideal of, xxiii–xxiv; and Hind Swaraj, 258–59; and Salt Campaign, xxiii–xxiv

violin lessons, 12, 133

V. M. Bagas and Others, Rex v., 306n33

Volksrust, 203, 233, 241, 246–47, 249–250

Voortrekkers, 58

voting rights. See franchise, Indian

Wacha, Dinshaw Edulji, 96

Waller, John Parker, 81–82, 86–92, 287n17; question of, 88, 94

Walton, Charles, 165, 176, 178

Ward, Charles, 224–25, 304n31

war veterans, Indian, 188–89, 210, 214

wealthy commercial clients: and DLA, 117–18; in Natal, xvi, 34, 36, 47, 51, 117–18, 131; and tramcars, 182; in Transvaal, 182

Weber, Thomas, xxv, 276n11, 276n13, 307n52

Weenen County, 75–76

Welch, John, 183–84

Wesleyan Church, 44, 65

Wessels (Justice), 162

Western civilization, 256–58, 308n20, 309n24

wholesalers, European, 106, 110, 252–53, 308n10

wills: and Indian law, 18, 70; and Natal, 70

wine, 4, 11–12

witnesses: and Adams case, 86–90, 92; and Asiatic Department, 165; and border-crossing resistance, 243–44, 307n55; and Camroodeen case, 76; Christian Indians as, 81–82; and DLA, 123, 125, 128; European, 72; Indian, 37, 60, 72, 76–78, 165, 193, 285n23; Indians viewed as untruthful, 37, 60, 72, 285n23; in Natal, 37, 60, 62, 69, 72, 76–78, 82, 86–90, 285n23; and Ramsundar case, 191, 193; and Sorabji case, 234; and trading without licenses cases, 240, 306n33; in Transvaal, 41, 165, 191, 193, 234, 240, 243, 306n33; witness intimidation, 77–78

Witwatersrand, 147

workers, Chinese, 147

workers, Indian: and collective actions, 73–75; as "coolies," 148–49, 156; in Natal, 73–75, 299n18, 304n2; and resistance to registration, 203; and strikes, 74, 299n18, 304n2; in Transvaal, 149, 152, 203. *See also* indentured Indians in Natal

workers, native: in Natal, 32, 147, 280n5; in Transvaal, 147

working class, European, 97–98. *See also* anti-Indian mob

World War II, xviii; failure of civil disobedience during, xxvi; and "Quit India" movement, xxii

Wragg, Walter: and *Abdulla* case, 76; and *Adams* case, 86; and anti-Indian legislation, 116, 120; and Gandhi's admission to bar, 57; and Islamic law, 70–71, 285n7; as vindictive, 285n7

Zulus, 153; Zulu Rebellion, 180, 197